THE ZONDERVAN 2016 PASTOR'S ANNUAL

For a *FREE* downloadable copy of the book, please visit:
http://downloads.zondervan.com/zpa2016

THE ZONDERVAN 2016 PASTOR'S ANNUAL

An Idea & Resource Book

T. T. Crabtree

ZONDERVAN®

ZONDERVAN

The Zondervan 2016 Pastor's Annual

Requests for information should be addressed to:
Zondervan, *3900 Sparks Dr. SE, Grand Rapids, Michigan 49546*

ISBN 978-0-310-49397-6

Cover photography: Superstock

Printed in the United States of America

15 16 17 18 19 20 21 / DCI / 20 19 18 17 16 15 14 13 12 11 10 9 8 7 6 5 4 3 2 1

CONTENTS

MISCELLANEOUS HELPS

Contributing Authors

Tom S. Brandon	AM	May 8, 15, 22, 29
		June 5, 12, 19
Harold T. Bryson	PM	October 5, 12, 19, 26
		November 2, 9, 16, 23, 30
		December 7, 14, 21, 28
James E. Carter	PM	July 17
T. T. Crabtree		All Messages Except Those Indicated Otherwise
Wayne Dismuke		Messages for Children and Young People
T Hollis Epton	PM	July 13, 20, 27
		August 3, 10, 17, 24, 31
Tom Geers	PM	September 7, 14, 21, 28
David R. Grant	PM	January 6, 13, 20, 27
		February 3, 10, 17, 24
		March 2, 9, 16, 23, 30
		April 6, 13, 20, 27
		May 4, 11, 18, 25
		June 1, 8, 15, 22
		July 6
James G. Harris	PM	July 3, 10, 17
	AM	December 4, 11, 18, 25
James F. Heaton	AM	July 31
		August 7, 14, 21, 28
		September 4, 11, 18, 25
Joe L. Ingram	AM	November 6, 13, 20, 27
Howard S. Kolb	PM	June 29
		September 4, 11, 18, 25
	AM	March 13, 20
Guy Lawyer		Funeral Meditations
L. E. Maples	PM	June 5, 12, 19, 26
	AM	March 6, 27
		April 10
		Messages on the Lord's Supper
		Weddings
Jerold R. McBride	AM	April 3, 17, 24
		May 1
		October 2, 9, 16, 23
G. Hugh Wamble	AM	July 3, 10, 17, 24
Fred M. Wood	PM	March 6, 13, 20, 27
		April 3, 10, 17, 24
		May 1, 8, 15, 22, 29

PREFACE

Favorable comments from ministers who serve in many different types of churches have encouraged me to believe that the *Pastor's Annual* provides valuable assistance to many busy pastors as they seek to improve the quality, freshness, and variety of their pulpit ministry. To be of service to fellow pastors in their continuing quest to obey our Lord's command to Peter, "Feed my sheep," is a privilege to which I respond with gratitude.

I pray that this issue of the *Pastor's Annual* will be blessed by our Lord in helping pastors to plan and produce a preaching program that will better meet the spiritual needs of the congregation to which they are called to minister.

This issue contains sermons by several contributing authors who have been effective contemporary preachers and successful pastors. Each of these authors is listed with his sermons in Contributing Authors. I accept responsibility for sermons not listed there.

This issue of the *Pastor's Annual* is dedicated to the Lord with a prayer that he will bless these efforts to let the Holy Spirit lead us in preparing "A Planned Preaching Program for the Year."

SUGGESTED PREACHING PROGRAM FOR THE MONTH OF

JANUARY

■ Sunday Mornings

The suggested theme for the first morning messages of the year is "Cultivating the Fruit of the Spirit." Encourage each child of God to recognize and respond positively to the person and purposes of the Holy Spirit who begins to dwell within a person at the moment of conversion.

■ Sunday Evenings

"Words of Correction and Counsel for New Disciples" is the theme for a series of messages based on Paul's epistle to the church at Corinth. The problems that these new converts from paganism faced are as contemporary as the front page of today's newspaper.

■ Wednesday Evenings

The book of Titus is the basis for a series of practical expository messages that can be very appropriate for individual believers and good for the congregation as a whole.

SUNDAY MORNING, JANUARY 3

Title: The Fruit of the Spirit Is Love

Text: "But the fruit of the Spirit is love" **(Gal. 5:22 RSV)**.

Scripture Reading: Romans 5:1–5

Hymns: "We Praise Thee, O God," Mackay

"The Haven of Rest," Gilmour

"Holy Spirit, Faithful Guide," Wells

Offertory Prayer: Heavenly Father, we thank you for the gift of your love demonstrated most clearly in the gift of your Son, Jesus Christ, and revealed to us by the ministry of your Holy Spirit. We thank you for the gift of eternal life and for the joy of knowing that our sins have been forgiven.

We thank you for an opportunity to serve and for the privilege of being used in ministries of mercy to help others. We come today bringing our tithes and offerings as expressions of our love and of our desire to share the good news of your love with others. Accept these gifts and bless them, we pray, in Christ's name. Amen.

Introduction

Much hate exists in the world. Husbands hate their wives, and wives hate their husbands. Parents hate their children, and children hate their parents. Brothers and sisters hate each other. People living in the same community have hostility in their hearts toward people who should be near and dear to them. Hate seems to have filled the world, for war and cruelty break out on all sides.

Do you have a problem with hate? Do you find it difficult to practice a spirit of goodwill toward others? Those of us who are honest will admit that we often find it easier to feel hostile toward others than to practice benevolence. Somehow we must deal with the problem of hate and replace hostility with love, or our world will cave in on us.

Christianity is built on love. At the heart of Christianity is the affirmation that God loves people. God requires his children to love him supremely and to love their neighbors as themselves.

Jesus condensed in capsule form the teachings of Moses and the prophets in the two great commandments (Matt. 22:35–40). From this distillation of the total teachings of the Old Testament, we learn three great truths:

1. Our first obligation is to love God supremely and steadfastly.
2. Our second obligation is to love self appropriately that we might have a proper measure by which to love our neighbors.
3. Our third obligation is to love our neighbors as we love ourselves.

The command to practice love in a world of hate comes to us clear as crystal. We should love God, ourselves, and others. We must love others in spite of the fact that they are unlovely. We must love those people whom we do not even like. How can this be possible?

The Scriptures declare that God not only requires that we love, but that he also provides us with both the ability and the disposition to love. "God is love" (1 John 4:8). God has manifested his love toward unloving people in the gift of his Son, Jesus Christ (vv. 9–10). Because God loves us, the apostle declares that we are both obligated and enabled to love one another (v. 10).

The Holy Spirit, who came to us in the moment of our conversion and who took up residence within our hearts (Gal. 4:6–7), came to pour out within our hearts the love of God (Rom. 5:5). God, who is described as love, "has given us of his own Spirit" (1 John 4:13 RSV). In describing the function of the Holy Spirit in the hearts of believers, Paul declared that the Holy Spirit has entered our hearts to produce the fruit of love (Gal. 5:22). God does not expect us to love in human strength alone. He has placed his Holy Spirit within us to make it possible for us to love God supremely, ourselves appropriately, and one another as we love ourselves.

I. We need a proper definition of love.

To make a proper response to the commands and invitations of our Savior, we need to understand the meaning of the words he used.

In the English language, the word *love* is greatly abused and misused. People say, "I love my family, football, work, flowers, poetry, popcorn," and so on.

In the Greek language, four words describe the act of loving.

A. *Eros.* From this word we get the words *erotic* and *romantic,* and it refers to the chemical reaction of a male to a female. This instinctual and sensual love always involves sexual attraction and interest. In New Testament times, this word was associated with lust; it does not appear in the New Testament Scriptures. Love on this level is self-centered.

B. *Philia.* The highest word in the Greek language for human love, this word represents brotherly love. Involving the body, mind, and spirit of people in a warm, tender, and intimate relationship toward others, this love is not necessarily permanent. The loveliness of the one who is loved serves as the basis for this love.

C. *Storge.* This word represents family love—the love of a husband for his wife and of a wife for her husband, the love of parents for children and of children for parents.

D. *Agape.* The New Testament writers coined a new word to describe a new quality of relationships and a new attitude toward others. This word *agape* describes God's attitude and actions toward people. *Agape* love is the Calvary kind of love. It is sacrificial, self-giving, unmerited love. It is love toward the unlovable. It is love whose source is in the heart of the lover.

II. The Holy Spirit reveals God's love for us and creates our love for God.

The word *agape* represents the attitude that we should have toward God and which as his children we should practice toward others. This love has been described as a persistent, unbreakable spirit of goodwill.

A. *God's love for us is unmerited on our part (Rom. 5:8; 1 John 4:10).*

B. *God's love for us is pure and productive of results in our lives (Rom. 5:1–5).*

C. *God's love for us is great.*

  1. God loved us when we were dead in sin (Eph. 2:1).
  2. God's love quickened us to spiritual life from spiritual death (Eph. 2:5).
  3. God's love for us extends into eternity (Eph. 2:7).

D. *God's love for us is eternal and unchangeable (Rom. 8:35–39).* As the Holy Spirit reveals to us the greatness of God's love for us, he creates within us a loving response toward God.

III. The Holy Spirit encourages us to have an appropriate love for ourselves.

I am not referring here to narcissism. In Greek mythology, there is a story of a young man named Narcissus. A beautiful youth, he saw his reflection in a pool and became so enamored with his own beauty that he fell in love with himself. The Holy Spirit does not encourage us to fall in love with ourselves, but rather to have a proper love for ourselves. As we love ourselves properly, will we be able to have proper love for our neighbors.

A. *Proper love for ourselves will enable us to accept ourselves as unique persons created by a loving God.*

B. *Proper love for ourselves will help us to forgive ourselves.* Some people cannot experience the forgiveness of God because they refuse to forgive themselves. Consequently, they beat themselves up and criticize themselves, creating a crushing burden of guilt. The refusal to forgive is due to a lack of love.

C. *Proper love for ourselves will encourage us to protect ourselves from self-destructive attitudes and habits.* People show improper regard for their physical well-being by eating too much. People who contaminate their lungs with nicotine do not show as much regard for their physical organs as they do for the tools with which they work or for the utensils with which they eat. People who destroy their reasoning through the use of drugs or alcohol show less concern for the highest part of their being than they show for the delicate mechanism of an automobile or another type of machinery.

D. *Proper love for ourselves will cause us to dedicate ourselves to the highest and best that we know.*

E. *Proper love for ourselves will challenge us to develop ourselves and to improve the quality of our lives that we might be of greater service to others.*

IV. The Holy Spirit enable us to love others.

Because of a lack of love for others, we try to avoid the unlovable. We try to ignore people who are in need. We refuse to become involved with others and try to live lives of isolated self-centeredness.

A. *To love our neighbors properly, we must accept them fully as being people for whom Jesus Christ died on the cross.* We must see them as the objects of God's supreme concern. They are valuable to God, and because God is concerned about them, we should be concerned about them.

B. *To love our neighbors properly, we must be willing to forgive their trespasses against us and against others.* Our neighbors make mistakes just like we do.

All of us sin. We have fallen short and missed the mark. Not one of us merits forgiveness. We can find it possible to be forgiving toward others only as we remember that Christ also forgave us (Col. 3:12–14).

C. *To truly love our neighbors, we must be willing to follow the example of the good Samaritan and assist them in their times of misfortune (Luke 10:25–37).*

D. *To love our neighbors supremely, we must reveal God's love to them by our lives and our words.* We can do this with the assistance of the Holy Spirit, who came to dwell within us to produce love within and to demonstrate love without.

Conclusion

Let the Holy Spirit do his wonderful work within you. He came unmerited and even uninvited as the gift of God's grace to you when you trusted Jesus Christ as Savior. Trust in his power to help you live by the principle of love. Listen to his voice as he encourages you to practice an attitude of benevolent kindness toward others. Cooperate with his leading, and rejoice in his work within you and through you.

If you have not yet received Jesus Christ as your own personal Savior, then listen to the Holy Spirit as he invites you to trust and receive Christ as Lord. He eagerly wants to help you come to know Christ as Savior, and today you should respond to him as he speaks to your heart (Heb. 3:7–8).

SUNDAY EVENING, JANUARY 3

Title: Saints Who Are Called to Be Saintly

Text: "To the church of God which is at Corinth, to those sanctified in Christ Jesus, called to be saints" **(1 Cor. 1:2 RSV)**.

Scripture Reading: 1 Corinthians 1:1–9

Introduction

God continues to speak to his people through the written Word, which we know as the Scriptures. God gave a message through the apostle Paul for the people of ancient Corinth, the capital city of Greece, which served as the gateway from the north to the south and from the east to the west. The members of the congregation to which Paul wrote his epistle were recent converts from paganism. His message to them in that day contains truth for us as we live in a modern pagan and secular world.

I. "Paul—called to be an apostle."

A. *Paul was a former Pharisee and persecutor of the infant church.*

B. *Paul had been called to be an apostle.*

1. He was not appointed to this position by people.
2. He was not elected by people to serve.

C. *Paul was an apostle "through the will of God."* He came with an authoritative message from God to the people of that day and to this day.

II. "Unto the church of God at Corinth."

A. *The letter is addressed to the church, a "called out group" of believers.*

B. *The epistle is addressed to "the church of God."*

1. The church in Corinth belonged to God.
2. The church did not belong to the pastors, to the trustees, even to the members of the congregation or to the parties within the church.
3. We need to recognize that we belong to God and that God does not belong to us.
4. The people, called to be saints, are said to belong to the church, and the church belongs to God.

III. "To them that are sanctified in Christ Jesus."

A. *The recipients of this epistle were people who had been converted to Jesus Christ.*

B. *By a divine act, they had been set aside and dedicated through Jesus Christ to be the servants of God.*

C. *The apostle assumed that they are committed to doing God's will.*

Soldiers, by the nature of their office, are available to their country and are under the orders of their officers. It could be said that they are sanctified for military service.

Many people consider themselves almost as the property of the company that employs them. They feel a loyalty to their company, and they are available to do the work of their company. In a sense they are sanctified to their company.

Those who are "sanctified in Christ Jesus" should consider themselves as belonging to him and available to him for the services that he might need for them to render.

IV. "Called to be saints."

A. *One of the titles given to New Testament disciples was the term* saint. This term was not applied in those days to those who were characterized by an excess of genuine piety.

B. *All believers are called to be saints.* That is, they are called to be dedicated ones who were available for the work of God.

C. *Believers are those who have been set apart by the call of God to service for God as they give themselves in obedience to God through Jesus Christ.*

As the children of God, we are the people of God. We are called the body of Christ and the servants of Christ. These are not only descriptive titles but also describe functions of those who are followers of the Lord Jesus Christ.

V. "With all that call upon the name of Jesus Christ our Lord."

A. *The church at Corinth was a family of believers.*

B. *The church at Corinth was a prayer group for the renewal of the spiritual life of the membership.*

C. *The church at Corinth was looked upon as the body of Christ through which he would carry on his work in the world.*

Conclusion

Paul's prayer for the people at Corinth was that they might be the recipients of God's grace and peace. God's grace is the unexpected and undeserved generosity of God toward the unworthy. The peace of God is the harmony and the tranquility and the prosperity that come as a result of a right relationship with God and with others.

Grace is God's attitude and purpose toward us in Christ Jesus, while peace is God's gift and God's achievement within us through Christ Jesus.

We are called saints, and we are called to be saintly.

WEDNESDAY EVENING, JANUARY 6

Title: An Overview of the Book of Titus

Text: "For this cause left I thee in Crete, that thou shouldest set in order the things that are wanting, and ordain elders in every city, as I had appointed thee" **(Titus 1:5).**

Scripture Reading: Titus 1

Introduction

The book of Titus is only three chapters, or forty-six verses, in length, and some people feel that this little book has been neglected. However, Titus is a classic piece of literature on church work.

In studying Titus, we will see that Paul offers counsel to persons in various situations. This first message will introduce the whole book, and details will be elaborated on in the messages that follow.

I. The dominant persons in the book are Paul and Titus, and the prominent place is Crete.

The first verse names the apostle Paul as the writer, and Titus is named as the recipient of the epistle (1:4). Verses 5 and 12 of chapter 1 tell that Crete is the place of concern. The latter part of the epistle identifies some other persons of less prominence.

II. Paul mentions a number of church problems and persons in various positions who deal with them.

A. *Some of the problems mentioned are things lacking in the church (1:5), unruly and vain talking (1:10), and liars.*

B. *The positions described in dealing with these difficulties are divided into two categories.*

1. Some are general, such as teachers (2:3), masters (2:9), and magistrates (3:1).
2. Others are more specific, such as servant (1:1), apostle (1:1), elders (1:5), and bishops (1:7).

III. Paul gives Titus certain orders to follow in connection with problems in the church.

These orders may be classified as counsel and exhortation. They include: "set in order" (1:5), "ordain elders" (1:5), stop wrong talk (1:11), "rebuke" (1:13), "speak ... sound doctrine" (2:1), "exhort servants to be obedient" (2:9), "put them in mind" (3:1), and "avoid foolish questions" (3:9).

Conclusion

Most churches today have at least some problems. The degree and number vary. A study of the epistle to Titus will give insight on how to recognize problems, face them, and deal with them.

SUNDAY MORNING, JANUARY 10

Title: The Fruit of the Spirit Is Joy

Text: "But the fruit of the Spirit is . . . joy" **(Gal. 5:22 RSV)**.

Scripture Reading: John 15:11; 16:22–24; 17:13

Hymns: "All Hail the Power of Jesus' Name," Perronet

"Praise Him! Praise Him!" Crosby

"Breathe on Me," Hatch

Offertory Prayer: Heavenly Father, for the breath, beauty, and meaning of life, we thank you. For your gifts to our bodies, minds, and souls, we thank you. For the gifts of forgiveness, new life, divine membership in your family, and your Spirit, we thank you.

For the gift of money through the work of our hands, we come to praise and worship you. By means of these tithes and offerings we share in your ministries of mercy and in the spreading of the good news of your love to the ends of the earth. Bless these tokens of our worship; through Jesus Christ we pray. Amen.

Introduction

A world that is dark with despair, disappointment, and grief stands in need of a religion of joy.

Every human heart hungers for joy. Humankind constantly seeks happiness. But not as deep or inward as joy, happiness results from things that happen in one's life or to the people whom that person loves. Many people seek happiness by acquiring cash, by enjoying pleasurable emotions, or by seeking gratification through people, places, or positions.

Many people have given no consideration at all to Jesus Christ as the source of deep, inward, satisfying joy. People ignore Jesus because a distorted concept of who he is has been spread. Christ sometimes has been misrepresented by people who claim to represent and interpret him to others.

I. When on earth, Christ Jesus knew fullness of joy.

Repeatedly our Lord spoke of joy. He experienced fullness of joy, and he desired that his disciples experience fullness of joy as well (John 15:11; 17:13).

Repeatedly the book of Acts refers to the joy of the early disciples. They rejoiced because of God's mighty work within them. They rejoiced as God saved the unsaved. They even rejoiced in the midst of persecution.

Paul encouraged the church at Philippi to rejoice in the Lord (Phil. 3:3). He repeated this word of encouragement in Philippians 4:1, 4. He spoke of these disciples in Philippi as being "my joy and my crown." One of John's purposes for writing his first epistle was to add to the joy of the recipients (1 John 1:4).

The source of this joy in the lives of the early disciples was the joy in the heart of Jesus Christ. We speak of the joy of Christ, and yet many people think of him as being sad rather than glad, as being solemn rather than radiant, as being melancholy rather than jubilant. Why is this?

Almost without exception, the poets and painters have pictured the sadness, the grief, the agony of the passion of our Lord as he suffered for the sins of the world. Many of the great artistic masterpieces picture the crown of thorns and the agony of the Christ. In many Catholic churches around the world, one can see the image of Christ with a crown of thorns around his brow or around his heart and a sad, melancholy look on his face. Yet the Scriptures speak of the fact that our Lord endured the cross because of the joy that was set before him (Heb. 12:2). When you take a fraction of a person's experience and universalize this fraction, you always get a false impression. This has happened to Christ; consequently, many people think of him in terms of his sorrow rather than in terms of his joy.

A. *Listen to the testimony of our Lord's enemies.* Falsehoods can reveal truth if we consider them from every angle. We can learn much from the critics of our Lord as they speak concerning him.
   1. Jesus' opponents called him a glutton. He was not, but they called him a glutton because he enjoyed banquets and feasts. Did you ever know a glutton who was a glum sourpuss? Usually people who enjoy a feast are joyful individuals.
   2. Jesus' opponents called him a drunkard. He was not, but he had such a free, uninhibited, jovial spirit that they assumed that he must be under the influence of some kind of alcohol.
   3. Jesus' opponents called him a friend of publicans and sinners. They resented the fact that he felt at home with lighthearted people who were concentrating on enjoying the moment rather than thinking about the ultimate issues of falsehoods.

B. *Consider the testimony of Jesus Christ concerning himself.*
   1. He refused to observe the practice of fasting as it was conducted by the religious authorities of his day. This would have involved wearing sackcloth and a long face. Acting in such a way did not illustrate the quality of life he came to produce.
   2. He spoke of himself as a bridegroom, and bridegrooms usually are happy and jovial.
   3. His words about trust in God and the destructiveness of worry should cause us to know that he rejoiced in a perfect faith in the loving Father.

Three references in the New Testament mention that Jesus wept, but these references are the exceptions rather than the rule concerning his life. Otherwise, they would not have been mentioned.

Jesus was the most radiant, winsome, joyous person who has ever walked across the face of the earth.

II. The sources of Jesus' joy.

Jesus spoke repeatedly concerning his joy. What were the sources of his joy?

Jesus' joy did not come from owning a lot of property and living a life of affluence. It was not the result of popularity with the crowds and applause of the multitudes. The joy of which he spoke was not the joy of security as people normally think in terms of a safe, secure position.

Jesus gave us at least six sources of his joy.

A. *Jesus experienced the joy of knowing God as a loving Father.* He always addressed the eternal as "Father," with one exception, and that was when he was on the cross suffering for our sins.

B. *Jesus knew the joy of being in perfect harmony with God's will.* No discord existed between his will and the Father's will. No rebellion existed in Jesus' heart against his Father's will. The peace and the joy of complete cooperation with God ruled his heart.

C. *Jesus experienced the joy of being a giver (Acts 20:35).* Jesus declared that the greatest joy comes to people who give rather than people who take. To find the greatest joy the human heart can experience, we must define our purpose for being in terms of being a giver.

D. *Jesus experienced joy because of his faith in the goodness and power of his Father.* Christ trusted his Father to the point of becoming incarnate in human flesh. He was willing to trust his Father to the point of going to the cross. He was willing to trust his Father to the point of entering the cold chamber of death. He trusted his Father, and this brought joy to his heart.

E. *Jesus experienced the joy of helping others come to know God the Father.* The angels might envy this privilege. Jesus came so that by means of his death on the cross he might bring us to God. Jesus lived, loved, served, sacrificed, suffered, died, and rose again that he might be the means of our salvation.

F. *Jesus lived in the joy of knowing about the heavenly home that awaits us.* He had spoken concerning the master who said to his servant, "Enter thou into the joy of your Lord" (Matt. 25:21). The home of the heavenly Father is a place of perfect holiness, happiness, and health. In this place, we will worship God without the limitations of our sinful humanity. In this place, we will exist with each other in perfect love. Our Lord rejoiced as he looked forward to the great homecoming in the home of the heavenly Father.

III. God desires joy for you.

When our Lord made his entrance into the world, the angel said to the shepherds, "Be not afraid; for behold, I bring you good news of a great joy which will come to all the people" (Luke 2:10 RSV). The magi came seeking the Christ, and when they saw the star, "they rejoiced exceedingly with great joy; and going into the house they saw the child with Mary his mother, and they fell down and worshiped him" (Matt. 2:10–11 RSV).

Christ Jesus came into the world that people might experience great joy: "Without having seen him you love him; though you do not now see him you believe in him and rejoice with unutterable and exalted joy" (1 Peter 1:8 RSV). "The fruit of the Spirit is love, joy...." Paul wrote to the Thessalonians, "You became imitators of us and of the Lord, for you received the word in much affliction, with joy inspired by the Holy Spirit" (1 Thess. 1:6 RSV).

Part of the ministry of the Holy Spirit, who came to abide within our hearts as the divine presence when we received Jesus Christ as Lord, is working to produce within us inward and overflowing joy.

A. *We can have the joy of knowing God as our heavenly Father (John 1:11–12; Rom. 8:16).* God the Father is greater and better than all of his other gifts to us. The Holy Spirit leads us to look up to and pray to the eternal God as our loving and gracious heavenly Father.

B. *We can have the joy of experiencing God's eternal and unchanging love (Rom. 8:35–39).* God's love for us is not conditioned on our being lovable. God loves us because God is love. By faith let us recognize this love, and with the help of the Holy Spirit let us respond to it.

C. *By the Holy Spirit we can have the joy of experiencing God's good work within us (Phil. 2:13).* The Holy Spirit came into our hearts to produce within us the fruit of the Spirit (Gal. 5:22–23). This description of the fruit of the Spirit portrays what it really means to be a genuine follower of Jesus Christ. These graces of the Spirit are for every believer.

D. *The Holy Spirit has come into our hearts to give us the joy of God's abiding presence in all of the crises and opportunities of life.* Our Lord promised to be with us always (Matt. 28:20). The apostle Paul bore testimony that one can make adjustments to all of life's circumstances through the power of the living Christ (Phil. 4:13).

E. *The Holy Spirit gives us the joy of a life that will not end by assuring us that the grave is not the goal of this life.* The indwelling Spirit acts both as God's sign of ownership and as his guarantee of our victory over death (Eph. 1:13–14).

Conclusion

How can this joy unspeakable be yours? If you have already permitted Jesus Christ to become your Lord and Savior, then evaluate what God has done for you. Recognize your spiritual birth into his family and your gift of his Spirit dwelling within you. Begin to cooperate with him as he works his wonderful work within you.

If you have not yet trusted Jesus Christ as Savior, then respond to the gentle leading of the Holy Spirit as he persuades you that Jesus Christ meets the deepest needs of your life. Trust yourself into the hands of the only Savior who can save you for time and eternity, and begin your journey toward fullness of joy.

SUNDAY EVENING, JANUARY 10

Title: The Faithfulness of God

Text: "God is faithful, by whom you were called into the fellowship of his Son, Jesus Christ our Lord" **(1 Cor. 1:9 RSV).**

Scripture Reading: 1 Corinthians 1:4–9; 4:1–2

Introduction

One of the great truths on which the saints of God through the ages have depended has been the faithfulness and the reliability of our God.

Paul began his epistle to the Corinthians with a word of greeting (1:1–3) and followed his greeting with an expression of gratitude (1:4–9). The apostle sought to minister to a city congregation by leading them to respond to a God who could always be depended on. He emphasized the reliable character of their God and urged them to respond with trust and faithfulness to a trustworthy God. He made several great affirmations that can bless our hearts and lives today.

I. You can trust the God who called you to salvation in the first place (1 Cor. 1:9).

A. *God called us to himself by his grace (1 Cor. 1:4).* Paul was called to be an apostle, and the members of his church were called to be saints.

B. *God called us to himself by the gospel (1 Cor. 15:1–4).* The gospel is the good news of God's unmerited love toward us and of unexpected love as far as we are concerned.

II. You can trust the God who continues his plan for our salvation (1 Cor. 1:9).

A. *God called us into a partnership with his Son, Jesus Christ, our Lord.* This partnership is to continue throughout all of our earthly journey, and we are to give ourselves in service to him with the assurance that nothing we do for him will be in vain (1 Cor. 15:58).

B. *God does more than keep sinners from going to hell (1 Cor. 15:10).* God comes into our hearts and lives to work out his good purpose for us and to help us achieve a life of peace, harmony, and productiveness.

C. *God is seeking to bring each of his children to spiritual maturity and competency.* In the church at Corinth, there was a serious neglect of the means of spiritual growth. These new disciples were not following the Word of God as it had been taught to them by the apostle and other spiritual leaders. They were neglecting to recognize and respond to the Holy Spirit's leadership (1 Cor. 3:16). Tolerance of deadly sin in their lives was destroying the power of their witness and discrediting the name of Christ within the church and within the city of Corinth (1 Cor. 5).

D. *Paul affirmed that they could trust God to give them victory over sin and a way of escape from the temptations that so easily beset them and would finally destroy them (1 Cor. 10:13).* From this affirmation, he spoke again of the faithfulness and the dependability of the God whom we worship.

III. You can trust God to complete his work of complete salvation.

A. *Christianity is based on a firm belief in the resurrection of Jesus Christ, who conquered death and the grave and demonstrated the reality of eternal life (1 Cor. 15:20–28).*

B. *It is our Christian faith that death itself will be defeated and that we will live with God throughout the endless ages of eternity (1 Cor. 15:51–57).*

Conclusion

On the basis of these great truths about the work of God in the past, the present, and the future, the apostle Paul challenged the believers in Corinth to glorify God in their bodies in the here and now (1 Cor. 6:19–20). He declared that we will glorify God in resurrected bodies forever.

This tremendous book of the New Testament that begins with an emphasis on the faithfulness of God comes to a climactic conclusion, urging the followers of Jesus Christ to respond to God with a steadfast, unmovable spirit of faithfulness in the assurance that all of our work for the Lord will not be in vain, but will be productive both in this life and for the life to come (1 Cor. 15:58).

WEDNESDAY EVENING, JANUARY 13

Title: A Faithful Henchman

Text: "Paul. . . . To Titus, mine own son after the common faith: Grace, mercy, and peace, from God the Father and the Lord Jesus Christ our Saviour" **(Titus 1:1, 4)**.

Scripture Reading: Titus 1

Introduction

Many times the name "henchman" has been used in a critical and/or derogatory way. However, this is not necessarily the meaning of the word. Webster defines it as "an attendant, squire, or page." A henchman is a trusted follower and supporter. Titus comes under the concept of being a follower and supporter of Paul. Thus the title "A Faithful Henchman" is given to him.

Not a great deal is known about Titus, but he was a star in Paul's opinion. He was one of the most trusted and valuable helpers Paul had, and Paul called him "my true son" (1:4 NIV).

I. Look at the kind of man Titus was.

A. *He was a companion in an awkward and difficult time.* When Paul was having a difficult time, Titus was by his side and was a faithful friend. When

Paul paid his visit to Jerusalem to a church that suspected him and was prepared to mistrust and dislike him, he took Titus with him (Gal. 2:1).

B. *He was a man for a tough assignment.* When the trouble at Corinth was at its worst, Paul sent Titus there with one of the harshest letters he ever wrote (2 Cor. 8:16). It took a person with real character to fulfill such an assignment, but Titus had the strength of mind and the toughness of fiber that enabled him to face and handle a difficult situation.

There are two kinds of people in the world. One is the kind that can make a bad situation worse. The other is the kind that can bring order out of chaos and peace out of strife. Titus was of the latter.

C. *Titus was a man with a gift for practical administration.* Because of Titus's talent, Paul chose Titus to be the one to organize the collection for the poor members of the church at Corinth (2 Cor. 8:6, 10). We ought to thank God for people to whom we can turn when a job needs to be done.

II. Paul gave Titus some affectionate names.

A. *Paul called him his true son.* This title probably means that Paul was instrumental in the conversion of Titus. An experience of this nature brings joy to any Christian.

B. *Paul called him his brother (2 Cor. 8:23).* When a child in the faith becomes a brother in the faith, it is a great day.

C. *Paul said that Titus walked in the Spirit (2 Cor. 12:18).* Paul knew Titus would deal with things as he himself would. Paul had a lieutenant to whom he could commit his work and know it would be done right. Therefore Paul sent Titus to Crete to be a pattern for the Christians there (Titus 2:7). Titus was not just to talk to them about what a Christian should be, but was to show them what one should be. No greater compliment can be paid to a person than this.

Conclusion

Titus is a good example for all. Everyone needs to develop the character of trustworthiness and dependability.

SUNDAY MORNING, JANUARY 17

Title: The Fruit of the Spirit Is Peace

Text: "But the fruit of the Spirit is love, joy, peace" **(Gal. 5:22 RSV).**

Scripture Reading: Isaiah 9:6; Luke 2:13–14; John 16:33

Hymns: "I Know Whom I Have Believed," Whittle

"Saviour, Like a Shepherd Lead Us," Thrupp

"The Solid Rock," Mote

Offertory Prayer: Holy heavenly Father, we thank you for the many gifts that have come to us through faith in our Lord and Savior, Jesus Christ. We thank you for your gift of love and for the joy that we receive through Christ. We thank you for the peace resulting from the right relationships that he has helped us to establish. We bring our tithes and offerings praying your blessings on them so that others might come to know this love, joy, and wonderful peace through him. Amen.

Introduction

The Bible says much about peace. Our Lord spoke of his gift of peace: "Peace I leave with you; my peace I give to you; not as the world gives do I give to you. Let not your hearts be troubled, neither let them be afraid" (John 14:27 RSV).

Paul spoke of the peace that comes from God. "Therefore, since we are justified by faith, we have peace with God through our Lord Jesus Christ" (Rom. 5:1 RSV). He defined the kingdom of God in terms of "righteousness and peace and joy," and encouraged us to "pursue what makes for peace and for mutual upbuilding" (Rom. 14:17–19 RSV). We are exhorted, "If possible, so far as it depends upon you, live peaceably with all" (Rom. 12:18 RSV).

One of the great beatitudes congratulates those followers whose lives result in bringing people into a right relationship with God and into right relationships with other human beings (Matt. 5:9).

All people desire peace. While Alexander the Great or Julius Caesar could produce a world at peace, the world hungers for peace of heart. The peace that they produced was a peace created by subjection and suppression. The statesmen and diplomats of the world work for outward peace, while Christ produces peace within individuals.

I. There are many definitions of peace.

A. *A modern understanding of peace is "an absence of war and trouble."*

B. *The pagan philosophers of the past offered suggestions concerning the pathway to peace.* The peace they describe is more negative in nature than positive.

1. Some philosophers suggested that to find peace, a person had to eliminate desire—to cultivate a detachment from things.
2. Some scholars suggested that to find peace, a person had to avoid personal emotional involvement. Attaining such peace would require living in isolation from other human beings.
3. Some thinkers suggested that to find peace, a person had to develop self-sufficient independence. Many people seek for this kind of peace through money and power. They seek to insulate themselves against life and against dependence on others. The great philosopher Epicurus has been quoted as saying, "Peace is the absence of pain in the body or trouble in the mind."

C. *The Hebrew writers of the Old Testament understood peace to be positive and beneficial.* The normal Hebrew greeting was "*Shalom.*" This common greeting expressed a wish for everything that would make for a person's highest good. The Old Testament concept refers to serenity, the perfect contentment of life that results from complete happiness and complete security.

D. *In its basic nature, peace describes the perfection of relationships.*
   1. *Peace* is the word used for human friendship (Jer. 20:10).
   2. *Peace* is the word used for right relationships between nations.
   3. *Peace* is the word used for right relationships between people and God.
   4. *Peace* is the word used for right relationships within the home (1 Cor. 7:15).

II. Christ brings peace.

The prophet Isaiah looked forward to the coming of the Messiah and called him the "Prince of Peace." For Jesus to be the Prince of Peace, individuals must make him King of Kings and Lord of Lords in their hearts and over all of their relationships.

A. *Jesus Christ came and died for our sins that we might be restored to a right relationship with God.* This position of acceptance in God's sight comes to us by an act of God when we trust in Jesus Christ as Lord and Savior (Rom. 5:1).

B. *Peace is the gift of Christ.* Christ spoke to his disciples immediately before his crucifixion, saying, "My peace I give to you" (John 14:27 RSV). Our Lord related perfectly with God and enjoyed perfect inward peace as he approached his passion. He desired that his disciples possess this same kind of relationship with God.

   Following his resurrection from the tomb, our Lord bestowed the gift of peace on his disciples (John 20:19, 21, 26).

C. *Peace is said to be the fruit of the indwelling Holy Spirit (Gal. 5:22).* In the moment of conversion, God bestows on us the gift of a new nature and plants within us the divine Holy Spirit. The Holy Spirit assures us of salvation. The Holy Spirit acts as the guarantee of our ultimate victory over death. The Holy Spirit provides us with guidance and helps all along the road of life. One of his primary functions is to produce peace within us—that is, to work within us to bring about a perfection of relationships, both with God and with our fellow human beings.

We must not think of peace in terms of stagnation or deadness. Peace is positive and constructive and even aggressive as the Holy Spirit helps us establish right relationships with all of the people with whom we come into contact.

III. The Holy Spirit and the foes of peace.

The Holy Spirit enters the heart of the new believer to help the believer put off all of the works of the flesh that are self-destructive and hurtful (Gal. 5:16–21).

One who follows a life of immorality, impurity, and licentiousness cannot possibly experience the peace of God. A person who is guilty of idolatry, sorcery, or enmity, of creating strife, jealousy, and anger cannot possibly know the inward peace of God. Someone who lives a life of selfishness and dissension, being controlled by a divisive spirit and an envious attitude, cannot possibly know the way of peace. One who succumbs to a life of drunkenness and carousing will know inward turmoil and disturbance throughout all of life. The Holy Spirit is deposited within us to help us see the evil destructiveness of these ways of living that characterize the lives of many people before they are converted.

To produce the fruit of peace, that is, right relationships, the Holy Spirit will create some inward turmoil within the heart of the believer unless the believer is cooperating with him to reflect the glory of Jesus Christ.

IV. The Holy Spirit as a producer of peace.

The Holy Spirit made us aware of our need for Jesus Christ as Savior and brought about the miracle of the new birth when we trusted Jesus Christ as Lord and Savior.

The Holy Spirit is now working within us to help us establish right relationships in every area of life.

The Holy Spirit enables us to love unlovable people in such a way that brings inward peace to us (Rom. 5:5). With the help of the Holy Spirit, we can accept them as they are, forgive them for their shortcomings, endure them when they irritate us, and help them rather than hurt them.

The Holy Spirit will help us focus our lives on the things of eternal significance so that we will not live a divided and destructive life (Gal. 5:24–25).

Conclusion

To enjoy the peace of God bestowed on us by Christ and produced within us by the Holy Spirit, we must receive it as a gift and cooperate with the Holy Spirit as he seeks to help us avoid the foes of peace. We must follow his leadership as he leads us in establishing and maintaining right relationships with our relatives, neighbors, friends, and even strangers. The Holy Spirit will lead us to trust in the Lord with all of our heart both in the present and in the future. He will replace fear with faith.

The Holy Spirit works continuously to help us maintain a right fellowship with God, a right evaluation of self, and a right appreciation of others. He is seeking to give us the inward peace that our heart hungers for.

SUNDAY EVENING, JANUARY 17

Title: Three Classes of People

Text: "Brothers and sisters, I could not address you as people who live by the Spirit but as people who are still worldly—mere infants in Christ" **(1 Cor. 3:1 NIV)**.

Scripture Reading: 1 Corinthians 2:14–3:4

Introduction

A vast difference can be observed between the character and quality of the daily lives of those who profess to be followers of Jesus Christ and those who do not. The explanation for this difference is revealed in the passages of Scripture under consideration today. The human family is divided into three groups. First, Paul speaks of unspiritual, or natural, people. Second, he speaks of spiritual people. And third, he speaks of carnal, or fleshly, people.

The New Testament focuses on the theme of improving the quality of human life. This improvement is experienced by those who meet certain conditions and make certain responses to the good news of God's love.

I. Unspiritual, or natural, people (1 Cor. 2:14).

By the unspiritual person, Paul is referring to the unregenerate, unconverted unbeliever who does not know God.

A. *The natural person is destitute of the working of the Spirit of God.* He or she does not understand, recognize, or appreciate the work of the divine Spirit.

B. *To the natural person, the preaching of the cross is foolishness (1 Cor. 1:18).*

C. *The natural person has been blinded to the light of the good news of God's love by the evil one (2 Cor. 4:3–4).*

The wisdom of this world or the knowledge of science does not equip one to understand or to appreciate the things of God. God is not real to the natural person.

II. People of the flesh, or carnal, people.

Paul writes to the church at Corinth and rejoices in the many rich gifts that God has bestowed on them. He also congratulates them for some matters in which they have achieved a degree of success.

Paul's primary emphasis in the book of Corinthians is an effort to correct them in their attitudes and actions as disciples of Jesus Christ. He writes to complain and to counsel concerning the fact that these new converts continue to be babes in Christ, or carnal. He grieves and complains because they are acting as if Jesus Christ had not been permitted to come into their hearts and lives (1 Cor. 3:3).

A. *These people of the flesh are still babes in Christ.* They are immature. They have not grown in the grace and in the knowledge of our Lord and Savior Jesus Christ (1 Cor. 3:1–3).

B. *These converts are still dominated by the desires of the flesh.* They have not let the Holy Spirit cleanse them of the attitudes and activities that were normal for their unconverted life.

C. *The divisions and strife among them indicate that they are still immature and under the control of their lower nature (1 Cor. 3:4).*

III. Spiritual people.

The apostle is eager that all of the converts to Christ in Corinth make a positive response to the Lord Jesus by cooperating with his Holy Spirit and letting the Spirit bear his fruit in their hearts and lives.

A. *The spiritual person recognizes and appreciates the deep things of God (1 Cor. 2:9–10).* Verse 9 often is used as a description of heaven, but in reality it is a description of the present experience of those who have trusted Christ and who are following the leadership of the Holy Spirit.

B. *The spiritual person believes the deep things of God (1 Cor. 2:12).* Only as the child of God responds in a spirit of cooperation with the inward work of the divine Spirit can he or she enter into the spiritual heritage of a child of God.

C. *The spiritual person continues to receive the rich gifts of God (1 Cor. 2:12).* The gift of eternal life as well as the gift of the Holy Spirit comes in the moment of conversion. God, the loving Father, continues to bestow the rich gifts of the Spirit on his children who trust him and obey him and seek to be his blessing to others.

Conclusion

If you are among the unspiritual, the unsaved, our loving Lord would invite you to be converted this day and to enter into God's family through faith in him.

If you continue to be a babe in Christ, controlled by the appetites of your lower nature and defeated in your desire to live a victorious life, there is hope for you if you will nourish your soul on the milk of God's Word and cooperate with the Spirit as he works within you.

WEDNESDAY EVENING, JANUARY 20

Title: A Servant of God

Text: "Paul, a servant of God, and an apostle of Jesus Christ, according to the faith of God's elect, and the acknowledging of the truth which is after godliness" **(Titus 1:1)**.

Scripture Reading: Titus 1

Introduction

In Paul's letter to Titus, he referred to himself as a servant of God. The word *servant* means "bond slave," and as a slave Paul belongs to Jesus Christ.

I. The title is mingled with humility and pride.

A. *The first thing to consider is the humility.* Being a bond slave of Jesus Christ means that one is the undisputed possession of God. The service one renders is to God. A Christian cannot serve both God and mammon.

A bond slave may not exercise his or her will; all decisions are made by the master. In Paul's case, the Lord had complete control over him and his time. Paul was totally submitted to God.

B. *The second thing to consider is the pride.* The Old Testament prophets wore the title "slaves of God." Many people consider Moses the greatest man who ever lived, other than Jesus. He was called the slave of God (Josh. 1:2). The successor of Moses, Joshua, claimed the same title (Josh. 24:29).

One mark of pride was that God's will was revealed to his servants (Amos 3:7) and they in turn spoke God's message to Israel (Jer. 7:25). This title gave Paul the right to walk in the succession of these other great men of God. He, too, was a bond slave of Jesus.

As Paul bore the title, so can all Christians of today. When people enter the church, they do not enter an institution that began yesterday, but one that is centuries old. Anyone who works for the Lord as a teacher, preacher, or in some other capacity is in rich tradition.

II. The title "servant of God" carries with it privileges and obligations.

A. *It is a privilege to serve Jesus because of what he has done for us.* The greatest story ever told is the story of Jesus, and the most wonderful experience a person can have is living in a personal relationship with Jesus. Thus we are privileged to be able to share this good news with others.

B. *Second Corinthians 4:5 says, "What we preach is not ourselves, but Jesus Christ as Lord, and ourselves as your servants for Jesus' sake" (NIV).* This is an obligation to unconditionally serve Jesus Christ anywhere, anytime, whatever the circumstances.

C. *The bond slave has a resource from God that is always enough.* The Lord has promised to be with his servants always, even to the end of the age (Matt. 28:20). He also has promised to supply all the needs and to give sufficient grace.

Conclusion

Christians have many titles given to them by their fellow humans and by our Lord, but there is no greater title than "servant of God." May all who hear this message wear the title well.

SUNDAY MORNING, JANUARY 24

Title: The Fruit of the Spirit Is Patience

Text: "The fruit of the Spirit is love, joy, peace, patience . . ." **(Gal. 5:22 RSV).**

Scripture Reading: Colossians 3:12–17

Hymns: "Guide Me, O Thou Great Jehovah," Williams
"Take My Life, and Let It Be," Havergal
"More Like Jesus Would I Be," Crosby

Offertory Prayer: Holy Father, we rejoice in this day that you have made, and we are glad for it. We serve you with joy. We bring tithes and offerings to show our love for you and to show our desire to share the message of your love with people everywhere. Accept these gifts and multiply them to the furtherance of your kingdom into lives of men and women, boys and girls. We pray in Christ's name. Amen.

Introduction

When we trusted Christ as Savior, we received the gift of eternal life. We became children of God, members of his family. The Holy Spirit was given to us to dwell within us. He assures us of our place in the family of God and of our salvation, and he transforms our personalities and enables us to reflect the grace of God and the beauty of the Lord Jesus Christ. God wants to do more than merely take our souls to heaven when we die. He wants to demonstrate in us and through us the heavenly quality of life here and now.

The first fruit of the Spirit is love. The Holy Spirit pours out divine love within our hearts and enables us to love unlovely people. The second fruit of the Spirit is the joy of Christ. The Holy Spirit seeks to fill us with the joy that Christ experienced because of his perfect relationship with God and his total involvement in a ministry to humankind. The third fruit is peace. By helping us to establish right relationships with God, other people, and material things, the Holy Spirit seeks to bless us with an inward tranquility that surpasses human understanding. The fourth fruit is patience, or long-suffering. The Greek word from which this translation comes means to be long-tempered rather than short-tempered. Repeatedly the Old Testament ascribes this trait to God. God is often described as being very slow to anger (see, e.g., Ex. 34:6; Neh. 9:17; Ps. 103:8).

I. Do you have a short temper?

The Holy Spirit helps us overcome or subdue a short temper. The Holy Spirit wants to enable us to restrain both our attitudes and actions when otherwise we might "lose our tempers and blow our stacks."

How do you keep from losing your temper? Or do you even try? Do you try to control your tongue and withhold harsh words toward others? How do you respond or react to the unexpected disappointments in life? Have you developed a reputation for a hasty reply to people who are unkind to you?

II. How do you react to mistreatment and disappointment?

Those living with other people cannot escape some degree of misunderstanding, mistreatment, and even deliberate misrepresentation. Our reaction to undeserved mistreatment indicates the degree of our spiritual and emotional maturity. Christ Jesus gave us the Holy Spirit to aid our responses when we are either mistreated or disappointed in life.

A. *Some people may respond to mistreatment by retreating into a state of depression.* Depression is anger turned inward on the self and can be very destructive.

B. *Some people respond to mistreatment by developing and harboring resentment.* This reaction becomes exceedingly costly to the individual who has been injured.

C. *Some people may respond to mistreatment or disappointment by some act of retaliation toward the person responsible for causing the hurt.* This response could result in anything from an unkind word to an act of murder.

D. *Some people may respond to mistreatment by determining to seek revenge at some time in the future.* Following this path includes harboring hostility that will eat out one's heart, disturb one's soul, and hinder one's prayers.

III. The Holy Spirit aids and encourages us to respond to mistreatment and disappointment with patience.

A. *Without patience we will find it exceedingly difficult to forgive others.* The wise man said, "Good sense makes a man slow to anger, and it is his glory to overlook an offense" (Prov. 19:11 RSV). We learn a great truth when we discover that Jesus taught the injured to be forgiving for their own good rather than for the good of the one who caused the injury. Jesus encouraged unlimited forgiveness (Matt. 18:21–22).

B. *Unless we practice patience, we will not be able to enjoy warm and continuous fellowship with others.* Short-tempered and hotheaded people will always find something about which to be upset. "A hot-tempered man stirs up strife, but he who is slow to anger quiets contention" (Prov. 15:18 RSV).

C. *Unless we practice patience, we will rob ourselves of the understanding and the insight we need to face life.* "He who is slow to anger has great understanding, but he who has a hasty temper exalts folly" (Prov. 14:29 RSV). To jump to a conclusion and to respond with anger to the various situations of life will prevent one from seeing through and understanding the significance of words and events.

IV. The importance of Christian patience.

We sometimes wonder why we do not have a more powerful impact on the non-Christian world. We sometimes wonder why our Christian testimony makes no impact on people around us. Could it be that we have thought of being Christian merely in terms of regularly attending worship and living life from a negative rather than a positive constructive viewpoint? Could it be that we have been so short-tempered and difficult to get along with that we have nullified our Christian witness to others?

A. *If we would be worthy of the name Christian, and if we would properly represent Christ, we must let the Holy Spirit enable us to be patient with others (Eph. 4:1–3).*

B. *Patience is said to be a vital part of the uniform of the true disciple of Jesus Christ (Col. 3:12–14).* Our Lord was very patient with people. He did not respond with harshness toward disappointing circumstances in life. Our Lord possessed a spirit of self-restraint and forbearance that enabled him to refrain from retaliating when he was mistreated.

C. *Genuine disciples of our Lord should practice patience toward all kinds of people.* In Paul's epistle to the Thessalonians, we hear him say, "And we exhort you, brethren, admonish the idler, encourage the fainthearted, help the weak, be patient with them all" (1 Thess. 5:14 RSV).

The Holy Spirit seeks to pour out on us the love of God. This love will enable us to love unlovely people and to imitate Jesus Christ, our Lord, in the response that we make toward people who mistreat us, people who disappoint us, and events that would depress us.

The Holy Spirit encourages us never to lose faith and hope, nor to give way to despair but to press on, hoping for the best.

Conclusion

Our God is very patient with us even when we fail. He continues to be forgiving and to work within us to produce something good. He does not give up hope. He still has a gracious plan for our lives.

God's patience should encourage us to change our attitudes toward him and to come to him with trust and a desire to obey him (Rom. 2:4).

God's patience continues to keep the door of opportunity open for people who come to him by faith for the gifts of forgiveness and new life (2 Peter 3:9).

SUNDAY EVENING, JANUARY 24

Title: Spiritual Birth and Spiritual Growth

Text: "I fed you with milk, not solid food" **(1 Cor. 3:2 RSV)**.

Scripture Reading: Hebrews 5:12–14; 2 Peter 3:18

Introduction

Retardation has been defined by Webster as "slowness in development or progress." Mental or physical retardation usually comes to mind when we hear the word *retardation*, but tonight we are going to consider spiritual retardation.

Throughout the centuries the church has been plagued with spiritual retardation. Spiritual retardation was one of the major contributing factors to the ineffectiveness of the church in Corinth to be the force for Christ that it could have been. Spiritual retardation hinders the church today from being what God wants it to be.

Paul addressed the people to whom he wrote as "brothers and sisters" (1 Cor. 3:1 NIV). They were the children of God.

I. How do we become children of God?

A. *Some say by ceremony or initiation.* Paul denied this position (1 Cor. 1:14, 17).

B. *Some say by the obtaining of wisdom or intellectual enlightenment.* Paul denied this explanation (1 Cor. 1:18–24).

C. *Some suggest that we become children of God through the practice of benevolence and philanthropy.*

D. *Some say that we become children of God through moral and ethical excellence.*

E. *Jesus taught that we become the children of God by a spiritual birth (John 3:3, 5, 7).*

1. The new birth is a divine change produced by the Holy Spirit.
2. The new birth is a spiritual change wrought within the soul.
3. The new birth is a complete change.
4. The new birth is a permanent change.

The new birth is experienced when we make a genuine faith response to Jesus Christ as Lord and Savior.

II. The spiritual birth experience is the beginning point rather than the climactic conclusion.

Some make the tragic mistake of believing that spiritual birth produces spiritual adults. Spiritual birth, like physical birth, produces infants.

A. *Continued infancy is a tragedy in the physical realm.*

1. Continued infancy produces brokenhearted parents.
2. Continued infancy produces frustrated, unhappy children.

B. *There are many foes to spiritual growth.*

1. We live in a hostile environment that is not conducive toward spiritual development and growth.
2. Believers continue to possess inward inclinations that handicap them at the point of spiritual growth. The receiving of the new nature in the spiritual birth does not eradicate the fleshly nature.
3. Believers are confronted with satanic opposition as they seek to serve God and as they seek to grow toward spiritual maturity.

III. Divine encouragements to spiritual growth.

The heavenly Father is tremendously concerned that his children grow. He has made provisions for this growth.

A. *The gift of a new nature from God (2 Peter 1:4).*

B. *The gift of God's divine Spirit to dwell within (Gal. 4:6).*

C. *The gift of the milk of God's divine Word to nourish and to strengthen (1 Cor. 3:2; 1 Peter 2:2).*

D. *Through the family of God found in the local congregation, God helps each of his children grow toward spiritual maturity.*

E. *God has given us the opportunity to serve and to be a blessing to others.* To respond to his leadership will assist us in our growth toward spiritual maturity.

Conclusion

It is not the will of our heavenly Father that we remain in spiritual infancy. By responding to his Spirit and by utilizing our opportunities for growth, we can move forward in such a manner as to bring joy to our hearts, good into the hearts and lives of others, and pleasure to the heart of our Father God.

WEDNESDAY EVENING, JANUARY 27

Title: An Apostle of Jesus Christ

Text: "Paul, a servant of God, and an apostle of Jesus Christ, according to the faith of God's elect, and the acknowledging of the truth which is after godliness" **(Titus 1:1).**

Scripture Reading: Titus 1

Introduction

A young man felt that he was called to be a minister. He was asked how he came to make such a decision. His answer was that after hearing a certain sermon in a school chapel service, he felt that God was calling him. He was then asked the name of the preacher who wrought such an effect on him. His answer was, "I do not know the preacher's name, but I know that God spoke to me that day."

An apostle of Jesus Christ is one who is sure God has spoken to him. Paul had this assurance, and because of this, he was an apostle.

I. What does it mean to be an apostle?

A. *It means to belong to Jesus Christ.* Paul's life was not his own. He had no choice but to live as Jesus wanted him to live. He was Jesus' possession.

B. *To be an apostle means to be commissioned or sent by Jesus.* The word *apostle* comes from the Greek word meaning "to send" or "dispatch." It means an envoy or an ambassador. The duty of an ambassador is to form a liaison between the country he or she represents and the country to which he or she is sent. An apostle receives authority from God; that authority cannot be taken, earned, or achieved.

C. *To be an apostle means that power and authority have been delegated to a person by Jesus.*

II. Paul felt that being an apostle carried with it some marks of distinction.

A. *It was an honor.* It is an honor to do anything for God. Paul was honored in this way according to the will of God. All Christians are chosen by God.

B. *It was a responsibility.* God chose Paul because he wanted him to do something. God also wanted to do something with him and through him. He wanted to make Paul an instrument through which the tidings of a new life would go out to people. Paul, as an apostle, stood in Christ's stead.

C. *It was a privilege.* As it is a privilege to represent one's country as an ambassador, so it is a privilege to represent Christ to one's fellow humans. It is also a duty. There is no greater privilege than to tell others of eternal life through Jesus Christ. This is the business of an apostle.

Conclusion

The apostleship of Paul was the explanation of his ability to toil and suffer. He was sure his task had been given to him by God, and this was his motivation. Since God gives this same task to every Christian, we should be motivated to be more diligent in our work for the Lord.

SUNDAY MORNING, JANUARY 31

Title: The Fruit of the Spirit Is Kindness

Text: "But the fruit of the Spirit is love, joy, peace, patience, kindness . . ." **(Gal. 5:22 RSV).**

Scripture Reading: Luke 6:35–36; Ephesians 4:30–32

Hymns: "We Have Heard the Joyful Sound," Owens

"Break Thou the Bread," Lathbury

"Amazing Grace," Newton

Offertory Prayer: Dear heavenly Father, thank you for your kindness that has brought us the gift of salvation through Jesus Christ. Thank you for your kindness revealed in the forgiveness of our sin and in the gift of new life. Today we come bringing our love and gratitude, our tithes and offerings as a response from our heart for your kindness. Accept these gifts, and bless and multiply them to the advancing of your kingdom and for the good of humankind, we pray in Christ's name. Amen.

Introduction

God wants to bring about some changes within all of us, for he is trying to make us better men and women.

God sent his Son to save us from the consequences of sin and to demonstrate the quality of life that he intended for humanity from the beginning.

God sent his Holy Spirit to dwell within us to deliver us from the power of evil in the world. This precious Holy Spirit has come to reproduce within us both the character of Christ and the abundant life that Christ makes possible for those who trust him.

Christ came to do more than die for our sins. Intending to do more than taking us to heaven when we die and saving us from eternity in hell with the devil and his angels, Christ purposed to help us break with attitudes, ambitions, and actions that are both self-destructive and harmful to others. He came to give us a new pattern of thinking and a new program of action that lead to abundant life in the here and now.

Christ achieves his purpose in us through the gift of his Holy Spirit. Paul encouraged the Philippian Christians to work diligently because God was at work in them (Phil. 2:12–13). God sent his Holy Spirit to bring about a divine change within us. This change occurs when we look to the Lord and cooperate with him as he works out God's good purpose within us (1 Cor. 3:18).

Paul listed the inward graces or virtues that the Holy Spirit wants to produce within us. These graces include love, joy, peace, patience, kindness, goodness, faithfulness, gentleness, and self-control.

Today we will give primary consideration to the fruit of the Spirit expressed in kindness. The famous poet William Wordsworth said, "The best portion of a good man's life is his little, nameless, unremembered acts of kindness and of love." Washington Irving described the kind heart in beautiful words: "A kind heart is a fountain of gladness, making everything in its vicinity freshen into smiles." Mark Twain declared that "kindness is the language which the deaf can hear and the blind can see." Paul described Christian love by saying, "Love is patient and kind" (1 Cor. 13:4 RSV).

Paul's list of the fruit of the Spirit provides us with a verbal portrait of what Jesus Christ is like and what his disciples can be like with the help of the Holy Spirit. We must not only verbalize the message of Christ, but by the lives we live, we must reveal the reality of Christ within us. Our actions must speak louder than our words.

I. Christ was known for his kindness.

A. *Christ expressed kindness at a wedding feast when the refreshments ran short.*

B. *Christ expressed kindness to a widow at Nain whose only son had died.*

C. *Christ was kind to a poor leper who hungered for health and for human affection. The Scripture tells us that our Lord "touched him." This touch indicated the kindness of his heart.*

D. *Christ was exceedingly kind to Zacchaeus, a tax collector who was hated and despised by his neighbors.*

E. *Christ was expressing the kindness of his heart when he fed the hungry who followed him.*

F. *Christ showed kindness and compassion to a woman who was brought to him being charged with the sin of adultery.* The record tells us that "Jesus bent down and wrote with his finger on the ground." He would not embarrass her by staring at her in her humiliation. While not condoning the evil of her act, he did not condemn her, but he encouraged her to live a more productive life in the future.

G. *Christ was kind to the thief on the cross who pled for consideration.*

H. *Christ was kind to his mother while he was dying on the cross.* He made provisions for her future care.

I. *Christ was kind to the apostle Peter following his resurrection.* Jesus' three questions concerning Peter's love were not intended to embarrass him, but to provide him with an opportunity for restoration to fellowship and usefulness.

II. The Holy Spirit seeks to lead us to act kindly toward others.

A. *Unkindness is a characteristic of the godless life.* When Paul described those who did not know God, he said, "There is none that doeth good, no, not one" (Rom. 3:12).

B. *Kindness is not instinctive.* Kindness must be developed and cultivated. When Paul spoke to the Christians in Colossae concerning the garments that the children of God should wear, he encouraged them, among other things, to "put on kindness."

C. *The command to be kind is clear and definite.* "Be kind to one another, tenderhearted, forgiving one another, as God in Christ forgave you" (Eph. 4:32 RSV).

1. Kindness leads to tactfulness.
2. Kindness seeks to be helpful.
3. Kindness is being appreciative.
4. Kindness includes being constructive.
5. Kindness looks for the good in others.
6. Kindness shows forgiveness and mercy.
7. Kindness means treating others the way God has treated us.

Conclusion

God's kindness made provision for our salvation from sin. "When the goodness and loving kindness of God our Savior appeared, he saved us, not because of deeds done by us in righteousness, but in virtue of his own mercy, by the washing of regeneration and renewal in the Holy Spirit, which he poured out upon us richly through Jesus Christ our Savior, so that we might be justified by his grace and become heirs in hope of eternal life" (Titus 3:4–7 RSV).

By many deeds of kindness, God seeks to bring about a radical change within the minds of people. This change moves people from distrust to trust and from rebellion to a life of responsible cooperation with his good purpose. Paul warned us against presuming on the kindness of God to the extent that we bring about our own doom. He encouraged us to recognize in God's kindness that he is seeking to lead us to forsake destructive ways and to trust him for abundant life (Rom. 2:4).

God will continue to deal with us in terms of divine kindness after we have entered the eternal. He will continue to show "the immeasurable riches of his grace in kindness toward us in Christ Jesus" (Eph. 2:7 RSV). Because God has been so kind to us, we should respond to others in terms of kindness.

Be kind to yourself by putting your faith and trust in Jesus Christ as Lord and Savior. Be kind to yourself by responding to the Holy Spirit's work within you. Be kind to others as the Spirit leads, and you will find life to be much more beautiful and satisfying.

SUNDAY EVENING, JANUARY 31

Title: You Are God's Garden

Text: "For we are fellow workers for God; you are God's field, God's building" **(1 Cor. 3:9 NIV)**.

Scripture Reading: 1 Corinthians 3:5–9

Introduction

Paul uses many different figures of speech to describe the church and individual believers. In our text, he describes the members of the church as being fellow workers and partners together in the service they render for God. He then mixes his terminology and describes the church, the people of God, individual Christians, as God's field or God's garden, as well as God's building. Let us focus our minds on the significance of thinking about ourselves as God's garden.

For the garden that God is cultivating, he provides the soil, the seed, the sunshine, and the showers. All of these are essentials for growth.

I. If we are God's garden, we should sow the good seed of his Word with dedication.

God is eager for our lives to be both beautiful and productive. Receiving his divine truth as authoritative will produce a transformation in our lives.

II. If we are God's garden, we need to cultivate the struggling plants.

Gardens do not grow accidentally or automatically. The plants need to be cultivated, encouraged, and nourished. Similarly, believers need to cultivate the new affections, aspirations, and desires that the Holy Spirit puts within us.

III. If we are God's garden, we need to be on guard against the foes of growth.

Experienced gardeners know that pests such as groundhogs, moles, rabbits, and a great variety of insects threaten both the beauty and the productiveness of a garden. Likewise, there are many foes to spiritual growth, and these must be guarded against. We must watch our minds lest we harbor evil and destructive thoughts. We must watch our affections lest we love that which will bring hurt and harm.

IV. If we are God's garden, we need to enlist as much assistance as possible.

Even experienced gardeners sometimes need expert advice on problems associated with the growth of plants. Similarly, each of us needs the assistance of mature brothers and sisters in Christ to grow toward spiritual maturity. We need the inspiration and motivation that can come as a result of hearing the testimony of those who have lived through some of the crises of life that are bound to come to each of us.

V. If we are God's garden, we need to fertilize as we have opportunity.

There are many different kinds of fertilizers that stimulate growth and aid in producing a great harvest. Likewise, believers should use prayer, respond to the leadership of the Holy Spirit, and be regular in our worship habits, for these activities fertilize the growth of our spiritual life.

Conclusion

As God's garden, we can look forward to the harvest when we produce much fruit for the glory of our Lord (John 15:5–8; Gal. 5:22–23). We must not become weary in the struggles of life if we want to reap a harvest that will be pleasing to our Lord (Gal. 6:9). God is at work in us to help us to be both a beautiful and a productive garden (Phil. 2:13). You can be beautiful in the eyes of God, in the eyes of others, and in your own eyes as you respond to the opportunity to be God's garden.

SUGGESTED PREACHING PROGRAM FOR THE MONTH OF
FEBRUARY

■ Sunday Mornings

Continue the series of messages based on Galatians 5:22–23 using the theme "Cultivating the Fruit of the Spirit."

■ Sunday Evenings

Continue throughout February with messages from 1 Corinthians on the theme "Words of Correction and Counsel for New Disciples."

■ Wednesday Evenings

Continue the series of studies on Paul's epistle to Titus, in which he gave Titus practical suggestions concerning the church, its leadership, its needs, and its opportunities.

WEDNESDAY EVENING, FEBRUARY 3

Title: An Apostle's Gospel

Text: "In hope of eternal life, which God, that cannot lie, promised before the world began" **(Titus 1:2)**.

Scripture Reading: Titus 1

Introduction

We have discussed in two previous messages on Titus titles that Paul gave himself—"servant" of Jesus Christ and "apostle" of Jesus Christ. Now we turn our attention toward the gospel of an apostle.

I. The foundation of an apostle's gospel is the hope of eternal life.

A. Christians have a new kind of life to offer. This offering is a share of God's life. He alone gives it, and his instrument for giving this life is the believer. This offer is God's power for humanity's frustrations, God's serenity for our unrest, God's truth for our guessing, God's goodness for our failure, and God's joy for our sorrow.

B. Christians should take pride in such a privilege. A salesperson should take pride in the product he or she offers. Nothing greater than the gospel of Jesus Christ exists. It is an honor and privilege for the Christian to serve such a cause.

II. The apostle must do two things so that others can receive the offer of eternal life.

A. The apostle is to awaken faith in people. To Paul, faith meant total and absolute trust in God. The first step in the Christian life is to realize that one can do nothing but receive the offer of God. Evangelization, the first duty of the Christian, consists in persuading others to accept God's offer.

B. The apostle is to equip others with knowledge. Christian evangelism and Christian education must go hand in hand. The Christian life cannot survive on a wave of emotion. It involves daily loving Christ more and understanding him better.

III. The result of this faith and knowledge will be a truly religious life.

A. Faith will result in life that is eternal, abundant, and God-given. Christian knowledge is not merely intellectual but also contains a divine insight into knowing how to live the life God gives.

B. The religious life is the life people have when they are on right terms with God, themselves, and others. This life enables people to cope with the great moments in life. It also enables us to discharge our duties. Jesus Christ lives his life in the apostle, and he enables the apostle to live his life.

Conclusion

It is an honor and privilege to be an apostle. As God sends people forth, those people are to share the gospel—the good news about Jesus—to those to whom they are sent.

SUNDAY MORNING, FEBRUARY 7

Title: The Fruit of the Spirit Is Goodness

Text: "But the fruit of the Spirit is love, joy, peace, patience, kindness, goodness . . ." **(Gal. 5:22 RSV)**.

Scripture Reading: Micah 6:8; Romans 12:9–21

Hymns: "Ye Servants of God," Wesley

"Crown Him with Many Crowns," Bridges

"All the Way My Savior Leads Me," Crosby

Offertory Prayer: Gracious and loving Father, today we have many reasons for rejoicing in your love and grace. Thank you for the blessings of the past week and for your presence with us during this hour of worship. Thank you for the work of your Spirit within us. Thank you for the blessings you have in store for us both during this hour of worship and as we face the future. We present our tithes and offerings as we recognize your divine lordship and your kingdom's need for our financial resources. May your blessings be on these tokens of our love and gratitude. Use them for your glory and for the good of those in need, we pray, in Christ's name. Amen.

Introduction

Like the apostle Paul, all of us have a problem with evil. We hear Paul speaking to the Roman Christians concerning this: "I know that good itself does not dwell in me, that is, in my sinful nature. For I have the desire to do what is good, but I cannot carry it out. For I do not do the good I want to do, but the evil I do not want to do—this I keep on doing. Now if I do what I do not want to do, it is no longer I who do it, but it is sin living in me that does it" (Rom. 7:18–20 NIV). People who have evil natures and live in an evil world cannot easily be good and do good in all circumstances.

Our Savior once commanded "Do good to them that hate you" (Matt. 5:44). And Paul encouraged the Galatian disciples to do good: "So then, as we have opportunity, let us do good to all men, and especially to those who are of the household of faith" (Gal. 6:10 RSV).

It may be surprising when one looks at the Scriptures closely to discover why our Lord was able to do good under all circumstances. The Scriptures tell us, "God anointed Jesus of Nazareth with the Holy Spirit and with power; how he went about doing good and healing all that were oppressed by the devil, for God was with him" (Acts 10:38 RSV). Our Lord was anointed and filled with the Holy Spirit, and God was with him. Here we find the key that enabled the disciples of our Lord to practice benevolent goodness toward others rather than live by an evil principle. In considering the fruit of the indwelling Spirit, today we look at the broadest and the most general of the nine fruit when we look at goodness.

Goodness can be defined as "the generosity that is undeserved." To be good means to be generous, liberal, openhanded. Goodness is the opposite of evil. Christ came to lead us to goodness and away from that which is evil. Goodness relates to a quality of life and a quality of relationships. Christ came to help us to be good men and women, good brothers and sisters, good children, good employers and good employees, and so on.

The New Testament provides us with a beautiful example of a good man named Barnabas. He was known as the "son of encouragement" because he cheered the hearts of others.

I. Barnabas was filled with the Holy Spirit (Acts 11:24).

A. Barnabas was God-conscious. God was real to him. His life was open to God, and he was aware of God's presence. He did not ignore God.

B. Barnabas was God-controlled. He had made a proper response to the indwelling Spirit who came in the moment of his conversion. Being filled with the Holy Spirit allows one to be aware of God's presence and to be obedient to his leadership. One filled with the Spirit will trust God for guidance and help each step of the way throughout each day.

Paul encouraged each of us to "walk by the Spirit" (Gal. 5:16 RSV).

We should be "filled with the Spirit" (Eph. 5:18). We are warned not to "grieve the Holy Spirit" (Eph. 4:30 RSV) or "quench the Spirit" (1 Thess. 5:19 RSV). We must cooperate with the Holy Spirit as he works within us to reproduce the character of Jesus Christ.

II. Barnabas was filled with faith (Acts 11:24).

A. Barnabas sincerely and steadfastly believed in God's love and in God's power in his life. Because of his trust in the loving care of his heavenly Father, Barnabas enjoyed an inner security that enabled him to be good and gracious and kind and generous toward others.

B. Barnabas had faith in himself because he had faith in the love of his Father and in the power of his Christ and in the presence of the Holy Spirit.

C. Barnabas demonstrated faith in others. He put faith in Saul, the new convert, when others were not willing to trust him (Acts 9:26–27). Later he demonstrated faith in John Mark, the quitter (cf. Acts 12:25; 13:13; 15:36–39). The faith he demonstrated in Mark was most productive, and Paul later recognized this with appreciation (2 Tim. 4:11).

D. Barnabas believed that he lived in a world that belonged to God. A popular hymn goes, "My faith is rich in houses and land; he holdeth the wealth of the world in his hands." Barnabas could have joined with the lyricist William C. Martin, who said:

I trust in God wherever I may be
Upon the land or on the rolling sea;
For come what may, from day to day,
My heavenly Father watches over me.

III. Barnabas was filled with goodness (Acts 11:24).

A. Barnabas demonstrated the goodness of his heart in an expression of noble generosity (Acts 4:36–37).

1. Not a slave of the material realm, Barnabas found security in the spiritual realm. He believed that God would take care of the deep needs of life. He did not grasp for treasures that would evaporate.

   Barnabas sincerely believed Jesus' philosophy that more joy comes from giving than can be found in getting and hoarding (Acts 20:35).

2. Barnabas believed that God would take care of his children. As missionary Jim Elliot said, "He is no fool who gives what he cannot keep to gain that which he cannot lose."

3. Barnabas was a man who was willing to play second fiddle for the glory of God and for the good of others (Acts 11:25–26). When things were moving in a great way, Barnabas recognized the need for Paul's services. He secured Paul's help, and from that point forward, Paul occupied center stage as far as personalities were concerned. At no point do we find any evidence that Barnabas resented playing a supportive role.

B. Barnabas majored on looking for the good in others. He saw something in Saul of Tarsus, the new convert, that the others in the Jerusalem church could not see. Later he saw something in John Mark, the quitter, that even Paul the apostle could not see. The goodness of his heart sought that which was potentially good in others.

C. Barnabas cheered people's hearts. In a time of great need, he practiced a noble generosity to the extent that he sold a piece of property and contributed the entire sum for the relief of suffering (Acts 4:36–37). This act cheered the believers in such a way that they called him "son of encouragement." He was a spiritual cheerleader who brought joy into the hearts and lives of others.

Conclusion

Barnabas was a good man because he cooperated with the Holy Spirit. He responded to God's love, grace, kindness, and goodness by letting these character traits be reproduced within his own life. He determined with the help of the Holy Spirit to relate to others by being kind, generous, gracious, and helpful to them.

The beauty of Barnabas's life attracted others to his Savior, and they came to know Jesus Christ as Lord and Savior. We read, "And a large company was added to the Lord" (Acts 11:24 RSV). Christ will come into your heart to deliver you from evil both around and within you. He will bestow on you the gift of his Holy Spirit, who will seek to help you be a good person in all your relationships. He waits for you to open the door and to invite him to enter. Be good to yourself by trusting Jesus Christ as your Savior, and begin cooperating with the Holy Spirit as he works within you.

SUNDAY EVENING, FEBRUARY 7

Title: Fellow Workers for God

Text: "For we are God's fellow workers . . ." **(1 Cor. 3:9 RSV)**.

Scripture Reading: 1 Corinthians 3:5–23

Introduction

Spiritual immaturity plagued the church at Corinth. The membership was composed of new converts who brought into the church fellowship many of the attitudes, ambitions, and activities they had known in their pagan life. It is not surprising that this church fell far below the ideal.

A partisan spirit expressed itself in division and strife as some of the people considered God's work to be nothing more than the work of leading people (1 Cor. 3:3–6). Paul tried to correct these problems by emphasizing that we are fellow workers together for God.

I. Laborers together for God—a most sobering thought.

God is the Lord of the harvest, and we are but laborers together with each other in his vineyard.

A. In a sense, God does not need coworkers.
   1. God alone is the Creator of the universe and the source of life.
   2. God, in Christ Jesus, has provided for us salvation as a free gift apart from the works of people.

B. God does need helpers who will serve as coworkers in carrying the good news of his love to a needy world.

   God could have written his message of love in the sky or communicated it through angels, but he has chosen to communicate it through people.

   Paul rejoiced in the privilege of being a planter of the good seed in the hearts of people. He declared that Apollos served to irrigate the seed but that God gave the increase.

C. While God gives the increase, the planter and the waterer can be of great assistance in helping the work of God prosper. The opposite is also true. By unfaithfulness and by shoddy methods of serving, we can hinder the movement of God.

II. Laborers together for God—a position of distinction and significance.

Often an outstanding physician will invite a young intern to serve as his or her assistant. The young doctor learns from the experience of the older doctor.

Often an outstanding coach will assemble around herself or himself younger coaches who not only render a service, but also learn all they can learn from the head coach.

In the work of serving our Lord, we have the privilege of working with each other and learning from each other in order that we might be more effective ministers to God's people.

We should rejoice at the honor and privilege we have of working for the Lord.

III. Laborers together for God—a sustaining encouragement.

In the work of the Lord, success is sure if we trust in him and sincerely put forth an effort to be used by him (1 Cor. 15:58). Our Lord will help us and work on our own minds and hearts that we might be worthy followers of him. Our God is at work in us and will work through us as we labor with others to extend his kingdom.

Conclusion

God is at work in our world, and he is in need of the cooperative activity of all of his servants. We have the privilege of being workers together for God.

WEDNESDAY EVENING, FEBRUARY 10

Title: Things Lacking in the Church

Text: "For this cause left I thee in Crete, that thou shouldest set in order the things that are wanting, and ordain elders in every city, as I had appointed thee" **(Titus 1:5).**

Scripture Reading: Titus 1

Introduction

In Titus 1:1 Paul claims the furtherance of the faith of God's elect and the increase in their knowledge of the truth as his purpose for writing the epistle. To carry out his purpose, Paul mentions that one of the first things he would do is amend the defects in the churches (Titus 1:5).

I. Consider the meaning of some terms.

A. The first term is that which was wrong.

1. The King James Version uses the phrase "that are wanting" in the churches.
2. The Revised Standard Version has "what was defective in the church."
3. The definition in one Greek lexicon is "to fall short or to be inferior; to do without or be in need."
4. Theologian William Barclay says the phrase means "deficiencies in the organization."
5. The Living Bible has "whatever needed to be done."

These various translations and interpretations provide evidence that the church had a need. It was faltering. It was not fulfilling the purpose for which it was established.

B. The second term is the instruction given to Titus: "set in order."

Medical writers typically used this term in referring to the setting of broken limbs or straightening crooked ones.

C. Titus is to set things in order by appointing elders.

1. Much discussion exists regarding who is an elder. Barclay concludes that elder and bishop are synonymous terms.
2. These people would be leaders. They are the pastors or staff members who work in the church.

II. What was the problem in these churches?

A. They had false teachers. These teachers gave an inadequate interpretation of the meaning of the gospel.

B. They had liars in the church. The teachers not only gave an inadequate interpretation; they also gave false interpretations.

C. They had gluttons.

D. They had lazy people.

III. Lessons can be found here for contemporary times.

A. One lesson to be learned is that of the importance of the church in God's plan. One of the divinely established institutions the New Testament mentions is the church. Placed on the earth with Christ as its head and referred to as his body, the church's purpose is to proclaim the gospel.

B. Another lesson is about the importance of church leaders. Church leaders need to do their best to see that the church is not wanting. This does not mean that they are always right. They need divine guidance and support and encouragement from church members. To do their jobs effectively, they must have cooperation.

Conclusion

The church is a divinely established institution, but it sometimes has problems. God is able to work through people to set his church in order.

SUNDAY MORNING, FEBRUARY 14

Title: The Fruit of the Spirit Is Faithfulness

Text: "But the fruit of the Spirit is love, joy, peace, patience, kindness, goodness, faithfulness ..." **(Gal. 5:22 RSV)**.

Scripture Reading: Matthew 25:14–21

Hymns: "All Hail the Power," Perronet

"Wonderful Words of Life," Bliss

"He Is Able," Ogden

Offertory Prayer: Heavenly Father, we are grateful for your unchanging faithfulness. We rejoice that our God is reliable. We thank you for your mercy and goodness toward us. We praise you for your generous provisions for us through Christ Jesus and through your Holy Spirit. Thank you for both spiritual and physical blessings. Today we bring tithes and offerings expressing our love and indicating our faith in the worthwhileness of your kingdom's work. Bless these gifts to the bringing of your kingdom into the hearts of people, we pray, in Christ's name. Amen.

Introduction

The new birth is a new creation of a believer's life that is wrought by the Holy Spirit. The new birth is the beginning of God's work within us rather than the crowning climax of God's work in us.

The Holy Spirit dwells within each believer's heart to produce Christlike character. The Holy Spirit came to pour God's love into our hearts and to enable us to live by the principle of love. He grants us the joy of Christ and makes living a radiant life possible for us. He produces the fruit of peace by continually working within us to establish right relationships with God, other people, and all of life's events. He teaches us patience that we might get along with ourselves and with others. He instills kindness within us that we might do generous acts for others. And he develops goodness in us that we might be a light to others.

The fruit of the Spirit that we consider today is the fruit of faithfulness. The Lord wants to help us become dependable, trustworthy, honest, reliable persons. The Holy Spirit seeks to instill God's character within us. Because God is faithful, his children should develop this trait.

I. God is the faithful God.

A. "God is faithful" (1 Cor. 1:9).

B. Moses affirmed the faithfulness of God: "Know therefore that the Lord your God is God, the faithful God who keeps covenant and steadfast love with those who love him and keep his commandments, to a thousand generations" (Deut. 7:9 RSV).

The prophet Jeremiah affirmed the reliability of the God of Israel: "Great is thy faithfulness" (Lam. 3:23). God's Word and his children's testimony through the ages indicate that he will dependably continue the task that he has begun. He is more reliable than the Rock of Gibraltar.

II. Our Lord was and is faithful.

We can count on the Lord Jesus being trustworthy, reliable, dependable, and honest at all times.

A. Christ is called the faithful witness (Rev. 1:5). Our Lord came to bear witness to the truth about God, life, and eternity. Faithful to his mission, Christ steadfastly set his face toward Jerusalem though he knew this would lead to a crown of thorns, a cross, and a cold tomb. Because of his utter faithfulness to the point of death, he has been highly exalted to the position of highest authority at God's right hand (Phil. 2:9–11).

B. Christ is called our faithful High Priest (Heb. 2:17). A priest is a bridge builder. He acts as a go-between. Our Lord came as the Lamb of God to take away the sin of the world, and he also came as the High Priest who offered himself as a sacrifice for our sins. As the faithful High Priest, he has entered into the Holy of Holies of heaven bearing his own blood as a sacrifice for our sins (Heb. 9:24–26). We can count on him to take care of our sin.

If we would truly follow the one who is the faithful Witness and the faithful High Priest, we must let the Holy Spirit produce this same spirit of faithfulness within us.

III. Paul praised his helpers as being faithful.

A. He spoke words of praise concerning Timothy, whom he described as "my beloved and faithful child in the Lord" (1 Cor. 4:17 RSV).

B. Paul praised Tychicus as "a beloved brother and faithful minister in the Lord" (Eph. 6:21).

C. Paul praised Epaphras as "our beloved fellow servant. He is a faithful minister of Christ on our behalf" (Col. 1:7 RSV).

D. Paul praised the former slave Onesimus as "the faithful and beloved brother" (Col. 4:9).

Paul found these men to be dependable, reliable, trustworthy, honest, and faithful.

Are you that kind of friend and that kind of servant of the Lord? Are others able to praise you with the term faithful? Have you found something outside yourself that is big enough to deserve your highest love and loyalty? Have you found something that demands your energy and your effort? If you would live the abundant life, you must find the one to whom you can be supremely faithful.

IV. To whom and what are you faithful?

Faithfulness is never a negative quality. Faithfulness calls for a positive, constant response on the part of one who has chosen to be faithful.

A. Faithfulness to God should come first.

B. Faithfulness to family should take precedence over other groups.

1. Faithfulness to one's marriage partner is supremely important.
2. Faithfulness to children is necessary.
3. Faithfulness to parents is a proper response for children.

C. Faithfulness to the church should come before all other institutions.

D. Faithfulness to our friends is important.

E. Faithfulness to the Bible is indispensable.

F. Faithfulness to your employer is profitable.

G. Faithfulness to yourself needs to be emphasized.

V. Some concluding thoughts concerning faithfulness.

A. Faithfulness is required (1 Cor. 4:1–2). Superior talent or unusual cleverness is not required. Instead, the person who would be trusted must prove to be faithful.

B. Faithfulness is rewarding (1 Cor. 15:58). Faithfulness is rewarding to you first of all. Faithfulness brings its own inward satisfactions and rewards.

C. Faithfulness will be recognized by our Lord. "Well done, good and faithful servant" (Matt. 25:21 RSV).

D. Faithfulness is requested and rewarded by our Lord. He said, "Be faithful unto death, and I will give you the crown of life" (Rev. 2:10 RSV).

Conclusion

We can rejoice that God is faithful in his person and in his promises. You can depend on him to forgive you when you confess your sins and renounce them. "If we confess our sins, he is faithful and just, and will forgive our sins and cleanse us from all unrighteousness" (1 John 1:9 RSV).

Jesus Christ will become your Savior if you forsake the sin of unbelief and come to him for forgiveness and new life. "The saying is sure and worthy of full acceptance, that Christ Jesus came into the world to save sinners" (1 Tim. 1:15 RSV).

Christ has promised to be with people who trust and obey him throughout all their days and in all their ways (Matt. 28:20).

You can count on Christ to come into your life if you open the door and invite him to enter. He would like to come in now (Rev. 3:20).

SUNDAY EVENING, FEBRUARY 14

Title: Temples of the Spirit

Text: "Do you not know that you are God's temple and that God's Spirit dwells in you?" **(1 Cor. 3:16 RSV)**.

Scripture Reading: 1 Corinthians 2:10–13; 3:16–17; 6:19–20

Introduction

To recognize and appreciate the greatness of our salvation, we must make a total response to God's great program for us. This is impossible if we do not recognize and respond to the indwelling presence of the Holy Spirit.

Repeatedly the apostle Paul addresses the saints at Corinth about their lack of awareness of the indwelling presence of the Holy Spirit. He assures them that he would not have them to be uninformed concerning the spiritual gifts of God to his children (1 Cor. 12:1).

Many of us today are uninformed concerning the mystery and the miracle and the meaning of the indwelling Holy Spirit. Some, because of false interpretations concerning the work of the Spirit, actually fear the fullness of his presence. Consequently, they avoid making any response to the Holy Spirit.

In Paul's epistle to the Corinthians, he makes a shocking declaration. He proclaims in a city of many temples that the church, the body of Christ, is the temple of the Holy Spirit, the dwelling place of the eternal Spirit of God. This was particularly significant in ancient Corinth, a city filled with magnificent temples to the various gods and goddesses worshiped by the Greeks and later by the Romans. Paul addresses the heart of each of these believers and says, "You are God's temple." He warns against the peril of being destructive toward God's temple and encourages his readers to build a noble temple for the glory of God.

I. We need to recognize that we are temples of the Holy Spirit.

Our bodies belong to God. The human body is not essentially evil. Potentially it is good, because it is the instrument through which we tell the story of God's wonderful love and by which we render services in his name. It is by means of our bodies that Christ is able to continue his ministry in the world.

Our Lord promised his disciples that the Holy Spirit would come to dwell within them permanently (John 14:15–18).

II. We need to rejoice that we are temples of the Holy Spirit.

A. It was the Holy Spirit who convicted us of our sin and of our need for the perfect righteousness that comes through faith in Jesus Christ. It was the Holy Spirit who warned us of the judgment that had already come on Satan in the death and resurrection of Christ and of the judgment at the end of the age that all who reject Christ face (John 15:8–13).

B. It was the Holy Spirit who presented Jesus to us as the Savior whom we needed (John 16:13–14).

C. It was the Holy Spirit who produced the new birth within us (John 3:5; Titus 3:5). The Holy Spirit came to dwell within us to assure us of divine sonship through faith in Jesus Christ (Rom. 8:16).

III. We need to cooperate fully with the Holy Spirit who has made a temple of our bodies (Acts 5:32).

The Holy Spirit does his most wonderful work in and through those who recognize his presence and who give themselves in loving cooperative obedience to divine leadership.

A. The Holy Spirit came into our hearts and lives to create conflict with our lower natures that we might not be dominated by the fleshly appetites that plague us all (Gal. 5:16–21).

B. The Holy Spirit wants to produce within each of us the fruit of the Spirit—that is, he wants to reproduce within us the character and the disposition of the Lord Jesus Christ (Gal. 5:22–23).

C. We must refrain from conduct that brings grief to the Holy Spirit (Eph. 4:30), and we must refrain from attitudes and actions that would quench the Spirit as he seeks to do the work of God in us and through us (1 Thess. 5:7–19).

Conclusion

With faith in the Holy Spirit who has come to dwell within us, we can face life with courage and cheer and hope. He will seek to reveal the grace and glory of our God through the temple in which he dwells.

WEDNESDAY EVENING, FEBRUARY 17

Title: The People Who Rectify Church Trouble—What Kind of People Are They? **(Part 1)**

Text: " … ordain elders in every city, as I had appointed thee" **(Titus 1:5)**.

Scripture Reading: Titus 1

Introduction

A previous message titled "Things Lacking in the Church" mentioned trouble in the church. This message also pointed out that Titus was told to "ordain elders in every city" (Titus 1:5). This message and the following two messages deal with what kind of people are to be used by God in rectifying church problems.

I. Take a look at the background of the need for elders in the church.

A. Crete was an island of many cities. Homer called it "Crete of the hundred cities."

B. The Christian church needs its organization and leaders. To function properly, a church must be organized. To organize is "to arrange or constitute in independent parts, each having a special function or relation with respect to the whole" (Webster). Before a church can ever fulfill the purpose for which it was instituted, it must have all the parts properly related. Leaders are essential for this organization.

C. The congregation plays a role when church trouble is rectified. No leader can rectify trouble without the help or response of the membership. The congregation can do at least three things to assume its role in rectifying trouble.

1. "Its first duty is to listen to the preaching in a receptive and responsive manner. Nothing so kills a sermon or disheartens a preacher as an apathetic congregation. 'He that hath ears to hear, let him hear' " (Frank Colquhoun, *Christ's Ambassadors* [Philadelphia: Westminster, 1965], 91).
2. "The congregation has another responsibility: to pray for the preacher and for the ministry of the Word" (ibid., 92).
3. "There are other ways in which the laity can be of help. One of these is by encouraging the parson in his preaching ministry—and often he needs such encouragement" (ibid.).

II. Church workers—people who rectify church trouble—should teach and train their own families in the faith.

A. This category is twofold. The first of these two categories is clean living in the marital relationship. Church leaders must have only one spouse (Titus 1:6). A husband and wife must have a right relationship before the church leader can be used satisfactorily in correcting church problems. The second category consists in having right relationships with one's children. Before becoming what one ought to be in the church, one's own children need to be led to be believers. Titus says children as believers should not be open to the charge of being riotous or unruly. The word riot is used for profligacy, debauchery, or completely given to dissipation. It includes being wasteful to the point of dissipation. Neither should the children be insubordinate. They must be under control.

B. The lesson here is that Christianity begins at home. The home is the basic unit of society. As the home goes, so goes society. To be engaged in church work at the expense of the home is not right.

C. How is a rectifier of church problems to have the right kind of home?
   1. Make sure genuine love exists.
   2. Avoid legalism. The spirit far exceeds the law.
   3. Make time qualitative. This is more important than quantitative.
   4. Be genuine in living. Hypocrisy cannot be concealed at home.
   5. Watch your conversation.

Conclusion

Making the church stronger is a great need in the world today. It is also a big challenge to the church. Overcoming the problems in the church adds to the challenge of making it stronger. All Christians should pray that God will raise up the kind of people who meet the qualifications of being a church rectifier.

SUNDAY MORNING, FEBRUARY 21

Title: The Fruit of the Spirit Is Meekness

Text: "But the fruit of the Spirit is love, joy, peace, patience, kindness, goodness, faithfulness, gentleness ..." **(Gal. 5:22–23 RSV)**.

Scripture Reading: 1 Corinthians 3:17–18

Hymns: "God, Our Father, We Adore Thee," Frazer

"How Sweet the Name of Jesus," Newton

"Have Thine Own Way, Lord," Pollard

Offertory Prayer: Holy Father, today we thank you for life with its privileges and responsibilities. Even more, we thank you for spiritual life that is through faith in Jesus Christ and is maintained by your Holy Spirit.

Help us to accept and wisely manage all the things you give us.

Today we bring tithes and offerings. Accept these gifts of our love and bless them. Use these gifts to take your kingdom to people and agencies and institutions. In Jesus' name. Amen.

Introduction

Our loving heavenly Father has something wonderful for each of us. He sent his Son, not only to save us from eternal separation from God, but to enrich, enlarge, and improve our lives. When the Holy Spirit entered our hearts, he came to transform us from within.

We have been considering the fruit that the Holy Spirit produces in the lives of people who cooperate with him. Today we examine the fruit called meekness or gentleness and sometimes humility. No single English word fully translates the meaning of the Greek word *prautes*. Hence, a problem results when we try to understand exactly what the apostle was referring to as a fruit of the Spirit.

Many people think the term meekness refers to a person with no fortitude and with a very poor self-image. This understanding of meekness does not represent the quality that the Holy Spirit is seeking to produce within us. In the New Testament, meekness or gentleness or humility is a positive quality expressed in both attitude and action. The New Testament concept of meekness reflects in our attitude toward our fellow humans and toward God's dealings with us.

I. The use of the term meekness.

A. Christ used the term meekness to describe his own disposition (Matt. 11:29).

B. The term meekness described Christ as the King Messiah when he entered the city of Jerusalem in his triumphal entry (Matt. 21:5; cf. Zech. 9:9). Christ came in humility and gentleness. Shortly after his triumphal entry, he entered and cleansed the temple area. This incident does not even hint at weakness.

C. Christ used the term meekness in the third beatitude (Matt. 5:5). Apart from meekness, one cannot progress in the Christian life.

D. Meekness is listed as a part of the spiritual garment of the genuine follower of Jesus Christ (Col. 3:12; 1 Peter 3:8).

Meekness, an inwrought grace of the soul, is exercised chiefly toward God. A meek believer accepts all of God's dealings as good (Rom. 8:28). Not every event fulfills God's ideal will, but nothing can touch the believer without God's permission. Meekness is assuming that God will work to bring good out of every situation.

Meekness is not weakness. Christ was meek, but he was not weak. Christ was meek because he had the infinite resources of God at his disposal.

Meekness toward God includes complete openness to his suggestions and corrections. It involves instant responsiveness to his wishes.

II. Great examples of meekness.

A. Christ was meek (Matt. 11:28–29; 21:5). Christ was not weak. He was meek toward God in that he was completely open and instantly responsive to God's will for his life.

From an external viewpoint, some people may consider Jesus' attitude of meekness to be weakness because he submitted to a series of unjust trials and a horrible death on the cross. In reality he was demonstrating both the divine love for people and his submission to Father God's will as he went to the cross. The cross most highly expressed meekness.

B. Moses exemplified meekness (Num. 12:3). Not much about Moses was weak. He was a strong, stalwart, courageous individual. He was called meek because he was open to God's guidance and obeyed God's will.

C. Paul demonstrated a meek attitude when he faced Nero's trial (Phil. 1:19–20). Not murmuring or complaining about his fate, Paul accepted his situation as an opportunity to glorify Jesus Christ and to help other people come to know Christ through his sufferings.

III. Commands concerning meekness.

Not instinctive qualities, meekness, gentleness, and humility must be acquired and maintained.

A. We should receive the truth of God's Word with a meek spirit of instant responsiveness (James 1:21).

B. We should witness to others with a meek attitude (1 Peter 3:15).

C. We should restore the wayward brother with gentle meekness both toward God and toward the offender (Gal. 6:1).

D. Ministers should desire meekness (1 Tim. 6:11), and they should practice gentle meekness when correcting wrongdoers (2 Tim. 2:24–26).

IV. Illustrations of meekness.

Perhaps some illustrations can help us to understand a meek attitude. A meek person is completely open, teachable, and instantly responsive.

A. Power steering on an automobile illustrates openness and responsiveness to the wishes of the driver.

B. A horse that is sensitive to the bridle bit and that responds to the rider's wishes without hesitation could be called meek.

C. A football team's quarterback illustrates meekness when he watches the coach's signals during a game and listens to the coach's instructions during a conference regarding plays he is to use. With the coach in charge of the game, the quarterback calls the signals the team will then play.

As followers of Jesus Christ, we need to let him sit in the driver's seat. In playing the game of life, we need to let Jesus Christ call the plays for us.

V. God's provisions and promises for the meek.

A. God offers and promises guidance to the meek and humble (Ps. 25:9).

B. God offers and provides true prosperity to the meek (Ps. 37:11).

C. God offers and promises ultimate victory to the humble and meek (Ps. 149:4).

Conclusion

In one of the most gracious invitations in all of Scripture, Christ described himself as meek, gentle, and lowly in heart. Christ was declaring that he would be open and responsive when people brought their needs to him. He was also declaring that he would deal with their needs gently, kindly, and graciously.

Only the Son of God could extend such an all-inclusive invitation. No matter what your spiritual condition may be, come to him with confidence, trusting him for salvation, satisfaction, security, and a life of significant helpfulness to others.

SUNDAY EVENING, FEBRUARY 21

Title: The Priority of Faithfulness

Text: "Moreover it is required of stewards that they be found trustworthy" **(1 Cor. 4:2 RSV).**

Scripture Reading: 1 Corinthians 4:1–5

Introduction

One of the great emphases of the apostle as he writes to the followers of Christ at Corinth is on the trustworthiness of the God who has revealed himself in Jesus Christ. Paul declares that they worship a God who is faithful and dependable (1 Cor. 1:9). He also declares that God can be depended on to be with them in any trial so that they might bear their burdens triumphantly (1 Cor. 10:13). He further encourages and motivates them to be zealous in service with the assurance that their labor for the faithful God will not go unrewarded (1 Cor. 15:58).

This great emphasis on the faithfulness of God is more significant when one recognizes that each disciple is a servant of Christ and a steward of the mysteries of God (1 Cor. 4:1). The mysteries of God are the great truths that God has chosen to reveal by means of his Holy Spirit. These mysteries, or truths, are those blessings from God that cannot be discovered by human reason or by laboratory processes. They are truths revealed by divine initiative. Paul considers himself, and he would consider each of us, a steward of these mysteries.

A steward is a manager or a supervisor entrusted with that which belongs to another. Paul declares that the requirements for being a good steward are faithfulness, reliability, dependability, and trustworthiness. It is not required that a steward be brilliant or successful. It is required that each one be faithful. Faithfulness is the will of God for us and is possible for each of us.

I. Stewards must be faithful to God in the use of time.

Time is one of the precious gifts that God places at our disposal. It can be divided into at least three categories.

A. Time to work. In the Old Testament, God's plan was that people should work six days and earn their livelihood. People who have to work more than six days a week need either to reexamine their methods or reevaluate their goals.

B. Time to rest. The Sabbath originally was a day for rest and relaxation. Every day was to be a day of worship dedicated to God. The Sabbath was a day in which people were to be released from the routine and labor of earning a living in order that they might be refreshed.

C. Time to serve. Our Lord declared that the Sabbath was made for man and not man for the Sabbath. The Sabbath is not an institution that is supposed to be a burden. Jesus violated the traditions surrounding the Sabbath in order that he might minister to others. Those who would find the highest possible joy in life must dedicate much of their time to being of service to the Lord and to others.

II. Stewards must be faithful in the use of talents.

A. Our talents should be considered as the gifts of God to be used for his glory and for the joy and the good of others.

B. Talents must not be exploited merely for self-centered advancement.

C. Every talent carries with it a responsibility.

God does not expect us to excel in the sense that we win the race and outachieve competitors. Our God has given us our talents to develop and to use. If we would please him, we must be reliable and dependable in the use of the talents with which he has endowed us.

III. Stewards must be faithful to God in the use of treasure.

Money represents life in crystallized form and can do wonderful things.

A. It is God who gives us the power to get wealth (Deut. 8:18).

B. God expects us to earn our money by honest and helpful means.

C. God requires that we share our income with the work of his kingdom. In the Old Testament, the law required of the Israelites that they bring a tithe of their increase into the storehouse for the work of God. In the New Testament, love requires that we put our total selves at God's disposal. Those who never learn to bring the tithe will find it exceedingly difficult to give their total selves into the service of God.

IV. Stewards must be faithful to God in the handling of trouble.

Not all trouble and not all trials come to us by the ideal will of God. Some trouble comes to us because of our own selfishness, ignorance, or foolishness. We can let trouble cause us to become bitter, hostile, and rebellious. We can let trouble cause us to become discouraged, depressed, and defeated. But Paul declares that God will be at work in all things for good to those who love God and who are seeking to live out his purpose in their lives. To be a good steward, we must remember to be faithful to our Lord, especially when trouble comes.

V. Stewards must be faithful to God in the giving of Christian testimony.

To us has been committed a trusteeship with the mysteries of God—the great truths that God has revealed by means of his Spirit through Jesus Christ.

A. We must use the language of our lives, but merely to live a good life is not enough.

B. We must use the language of our lips to communicate the divine concern and the wonder of the divine love. To be silent in the presence of great spiritual need is inhuman, unnatural, and unchristian.

Conclusion

It is not required that stewards be naturally intelligent. It is not required that stewards be highly educated. It is not required that stewards be unusually clever. It is not required that stewards be innovative and creative. But it is required that stewards be trustworthy, reliable, dependable, and faithful. Each one has the capacity to be faithful and trustworthy.

WEDNESDAY EVENING, FEBRUARY 24

Title: The People Who Rectify Church Trouble—What Kind of People Are They? **(Part 2)**

Text: "For a bishop must be blameless, as the steward of God; not self-willed, not soon angry, not given to wine, no striker, not given to filthy lucre" **(Titus 1:7)**.

Scripture Reading: Titus 1

Introduction

This is the second of three messages on the people who rectify church trouble. Last week's message dealt with the lives of people and their families and also with the responsibility of the church as it responds to the leader's work. This evening's message is a continuation of the same subject, and the main thought is directed to the concept "the steward of God."

I. The person must be unaccused as God's steward.

The word in the King James Version is "blameless." Probably a better word is unaccused.

A. The word steward means overseer. The meaning is similar to that of a manager of a house, and the word economics derives from this Greek term.

B. These people should be unaccused. They are to be blameless. Verses 6 and 7 mention that they are to be blameless in their own homes. When they achieve the record indicated in verses 7–9, they will be blameless. Such people should also possess integrity, kindness, understanding, compassion, and perception.

II. Verse 7 lists five negatives that the people who rectify church trouble must avoid.

A. They should not be self-willed. That is, they must not be given to pleasing themselves. They must not assert their own opinions or rights while being reckless with the rights of others. They should not be of unpleasant character. They are not to be intolerant or condemning of things they cannot understand.

B. They should not be angry people. People who nurse within their hearts long-lasting anger against any other person should not bear office in the church.

C. They should not be given to drunken and outrageous conduct. The word for "drunken" pertains to an overindulgence in wine. No doubt, this would refer to the modern-day overuse of alcoholic beverages. But another wider meaning applies to outrageous conduct of one who acts without self-control.
D. They should not be strikers. Church people will be unable to right wrongs in a church if they permit themselves to come to physical blows. They should not exercise violence in action or in speech. Such violence would indicate an abandonment of the first essential of working in a church: love. When people abandon love and resort to violence in action or speech, they should not hold offices in the church.
E. They should not be given to filthy lucre. Officers in the church must not seek gain in a disgraceful way, and they must not do things for personal gain with God's money. Those who gain material things in a dishonest or dishonorable manner are promoters of trouble and not ones who rectify.

Conclusion

Being an officer in a church is a distinct honor and challenge. People who are responsible for correcting difficulties in a church must have character above reproach.

SUNDAY MORNING, FEBRUARY 28

Title: The Fruit of the Spirit Is Self-Control

Text: "But the fruit of the Spirit is love, joy, peace, patience, kindness, goodness, faithfulness, gentleness, self-control . . ." **(Gal. 5:22–23 RSV)**.

Scripture Reading: Galatians 5:16–26

Hymns: "Love Is the Theme," Fisher

"Holy Spirit, Faithful Guide," Wells

"Yield Not to Temptation," Palmer

Offertory Prayer: Holy Father, we come today to thank you for all of the perfect gifts that you have bestowed on us and within us. We thank you for Jesus Christ our Savior. We thank you for your divine Spirit who sustains us and leads us to a deeper and fuller life. Thank you for the opportunity to serve. Thank you for your blessings on the work of our hands. Thank you that we have tithes and offerings to bring today as a token of our love and as an indication of our desire to participate in your work beyond the range of our own immediate presence. Bless these gifts and use them for your glory, we pray, in Christ's name. Amen.

Introduction

Paul concludes his list of the fruit of the Spirit by adding "self-control" at the end. This particular expression of the fruit of the Spirit is altogether significant when we recognize the context of this statement as including the works of the flesh described in Galatians 5:18–21. From the dawn of human history, people have sought to makes laws and place restrictions on the lower appetites, inclinations, and actions of those who give themselves to a life of selfish dissipation and uncontrolled behavior.

History provides us with a documentary record that shows that external laws that prohibit and restrict and penalize have not solved the problem of controlling the evil inclinations of people. Laws that restrict and penalize are absolutely essential for maintaining a stable society. However, humanity's greatest need is not for external control, but for inward self-control.

The Scriptures do not hold out any hope for the solution to our human problems through external laws and controls. The Scriptures teach us that each individual must develop internal spiritual controls to help overcome evil inclinations and make it possible to govern oneself.

The writer of Proverbs declares, "He who is slow to anger is better than the mighty, and he who rules his spirit than he who takes a city" (Prov. 16:32 RSV). The tragedy of a person without self-control is described by the wise man as follows: "A man without self-control is like a city broken into and left without walls" (Prov. 25:28 RSV).

Most of us have far greater difficulty at the point of controlling ourselves than we do at any other point in life.

I. Self-control is one of the perfect gifts of God for each of us.

It is God's will that we live with control over ourselves. The Holy Spirit came to give us that strength of soul that is necessary for a person to take control over self. A mastery of self always adds dignity and poise to one's character.

A. We can believe that the Holy Spirit wants us to maintain control over our attitudes, our appetites, our ambitions, and our actions.

B. We can believe that the Holy Spirit will assist us to maintain control over our emotions, our moods, our imaginations, and our thoughts.

C. We can believe that the Holy Spirit will assist us in maintaining control over our temper, tongue, talents, treasure, and time.

II. Self-control is basic to the Christian life.

A. A disciple is one who has voluntarily accepted the discipline of being a follower of Jesus Christ. The word disciple and the word discipline have the same base root meaning. Those who consider themselves to be disciples fool themselves if they do not recognize that this involves the discipline of being a genuine follower of Jesus Christ.

If we would learn the art of self-mastery, we must begin by yielding ourselves to the one great Master, Jesus Christ.

B. The Holy Spirit wants to give us the self-restraint, self-control, self-denial, and self-discipline that will enable us to restrain ourselves in the presence of temptation in its every form.

C. Self-control is a part of our spiritual heritage. The Holy Spirit is eager to assist us in living a victorious Christian life.

III. Self-control is inward and voluntary.

A. All of us must accept responsibility for all that we are and for all that we do. We must not deceive ourselves by blaming others for our lack of self-control.

B. No external force can compel us to practice self-control. This is a way of life that we must choose for ourselves, and we must depend on the Holy Spirit for assistance.

IV. Self-control is exceedingly difficult.

A. We live in a world that encourages us to give full release to our every wish. High-pressure advertisements stimulate us to want far more than we need.

B. Our own fleshly nature with its many appetites constantly demands to be satisfied. A wise teacher said, "Character is developed only as a man resists his inward inclinations toward evil." A man must keep a tight rein on himself and never relax it.

C. The devil constantly will tempt and seek to promise the fulfillment of every desire that we have providing we let him control our lives. These factors, when combined, present a real problem to the person who recognizes the need for self-control.

Self-control is not a permanent achievement so much as it is a way of life to be practiced moment by moment.

V. The self-controlled life is a Spirit-controlled life.

If we want to experience this fruit of the Spirit and be in control of our faculties, our inclinations, our appetites—every aspect of our life—there are certain essential responses that we need to make toward the indwelling Spirit.

A. We must recognize the abiding presence of the Holy Spirit who has come to be with us always.

B. We must believe in the benevolent purpose of the Holy Spirit and not distrust him as he seeks to place divine restrictions on us.

C. We must listen to the voice of the Holy Spirit as he speaks to us through the Word of God and through our consciences as well as through the circumstances of life.

D. We must rely on the guidance of the Holy Spirit as he seeks to enable us to understand truth about God and about life (John 16:13).

E. We must trust in the power of the Holy Spirit as we face life (Acts 1:8).

F. We must cooperate with the Holy Spirit as he works within us from day to day (Phil. 2:13).

Conclusion

God wants to set us free from the control of destructive forces, powers, habits, attitudes, and appetites. Christ came to save us from the insanity of a life of sin and self-destruction, so if we want to gain mastery over ourselves, we must first of all let Jesus Christ become our Savior and our Lord. Then day by day we are to be filled with the Spirit and to walk in the Spirit. "The fruit of the Spirit is ... self-control."

SUNDAY EVENING, FEBRUARY 28

Title: Facing Judges in Three Courts with Confidence

Text: "Therefore do not pronounce judgment before the time, before the Lord comes, who will bring to light the things now hidden in darkness and will disclose the purposes of the heart. Then every man will receive his commendation from God" **(1 Cor. 4:5 RSV)**.

Scripture Reading: 1 Corinthians 4:1–5

Introduction

Most of us dislike the idea of having to go to court for any reason. Perhaps this is due to guilt feelings. Yet at some time in life nearly all of us will have some dealings with one of the courts of our country. There are many different kinds of courts. There is a magistrate's court and a justice of the peace court. At a higher level there are district or circuit courts for both civil and criminal cases. The next level is the court of appeals, or appellate courts, that handle cases appealed from lower courts. There are special state courts like a police court, a municipal court, a traffic court, a domestic relations court, a juvenile court, and a probate court. Each state has a supreme court, and the highest court of all in our country is the United States Supreme Court.

In our Scripture reading, the apostle Paul speaks of three courts before which all of us will appear. He speaks of the court of public opinion, the court of personal opinion, and the court of our Creator (4:3–5).

Is it possible to face these three courts with confidence? Since there is no way by which we can avoid these courts, we must face them with confidence.

I. Facing judgment in the court of public opinion with confidence.

A. The desire for public approval is basic to human nature. This is true in the realm of business, politics, and even religion.

B. Favorable public opinion is essential to survival for individuals and institutions.

C. The public whose opinion is desired is of supreme importance. Some people let the desires and the opinions of their peer group determine their every attitude and action. This can be very harmful. Do you take a poll of public opinion before you make moral decisions? To do so can be deadly. Public opinion matters, but it should always be secondary to one's personal opinion and, of course, to God's judgment. We must beware lest we let the desire for public approval become primary.

II. Facing judgment in the court of your personal evaluation of self (I John 3:21).

To be happy, we must have a good opinion of ourselves. Those with low self-esteem are miserable and in most cases ineffective in what they do. It is of tremendous importance that we evaluate self and that we conduct self in such a manner as to be able to hold our head up and not be ashamed.

A. In the court of our personal opinion, we face the peril of self-deception. Repeatedly the Bible warns us against the peril of self-deception. The wise man tells us that every man's way is right in his own eyes, but the Lord sits in judgment on our motives as well as our methods. He affirms that there is a way that appears to be right, but the end thereof is the way of death and destruction.

B. In the court of our personal opinion, we face the peril of self-destruction. If we are introspective and perfectionistic in our self-expectations, we are in for much misery.

1. Total knowledge, total recall is possible. This can produce guilt and negative conclusions concerning oneself.
2. We often make unfavorable comparisons of ourselves with others.
3. We have a tendency to be unwilling to accept ourselves as being of great worth in the sight of God. A great Greek philosopher said, "Know thyself." Jesus would tell us that as well as loving God and our neighbor, we also should have a proper love for ourselves. Those who do not love themselves properly have no measuring stick by which to determine the manner in which they are to love their neighbors.

To face the court of our personal opinion of ourselves with confidence, we need to evaluate ourselves as being of infinite worth in God's sight. We need to accept ourselves as unique persons made in the image of God and for a noble purpose. We should dedicate ourselves to something bigger than ourselves.

III. We can face judgment and the final court of God with confidence.

Someone may hasten to ask, "How is this possible?" And that is a good question.

A. All of us are sinners, and when weighed in the balance of righteousness, we are found wanting. There is not one single person among us who can stand before a holy God in our own righteousness and be accepted.

B. The Bible teaches that many will be rejected in the final day of judgment. Those who will be rejected are those who were unwilling to trust God and to accept his forgiveness. Those who will be rejected are those who have shut God out of their lives and, in doing so, have shut themselves out from acceptance by our Creator, who would love to be the heavenly Father of each one.

C. In this final court before God, some will be accepted. These are those who are said to be justified by faith in Christ Jesus (Rom. 3:28; 5:1; 8:1, 33–35).
D. On the final day of judgment, some will be rewarded. The Bible teaches us that the children of God who are faithful, obedient, generous, serving, and merciful will be rewarded by the heavenly Father. Our Lord promised a reward to those who serve (Rev. 22:12).

Conclusion

God, our Creator, has created us with an inward desire to experience approval. We need the approval of the public. We need the approval of ourselves. Even more so, we need the approval of our God, which is available through faith in Jesus Christ. Rewards will come as we give of ourselves in faithfulness to him.

SUGGESTED PREACHING PROGRAM FOR THE MONTH OF MARCH

■ Sunday Mornings

As you approach Easter, use a theme that celebrates the death and resurrection of our Lord—"Facing the Cross and the Empty Tomb."

■ Sunday Evenings

Begin a thirteen-part series with the theme "Messages of Joy" from Paul's letter to the Philippians.

■ Wednesday Evenings

Continue the series of studies on Paul's epistle to Titus as he gives practical suggestions concerning the church, its leadership, its needs, and its opportunities.

WEDNESDAY EVENING, MARCH 2

Title: The People Who Rectify Church Trouble—What Kind of People Are They? **(Part 3)**

Text: "But a lover of hospitality, a lover of good men, sober, just, holy, temperate; holding fast the faithful word as he hath been taught, that he may be able by sound doctrine both to exhort and to convince the gainsayers" **(Titus 1:8–9)**.

Scripture Reading: Titus 1

Introduction

This is the third message on the people who rectify church trouble. The first message dealt with their being family-oriented and the church's response to their ministry. The second one concerned what church leaders ought not to be. This one deals with what church leaders ought to be.

The Moffatt commentary says, "He must be a kindly, sensible, honest, clean-living person. No demand is made for any rare qualities, moral or religious. The writer has in mind an average Christian community and the worthy, capable men who are sure to be found in it" (E. F. Scott, *The Pastoral Epistles* [New York and London: Harper and Brothers, n.d.], 156).

I. First, consider qualities in relation to other people.

A. They must be lovers of hospitality. Church leaders should love strangers. The reason for this love of strangers is obvious when one understands the deplorable conditions of public lodging during the time of Paul and

Titus. Places to stay were terribly expensive and dirty, and immoral activities took place within them. The wayfaring Christian needed an open door within the homes of the Christian community. Even today, Christians away from home need Christian fellowship and friendship.

B. They must love goodness. This word is comprehensive and applies to good things, people, and actions. The idea is to be helpful to others.

II. The second consideration is the qualities the church leaders must have on the inside.

A. They are to be sober. Sober people have entire command over their passions and desires at all times. Christian officeholders must be people who wisely use and control every instinct and every passion of their beings.

B. They are to be just. Church leaders give God and humanity the respect and reverence they are due. Their conduct meets the approval of the divine Judge.

C. They are to be holy. The word holy means to be different or set apart. Holy people are different from average worldly people. The term applies to the fundamental decisions of life. It refers to things that go beyond any man-made law or regulation. Their character is unspotted in moral and religious obligations.

D. They must be temperate. They must master themselves before serving others well. This is one of the fruits of the Spirit mentioned in Galatians 5:22.

III. The third quality relates to the church.

A. This qualification is summed up in the term "holding fast the faithful word" (Titus 1:9). Here Christian workers must be unaccused.

B. People who rectify church trouble must be able to encourage the church members.

The Navy has a rule that says, "No officer shall speak discouragingly to any other officer in the performance of duties." No better words could be said of church workers. Something is wrong when a religion's teaching or preaching discourages others. Church leaders should not drive people to despair but should lift them up in hope.

C. They must be able to convict opponents of the faith. This means that the leaders must be able to rebuke people such that they are compelled to see and admit the error of their ways. They bring people to a confession, if possible, but at least to a conviction of sin. Church leaders should not humiliate people, but they should enable people to see, recognize, and admit the duty and truth to which they have been either blind or disobedient.

Conclusion

Any time a church gets ready to elect elders, bishops, deacons, preachers, teachers, or any other officers, it needs to take seriously the qualifications mentioned in this passage.

SUNDAY MORNING, MARCH 6

Title: The New Birth

Text: "Except a man be born again, he cannot see the kingdom of God" **(John 3:3)**.

Scripture Reading: John 3:1–3

Hymns: "Jesus Saves," Owens

"At Calvary," Newell

"When I Survey the Wondrous Cross," Watts

Offertory Prayer: Our heavenly Father, we are grateful for these moments that are made sacred by your divine presence. Just to be still and to have our hearts refreshed in the knowledge that you are the true and living God provides for us new assurances of joy and peace. We give you grateful thanks for the unnumbered blessings of life that you have so generously showered on us. Day after day you have remembered us, not only with your love and tender mercy, but also with temporal blessings that have filled the cup of life to overflowing. In gratitude for these remembrances from heaven, we come now to dedicate what we are and what we have to your service. Multiply these tithes and offerings according to the needs of those who serve you around the world. Make our hearts glad that we can share in the outreach ministry of the gospel to the ends of the earth. Bless us as we give in Jesus' name. Amen.

Introduction

Intelligent people seek knowledge from dependable sources. Nicodemus was a wise man, a teacher who was sincerely seeking the truth. We can admire his honesty, because it is evident that he was dissatisfied with the apparent failure of his own belief to fill his soul with security and peace. Now he had come to a greater miracle worker and teacher. He had not come because of the miracles alone, for miracles are not enough to prove Christ's deity—prophets and apostles had sometimes performed them. However, deeds that exhibit the power of God do prove that God is with the person who works them. So it was reasonable that Nicodemus should seek the favor and counsel of the Master Teacher. This most famous conference produced at least three things that applied to the needs of an earnest inquirer, just as they apply to our hearts today.

I. The heart of true religion.

Jesus pointed out the primary truth to Nicodemus by saying, "Except a man be born again, he cannot see the kingdom of God" (John 3:3). This truth needs to be emphasized again and again in our modern approaches in meeting the needs of people. People have tried to devise plans for the betterment of the human race and have failed miserably.

A. Through education people have sought to enlighten the mind with certain processes of thinking that would make possible desirable relationships among the nations of the world.

B. Through legislation people have sought to impose mandatory procedures that would bring punishment for failure to obey the law.

C. Through better social conditions, better homes, better roads, better schools, better playgrounds, better libraries, and so on, people have sought to build a utopia in which they make mastery of things the mark of achievement for the human race.

While these things may be good, they can never meet the total need of the human heart. People need the life that comes from above. They need a transformation of the mind by the Word of God to make them think right. They need a conversion of the heart to make them love right. They need a conversion of the will to make them obey the commands of the Author of life.

The heart of true religion is found in Jesus Christ. He, and he alone, imparts the new life.

II. The mystery of true religion.

There is mystery in God's creation. Scientists tell us that snow is crystallized water and that water is composed of a proportionate amount of hydrogen and oxygen. We cannot see these elements, but we can see that they are combined to produce water, without which we cannot survive.

Likewise, people cannot see the Holy Spirit or the human soul. How the Holy Spirit operates and accomplishes his work of regeneration we do not know. Scientific tests cannot be applied to him. Yet we can be sure that he works, because we can see the effects produced in the lives of people. Selfish, evil people who are slaves of sinful habits are completely changed and given power to live triumphantly.

Such transformations are beyond the explanation of the most brilliant psychologists. Regeneration can be explained only by the presence of that divine force that permeates deep into human character. The inner change that accompanies conversion is real. Millions of people testify to having found the Holy Spirit, the one potent factor that cleanses, transforms, and changes them into a happy, hopeful, decent people.

III. The mystery of redemption.

John 3:16 is the gospel in a nutshell. It is the story of how redemption cost God everything. It is a message given freely to all who will accept it. We do not need to understand the mystery of the atonement in order to partake of its benefits. In substance, God's Word says, "Believe ... or perish." This is the eternal watchword of truth.

Just as God brings new life in the springtime to plants that have been dormant all winter, so also he brings new life to spiritually dead people who come confessing their need of Christ as Savior and Lord. No other wonder can compare with the joyous experience of heaven's pronouncement of new life for the believing heart.

If matter that is cold and mute and lifeless can be changed by the force of nature into a multitude of forms, why would we believe that our heavenly Father forsakes the need of his highest creation in their hope for redemption? God has demonstrated his love for us through the sacrifice of his Son on Calvary. His gift of healing, cleansing, and forgiveness is offered to all who believe in the Lord Jesus Christ and confess him before others.

Nicodemus was a conscientious Pharisee. He expected his salvation to come through ceremonial obedience. He was no doubt strict in observing all traditional requirements of his day and was ready for any task Christ might impose: to fast more often, to offer longer prayers, to bring his body into severe subjection. He was a type of those in every age who would make themselves better before God and to this end are full of resolutions, daily penances, and pious works. Christ does not condemn any of these things. He simply declares them to be insufficient and says, "You must be born again" (John 3:7 NIV). The old nature does not furnish a foundation on which to rest hopes of recovery and life. A new life must begin. The old heart is depraved and must be made anew. Our own righteousness is like a robe of rags—it cannot be patched or made over. We must have an entirely new robe, the robe of Christ's righteousness.

The doctrine of the new birth is for Christians a sure anchor. The Spirit who has begun a good work will carry it on until the day of Christ Jesus (Phil. 1:6), and all who trust Christ for salvation can know that their salvation is safe in him.

Conclusion

You may be asking, "How may I secure the new birth? If this assurance is born of God, what can I do about it? Must I simply wait until the Spirit moves on my soul and begets in me the image of Christ?" No, not at all. The Savior did not leave Nicodemus and does not leave us helpless in the darkness about such an important issue. In his own discourse, Christ passes naturally from the work of the Spirit to his own work and that of the Father, and to the duty of people. "For God so loved the world, that he gave his only begotten Son, that whosoever believeth in him should not perish, but have everlasting life" (John 3:16). "As Moses lifted up the serpent in the wilderness, even so must the Son of man be lifted up: that whosoever believeth in him should not perish, but have eternal life" (John 3:14). Your part is to believe in the Lord Jesus Christ, and you will be saved. If you have never done so, do it now.

SUNDAY EVENING, MARCH 6

Title: Christian Friends Bless Our Lives

Text: "I thank my God upon every remembrance of you" **(Phil. 1:3)**.

Scripture Reading: Philippians 1:1–5

Introduction

Since we will be dealing with Paul's letter to the Philippians for a number of Sundays, an introduction to the entire letter is in order. Paul founded the church at Philippi on his second missionary journey. Some of the first members included Lydia and her friends, the girl possessed with the spirit of divination, and the Philippian jailer. After Paul left the city, the church stayed in contact with him and often took care of his needs. After a while, however, they lost touch with him. When, later in his life, Paul went to Rome as a prisoner, they once more established a relationship with him.

The immediate occasion for the writing of Philippians was Paul's receiving a gift from the Christians at Philippi. They sent it by Epaphroditus. He became sick en route to Rome, and it became necessary for Paul to care for him. The people at Philippi were distressed because their well-intentioned deed turned out to be a hardship for Paul. When Paul learned of their feelings, he wrote to the church. Paul wanted to let them know that the kindness they expressed to him more than offset any difficulty he had in caring for their messenger.

The book is a "love letter" by Paul to his favorite church. It is intensely personal—filled with various forms of the word joy. One of the earliest statements concerns Paul's delight as he remembered his friends at Philippi.

I. Friends are important.

Elizabeth Barrett Browning once asked Charles Kingsley, "Tell me the secret of your life that I too may make mine beautiful." He replied, "I had a friend." Few of us realize how important our friends are and what a contribution they make to our lives. Someone has said that we are fortunate if, when we come to the end of our way, we have even two or three true friends. Paul possessed happy memories as he looked back across the years. Although he had been away from the Philippians for a long time, he thanked God for his friends and remembered them often in prayer.

II. Our friends in Christ are our dearest friends.

A tremendous difference exists between acquaintances and real friends. Often we meet people in business life and sometimes share social activities with people who do not know Christ the way we know him. Such friendships may, on the surface, seem meaningful, but they do not stand the tests of time. When a true crisis comes, the friend who knows Christ is able to share with us the deeper meaning of these experiences.

Paul loved his Christian friends. He mentioned them often in his letters. Several times he associated his friends with him as cowriters of letters to the churches. As often as possible, Paul mentioned the good points his friends had. Even when disappointed with someone, Paul made special mention if that person came back later and proved useful. For instance, after John Mark turned back on the first missionary journey, Paul refused to take him on the second journey, but years later he included Mark in a list of his friends when writing to Philemon. Also, he wrote to Timothy, "Take Mark, and bring him with thee: for he is profitable to me for the ministry" (2 Tim. 4:11).

III. To make friends and keep friends, we must be a friend.

The writer of Proverbs reminds us, "A man that hath friends must shew himself friendly" (18:24). This means more than merely performing the niceties of social functions. To show ourselves friendly means we must act unselfishly toward others. Often we must take the first step toward establishing the relationship. Jesus said of himself that he came "not to be ministered unto, but to minister" (Mark 10:45). Every Christian should have this attitude toward life. We should not seek what we can get from our friends, but rather what we can do for our friends. In this way, we gain friends. No one enjoys being with a selfish person. Jesus said that we are his friends if we do the things he commands us to do. This means that friendship carries obligations.

IV. The greatest friend is Jesus.

The writer of Proverbs also said, "There is a friend that sticketh closer than a brother" (Prov. 18:24). This marvelous Old Testament passage alludes to our Savior. No one else stays so close to us as the Savior. He delivers from sin, but he does more. Jesus stays with us through every step of life's journey. He motivates us to service and gives strength for the performance of deeds.

A large transport was crossing the Atlantic during World War II. The captain saw a submarine rise and let loose a torpedo straight at his ship. He shouted through the speaker, "Men, this is it!" A small escorting destroyer was nearby. Its captain saw the submarine and the torpedo. Without hesitating a moment, he ordered, "Full steam ahead." The destroyer went into the path of the torpedo and took the full impact. The destroyer was blown apart. Every crew member was lost. The transport captain said later, "The captain of that destroyer was my best friend. I understand more clearly now a verse in the Bible, 'Greater love has no man than this, that a man lay down his life for his friends.'" Jesus laid down his life for his friends, but he did more. He died for his enemies as well. In fact, this is the way he makes his enemies his friends.

Thank God for our friends! We rejoice afresh with each memory of them. Thank God even more for the Friend who laid down his life for us!

Conclusion

Memories can either bless or burn! Memories that recall past joys linger to make our life happy in retrospect. We can and should devote perennial gratitude to God. This type of memory enriches our moral worth.

As people reflect on us, do they remember the good things we have done for them and the many ways we have strengthened their lives? Do we likewise think often with gratitude about those people who have meant much to us? In all probability, if we reflect with thanksgiving on the contribution that friends have made to us, people are praising God that they have known our friendship in days past.

The greatest memory, however, is of a time when we met Jesus as Savior, Lord, and Friend. To say that we remember a time in our lives when Jesus became our personal Friend will be the greatest memory we can have. As we love him, joy will be constant and abiding.

WEDNESDAY EVENING, MARCH 9

Title: False Teachers: What They Do and How to Handle Them

Text: "For there are many unruly and vain talkers and deceivers, specially they of the circumcision: whose mouths must be stopped, who subvert whole houses, teaching things which they ought not, for filthy lucre's sake" **(Titus 1:10–11)**.

Scripture Reading: Titus 1

Introduction

In the three immediate messages before this one, attention was given to the kind of persons that can be used to correct church problems. This message will study what the trouble in Titus's church was. This passage of Scripture has an interesting parallel to the modern church.

I. The troublemakers are referred to in the Scripture passage as the circumcised.

Paul said that these people (Jewish leaders) upset households by leading people away from the truth. Their fundamentally unsettling teaching led to doubt and questioning, whereas true teaching results in greater certainty. Their influence over people brought dissension and misery (see also 1 Tim. 3:6). Their motive was money—either fees or gifts—and they were more concerned with what they could get out of people than with what they could put in.

Paul also wrote to Timothy of things that were applicable to these troublemakers.

A. "These teachers ... spend their time arguing and talking foolishness. They want to become famous as teachers of the laws of Moses when they haven't the slightest idea what those laws really show us" (1 Tim. 1:6–7 TLB).

B. "Don't waste time arguing over foolish ideas and silly myths and legends.

Spend your time and energy in the exercise of keeping spiritually fit" (1 Tim. 4:7 TLB).

II. For the church to be made strong, the mouths of these troublemakers must be stopped.

A. Their mouths need to be controlled like a bridle on a horse or a muzzle on an ox.

B. Violence is not to be used to control them. Rather they are to be kept firmly within bounds.

Conclusion

It is a shame that troublemakers can get into a church. But they do, as evidence on all sides shows. The churches of today need to deal with them in a gentle spirit, yet in a firm, sincere manner.

SUNDAY MORNING, MARCH 13

Title: The Cross of Jesus Christ

Text: "And I, if I be lifted up from the earth, will draw all men unto me. This he said, signifying what death he should die" **(John 12:32–33)**.

Scripture Reading: John 12:27–36

Hymns: "Wonderful, Wonderful Jesus," Russell

"Christ Receiveth Sinful Men," Neumeister

"Though Your Sins Be as Scarlet," Crosby

Offertory Prayer: Heavenly Father, we pray that you would open our eyes and help us to see the grace and the graciousness of your gift to us through Jesus Christ. Help us to recognize and appreciate more your generosity toward us. As you have given your best for us, even so today we offer our best to you. Help us to bring the firstfruits of both our love and labor to the altar of worship. May your blessing be on these tithes and offerings. Bless not only the gifts but the givers, through Jesus Christ our Lord. Amen.

Introduction

Crucifixion is the cruelest form of execution known to man. It was practiced by the Romans from the Punic Wars of the second and third centuries BC, and Roman citizens were exempt from its torture and cruelty. Crucifixion was so brutal and excruciating that it was reserved for rebels, slaves, thieves, and criminals.

Jesus Christ was crucified on a cross. He was nailed to the cross at 9:00 in the morning, and he died at 3:00 in the afternoon. Strange portents accompanied the crucifixion of Jesus Christ: (1) darkness covered the land from 12:00 until 3:00 (Luke 23:44; Amos 8:9); (2) the curtain of the temple was rent in two from top to bottom (Luke 23:45; Heb. 9:11–12; 10:19–22); and (3) an earthquake split the rocks and opened graves, and a large number of saints came forth from the graves and appeared to many in Jerusalem (Matt. 27:51–53).

While on the cross, Jesus spoke seven times. Three of his utterances have to do with others: "Father, forgive them; for they know not what they do" (Luke 23:34); "Today shalt thou be with me in paradise" (Luke 23:43); and "Woman, behold thy Son.... Behold thy mother" (John 19:26–27).

Four of the utterances of Jesus Christ from the cross have to do with himself: "My God, my God, why hast thou forsaken me?" (Mark 15:34; cf. Matt. 27:46); "I thirst" (John 19:28); "It is finished" (John 19:30); and "Father, into thy hands I commend my spirit" (Luke 23:46).

When the centurion witnessed how Jesus died, he exclaimed, "Truly this man was the Son of God" (Mark 15:39). And the women who supported the ministry of Jesus Christ in Galilee and those who came to Jerusalem stood afar off beholding all of these things.

Let us turn our hearts again to the cross of Jesus Christ for its message to us.

I. The cross of Jesus Christ is revealing.

A. The death of Jesus Christ on the cross reveals God's concern for sinful people (Matt. 20:28; Luke 19:10; John 12:32–33; Rev. 13:8).
B. The death of Jesus Christ on the cross reveals the awfulness of sin (Rom. 3:23; 6:23).
C. The death of Jesus Christ on the cross reveals God's love for sinners (John 3:16; 15:13; Rom. 5:8).

II. The cross of Jesus Christ is sacrificial, saving, and atoning (Matt. 20:28; Luke 19:10).

To understand the cross of Jesus Christ, we need to understand what kind of death he died on the cross.

A. The death of Jesus Christ on the cross was predicted (Rev. 13:8; 1 Peter 1:18–20).
B. The death of Jesus Christ on the cross was shameful (John 19:23–24; Heb. 12:2).
C. The death of Jesus Christ on the cross was voluntary (John 10:17–18).
D. The death of Jesus Christ on the cross was substitutionary (1 Peter 2:24; Titus 2:14; Isa. 53:4–10; 2 Cor. 5:21). Jesus Christ died on the sinner's behalf. He offered himself for sinners (Heb. 10:14) that they might be saved. His death was sacrificial, saving, and atoning.

III. The cross of Jesus Christ is offensive (1 Cor. 1:23; Phil. 3:18–19).

If we are faithful to the truth of God as revealed in the cross of Jesus Christ, the cross will be an offense and a stumbling block to those who are trying to be saved by their works. The cross of Jesus Christ proclaims liberty (Gal. 5:1). It sets people free from the yoke of works. The cross becomes a stumbling block to those who refuse to be saved by grace alone (Eph. 2:8–9).

It is possible to become an enemy of the cross of Jesus Christ. Those who love sin, live in sin, and serve sin are enemies of the cross. Those who love songs of the nativity but do not care about the songs of redemption are enemies of the cross.

What is the cross of Jesus Christ, and why is it offensive? Two reasons:

A. The cross of Jesus Christ is the power of God (1 Cor. 1:17–25). When Christ crucified is preached, the power of God is demonstrated in the saving of souls. To believe in the cross of Jesus Christ is to put yourself in touch with the power of God that delivers from all iniquity and saves with an everlasting salvation.

B. The cross of Jesus Christ is the wisdom of God. When we are saved by the cross of Jesus Christ, we can see the wisdom of God in planning humanity's salvation by the gift of his Son. A true vision of the Crucified One enables us to say, "O the depth of the riches both of the wisdom and knowledge of God" (Rom. 11:33).

To flee to the cross of Jesus Christ is to put yourself in the power and wisdom of God.

IV. The cross of Jesus Christ is triumphant.

The victory of the cross of Jesus Christ is seen in many places throughout the Bible.

A. The cross of Jesus Christ triumphs over the law (Col. 2:14).
B. The cross of Jesus Christ triumphs over sin (Heb. 9:26).
C. The cross of Jesus Christ triumphs over death (Heb. 2:14–15).
D. The cross of Jesus Christ triumphs over the devil (John 3:8; Rev. 12:10–11).
E. The cross of Jesus Christ triumphs over all (Col. 2:15).

Has Jesus Christ triumphed in your life?

V. The cross of Jesus Christ is primary.

A. The cross of Jesus Christ was primary in his life (Luke 9:51).
B. The cross of Jesus Christ is primary in becoming a believer (John 3:16; Matt. 16:24).
C. The cross of Jesus Christ is primary in glorying God (Gal. 6:14).

Conclusion

Come to the cross of Jesus Christ. Isaac Watts wrote:

When I survey the wondrous cross
On which the Prince of glory died,
My richest gain I count but loss,
And pour contempt on all my pride.

SUNDAY EVENING, MARCH 13

Title: God Never Gives Up

Text: "Being confident of this very thing, that he which hath begun a good work in you will perform it until the day of Jesus Christ" **(Phil. 1:6)**.

Scripture Reading: Philippians 1:6–7

Introduction

Paul was a man who dealt in assurances. He never left anyone in doubt concerning his position on a subject. No matter how great the difficulty, Paul was optimistic concerning the outcome. Paul derived his zeal not from his personal frustration, but from the certainty that he was on the "winning side." Not a person of presumptuous pride, Paul trusted completely in his message and, even more, in the one who stood behind it.

After his personal greetings, Paul encouraged his friends by assuring them that their labor in the Lord was not in vain. Their contributions to the gospel would be rewarded. Although he was perhaps thinking primarily of monetary gifts from the Philippians, we should not limit the meaning of his words. The word translated "fellowship" includes the sympathy and compassion expressed by the gifts. Paul is referring to the various services the people at Philippi had provided to help him spread the good news of Jesus Christ. This fellowship with Paul had begun the first day they knew him and continued as long as they were able to keep in contact with him. He was rejoicing in their friendship, and he sent them a great promise from prison.

I. God works constantly.

Although Paul followed Jesus, he carried into his Christian faith some great convictions from the Old Testament. One truth the Old Testament prophets continuously stressed was that God was working in the world. Perhaps the greatest heresy imaginable to an Old Testament prophet was that God had abdicated his creation. God is present even when he seems most invisible. To Paul, God could both bring down and raise up. He could destroy that which needed to be destroyed but build on the ruins an even greater edifice. Paul's God brought judgment for redemptive purposes rather than punitive ones. His sovereign grace led people to repentance, and this, through the Holy Spirit, led to their transformation.

God's Spirit moved over the void and brought creation. Throughout history, even today, God continues to transform the chaos of the cosmos into a new creation. Perhaps we need nothing more than a fresh realization of the sovereignty of God supplemented by an understanding that he is merciful and forgiving to repentant people.

God is always beginning a new work. The world continuously changes, but God channels these changes into constructive and meaningful events. Someone has said that the very word history means "His story."

II. God works to save individuals.

People cannot meet their own needs. Standing against the secular philosophy that puts a person's salvation in his or her own hands is the inescapable fact that God controls both our beginning and our ultimate destiny. God brings about regeneration and is able to complete the work that he has begun. Only God can justify people. Paul asks, "Who shall lay any thing to the charge of God's elect? It is God that justifieth" (Rom. 8:33). God declares the sinner righteous on the basis of Christ's work on Calvary. Our personal growth as Christians is contingent on the fact that we have had a personal experience in salvation. God will continue the good work he has begun throughout our Christian lives. Sanctification is both an act and a process. God's Holy Spirit sets us apart, and then we continue to grow as we commit ourselves progressively to the lordship of Jesus Christ and the leadership of the Holy Spirit. God began the work. God will continue the work. Paul's words are both a comforting assurance and a constant challenge. No Christian has reached perfection. God works constantly to bring us to maturity. Therefore we need to have our complacency disturbed often. The saving grace by which we began our spiritual experience will never be destroyed. The God who saved us from the penalty of sin is, day by day, saving us from the power of our sin and leading us to become more like our Savior.

III. God works in the churches.

Every local congregation is precious in God's sight. He loves each one as a bridegroom loves his bride. He expects each local congregation to be a body through which he can do his work in the world.

The church at Philippi was a work of God's grace. When Paul entered the city, not enough spiritually minded people were there to form a synagogue to study the Old Testament. He found a group of women praying by the riverside. From this humble beginning, others were added. We do not know how large the Philippian church became numerically, but we know it was one of great spirit. Paul was convinced that the "gates of hell" would not prevail against the Philippian congregation. God would continue the good work that he had begun in the church.

Those who serve in local congregations need to be reinforced constantly with this great truth. A pastor is not alone in his work. God is with him. The congregation is not without help. The Holy Spirit attends every assembly of born-again believers. Where even two or three are gathered together to worship, God is with them. The ultimate success of a church does not rest in the human strength of the members, but rather in the power of God. The permanence of the church's existence depends on God's power. Of course, the members must be in harmony with the great principles by which God operates, but the ultimate success depends on God's strength, not on human strength.

How much persecution the church at Philippi had endured, we cannot be certain. Most of the churches in the first century suffered at the hands of unbelieving Gentiles. On the other hand, they progressed remarkably in the pagan environment that surrounded them. The members gave a unique witness, and many lost their lives because of their testimony for Christ. They were not nearly as concerned about ecclesiastical structures as they were about the communication of their faith. God had spoken to them and was working through them. This assured their continuity.

IV. Until the Day of Christ.

Like the Old Testament prophets who constantly looked forward to "the day of the Lord," Paul hoped for the return to earth of Jesus, his Savior and Lord. This event would consummate history in a climactic and comprehensive manner. To Paul, everything done for Jesus was worthwhile because he would eventually win the victory.

Paul's concept of being saved thus included a third element. Not only have we been saved from the penalty of sin and are being saved from the power of sin, but at Christ's coming we shall be saved from the presence of sin. Paul was convinced that Christ works all things to his glory both in the lives of individuals and in the churches. Nothing can happen outside the ultimate will of God. The satanic forces of unrighteousness may win a few skirmishes, but Christ will win the conflict. The central theme of the last book in the New Testament, Revelation, is that victory belongs to the Lord and his people. Paul concludes his great chapter on the resurrection with a plain, simple exhortation to faithfulness: "Therefore, my dear brothers and sisters, stand firm. Let nothing move you. Always give yourselves fully to the work of the Lord, because you know that your labor in the Lord is not in vain" (1 Cor. 15:58 NIV).

Christians place their hope in final consummation. We should not stand idly by and imagine that we can do nothing either to make this a better world or to develop our own Christian lives. At the same time, however, we need to recognize that our supreme mission consists in leading individuals to redemption in Christ Jesus. This provides the best way to improve the world. In fact, leading people to Christ is the only way the world will become as God wishes it to be. Peace on this earth will come only as peace rules the hearts of enough people to affect the world and its social order. Yet deep in the heart of all born-again believers should be the conviction that their ultimate hope for a new world is the glorious return of the Lord.

Conclusion

Since God always completes what he begins, humanity's possibility always exceeds their ability. Life is similar to rowing a boat: we move forward, but at the same time, we look backward so as to gain perspective. Not absolutely certain of the future, our only certainty is the existence of a divine purpose for us. This purpose began before we came on the scene and will continue to direct us if we cooperate with the one who leads. Truly creative people never achieve their goals. When they come near to their goal, imagination makes their mouths water for higher aspirations and for longings yet unfulfilled.

God is in all of this striving! He wants us to never be satisfied, but to ever desire "more stately mansions" for the soul. Indeed, we do not know what the future holds, but we do know the one who holds our future!

WEDNESDAY EVENING, MARCH 16

Title: The Correction of Deceivers

Text: "Even one of their own prophets has said, 'Cretans are always liars, evil brutes, lazy gluttons.' This testimony is true. Therefore, rebuke them sharply, so that they will be sound in the faith and will pay no attention to Jewish myths or to the commands of those who reject the truth" **(Titus 1:12–14 NIV)**.

Scripture Reading: Titus 1

Introduction

Titus 1:5 appears to be the most important part of the epistle. The people referred to in Titus 1:5 are the cause of trouble in the church. This passage tells how to handle such people.

I. One of their own prophets used three terms to describe them as troublemakers (Titus 1:12).

A. They were liars (1:12). A lie is a falsehood uttered or acted to deceive. A liar, then, is a person who speaks or acts with the purpose of deceiving. This deception can take the form of outright telling lies or of telling half-truths. Commentaries say that one particular lie circulated in Crete—namely, that the tomb of Zeus was on the island. John 8:44 says the devil is the father of lies.

B. They were evil brutes (1:12). They were lazy animals, prowling around for prey (1 Tim. 3:6).

C. They were lazy gluttons (1:12). They wanted to be filled without the exertion of earning a living by honest work.

II. These people should be corrected by sharp rebukes (Titus 1:13).

A. The tense of this verb "rebuke" suggests continuous action. This rebuking should be continuous, not once and for all. Titus had been doing so, but the elders were to take over this role.

B. The term "rebuke sharply" literally means to speak sharply. The meaning is similar to cutting off with one blow as with an ax. These people need to be convicted of their wrongdoing.

III. The reasons for rebuking these troublemakers.

A. For the good of the church. People who are liars, loafers, and gluttons cause trouble in a church. They present the wrong image to outsiders and disturb the harmony inside the church.

The troublemakers must be stopped, or else a church will not accomplish its mission.

B. For the good of the troublemakers themselves. For people to be healthy mentally or spiritually, they cannot maintain the character mentioned in these verses. Unhealthy faith produces unhealthy doctrine.

Conclusion

One of the most difficult assignments given to the church consists in dealing with troublemakers according to God's will. We must seek the Holy Spirit's wisdom and guidance in dealing with them.

SUNDAY MORNING, MARCH 20

Title: The Love of Jesus Christ

Text: "Now before the feast of the passover, when Jesus knew that his hour was come that he should depart out of this world unto the Father, having loved his own which were in the world, he loved them unto the end" **(John 13:1)**.

Scripture Reading: John 12:12–16; Ephesians 5:1–2

Hymns: "All Hail the Power of Jesus' Name," Perronet

"Jesus, Keep Me Near the Cross," Crosby

"There Is a Green Hill Far Away," Alexander

Offertory Prayer: Holy Father, because you have freely given us the rich gifts of heaven, we bring to you the gifts of the earth. Because you have given us gifts of eternal significance, we bring to you temporal gifts with a prayer that you will bless them with eternal significance. Bless the use of these tithes and offerings for the preaching of the gospel. Through Jesus Christ our Lord. Amen.

Introduction

No truth in the Bible comes home to us with such force and with such power and tenderness as the love of God through Jesus Christ. Jeremiah the prophet wrote concerning the love of God: "I have loved thee with an everlasting love" (Jer. 31:3). John the apostle wrote concerning our Lord's love for his disciples: "When Jesus knew that his hour was come that he should depart out of this world unto the Father, having loved his own which were in the world, he loved them unto the end" (John 13:1). Paul the apostle wrote in Ephesians concerning Christ's love for us: "And walk in love, as Christ also hath loved us, and hath given himself for us an offering and a sacrifice to God for a sweet-smelling savour" (Eph. 5:2).

There is no question about it: Christ loves us. Let's look at the great love of Christ as revealed in his Word.

I. The love of Jesus Christ is a personal love (John 15:13; 16:27; Rom. 5:8; Gal. 2:20).

God is love, and all love starts with him and ends in him. Jesus Christ came to reveal the Father. He came into this world because he loves us personally, individually. God's love for me, Christ's love for me, the Holy Spirit's love for me opens the way for me to love God and everyone else. As Augustine said, "God loves us every one as though there were but one of us to love." The songwriter Charles Gabriel expressed our awe at God's love this way:

I stand amazed in the presence of Jesus the Nazarene,
And wonder how he could love me,
A sinner, condemned, unclean.

II. The love of Jesus Christ is a universal love (John 3:16).

Jesus Christ loves all people everywhere. He loves people of all races, in all lands, as John 3:16 expresses. Someone has said, "If all the Bible were destroyed except John 3:16, anyone anywhere could be saved by believing this oft-quoted and cherished verse."

III. The love of Jesus Christ is a powerful love.

A. The love of Jesus Christ is powerful in seeking sinners (Luke 19:10; Matt. 20:28).

B. The love of Jesus Christ is powerful in saving the lost (Rom. 5:8).

Oh, the love that drew salvation's plan!
Oh, the grace that brought it down to man!
Oh, the mighty gulf that God did span at Calvary!

—*William R. Newell*

C. The love of Jesus Christ is powerful in securing saints, in taking saints all the way (Rom. 8:34–38).

IV. The love of Jesus Christ is a demanding love.

A. The love of Jesus Christ demands my love (Ex. 20:5).

B. The love of Jesus Christ demands commandment keeping (John 14:23).

C. The love of Jesus Christ demands communication, signification (John 21:25).

We are to witness to the love of Jesus Christ. Jesus said to Simon Peter, "Feed my lambs" (John 21:15); "Feed my sheep" (v. 16); "Feed my sheep" (v. 17).

V. The love of Jesus Christ is a stimulating love.

Many great doxologies can be found in the Bible. Some of them are Romans 11:36; Ephesians 3:20; 1 Timothy 1:17; Hebrews 13:20–21; 1 Peter 4:11; and Jude 24–25.

The first doxology found in the book of Revelation reads, "Unto him that loved us, and washed us from our sins in his own blood" (Rev. 1:5). In the King James Version, the words are "loved us." However, in the original language the words are in the articular present and mean that he loved us before the foundation of the world, and he is still loving us. He loves us continually and forever.

Paul said, "For the love of Christ constraineth us" (2 Cor. 5:14). The love of Jesus Christ keeps us at our task regardless of what people may think or say.

VI. The love of Jesus Christ is a satisfying love (Rev. 1:5).

At the end of the first doxology in Revelation 1:5–6, we find these words: "To him be glory and dominion for ever and ever. Amen" (v. 6). John the apostle knew that Jesus Christ loved him, and it made his heart sing; it made him shout praises; it satisfied him.

Paul Gerhardt wrote the words:

O let Thy love my soul inflame,
And to this service sweetly bind.
Transfuse it through my inmost frame,
And mold me wholly to Thy mind!

VII. The love of Jesus Christ is a triumphant love.

Paul said, "In all these things we are more than conquerors through him that loved us" (Rom. 8:37). In the Song of Songs we find these words: "He brought me to the banqueting house, and his banner over me was love" (2:4). If we are triumphant over the trials and tribulations of life, it is because the love of Jesus Christ has enabled us to triumph.

Conclusion

The love of Jesus Christ is the greatest thing we can experience, the greatest thing that can happen to us. The one thing all men, women, boys, and girls need to know is this: "Jesus loves me, this I know, for the Bible tells me so."

SUNDAY EVENING, MARCH 20

Title: A Pastor's Prayer for His People

Text: "And this I pray, that your love may abound yet more and more in knowledge and in all judgment; that ye may approve things that are excellent; that ye may be sincere and without offence till the day of Christ" **(Phil. 1:9–10)**.

Scripture Reading: Philippians 1:8–11

Introduction

Few people have been as multidimensional as Paul. He was capable in a number of areas. He excelled as a preacher, writer, evangelist, missionary, and administrator. Perhaps the most characteristic thing about Paul, however, was that he had a pastor's heart. He established churches and remained with some of them for a considerable length of time but with others only a short time. Wherever he went, however, he always dealt with the church from the standpoint of a pastoral relationship.

To the Philippians, Paul was an "absentee pastor." The church, no doubt, had its own spiritual leader on the field with them. Paul, nevertheless, felt that the Philippian church was in a real sense "his own" and did not feel out of place in offering spiritual advice to the church as though he were the pastor.

Every pastor has certain goals for the people to whom he or she ministers. Pastors take pride in their spiritual growth and are discouraged when they fail to develop in Christian insight. In the following verses, Paul lays bare his heart concerning his fondest dreams for these dearly loved people.

I. That your love may abound yet more and more.

A phrase that has come down from the first century is, "How these Christians love one another!" One need only to read 1 Corinthians 13 to see how strongly Paul felt about love as a Christian virtue. He does not use any of the lesser Greek words for "love" in this passage but the one that means divine love *(agape)*. Paul knew that the only way Christians can love one another is if they have a spontaneous overflow of love for Jesus Christ.

Paul understood the importance of Christian fellowship. He knew that the spirit of a church was the true index to its greatness. Proper motivation for service comes only when people have fellowship based on their relationship with their Savior and Lord.

Paul wanted the Philippian Christians not just to love but to grow in love. He understood love as the practical principle by which the fruits of faith become a reality in one's life. People who love are born of God and know God (1 John 4:7). No truth is emphasized so strongly in the New Testament. When we love properly, we evaluate the various priorities of life that clamor for our attention and allegiance.

II. That you may approve things that are excellent.

Paul believed fervently that proper love would submerge the lower cravings of life. People would then yield themselves to the best and the highest in daily living. Paul certainly meant that Christians should choose the good in contrast to the evil, but he probably meant even more. They should choose the highest degree of good. An old truism says, "The good is the enemy of the best." Paul wanted the Philippians to have a sense of what was vital. He wrote to the Thessalonian church, "Prove all things; hold fast that which is good" (1 Thess. 5:21). The Greek word Paul uses for "prove" or "test" is the word used for testing a coin to see if the metal is genuine, pure, and unalloyed rather than false. The phrase actually relates to the previous one, because love is never blind. Real love can see the difference between the true and the false.

Christians who set their hearts on that which is highest will never be led astray by side issues. They will have a proper sense of priorities. Instinctively, they will choose those things in everyday living that both glorify God and make their own lives happy and useful.

III. That you may be sincere and without offense.

The opening word of this phrase is best translated "in order that," showing the definite relationship between "approving things that are excellent" and "being sincere and without offence" (Phil. 1:10). Some people live by a strict moral code, but by their arrogant and self-righteous attitudes, they turn people away from Christ rather than toward him. The proper kind of "choosing of the excellent" is rooted and grounded in the love that Paul mentions in Philippians 1:9. When love produces discernment, and discernment leads to proper choices, the result is a sincerity that causes others to know the Savior who inspires such righteous and yet winsome living. The word translated "sincere" comes from a combination of two Greek words. The first is "sunshine," while the other is the verb "judge." The word means that which is being viewed in the full light and found to be clear and pure. In the Latin language, the word "sincere" is "without wax." Ancient merchants sold statues in the marketplace. If the statues had defects or flaws, the merchants filled them with wax. If a thing was completely without flaws, it was said to be *sine cere* or, in other words, "without wax." One can clearly see the derivation of the English word from the two Latin words.

Paul was concerned that the Christians at Philippi should never cause other people to stumble in their moral lives because of their inconsistencies in actions or attitudes. In this context, the word Paul used is best understood as "freedom from offensiveness." In other places, however, the word has the idea of not jarring or shocking anyone. Living an example of the gospel is certainly our need today as much as it ever could have been in ancient Philippi. The world is looking to the Christian not so much for advice on how to live as an example of how to live.

The light of God shines on a truly sincere person, and such a person is unimpeded by either duplicity or sin. This person sincerely searches after truth. Such a person of genuine sincerity, upon arriving at the living truth as embodied in Jesus Christ, will humbly accept the revelation God has made in his Son. When someone who sincerely searches after truth comes face-to-face with Jesus, that person will find that the seeking has not been in vain.

IV. Until the day of Christ.

Although no one could accuse Paul of being a radical regarding eschatology, he referred often to the second coming of Jesus Christ. No doubt exists that Paul expected Christ to come during his own lifetime. This belief was in harmony with what Jesus taught—we should be expecting him at any hour. To Paul, the present life prepares one for that moment when Jesus Christ will appear to claim his own and judge those who have rejected him. No greater incentive to moral purity can be found than the consciousness of Christ's imminent coming.

The particular grammatical construction of this verse is such that the word translated "until" means more specifically "in view of" that glorious day. Paul meant that our living should be such that it will withstand the scrutiny of that great day. The preposition used emphasizes the ability to stand the testing. If the Christians in Philippi lived with a sense of that which is vital, they would have no fear of being tested by God at the second coming of Christ. One who is familiar with the writings of Paul will remember that this great and glorious day was never far from his thoughts.

Conclusion

All of these aspirations result in the concluding verse of this section (Phil. 1:12). The Christian life consists not merely of personal piety, although that is important, but rather of service. This service includes the giving of oneself to bring people to faith in Christ as personal Savior and Lord. A significant fact about the original language of this verse is that Paul says literally, "having been filled with the fruit of righteousness through Jesus Christ," suggesting an interesting interpretation. All of our Christian growth is due to having been personally forgiven by the one who literally "bought our righteousness" when he died on the cross for our sins. These two ideas merge into one—we are to serve him as a fruit of having been redeemed by him.

WEDNESDAY EVENING, MARCH 23

Title: Two Kinds of Minds

Text: "Unto the pure all things are pure: but unto them that are defiled and unbelieving is nothing pure; but even their mind and conscience is defiled. They profess that they know God; but in works they deny him, being abominable, and disobedient, and unto every good work reprobate" **(Titus 1:15–16).**

Scripture Reading: Titus 1

Introduction

A student of God's Word will recognize immediately that this passage has several parallels in the New Testament; this discussion, however, focuses on two verses in Titus.

The background related to this passage is important. Paul has talked about trouble in the church and how to correct it. These two verses also concern church trouble. Notice the subject "Two Kinds of Minds."

I. The first kind of mind is the "pure."

Scripture says, "Unto the pure all things are pure" (Titus 1:15).

A. This is a categorical statement. The writer does not elaborate on this statement.

B. Why does he not elaborate on his statement?

1. Because he is dealing with negatives, or problems, he does not elaborate.
2. Another reason for his lack of elaboration is that the statement speaks for itself. The pure people have been bestowed purity by Christ's atonement. They have been regenerated.

II. The second kind of mind is the "impure."

This kind of mind is opposite the pure mind.

A. Paul describes the impure with two words. They are the corrupt, unbelieving people who have not been cleansed by faith in the blood of Jesus Christ.

B. Two words mentioned refer to how one makes decisions and arrives at conclusions. Paul uses the words "mind" and "conscience" (1:15). Humans use their minds, or intellect, to think and direct their wills. The conscience refers to inner moral judgment of what is right or wrong. The Scripture passage makes clear that the conscience has lost its ability to discriminate.

C. Paul uses four things to elaborate on this idea.

1. They profess to know God but deny him by their deeds. The words "to know" mean to be fully informed about God. Their deeds or works contradict their profession. With their deeds they flagrantly deny God.
2. They are abominable. These people who are foul in thought, word, and action are repulsive to both God and man.
3. They are disobedient. Because they profess to know God but do not obey him, these people are repulsive.
4. They are reprobates in regard to works. God sees their counterfeit work as useless. They are the stones the builders reject.

Conclusion

For people to be right in God's and humanity's eyes, they need to have their minds and consciences cleansed by the blood of Jesus Christ. They need to remain in God's Spirit.

SUNDAY MORNING, MARCH 27

Title: The Resurrection Speaks

Text: "He is not here: for he is risen, as he said, Come, see the place where the Lord lay" **(Matt. 28:6)**.

Scripture Reading: Matthew 28:1 – 10

Hymns: "Christ Arose," Lowry

"He Lives," Ackley

"My Jesus, I Love Thee," Featherston

Offertory Prayer: Eternal Father, we come before you with hearts filled with gratitude and thanksgiving for the blessings of the faith that prompts our souls to bow before you on this glorious Easter Sunday. You have given so completely of yourself in offering to a weary world the hope that assures the forgiveness of our sins through simple faith in Christ Jesus, our Lord. We thank you for the message of this day that gives to us the eternal guarantee that life moves out beyond the borders of time into the heavenly place that you have prepared for those who love you. We stand in your holy presence rejoicing in all that you have done through Calvary and the empty tomb. Just as you have shared your joy in the giving of your Son for world redemption, so we dedicate ourselves to sharing the glad tidings of great joy with humankind everywhere. We humble ourselves, Father, in bringing to you our heart's best love and our life's best service. May our tithes and offerings give substance and power to the outreach of the gospel message during these significant days of world history. We pray in the name of the risen, living Christ, the hope of all people. Amen.

Introduction

On a glorious Lord's Day morning nearly two thousand years ago, a group of faithful women visited a tomb that held, as they believed, the cold and breathless body of their beloved leader and teacher.

They went to the tomb that morning in the same frame of mind with which we go to cemeteries to lay our own dear loved ones to rest—their hearts were full and heavy. How exceedingly difficult it was for them to reconcile themselves to the fact that they had been separated from Jesus, the divine Lord!

When they reached the sepulchre, their discovery greatly disturbed them. They saw that the stone had been rolled away from the opening to the tomb, and they hastily concluded that the body had been removed. Impelled by grief, they stood within the rock-hewn burial place to behold a vision of angels who were clothed with dazzling garments.

As they stood there in their sorrow, a voice spoke to them and said, "Fear not ye: for I know that ye seek Jesus, which was crucified. He is not here: for he is risen, as he said. Come, see the place where the Lord lay. And go quickly, and tell his disciples that he is risen from the dead" (Matt. 28:5–7).

The resurrection still speaks today. What does it have to say to modern-day disciples? What does it have to say to people who have lost their way?

I. The resurrection speaks of a living Lord.

It was not Christ's death that proved his mission or his messiahship. Had our Lord remained in the grave and returned to dust, our darkness would be as deep as that which reigned for three hours after the crucifixion. There would be no hope for deliverance from sin and death.

But death could not hold him. His resurrection was his triumph. It was proof of all he claimed to be, the token that his work was accepted by the Father.

There is no record in history more firmly established by the word of trustworthy witnesses than these facts: that Christ died, was buried, and arose from the dead on the third day. Men and women of unimpeachable character have borne witness that they saw him, knew him, ate with him, and talked with him as he moved among them in his resurrection body. Luke, the beloved physician, says, "He shewed himself alive after his passion by many infallible proofs" (Acts 1:3).

No fact in history is more certain than this: Christ lives.

II. The resurrection validates Christianity.

It would be difficult to account for the life of Jesus Christ if we found the record in any other book than the New Testament. But Christianity has grown out of the soil of the historical past. Its mystical revelation evades human invention. Christ's whole life was attended by the miraculous.

The disciples did not believe that they would ever see Jesus again. They believed that he was dead. But their minds and spirits experienced a great change during the three days that his body lay in the tomb of Joseph of Arimathea.

Now the disciples believed that Jesus had risen from the dead. Their faith in the reality of our Lord's victory over death is to us of greater significance than any other form of evidence. To say that they spent their lives enduring hardships, suffering privation and even death just to support an exquisite fable would be an insult to human intelligence. The foundation of the Christian movement is Jesus Christ crucified, buried, and risen in glorious power. "For since by man came death, by man came also the resurrection of the dead. For as in Adam all die, even so in Christ shall all be made alive" (1 Cor. 15:21–22).

III. The resurrection guarantees the redemption of the soul.

The argument of the apostle Paul is this, "If Christ be not raised, your faith is vain; ye are yet in your sins" (1 Cor. 15:17). For if Christ is not risen, then the chief cornerstone is taken out of the Christian system and the hopes that men have built on Jesus crumble to the ground.

The faith that saves rests solely on the historic foundation of the resurrection of Jesus Christ from the dead. Our faith is in Jesus Christ, the risen Lord, "who was delivered for our offences, and was raised again for our justification" (Rom. 4:25).

IV. The resurrection is the foundation for the hope of life beyond the grave.

Our Lord's resurrection is the promise of other resurrections. It is on this truth that the doctrine of the future life is established. It proclaims with finality that life here and life beyond the grave is one and continuous. It is unbroken by death. The same Jesus who was taken from the disciples by death was given back to them by the resurrection.

When our loved ones die and pass into that silent land, what hope do we have that we shall see them again? None but the words of the risen Christ, who said, "I am the resurrection, and the life: he that believeth in me, though he were dead, yet shall he live: and whosoever liveth and believeth in me shall never die" (John 11:25–26).

Conclusion

The voice of the Holy Spirit still speaks to the followers of the living Lord. "Go quickly, and tell . . . that he is risen from the dead" (Matt. 28:7). The foundation of the message we proclaim to a world that has lost its way is found in the assurance that we worship and serve a risen, living Savior. Like the early Christians who went everywhere preaching "that Christ died for our sins according to the scriptures; and that he was buried, and that he rose again the third day according to the scriptures" (1 Cor. 15:3–4), so should our witness be today.

Again and again our hearts need to be reminded that the resurrection is the only assurance of eternal life. Like all mysteries encompassed in the supernatural power of God, we may not understand them, but we can embrace them for our comfort and peace.

No greater joy can come to the heart of a Christian than that sacred moment when an unbeliever confesses his or her faith in the saving power of the risen, living Lord. No greater challenge can inspire the spirit of a believer than the opportunity to share in the hope of the Christian gospel. To hear the response to God's invitation, "Lord, I believe," is still the reason why we would never fail to offer to lost people the assurance of salvation in the name of the living Christ.

Thomas Yuen was a devoted follower of a pagan Chinese faith. His attendance at Christian services revealed that he was not satisfied in the religious faith that he had embraced since he was a child. For several weeks, he found his way to a fellowship of Christian believers where he heard the message of a faithful pastor as he proclaimed the redeeming, saving power of Christ in making people whole. One Lord's Day morning, Yuen's heart responded to the Spirit's invitation to trust in Jesus Christ for salvation. It was a glorious moment as he confessed before the people, in broken English, "I believe in Jessee, I believe in Jessee."

Some weeks later, following his baptism, Thomas Yuen underwent open-heart surgery. Again, the pastor found real joy in ministering to his spiritual need in these critical days. Each time the pastor prepared to leave Yuen's bedside, Yuen never failed to request prayer and give his testimony, "I believe in Jessee."

One evening an attending nurse called the pastor to inform him of Thomas Yuen's critical condition. Within minutes the pastor was at the hospital to hear the words of this man as he said, "Tonight I think of go see Jessee." And this he did in the hope and confidence that the Christ he had trusted would greet him at the portals of his heavenly home. This same Jesus can be your hope of eternal life. Accept him, and trust him today.

SUNDAY EVENING, MARCH 27

Title: Burdens Can Be Blessings

Text: "I would ye should understand, brethren, that the things which happened unto me have fallen out rather unto the furtherance of the gospel" **(Phil. 1:12)**.

Scripture Reading: Philippians 1:12–19

Introduction

Paul always wanted his hearers or readers to know all the facts. He never failed to face reality, and he sought to lead others toward the healthy-mindedness of accepting and coping with things as they were.

Paul was in jail. True, it was not the dungeon in which he was later confined; it was a rented house. Nevertheless, he was under constant guard and was truly a prisoner. Paul never ignored this fact, but neither did he use it to play on the sympathies of people. In fact, he did the opposite. Paul did not want any sympathy because of his confinement and the consequent limitation of his physical activity. This section in his letter deals with the fact that even in the midst of burden and disappointment distinct advantages had come to him.

I. "Ye should understand."

Many people miss out on great blessings in life because they do not understand an event and make no effort to explore the facts concerning it. Suppose Moses had turned away from the burning bush because it was something he did not understand. He would have missed the greatest blessing and opportunity of his life. Since Paul was in prison, he could no longer move about freely preaching the gospel of Christ. Suppose he had become bitter and blamed God for it. He would have ceased to make any effort toward sharing the good news about Christ. He might have decided his ministry was over and allowed cynicism to take over his life. Paul, however, refused to adopt this position. He reasoned that if God had placed him in jail, there was a divine purpose for it. He shared the viewpoint of the one who wrote:

The world will never adjust itself
To suit your whims to the letter;
Some things will go wrong your whole life long,
And the sooner you know it, the better.
It's folly to fight with the Infinite
And go down at last in the wrestle;
The wiser man shapes into God's plan
Like water shapes into the vessel.

—*Ella Wheeler Cox*

II. "The furtherance of the gospel."

Paul frankly stated his feelings about the disasters that had come to him. He refused to be a defeated man at the end of a strenuous career. He would not accept the fact that he had been confined to prison merely to await probable execution and that he had only a faint hope for release. He began to tell people near him of his personal experience with Jesus on the Damascus road and of his newfound faith. Similar to our own era, the time in which Paul lived was one in which people had become disillusioned with the shallow substitutes for reality. They longed for something that would give them confidence concerning the meaning of life and hope for a future beyond the grave. Christianity provided the only answer, and Paul delivered the message with a certainty that made the people realize their craving for inner peace would be met only in Jesus Christ. Paul believed there was only one issue in life: in the world of uncertainty, only Christ can bring that which will give one something to "die by and live for."

As Paul delivered this message to people about him, a strange thing happened. The soldiers, impressed by Paul's strength of character, wanted to know more about his Savior and Lord. As his guards accepted Christ, the word spread. Paul became an object of interest. Through those people whom Paul contacted, the gospel was spread even further.

The word Paul used for "furtherance" describes the progress of an army. In other places, this term means cutting away the trees and undergrowth and removing the barriers that would ordinarily hinder an army's progress. This is significant in Paul's case. If he had tried to "crash" the emperor's inner circle, he never could have succeeded, because too many obstacles blocked the way. Since he was a prisoner, however, he could see these people face-to-face and witness to them. Surely his decision, while in Caesarea, to appeal to Rome, was God's will at work in his life, although he did not realize it at the time. The trip to Rome gave him an even greater field of service for his Lord.

III. "Waxing confident by my bonds."

Paul encouraged his readers by saying, "And many of the brethren in the Lord, waxing confident by my bonds, are much more bold to speak the word without fear" (Phil. 1:14). People have far more influence on others than they realize. Although Paul was a prisoner, his strong faith encouraged believers who were weaker. Other Christians who came in contact with Paul were hesitant to stand firm for their faith, but Paul, by his boldness, gave them renewed strength. An outstanding Christian tells how, as a young man, he was at a social activity when alcoholic beverages were served. He had not expected this and did not want to drink. At the same time, it seemed everyone else at the table was allowing the waiter to pour a drink. He saw a young lady there whom he respected and decided he would see what she did. When she smiled sweetly and turned her glass upside down, indicating she did not care for a drink, he immediately did the same. That girl later became his wife, and they lived many years together and served the Lord in an outstanding way. Her firmness of strength gave him the courage to act out his conviction. How important is our influence!

IV. "Some preach Christ even of envy and strife."

Paul continued, "Some indeed preach Christ even of envy and strife; and some also of good will" (Phil. 1:15). Paul could have been more disturbed had he allowed himself to be, by the people who were seeking to discredit him personally. It seems incredible that there should have been jealousy and envy among the Christians when they were all facing such difficulty. Paul does not expand on this or give us any details but merely mentions that people seemed to be adding to his bonds by the manner in which they delivered the message of Christ. Although we cannot be sure, these people may have been the Christians who had been influenced by the Judaizers and who were opposed to Paul's message of salvation by grace without either the ceremonies or the good deeds of the law.

Paul's philosophy is excellent for us today. Don't fight your opposition, especially if you are in the Lord's work. People come to Christ not because of our arguments or cleverness but because of a personal experience with Jesus. Jesus can meet the needs of humanity and can transform one's life even though the messenger may be slightly confused concerning details of how Jesus does it. Let Christ be received, and his transforming power will change hearts!

V. "My salvation ... the Spirit of Jesus Christ."

Paul knew that if he kept his spirit in tune with the Lord, he would be vindicated. He wrote, "For I know that this shall turn to my salvation through your prayer, and the supply of the Spirit of Jesus Christ" (Phil. 1:19). Some scholars believe the expression "my salvation" refers to Paul's personal relationship with the Lord, while others feel he was speaking of his deliverance from prison. In a sense, both may be true, but Paul probably was indicating that if the Philippians continued to pray for him and he continued to manifest a sweet Christian spirit, he would be victorious in his forthcoming trial in the Roman court. This is always the way to meet opposition—with firm conviction and a sweet spirit. We should never compromise with our basic beliefs, but also we should not become militant and discount the Christian message through an obstinate attitude.

Adversity can strengthen us. We can turn our burdens into bridges. A biologist watched an ant carrying a piece of straw. The ant came to a crack in the ground. The ant put the straw across the crack and walked over on the straw. The straw was a burden, but the ant used the burden as a bridge. Wise people let their burdens bear them up instead of weigh them down. The ancient poet Horace said, "Adversity has the effect of eliciting talents which in prosperous circumstances would have lain dormant."

Conclusion

Many people have won victories over circumstances and have made contributions to the world that have blessed the lives of millions. Milton's blindness, Beethoven's deafness, and David Livingstone's fever-stricken body were conquered and molded into personal victories as they found and did God's will. Faith is not the ability to explain things but is a spirit that dares to venture even when it does not have the key to the puzzle.

Whatever the sorrow or time of crisis, we can profit from it. God's will is perceived more clearly during the dark night of discouragement than in the noontime of prosperity.

WEDNESDAY EVENING, MARCH 30

Title: The Christian Character of Old Men

Text: "But speak thou the things which become sound doctrine; that the aged men be sober, grave, temperate, sound in faith, in charity, in patience" **(Titus 2:1–2)**.

Scripture Reading: Titus 2

Introduction

Against the background of acknowledged corruption in Cretan life, Paul urged Titus to call the people to high standards of Christian living. In Titus 1 Paul pointed out what the trouble was and suggested one approach for correction. Now in chapter 2 he mentions the second approach—namely, to call the church people to high conduct. He addresses them by ages or stations in life.

The first age group is the old men. The question is, just what is old? It seems that it is a comparative thing—the "old" men are simply older than the others.

I. Paul is emphatic in saying that sound doctrine should be exercised.

A. Sound doctrine is based on a scholarly, Spirit-led interpretation of the Word. A damnable thing in any church is a deviation from true doctrine.

B. This is in contrast to false teachers already mentioned in the epistle.

II. Paul gives six requirements for the character of old men, and he divides these into sections.

A. The first section is in regard to ethics.

1. They should be sober. This is a word that continues to show itself in this epistle. The word is especially applicable to drink, but it also applies to thought, word, and act. It means not to be swept off one's feet by flighty teaching.

   It is combined with watchfulness and prayer. The older person should be a balance wheel of every congregation.

2. They should be grave. That is, they should be serious. This does not mean that the elders should not be happy. It just means they should be seriously committed to the work of the Lord. They should be serious about Bible study and soul-winning.

3. They should be temperate, or prudent. They are to govern every instinct and passion until each has its proper place. They are to have the same influence on the church.

B. The second section deals with the spiritual walk. This has been referred to as the trilogy of graces.

1. They must be sound in faith. Their faith is to be healthy. A close walk with God will give this. Faith cheers hope and promotes steadfastness.

2. They must be filled with love. Their love is to be healthy. A great danger is to drift into censoriousness, criticism, and fault-finding. Real agape

love comes from years of close fellowship with God. When practiced, it binds a congregation together.

3. They must have patience. Other words that mean the same are fortitude and endurance. A strong faith endures the things that are unpleasant and accepts the inevitable.

Conclusion

Older people who have walked with God for a long time should have sound judgment. They are better able to evaluate and then to respond in the right way.

SUGGESTED PREACHING PROGRAM FOR THE MONTH OF APRIL

■ Sunday Mornings

In the post-Easter season, continue to celebrate the resurrection of our Lord with the series "Real Life in the Here and Hereafter." This series will continue through the first Sunday in May.

■ Sunday Evenings

Continue the series of messages based on Paul's epistle of joy—Philippians.

■ Wednesday Evenings

Continue the series of studies from the book of Titus. The section for consideration emphasizes the supreme importance of Christian character.

SUNDAY MORNING, APRIL 3

Title: At the Cross

Text: "And when they were come to the place, which is called Calvary, there they crucified him, and the malefactors, one on the right hand, and the other on the left" **(Luke 23:33)**.

Scripture Reading: Luke 23:33–49

Hymns: "At the Cross," Isaac Watts

"Down at the Cross," Elisha A. Hoffman

"The Old Rugged Cross," George Bennard

Offertory Prayer: Our heavenly Father, you have instructed us to bring our tithes and offerings into your storehouse. This we do with joy and gratitude. We ask you to make your storehouse a place of worship where you are honored and praised. May we be good stewards of all you have committed to us. Some of our gifts will make possible the sharing of the gospel in faraway places. Some of our gifts will minister to the lost, the poor, and the needy right around us. But all of our gifts are given in honor of you, our Lord and Savior. Take our tithes and offerings and ourselves and make of them whatever you will. In Jesus' name we pray. Amen.

Introduction

In Charles Rann Kennedy's drama of the last days of Jesus, *The Terrible Meek*, the captain says, "Something has happened here upon this hill today. It is something that will shake all the empires and kingdoms of this world unto the dust. The earth is His, the earth is theirs, and they made it—the meek, the terrible meek, the fierce, agonizing meek are about to enter into their inheritance" (Charleston, SC: Bibliolife, 2009, n.p.).

Across the centuries, people have looked back to Calvary because of the cross. Something happened that made all the difference in the world before and after the cross. Before the cross, women had no rights, children were disposable, there were more slaves than free people, and there was no clear revelation of God. After the cross, there is a perfect revelation of God, women are more respected, children are normally cherished, and souls are set free.

At the cross:

I. We hear the cry of Jesus.

"Father, forgive them; for they know not what they do" (Luke 23:34).

A. Which intercedes for the undeserving. In this first word from the cross, we see that Christ's thoughts are turned away from himself to his enemies—to the governor who had issued the order to crucify him, to the religious leaders who were the instigators of the crime, to the Roman soldiers who nailed him to the cross, and to the multitude who were stirred up by their religious guides. Though they are undeserving, Christ still intercedes for them. Thank God that he does not wait until we are deserving before he intercedes for us!

B. Which reveals the boundless love of God. For Christ to be able to pray for those responsible for his death revealed God's love as it had never been revealed before. Christ reveals God's love to be offered to those whom no one else loves. The crowd saw the thieves as "malefactors" to be hated, but Christ saw them as "men" to be loved and saved.

II. We feel the temptation to compromise.

"The people stood beholding. And the rulers also with them derided him, saying, 'He saved others; let him save himself, if he be Christ, the chosen of God'" (Luke 23:35).

"Let him now come down from the cross, and we will believe him" (Matt 27:42). If ever the temptation to compromise was overwhelming, it was on the cross. We confront the same temptation to compromise today. We are called to compromise on the issues of same-sex marriages, homosexuality, and the legalization of marijuana. Many of our national leaders have embraced the call to compromise on these and other moral issues.

We feel temptation:

A. When our personal welfare is at stake. The very life of Christ was involved. To answer the call and come down from the cross would save his life. To turn a deaf ear to the call would cost him his life. When telling a white lie or going along with the crowd or failing to report all your income on your taxes becomes appealing to you, you are feeling the call to compromise.

B. When others make fun of us. "And the rulers also with them derided him" (Luke 23:35). Most of us can take anything except ridicule. When we take a Christian stand openly, we are afraid that others may make fun of us.

C. When what we may gain is appealing. "Come down from the cross, and we will believe" (Matt. 27:42). At the beginning and the end of Christ's earthly ministry, he was called to compromise. At the beginning of Christ's ministry, Satan said to him, "Turn these stones into bread" (see Matt. 4:3 and Luke 4:3), and at the close of Christ's ministry, Peter said, "Anything, but not the cross" (see Matt. 16:22). Did not Christ want people to follow him? Yes, but only by the way of the cross.

III. We witness the crisis of decision.

"One of the malefactors ... railed on him, saying, 'If thou be Christ, save thyself and us'" (Luke 23:39). The other thief said, "Remember me when thou comest into thy kingdom" (v. 42).

In this crisis you:

A. May question the claims of Christ. "If thou be the Christ" (Luke 23:39). Until you accept Christ as the Messiah, you are saying, "I don't believe you enough to trust my soul to you."

B. May make an open confession. "And we indeed justly: for we receive the due reward of our deeds: but this man hath done nothing amiss" (Luke 23:41). This thief not only confessed his guilt, but he also declared his belief that Christ was all he claimed to be. You can tell by the way a man dies how he has lived. And as this thief saw how Christ died, he was compelled to believe that Christ was indeed the Messiah.

IV. We see the contract of salvation.

"And he said unto Jesus, 'Lord, remember me when thou comest into thy kingdom.' And Jesus said unto him, 'Verily I say unto thee, Today shalt thou be with me in paradise'" (Luke 23:43–43).

A. There is our part. Our part is to admit our need. This the thief did openly. This is repentance. Our part is to believe that Christ is all he claims to be. This is faith. And our part is to take the leap of faith. This the thief did when he said, "Remember me." He was saying, "Live or die, sink or swim, I am dying trusting Jesus!"

B. There is God's part. "Today shalt thou be with me in paradise" (Luke 23:43). The world said, "He is incorrigible—crucify him!" Christ said, "He is a man made in the image of God—redeem him!" Christ accepts us, for he is our maker.

God's part is to save. When we believe on the Lord Jesus Christ, the promise is that we are saved. When we are saved, we have the assurance that we will be with Christ in paradise.

Conclusion

Salvation is open to all because of what happened at the cross. It is at the cross that

1. We hear the cry of Jesus.

2. We feel the temptation to compromise.
3. We witness the crisis of decision.
4. We see the contract of salvation.

Will you not enter into the contract of salvation today? Your part of the contract is to admit your need, to believe that Christ is all he claims to be, and to take the leap of faith.

SUNDAY EVENING, APRIL 3

Title: In the Meantime Live for Jesus

Text: "Only let your conversation be as it becometh the gospel of Christ" **(Phil. 1:27)**.

Scripture Reading: Philippians 1:20–30

Introduction

Paul faced a dilemma. He had been serving God for many years and was physically tired. He was certain of his heavenly home, not because of his righteous deeds, but because he had personally placed his faith in Jesus Christ as his Savior from sin. Paul's dilemma was whether or not his ministry was almost completed. Was God ready to take him to his heavenly reward, or did God have more work for him to do?

Paul had developed a personal philosophy. He prepared for the worst, but he hoped for the best. He determined to serve God with courage regardless of the external circumstances, leaving the "times and seasons" with God. As he faced the future, he possessed the same attitude toward it as he possessed toward the present.

I. "Living is Christ."

Most translations render this phrase as an infinitive—"to live" is Christ. The construction in the original language has an article preceding the infinitive. Some translators feel the force of Paul's statement is best brought out with a participle—"living" is Christ. No essential difference in meaning exists except perhaps that the emphasis of the participle rendering is on the present continuous action.

To Paul, Christians' lives should continue the incarnation—Christ's life in the flesh. In the conversion to Christianity, people are not only justified from their sins through the atonement of Christ; the presence of the Holy Spirit transforms them. God plants a seed within them, and they begin lives of spiritual growth. The ultimate aim of Christian character development is summarized in Jesus' words, "Be ye therefore perfect, even as your Father which is in heaven is perfect" (Matt. 5:48).

Growing Christians thus become more like Jesus each day. This pilgrimage goes beyond merely imitating Christ's life. It includes following him in love because of a new motivation. We become like that which we constantly admire. As we love Christ, we admire him and therefore become like him not only consciously but even unconsciously. Before he met Christ, Paul's energies had been scattered along many lines. Since his transforming experience on the Damascus road, he concentrated his mind, heart, and energy on one thing—surrendering his will to God's will as he understood it in Jesus Christ. In short, for Paul, living had become Christ. His religion was no longer a creed but personal fellowship with his Savior, Lord, and Friend.

II. "Dying is gain."

What is the primary purpose of bringing people to Christ? Is it merely to give them a new ethic? To be sure, when people are dedicated to the Christian way of life, they are constrained by a principle of life far superior to any other worldview. Most people, however, repent of sin and trust the Savior because they experience deep conviction concerning their personal deficiency and feel uncertain concerning their future life. Most people are saved because they want the promise of eternal life with Christ.

The New Testament says far more about the life to come than the Old Testament. This is because Christ is the "firstfruits of the resurrection." He was not the first person to rise from the dead, but he was the first person to rise from the dead through his own power and subsequently appear in his resurrected body.

For the Christian, dying is gain! Many things about heaven are unknown to us. Our natural curiosity prods us to inquire at every source for answers to our lack of knowledge. For instance, the Bible teaches us that there will be a resurrection of the dead in Christ at the return of Jesus. People who are saved will receive glorious bodies that will not be subject to time or space. These bodies in some ways will resemble our old bodies and yet will be far superior to them. Our new bodies will be a proper dwelling place for our eternal souls.

Yet the Bible is vague as to the "parenthesis" between our physical death and the Lord's coming. Paul speaks of being "absent from the body" and "being present with the Lord" when discussing our leaving the physical world in death. To us this parenthesis can be thought of as sleep, but that is our way of looking at it while we are in the flesh. In many places, the Bible clearly indicates that the soul is conscious during this intermediate period. The great evangelist Dwight L. Moody once said, "Someday you will read in the papers that Moody is dead. Don't you believe a word of it. At that moment I shall be more alive than I am now." The New Testament pictures heaven as a place of joy, peace, freedom from pain, presence with the Lord, and never-ending life.

III. Paul's crisis and his decision.

What must Paul do? Shall he continue living and therefore serving Christ, or shall he depart and be with Christ, which would be far better? Actually, the decision was not Paul's but rather belonged to the Lord. Paul, however, debated the alternatives deliberately within himself and reached a profound conclusion.

Knowing that continuing his earthly work would result in more fruit for the Lord and more growth for those whom he served, he decided God was leading him to more years in service. His trial was coming up shortly. He felt certain that he would be released.

Most scholars believe that Paul was released after the trial and went back eastward on another missionary journey. Some verses in the pastoral letters almost demand this conclusion. A few scholars believe that Paul made a westward trip as well—perhaps as far as Spain.

Paul gave a practical message to the Philippians. They should continue serving Christ whether the apostle came to see them or not. He urged them to stand together in fellowship and missionary endeavor, and he exhorted them to have courage in the face of opposition. He entreated them to remember that even suffering can be a privilege, especially when it is for the sake of Christ and his work.

Conclusion

Paul's advice to his friends at Philippi proves uniquely relevant for us today. Strange events are taking place in the world. A temptation exists for Christians to panic on one hand or go off on a tangent on the other hand. Some people claim to have a key to future events and capitalize on their so-called knowledge by exploiting gullible people who follow them blindly. Still others become frustrated with the seeming hopelessness of world conditions and become emotionally incapable of normal Christian living and service.

What will wise Christians do? They will follow Paul's simple yet profound advice to the Christians at Philippi. Whether God is about to wrap up history or not, we should serve him faithfully now. If God is ready to take us to heaven, we should be ready to go. If, however, he wants us to continue to live in this perplexed world, we need to be steadfast, unmovable, always abounding in the work of the Lord. Of one thing we can be certain—our work will never be useless nor fruitless if we are serving our Savior!

WEDNESDAY EVENING, APRIL 6

Title: The Christian Character of Old Women

Text: "The aged women likewise, that they be in behaviour as becometh holiness, not false accusers, not given to much wine, teachers of good things; that they may teach the young women to be sober, to love their husbands, to love their children" **(Titus 2:3–4)**.

Scripture Reading: Titus 2

Introduction

Keep in mind that old is a comparative word, referring here to women who are mature in age.

I. "Likewise" in Titus 2:3 is a connecting word.

It connects the character of the old women with that of the old men. Everything that was said about men is applicable to women. A quick review is in order.

A. Sober—that is, not swept off one's feet by flighty teaching. This applies to word or action.
B. Serious—seriously committed.
C. Temperate—having everything under control.
D. Sound faith—healthy in faith.
E. Filled with agape love.
F. Fortitude—endure the unpleasant.

II. Paul then adds information about the character of old women.

A. They are to behave in a holy manner. A word that could be used instead of behavior is decorum. It applies to conduct and to dress and gestures as well. First Timothy 2:9 refers almost exclusively to clothing. Our Titus passage also refers to looks and speech. The conduct described here is that which comes from inward integrity that orders outward conduct at all times.
B. These women are not to be false accusers. "They are not to foster discord by backbiting or speaking evil of someone. Otherwise they would be slanderers, and slanderers are those whose tongues are set on fire by hell. They are of the devil. Ephesians 6:11 identifies the devil as the chief slanderer.

   This sin is contrary to the great duties of love, justice, and equity between believers. This attitude springs from malice and hatred, envy and jealousy.
C. These women are "not to be given to much wine." A Christian must not be under the power and control of alcoholic beverages. Such destroys modesty and makes for immorality. It creates shame. It corrupts and destroys purity of body and mind.
D. These women are to be "teachers of good things." Older Christian women are to teach by the example of a good life and by doctrinal instruction in the home and elsewhere.

Conclusion

Older people have a tremendous influence in a church. It behooves all people who have reached a mature age to use their influence for good in the church. To exercise good, there are some things they need to avoid and some things they need to do.

SUNDAY MORNING, APRIL 10

Title: Eternal Life

Text: "For God so loved the world, that he gave his only begotten Son, that whosoever believeth in him should not perish, but have everlasting life" **(John 3:16)**.

Scripture Reading: John 3:1–17

Hymns: "Crown Him with Many Crowns," Bridges

"To God Be the Glory," Crosby

"Jesus Paid It All, "Hall

Offertory Prayer: Heavenly Father, our hearts are sensitive to your living presence as we worship you in this hour. Our souls rejoice in the constant assurance that you provide for our care and keeping each day of our lives. Because you have given your best in making our lives more joyful and more comfortable, we pray that we shall not be satisfied with giving less than our best in bringing our gifts to you. We dedicate all that we are and all that we have to the service of him who loved us and gave himself for our redemption. Multiply the usefulness of our offerings today as they undergird the outreach ministry of the gospel to the ends of the earth. We pray in the name of the Author of eternal life, Jesus Christ, our Lord. Amen.

Introduction

When does eternal life begin? This question is as old as the ages. Some say that this experience is set for some distant date in the future. Some believe that it will begin in the day of resurrection. Others believe that when the soul moves out of the body, eternal life will become a reality.

Whatever may be our human conceptions of eternal life and when it begins, we have but one authority to whom we can go for an answer to this question—Christ. Not once did he indicate that it was wise to postpone the acceptance of his Word of truth that guarantees the possession of eternal life. He always appealed to the hearts of people with an urgent calling. As Paul, the mighty messenger for the living Lord, said, "Behold, *now* is the accepted time; behold, *now* is the day of salvation" (2 Cor. 6:2, emphasis added).

Scripture leads us to believe that eternal life is an experience that begins the moment the soul trusts in Christ as personal Savior. Jesus wants people to become acquainted with the requirements of heavenly citizenship while they are still living on the earth. He wants them to know that all they shall possess in the way of assurance of everlasting life is totally dependent on their faith in him.

Eternal life is one of the great Bible doctrines. Let us notice the authority of eternal life, the nature of eternal life, and the results of eternal life.

I. The authority of eternal life.

Jesus was confident in his authority to offer eternal life to those who trusted him. "Verily, verily, I say unto thee, Except a man be born again, he cannot see the kingdom of God" (John 3:3), he said. This word of authority has the signature and testimony of God's power and is further expressed in Jesus' words in John 4:23: "The hour cometh, and *now* is, when the true worshippers shall worship the Father in spirit and in truth" (emphasis added). What wonderful attestation to the truth that has the power to break the silence of the grave!

Jesus insisted that proofs of eternal life always existed. At his words, the spiritually dead will be disturbed in their slumber and roused from their indifference. They will know that the summons of supreme power and authority is addressed to them (Eph. 5:14). Jesus always lays great emphasis on the divine force that is at work on the human heart and conscience. He is the one authority for our faith and practice.

II. The nature of eternal life.

Because of sin, people lost the peace, harmony, and happiness that arise from friendship with God. The soul left God like a wandering star from its central sun.

Moreover, this life is in and through Christ. Having lost the joy of spiritual life because of sin, it is evident that it must be recovered through a divine source, a divine channel, and under a new divine arrangement. Christ is this source to which people must turn for the hope of eternal life. He is our only hope for the future. He is the Way, the Truth, and the Life (John 14:6).

As we derive our natural life from Adam, we receive spiritual life from Christ, the Second Adam. Eternal life becomes ours as soon as we confess our sins and accept Jesus Christ as Lord and Savior. This world is the only birthplace, and the day of salvation is the only birthday of eternal life. All who enjoy eternal life in the heavenly place found it on earth.

Let us not forget that the life of the body has an end. But the life of the soul—spiritual life in Christ—is eternal. Only life that is found in the saving, redeeming love of Christ is worthy of the word "eternal." Only the Lord Jesus Christ has the power to open the windows of heaven so that the blessings and security of everlasting life can become a reality to the soul.

III. The results of eternal life.

Eternal life is immune to judgment. Much of the blessing of redemption consists not in what we will enjoy, but in what we will evade. The words of the great evasion are "shall not come into condemnation; but is passed from death unto life" (John 5:24). Eternal life and judgment are opposed to each other. The one is the result of faith, and the other is the result of no faith in Christ. Judgment is in the area of sin, but the believer has come out of that. "Who shall lay any thing to the charge of God's elect?" (Rom. 8:33). In this case, passing the final examination is preliminary to all things. Pass this one and you pass them all! Praise be to God!

This transition, passing from death unto life, is a beautiful thing, a wonderful experience. Think of it! There is a change of nature, a change of condition, a change of character, a change of prospect, and a change of worlds. This transition is divine. Everyone who undergoes this transition must experience the holy presence of the heavenly Father. The voice of God alone can call the names of those who are dead in trespasses and sin. The voice of God alone can bring them back to life.

This transition is real. It becomes evident in the life of believers; they are new creatures. Their affections are not attracted by the same things, and their minds are transformed by the Word of God. Indeed, they are different people—different in habits, temperament, character, and language. These are unmistakable evidences that something wonderful has happened in the soul that God has prepared for the endless joys of eternal life.

Conclusion

Oliver Goldsmith once said, "Ill fares the land, to hastening ills a prey, where wealth accumulates and men decay." The real decay begins to set in when people begin to magnify physical and temporal existence as all there is to life. The disposition to trample faith underfoot and kick God out the window is no new thing. But the day of accounting will be real for those who refuse to acknowledge the reality of the spiritual.

We hail progress in the fields of art, music, architecture, and science. But when we have said all this, we must admit there are some questions that are beyond the solution of mortal minds. While belief busies itself with logic and testimony, faith concerns itself with thanksgiving. Saving faith always has been an operation of the heart. Indeed, salvation and eternal life become the coveted possession of those who believe with the heart. But those who will not believe will walk out into a darkness from which there will be no return.

So let us thank God today for the assurance of sins forgiven through simple faith in Christ as Savior. Let us rejoice in the abundant provision that God has made for eternal life! Thank God for Jesus!

SUNDAY EVENING, APRIL 10

Title: Think Like Jesus Thought

Text: "Let this mind be in you, which was also in Christ Jesus" **(Phil. 2:5)**.

Scripture Reading: Philippians 2:1–11

Introduction

To Paul, two things characterized a church that was pleasing to Christ. First, the church should be in a spirit of unity. Second, the members should act from proper motivation.

Like-mindedness comes from having the same goals and, consequently, the same priorities. Paul reasoned that the Christian faith was the best base on which to operate if one wished to produce a spiritually homogeneous organization. He began this next section of his letter to the Philippians by suggesting that the members of the church at Philippi examine their own relationships with Christ and with other Christians in the congregation.

Motivation is a subtle matter. Satan uses many methods to hinder the work of God and discount the personal effectiveness of a Christian's witness. Someone once said, "If Satan cannot get us to do the wrong thing, he will get us to do the right thing with the wrong attitude and for the wrong motive." Paul warned the Philippian Christians of the ever-present temptation to think of themselves more highly than they ought to think. He urged his readers to focus unselfishly on the needs of their fellow Christians and minimize the fulfilling of their own personal wishes.

To think and act unselfishly is not easy. How does one acquire this skill? Rather than give a treatise on "how to do it," Paul turned to a personal example. Look at Jesus, and let his attitude toward life be yours in day-to-day activities.

I. Forget your own privileges.

No one had more status than Jesus Christ. He existed as God before his incarnation. He was, and still is, the second member of the Trinity. Jesus did not begin his existence in Bethlehem. He existed beforehand with the Father and the Holy Spirit.

Yet Jesus willingly left it all. He did not consider his equality with God a thing to be held on to tenaciously. Rather, he made himself of no reputation and took upon himself the form of a servant and was made in the likeness of humanity. Not only this, but he was willing to go to the cross to be a substitutionary sacrifice for our sins. Did any man ever show such a spirit of selflessness?

Christians should show this same spirit. Many years ago a wise man said, "Life is too short to be little." It is also too short to strut through as though we were privileged characters. We should recognize that we are "bound together in a bundle of life." Almost every sin, perhaps every sin, is rooted in our selfishness. Becoming a Christian includes actually dying to self. Christlikeness cannot exist in our lives until self is crucified.

II. Take the long look.

Jonathan Swift once said, "Vision is the art of seeing things invisible." William Wordsworth wrote:

> *To whom, in vision clear,*
> *The aspiring heads of future things appear,*
> *Like mountaintops whose mists have rolled away.*

Someone once asked Alfred Tennyson about his greatest desire in life. He immediately said, "A fuller vision of God." A churchman of the Middle Ages said, "Perfect blessedness ... consists in a vision of God."

All of these statements reflect our need to take a long look toward the issues of life. This is what Jesus did when he left the "glory place" for the "gory place." He left the splendors of heaven for the sufferings of earth. He did this because he envisioned a kingdom of love consisting of people who had been redeemed from their sins.

Shortsightedness never wins victories. A guide showing tourists through a large university pointed to a statue of Alexander the Great as a dreamy-eyed boy.

He said to the group, "He who conquers a world must first dream that he has conquered it."

Redeeming the world was Jesus' one purpose in life. He would not be led astray by shortcuts. The basic message of the three temptations Jesus faced early in his ministry was "Shall I take the long look, or shall I try to gain my kingdom by superficial methods?" Every preacher faces this dilemma with his local congregation as he projects a program for them. Christians face this matter in their personal lives. Worthwhile goals will not be achieved overnight. We must learn to labor, and we must learn to wait. Most of all, however, we must weigh all of life's issues, keeping in mind the long-range influence on our character and ultimate destiny.

III. Remain true to our commitment.

Jesus must have wanted to quit many times. His enemies sought to kill him, and his friends refused to understand him. Even his family seemed often to be a hindrance rather than a help. Yet Jesus had set his mind to a great task. He was completely dedicated to doing his duty. Not even a shameful cross could cause him to change his course.

Often we fail to distinguish between a burden and a cross. We speak of our cross as if it were a burden. Actually, a cross should not be endured reluctantly but taken up voluntarily. No one took Jesus' life from him. He laid it down gladly. In other words, he chose to make his cross part of his life. Likewise, we accept our cross as our personal responsibility to share in Christ's redemptive work in this world. Dedicated people have gladly accepted not only a goal in life but also a task that enables them to meet that goal.

Conclusion

If, as someone said long ago, "the mind is the measure of the man," where do you rate? The ideal man, as pictured by the psalmist, delights in the law of the Lord and meditates day and night in God's law. To a large extent, one's thought patterns determine that person's attitude toward life.

Although the Old Testament says much about the "heart," the Hebrews thought of the heart not only as the seat of affection but also as the home of one's thought processes. Likewise, the mind is more than the seat of one's intellectual processes. We both think and feel with our mind. For this reason, we use the expression that a person needs to "get right in his thinking." One writer has said, "We do not think our way into right living nearly so much as we live our way into right thinking."

Jesus is our supreme example in both attitude and action. Paul's amazing career resulted from his spirit being united with God's Spirit. This union was possible because he had sublimated every desire to the will of God as revealed in Jesus Christ. People are not naturally unselfish, nor do they naturally possess vision and dedication. People must surrender personally to Jesus Christ and become transformed by God's Spirit. This transformation is what Paul called "being saved" and what Jesus spoke of as a "new birth" or, as the literal Greek says, "the birth from above." When this event takes place, the new nature imparted to us enables us to think like Jesus thought and adopt his way of life.

WEDNESDAY EVENING, APRIL 13

Title: The Christian Character of Young Women

Text: "That they may teach the young women to be sober, to love their husbands, to love their children, to be discreet, chaste, keepers at home, good, obedient to their own husbands, that the word of God be not blasphemed" **(Titus 2:4–5)**.

Scripture Reading: Titus 2

Introduction

In the second chapter of Titus, Paul devotes a goodly amount of space to the Christian character of both genders of various ages, but to young mothers and/or wives, he gives the largest space.

I. The young woman is to love her husband and children (Titus 2:4).

A. Take a good look at the word love. It means to be devoted. A woman is to be devoted to her husband and children. She is to exercise affection as proof of love. If one has the kind of love mentioned here, she will do something to express affection, such as bestow a kiss.

B. The objects of love are husband and children. The young woman is to be affectionate toward her husband. She will find in this love the source of her strength, the husband will find the solace for his cares, and the children will find the guarantee for their happiness and welfare. A loving wife is a blessing to her husband (Prov. 12:4). She brings honor to him (31:23), secures his confidence (v. 11), and earns his praises (v. 28). She also is to be affectionate toward her children. This closes the generation gap more than any other one thing. It gives confidence and security to children.

II. The young woman is to be discreet (Titus 2:5).

A. The meaning of the word. This word means to show self-control. It is applicable to drink, thoughts, and actions.

B. The idea expressed in the word. The young woman is to be wise and careful in her conduct both at home and away. Webster defines the word "discreet" as showing good judgment in conduct.

III. The young woman should be chaste (Titus 2:5).

A. The meaning of the word. The Greek word simply means "purity." It means being innocent of unlawful sexual intercourse. It is to be pure in thought and act by exemplifying modesty. This is truly a great need in the church today.

B. The larger concept of the word. It means refraining from methods of dress or action that would cause the base nature of men to be tempted. It also means abstinence from premarital sex. It implies a general modesty that makes for true beauty and a great witness.

IV. The young woman is to be a keeper of the home (Titus 2:5).

A. The wife's business is her household. Religion gains no honor when home duties are neglected.
B. The husband's interests are preserved by her industry at home.
C. The word good is attached. The idea is one of kindness and/or good nature. It is thoughtfulness. It is doing what is right in the domain of the home.

V. The young woman should submit to her husband (Titus 2:5).

There will be harmony in the home when husband and wife show mutual respect toward one another.

Conclusion

This discussion points out vividly how Christianity is bound up in Christians faithfully living out biblical principles. The church will be judged by the world by the kind of families it produces.

SUNDAY MORNING, APRIL 17

Title: If I Should Die Before I Wake

Text: "And as it is appointed unto men once to die, but after this the judgment" **(Heb. 9:27).**

Scripture Reading: Ecclesiastes 3:2–8; Hebrews 9:27

Hymns: "In Times Like These," Ruth Caye Jones
"Rock of Ages," Toplady
"God Will Take Care of You," Martin

Offertory Prayer: Our heavenly Father, we humbly recognize that we live and move and have our being all because of you. Help us to be good stewards of the time you continue to give us. We want to live in such a way that when we die we will have no regrets. Accept our gifts as an expression of our love for you and an acknowledgment of our indebtedness to you. Amen.

Introduction

Now I lay me down to sleep,
I pray the Lord my soul to keep,
If I should die before I wake,
I pray the Lord my soul to take.

This child's prayer affirming God's watchful care over us in life and death was printed in *The New England Primer* printed in 1690. It has been quoted by millions of people through the years.

The wisest man who ever lived, King Solomon, asserted that there is "a time to be born, and a time to die" (Eccl. 3:2). The book of Hebrews affirms, "It is appointed unto men once to die" (Heb. 9:27).

It is estimated that sixty million people, or two every second, die each year. Yet many people live in denial of death.

Louis XV, king of France from 1715 to 1774, ordered that death was never to be spoken of in his presence. He sought to avoid every place and monument that in any way suggested death.

The fact remains that there is no avoiding death. And wisdom compels us to ask, "If I knew that I should die before I wake, what would I do?"

If I knew that when this day ends I would die, how would I live this day? Let me share with you some of my own thoughts.

I. I would make sure of my salvation.

"Make every effort to confirm your calling and election" (2 Peter 1:10 NIV).

A. I would make sure that I have repented of my sins. "Godly sorrow brings repentance that leads to salvation" (2 Cor. 7:10 NIV). At age nineteen, Al Johnson had joined two other men in robbing a Kansas bank. The case was closed by police after two former convicts who had been mistakenly identified by bank officers as the robbers were killed in a car crash. Al felt he would never be caught.

He married a Christian girl who knew nothing of his past crime. Then one day someone mailed him a tract titled God's Plan of Salvation. Under deep conviction, the realization struck him that he could be forgiven. With great repentance, he knelt in prayer and accepted Christ. After much prayer, he confessed his crime. Under the Kansas statute of limitations, he was set free.

Today Al is the manager of a service station, the father of three admiring children, and a faithful church member. He has paid back every dime he stole.

B. I would make sure I am trusting Christ alone. "No man comes to the Father except through me" (John 14:6 NIV). I do not want to trust in self, good works, baptism, or the prayers of others. Martin Luther dreamed one night that he was standing before the judgment seat of God. When Luther was asked to give an account of himself, Satan stepped forward and opened a large book in which Luther's every sin had been recorded. Luther said, "I was guilty of every sin." Suddenly one verse came to mind, and he said to Satan, "But one thing you have forgotten: 'The blood of Jesus Christ his Son, cleanses us from all sin.'" Satan picked up the heavy book and fled!

II. I would let others know I love them.

"We know that we have passed from death to life, because we love each other" (1 John 3:14 NIV).

The need to be told, "I love you" is a universal need!

Late one night the phone rang. A police officer was on the line. "We have your son. He was arrested for driving while intoxicated. You may want to come down and bail him out." The father quickly dressed and rushed to the police station. He was a professional man whose business allowed him little time with his family. But he did provide well for his family.

The father asked his son, "Why would you do this to your mother and me? We bought you a new car; anything you asked for we have given you."

The son said, "Dad, I appreciate all you have given me; it is more than any of my friends have. But, Dad, what I want is not what you can give me. All I want is you. I just need to know you love me."

If I knew I would die before I wake, I would let others know I love them.

III. I would forgive all who have ever wronged me.

"Be kind and compassionate to one another, forgiving each other, just as in Christ God forgave you" (Eph. 4:32 NIV).

President Abraham Lincoln was asked how he was going to treat the rebellious Southerners when they returned to the union of the United States. He answered, "I will treat them as if they had never been away." "Forgiveness" is treating others as if they have never wronged you.

IV. I would ask forgiveness from all whom I have wronged.

"First be reconciled to your brother, and then come and offer your gift" (Matt. 5:24 RSV).

It was not easy for the prodigal son to ask forgiveness from his father, but he did. He said humbly, "I am no longer worthy to be called your son" (Luke 15:21 NIV). He did not ask to be restored to his former position; he simply asked to be forgiven.

V. I would do what I had intended to do that day.

"Whatever your hand finds to do, do it" (Eccl. 9:10 NIV). If I planned to cut the grass, I would do it. If I planned to wash the car, I would do it. If I planned to work on a sermon, I would do it.

VI. I would anticipate seeing others who have gone on.

"Now we see only a reflection as in a mirror; then we shall see face to face" (1 Cor. 13:12 NIV). I will see my mother; my father; my wife, Elizabeth; and other family members. I will see church members with whom I have served and to whom I am indebted.

VII. I would anticipate seeing Jesus.

"They will see his face" (Rev. 22:4 NIV). "If I go and prepare a place for you, I will come back and take you to be with me, that you also may be where I am" (John 14:3 NIV). Each time a Christian dies, Christ "comes again" to receive that person to himself.

Conclusion

If you knew you would die before you wake, what would you do?

SUNDAY EVENING, APRIL 17

Title: Working Out What God Works In

Text: "Wherefore, my beloved, as ye have always obeyed, not as in my presence only, but now much more in my absence, work out your own salvation with fear and trembling" **(Phil. 2:12)**.

Scripture Reading: Philippians 2:12–18

Introduction

Paul had a unique ability to move quickly from the idealistic to the intensely practical. Philippians 2:5–12 contains a beautiful portrayal of Christ's self-humiliation and God's making him the "name above every name." This portrayal of the risen and exalted Christ should motivate Christians to dedicated service and complete surrender to God's will. Paul followed this passage with a call to complete commitment in Christians. He called them to dedicate themselves to service and to surrender completely, which is a difficult process. Nevertheless, we should strive constantly toward God's goal for us in redemption.

I. We are not justified from our sins by our good works.

Upon first reading Philippians 2:12, one might feel that Paul contradicts himself, because elsewhere in the Bible he clearly says that we are "saved by grace, through faith" and not through works.

At this point, we need to distinguish carefully between "justification" and "salvation." We also need to understand the other meaning and various uses of the word salvation in the New Testament. When we say people are justified from their sins by faith in Christ, we are speaking of an event that occurs once and for all in a person's life. To be justified is a legal term that means that God has accepted Christ's death on the cross, validated by his resurrection, as the substitute for our sin debt. The old hymn says, "Jesus paid it all." Once people have received pardon for their sins, they stand before God as "justified" people. Lawyers have a phrase, "once in jeopardy," which means that when a jury reaches a not-guilty verdict, the person who was tried can never be tried for that crime again. Likewise, when God has declared one free from sin's guilt based on

Christ's substitutionary death, he will never again condemn that person for sin. This scenario exemplifies "justification."

The word salvation has a broader context of meaning than the term justification. Actually, the New Testament uses the word in three senses. God saves us from sin's penalty, power, and presence. The first sense of salvation indicates a "one-time" transaction. Every born-again Christian can look back and say, "I have been saved." God saves a person from sin's penalty only one time. Actually, this initial act in the "salvation experience" corresponds to "justification."

The second stage in the salvation experience is a process. We are being saved from the power of sin. This stage comes in personal growth as we surrender to God's will for our lives and learn to give priority to things of the Spirit. This process goes on throughout our Christian life. The Christian should strive at constant growth toward Christlikeness. Unfortunately, our growth varies as we grow more in some periods of time than in other times. This variation in growth occurs because human beings still struggle with the old nature even while striving with the new nature that was implanted by God's Holy Spirit when they received Jesus as Savior.

The final stage in our salvation will occur in the future. When Jesus comes, we will be saved from the presence of sin. This sense of salvation also is a "point action" rather than a process.

Thus the New Testament word justification relates to one area of God's dealings with humanity, whereas "salvation" concerns the totality of humanity's relationship with God.

II. God does the work, not us.

When any truth is carried to an extreme, it becomes false teaching. Thus the battle of "Calvinism" against "Arminianism" has persisted through the years. The former puts the emphasis on God's sovereignty, while the latter puts the emphasis on a person's choice. Each position distinctively contributes to the understanding of the God-human relationship.

In the ultimate sense, every born-again Christian knows that God always takes the initiative in leading a person to himself through Jesus. Long before we thought of God, he had already thought of us. God was "working a work" in the dawn of history as he prepared the world for the coming of our Redeemer.

After urging the Christians at Philippi to work out their own salvation, Paul immediately reminded them that God was constantly at work in them. Many years ago, a great Christian said, "My life was changed drastically when one day I realized a great truth. It is not so much what I do for Christ that counts as it is what I allow him to do through me as I surrender myself to his purposes for me." God is far more interested in both his own kingdom and in our personal development than we ever could be—no matter how much we try.

A young minister once said to an older one, "I am overwhelmed at the possibilities of my church field. I am fearful lest I cannot do the job that needs to be done." The older minister replied, "Let me give you a verse from God's Word."

He then quoted the words of Jesus, "Fear not, little flock; for it is your Father's good pleasure to give you the kingdom" (Luke 12:32).

We should not use Paul's statement as an excuse to minimize our personal efforts, but should realize that God's grace, his free and unmerited love, makes us who we are. Paul testified, "By the grace of God I am what I am" (1 Cor. 15:10).

III. Proper growth demands right attitudes.

Paul always followed sound theology with practical applications. Philippians 2:14 concerns the spirit of the Philippian Christians in everyday living. Although some people have suggested that Paul's exhortation to Euodias and Syntyche in 4:2 implies a division in the fellowship, no evidence supports this view. In several places, however, Paul does emphasize the need for unity in the church. He strongly urges that the people serve God without bickering and divisions.

One cannot overemphasize the importance of unity in doing God's work. In fact, modern psychologists emphasize the importance of people being unified within themselves. We speak of a "whole person" today and of a "unified or integrated personality." On the other hand, we say that some people are a "civil war" within themselves. One of the major goals of all people should be "peace within themselves. "Jesus offers resources for attaining this aim. Peace with God results from the redemptive experience, and peace with oneself comes by growing toward the fullness of Jesus Christ. Paul called the latter "the peace of God, which transcends all understanding" (Phil. 4:7 NIV).

Conclusion

A farmer must first plant the crop. Then he "works it." Likewise, God plants the seed of spiritual life in the experience of regeneration, the new birth. Then we work to make that which is within us explicit in outward living. Years ago a minister said it in a way that, though it borders on oversimplification, expresses the truth succinctly. He said, "You must work out what God works in."

WEDNESDAY EVENING, APRIL 20

Title: The Christian Character of Young Men

Text: "Young men likewise exhort to be sober minded" **(Titus 2:6)**.

Scripture Reading: Titus 2

Introduction

In the message dealing with the Christian character of young women, we noted that Paul devoted the lengthiest passage to them. This is true, but it must be clarified. The word "likewise" in Titus 2:6 refers to the young women. So what is said about young women in Titus 2:4–5 also applies to men, plus what is discussed in Titus 2:6.

I. In discussing the character of young men, consider some introductory words.

A. What is meant by "young men"? The term means fresh and youthful—the age when one is in the prime and vigor of life. The modern term is likely young adults. This is suggested because of the comparison to the young women and the reference to wives and children and also because of the tremendous influence of this age group.

B. What is mean by "exhort"? This word represents continuous action. It means keep on doing it. The meaning of the word is to admonish or beseech.

C. What is meant by "likewise"? This is a connecting word. It connects the character of a young man with that of a young woman.

II. The young men are told to be sober-minded.

That is, they are told to have a sound mind, to be temperate.

A. Consider this exhortation as it relates to the age group under consideration. Young men are at the age of strong temptation, and they face temptations that are greater for them than for others. Their blood runs hotter, and their passions speak more commandingly. It also is the age when they have many opportunities to go astray. They are thrown into company where temptation is strong. Often they are away from home and do not have family members to help keep them straight. Yet they must assume responsibility. Still another reason for the exhortation is that this is an age at which men have confidence but are lacking in experience. They approach life more recklessly.

B. Why then should they be sober-minded? Because they are at an age when they have to make decisions without prior experience. This applies to home life, the business world, and the church. For young men to have influence for good in the church, it is imperative that they be sound in their thinking and temperate in all things.

Conclusion

Matthew Henry's quote says well what Paul is speaking to the young men.

> Here is the duty of young men. They are apt to be eager and hot, thoughtless and precipitant; therefore they must be earnestly called upon and exhorted to be considerate, not rash; advisable and submissive, not willful and head-strong; humble and mild, not haughty and proud; for there are more young people ruined by pride than by any other sin. The young should be grave and solid in their deportment and manners, joining the seriousness of age with the liveliness and vigor of youth. This will make even those younger years to pass to good purpose, and yield matter of comfortable reflection when the evil days come; it will be preventive of much sin and sorrow, and lay the foundation for doing and enjoying much good. Such shall not mourn at the last, but have peace and comfort in death, and after it a glorious crown of life. (Matthew Henry, Matthew Henry's Commentary, vol. 6 [New York: Revell, n.d.], 863).

SUNDAY MORNING, APRIL 24

Title: Living in the Meantime

Text: "And Nebuchadnezzar king of Babylon came against the city, and his servants did besiege it" **(2 Kings 24:11)**.

Scripture Reading: 2 Kings 24:11–15

Hymns: "Be Strong in the Lord," Linda Lee Johnson
"Lead On, O King Eternal," Ernest W. Shurteff
"Stand Up, Stand Up for Jesus," George Duffield

Offertory Prayer: We come into your presence today, Lord Jesus, with confidence that you care for us all the time, especially during the meantime. Yet there are times when we feel our meantime will never end. We feel life will never be the same again. We do not know how to cope with the meantime, let alone survive the meantime. Therefore, we come to you in total dependence. We offer our gifts and ourselves to you. Amen.

Introduction

Learning how to live involves learning how to live in the meantime. A significant portion of life is spent in the meantime—the meantime of plans and fulfillment, dreams and reality, uncertainty and assurance, planting and harvesting. Sometimes the meantime is the time that follows surgery, divorce, emotional breakdown, or the loss of a loved one.

How are we to live when a meantime invades our lives?

I. Do the next thing.

"Build houses and settle down; plant gardens and eat what they produce" (Jer. 29:5 NIV). When in exile, God's people were admonished to do the next thing by building houses, planting gardens, and eating the fruit of them.

Whatever it is that you would have done before the meantime, do it! If it is returning to work, do it. If it is cutting the grass, do it. If it is writing a letter, do it. Even if you don't feel like it, do the next thing.

Following the death of his wife, C. S. Lewis said, "I never realized that grief has within it such laziness." When you are living in the meantime, you may lack energy and the drive and desire to move forward.

During their captivity in Babylon, this is what Israel was experiencing. Their harps were hung on the trees. There was no music, no song to lift their spirits. This is why Jeremiah instructed them to "build houses and settle down; plant gardens and eat what they produce." They were to do the next thing. They needed to realize that life must move on.

II. Find something to celebrate.

"Marry and have sons and daughters; find wives for your sons and give your daughters in marriage, so that they too may have sons and daughters. Increase in number there; do not decrease" (Jer. 29:6 NIV). Weddings and births are occasions for celebration.

During the meantime there is always something to rejoice over. Recovering from spinal surgery as my wife battled ALS, there was one thing I celebrated each morning. I celebrated having less pain than the day before. You must look for it, but there is always something to celebrate.

Two days after my wife, Elizabeth's, death, I received the following note from a neighbor:

> *Please accept my deepest sympathy on the passing of your beautiful wife and friend. No person or experience will ever replace your happy days together.*
>
> *Living in the same neighborhood as you, I have frequently walked your street. At times your lights were on and your warm home was visible as my dog and I walked by. Your true love for your wife was very visible as you cheerfully cared for her needs in the kitchen area. Many times I had tears just seeing you two together and so in love. That is true love. How lucky you were to have each other and with such dedication. You will be blessed for caring for her in such a dear and compassionate way. Thank you for blessing me on my neighborhood walks.*

Elizabeth and I never ceased to celebrate each other even in our meantime.

III. Don't forget to pray.

"Then you will call on me and come and pray to me, and I will listen to you" (Jer. 29:12 NIV).

Difficult times are not easy times in which to pray, but pray you must!

For ten years, Elizabeth suffered with Lou Gehrig's disease, or ALS, a fatal nerve disorder. Three years is the average life expectancy of an ALS patient. By the grace of God, we were given ten years. Our prayer time was in the evening. One November evening in 2003, Elizabeth said to me, "I am praying that God will let me live through Thanksgiving when, for one last time, I can be with my children and grandchildren. Then I want to go home. I am not angry; I am just tired and want to go home." Then she said, "But I do not think you are praying that way."

I replied, "I am not praying contrary to your prayers. But if I were, your prayers would prevail because you are such a better Christian than I."

Nevertheless, nothing would bring her peace but for her to hear me pray. "Lord, I thank you for giving us forty-nine years together. Out of gratitude for these wonderful years, I am willing to give her back to you. Thank you, Lord Jesus."

Elizabeth's prayer was granted. She relished the time with her grandchildren. Having lost all use of her arms, the only way she could embrace them was for me to pull her limp arms around them. God heard her prayers and called her home on Sunday morning, December 1.

It isn't easy to pray in the meantime, but don't forget to pray.

IV. Walk on through it.

"Because the Sovereign Lord helps me, I will not be disgraced. Therefore have I set my face like flint, and I know I will not be put to shame" (Isa. 50:7 NIV).

Isaiah was moving on. He was moving forward. He knew the day would come when the exile would end and hearts would sing again. He knew the time would come when sadness would turn to joy and tears to laughter. When it seemed he had come to the end of the rope, he tied a knot and hung on.

In the meantime, God is working in your life. He is in charge of his world. So set your face like flint and walk on through it.

Conclusion

On January 22, 1998, Elizabeth made her final entry in her journal:

> This will most likely be my final entry. My writing is impossible. I am tired, so when I enter your heavenly land, I want to shout, "I am home; I can kick off my shoes and run! Thank you, Lord."

A few days before Elizabeth's death, I was lying beside her. With closed eyes, she said, "Can you believe that?" I asked, "What is it that you see?" Her only reply was, "Can you believe that?" I so much wanted to know what she saw. Like Paul, who was "caught up to the third heaven," she was not allowed "to utter" what she saw. Surely it was a glimpse of heaven.

Thank God! Elizabeth taught me how to live in the "meantime."

SUNDAY EVENING, APRIL 24

Title: How Well Do You Know Jesus?

Text: "That I may know him, and the power of his resurrection, and the fellowship of his sufferings, being made conformable unto his death" **(Phil. 3:10)**.

Scripture Reading: Philippians 3:1–10

Introduction

A woman in India was making a pilgrimage to a distant spot where she heard God was to be seen. She had already gone hundreds of miles and still had hundreds more to go. She would lie on the ground then rise and put her feet where her head had been, prostrating herself over and over again. She continued to travel in this way. Someone asked her what she wanted from this laborious pilgrimage. She answered with a great light in her eye, "Vision of him! Vision of him!"

Throughout history, humankind's greatest desire has been for a full revelation of God. Job voiced this universal longing when he cried, "Oh that I knew where I might find him" (Job 23:3). When Alfred Lord Tennyson was asked in his later years about his chief desire in life, he replied, "A clearer vision of God."

In tonight's Scripture reading, Paul, too, was nearing the end of his life. He had many years of ministry behind him, but his chief aim was still to know more about his Savior. His statement in verse 10 does not represent a desire to know Jesus as personal Savior. He had settled this matter many years ago on the Damascus road. Rather, he desired a closer walk with the Savior and a more meaningful fellowship with the one who had been his Lord and Friend throughout the years.

I. Christianity rests in a person, not in a system of thought.

In the first few verses of chapter 3, Paul discusses a problem that plagued most, if not all, of the churches he had founded. The Judaizers moved into the Gentile churches after Paul left, and they upset the Gentile believers' faith in Christ. These agitators insisted that salvation in Christ was not a matter of "free grace," but rather of "grace plus works." This teaching stemmed from the fact that they believed Christianity was merely another division of Judaism rather than a faith that could be accepted by Jew and Gentile alike without the forms and ceremonies of the Jewish religion.

This particular issue is not present in Christianity today, but the basic principle is still relevant. People are not saved by forms, ceremonies, ordinances, or even good deeds. Christianity is rooted in personal fellowship with Jesus Christ. Correct doctrine in teaching is important, but doctrine of itself does not bring salvation. Salvation comes through a personal experience with Jesus Christ.

If anyone could have been saved by laws and ceremonies, it would have been the apostle Paul. Yet he makes it clear that he gave up all of his claim to righteousness when he received Jesus as his personal Savior and accepted the work of Christ on the cross as the payment for his sin. Paul's legalism and dependence on his own righteousness were nailed to the cross the day he met Jesus on the Damascus road. His dependence on self was completely destroyed. He began to live in Christ, and Christ began to live in him. Paul expresses it in many ways and in many places, but never any clearer than when he says that he wished to be "found in him, not having mine own righteousness, which is of the law, but that which is through the faith of Christ, the righteousness which is of God by faith" (Phil. 3:9).

II. True knowledge grows.

There is no such thing as a static experience with truth. That which is vital is always growing. Paul recognized that his experience with Jesus must move forward in deeper dedication and discovery of new areas in which to serve God.

That which does not grow, retrogrades. Henry Wadsworth Longfellow was once asked the secret of his marvelous spirit and perpetual energy. He pointed to a tree and said, "I try to be like that tree and grow a little new wood every year." One of the most frustrating experiences we can have is to deal with people who are childish in nature and immature in attitude. They may have grown up physically, but they have refused to grow emotionally or spiritually. John Steen, in *Conquering Inner Space,* says, "What is immaturity? It is a board member pounding on the table, demanding his way of doing things. It is a college student telling his parents what is wrong with them emotionally.... It is a high school girl sulking and pouting over not getting a luxury she expected."

The life that continues to advance remains vital and useful to the end. When we stop breaking new ground, life goes stale. A true experience with Jesus will be the kind that desires further growth. The most dangerous time in a person's Christian life is when that person feels that he or she "has arrived." When we stop growing, our effectiveness decreases. The last words we have recorded from Simon Peter are "Grow in grace, and in the knowledge of our Lord and Saviour Jesus Christ" (2 Peter 3:18).

III. Knowing Jesus better.

What are some practical ways for coming into closer fellowship with Jesus? Paul spoke of "the power of his resurrection" and "the fellowship of his sufferings" and being made "conformable unto his death." These are tremendous concepts and worthy goals. How may they be implemented in daily living?

For one thing, the Christian must make much of the Bible, the written Word of God. Jesus is, of course, the living Word of God, but it is through the record of God's revelation to man, the Bible, that we come to know more about Jesus and experience him more deeply in personal fellowship. The great evangelist Dwight Moody is reported to have written in the flyleaf of his Bible, "This Book will keep you from sin or sin will keep you from this Book." The growing Christian life is the one that feeds constantly on the truths in God's Word. Horace Greeley once said, "It is impossible to enslave a Bible-reading people." Likewise, it is impossible to grow without knowing God's Word. William Lyon Phelps once told a group of Rotarians, "While I believe in a college education for all men, at the same time, I would rather have a thorough knowledge of the Bible without a college education than to have a college education and be ignorant of the Bible."

The growing life is one that also makes much of "the closet with the closed door." Jesus affirmed often during his ministry the necessity for a vital prayer life if one was to stay in close touch with the Father.

Other elements enter into the meaningful Christian life. We must watch ourselves with an uncompromising watchfulness against sin. An old cliché says, "We cannot run with the hare and the hound" and be consistent in Christian living. Moral purity in our personal lives is an absolute necessity if we are to grow in Christlikeness. Again, we must live in a spirit of unselfishness if we are to develop a deeper fellowship with Christ. Finally, we must be busy for Christ in deeds of service. To be a Christian is more than pietistic isolationism. It is to enter the arena of service for the Lord and learn the meaning of joyful participation in Christian activities.

Conclusion

To know Christ does not mean to be skilled in a theoretical or theological approach, nor does it mean a pietistic mysticism that separates itself from contact with the mundane things of the world. Rather, a genuine knowledge of Christ means possessing the certainty that comes from an experience of forgiveness and then building on that assurance a superstructure of daily fellowship with him overflowing into unselfish and Christlike deeds for others in the Savior's name.

The ultimate in Christian development is being usable in personal witness concerning Christ's redemptive work. The more winsome our personality through Christlike unselfishness, the more apt we are to be effective in leading others to forgiveness through the Savior.

WEDNESDAY EVENING, APRIL 27

Title: The Christian Character of the Church Worker

Text: "In everything set them an example by doing what is good. In your teaching show integrity, seriousness and soundness of speech that cannot be condemned, so that those who oppose you may be ashamed because they have nothing bad to say about us" **(Titus 2:7–8 NIV)**.

Scripture Reading: Titus 2

Introduction

In several messages prior to this one, we have discussed Christian character as Paul presents it in his letter to Titus. We have covered Paul's instructions for old men, old women, young women, and young men. Now we come to verses that deal with the character of church workers.

I. The first characteristic is to set a good example.

It is a pattern of good works or an example of good conduct.

A. The Scripture says a good example is to be set "in everything." This teaching applies to men and women in all stations of life.

B. The Scripture also says the worker is to be an example. The word example means "that which is to be followed or imitated." The word in the King James Version is "pattern." This means "anything proposed for or worthy of imitation. Anything designed as a guide or model for making things." Christians are to perform seemingly menial tasks with as much care as important tasks.

II. The second characteristic is to be sincere and serious in teaching.

A. Paul gives three words that summarize the principles and manner of teaching.
   1. "Integrity": It is to be pure in motive and not self-seeking.
   2. "Seriousness": This deals with the manner in which teaching is done.
   3. "Soundness of speech": It must be clear and firm.

B. Teaching must be done with dignity. Dignity does not imply aloofness, arrogance, or pride. It comes from the responsibility of being an ambassador for Christ.

C. Showing concern for one's students is just as important as what one teaches. No teacher can do his or her best by just mastering and presenting the subject matter. The teacher also must have the interest of the students at heart.

III. The third characteristic is to be sound in speech.

A. Paul uses the word sound nine times in his pastoral epistles and four times in succession in Titus (Titus 1:9, 13; 2:1, 8).

B. The word means pure, wholesome, or healthy. The church worker is to have healthy motives so that he or she cannot be condemned by those in opposition. The church worker represents the whole church.

Conclusion

Church workers have a wonderful opportunity, but they also have a grave responsibility. To do their job according to Paul's specifications, they must be right in mind, teaching, and speech.

SUGGESTED PREACHING PROGRAM FOR THE MONTH OF
MAY

■ Sunday Mornings

On the first Sunday of the month, we will conclude our messages on the theme "Real Life in the Here and Hereafter."

"Christ, the Church, and the Enrichment of Family Life" is the theme for a series of messages beginning on Mother's Day and coming to a conclusion on Father's Day.

■ Sunday Evenings

Continue the series of messages based on Paul's epistle of joy—Philippians.

■ Wednesday Evenings

Continue the series of expository studies on the book of Titus. The passages under consideration emphasize the importance of the development of Christian character in God's people.

SUNDAY MORNING, MAY 1

Title: Living after the Meantime

Text: "And now, behold, the LORD hath kept me alive, as he said, these forty and five years, even since the LORD spake this word unto Moses, while the children of Israel wandered in the wilderness . . ." **(Josh. 14:10).**

Scripture Reading: Joshua 14:6–14

Hymns: "Victory in Jesus," E. M. Bartlett

"Faith Is the Victory," John H. Yates

"Because He Lives," William J. Gaither

Offertory Prayer: Father, life can be difficult. At times it is a challenge just to carry on. In the meantime, hardships and difficulties crash unexpectantly into our lives. Dreams are shattered, and hope seems to vanish. But in times like these, you prove to be a very present help in times of trouble. Our offering today is given out of love and gratitude. Take it, bless it, and multiply it. Amen.

Introduction

Much of life is lived in the meantime—between dreams and reality, between hope and fulfillment, between the death of a loved one and moving on with life.

How does one live after the meantime? Surviving a meantime is one thing, but living after a meantime is quite different.

In the minutes following the catastrophic earthquake off the Indonesian island of Sumatra on December 26, 2004, a wall of seawater more than ninety feet high surged at two miles per second and inundated stretches of the remote western coast. Sections of that coast sank three to six feet.

The historic 9.3 magnitude earthquake is among the most powerful recorded since 1900 and left an estimated 288,000 people dead. The village of Lampuuk had a population of 6,500 before the disaster. Today only 700 remain.

Living through the tsunami was one thing. Living after the tsunami proved to be quite a different matter. So, how does one live after a meantime?

This sermon is born of the personal experience of one who has lived in the meantime and who now is learning to live after the meantime. In homiletics this is called "confessional" preaching. Drawing from my own experience and that of Caleb, I offer these principles for "living after the meantime."

I. Appreciate the past.

Don't hate the past. Don't live in the past. Don't worship the past. It is easy to worship the past when one has fond memories of a deceased loved one. It is natural to recall joyous moments of such a relation. But to worship the past is to live in the wilderness of the past.

So how are you to relate to the past? You cannot and do not want to erase it from your memory. Rather, you must appreciate the past.

A. Past blessings. "Praise the Lord, my soul, and forget not all his benefits" (Ps. 103:2 NIV). The reason past hurts stand out so much is because they are few. Our past blessings far outnumber our past hurts.

I have learned to appreciate my past blessings—the home in which I was reared, the church where I was saved and called to preach, the family God gave me, and the churches I served.

B. Past hurts. "I brought [Moses] back a report according to my convictions, but my fellow Israelites who went up with me made the hearts of the people melt in fear" (Josh. 14:7–8 NIV). Caleb shared his heart with his people. He was certain they could conquer Canaan. But his own "brothers" turned against him. How disappointed he was! How disillusioned! How hurt! Yet he learned to appreciate this past hurt. Because of it, his greatest victory would come when he was an eighty-five-year-old man!

"Give thanks in all circumstances; for this is God's will for you in Christ Jesus" (1 Thess. 5:18 NIV).

"I love you, son, and I am proud of you." These were the last words my father spoke to me as I left his hospital room. During my last visit with my dad, he repeated that line several times in a half hour. I wasn't listening at the right level. I heard the words but not the message and certainly not their profound intent. I believed my dad would live well into his nineties. His family had a history of longevity.

The doctor said Dad's pneumonia was clear and he could go home the next morning. As I made my way to the door, Dad once again said, "I love you son, and I am proud of you." Then he looked at me the way we often do when we say good-bye to a friend whom we feel we will not see for a long time—a lingering, loving look.

At 2:00 Wednesday morning the phone rang. It was the hospital. Dad had died in his sleep! I was speechless. This wasn't the way it was supposed to happen! I felt grief, pain, and remorse. My dad was always there for me, but I was not there for him. The hurt lingers on. But in learning to live after the meantime, I have learned to appreciate even this hurt.

II. Celebrate the present.

We are never too old to celebrate the present. In Joshua 14:10–11, Caleb says, "I am eighty-five years old and I can still travel and fight!" He was saying with David, "This is the day which the Lord has made; let us rejoice and be glad in it" (Ps. 118:24 RSV).

Yesterday is a canceled check; tomorrow is a promissory note; today is the only currency you have. Spend it wisely; celebrate it joyfully!

Jesus was criticized for celebrating life too much. He was too much of a party person. In fact, his enemies said, "[He] is a glutton and a drunkard" (Matt. 11:19 NIV). Jesus believed in celebrating the present.

To live in the future is to rob the present of any celebration. The question is not "Is there life after death?" The question is "Is there life before death?" Our fear should be that we will die before we ever live!

I must confess that one of the greatest problems I have struggled with all my life has been failing to celebrate the present, never really living for today, but always living for tomorrow.

III. Anticipate the future.

One is never too old to anticipate the future. Caleb at eighty-five said, "Give me this mountain" (Josh. 14:12).

At the age of eighty-four, my father went to Fortaleza, Brazil, with me. We stood on a hill overlooking hundreds of new homes without a single church. Missionary Jerold Golston, my father, and others formed a circle, joined hands, and prayed, claiming the hill for the Lord.

I never shall forget when the prayers ended, my father said, "Like Caleb, I am saying, 'Give me this mountain!' " On a retired preacher's income, my father bought the hill and paid for the first unit. Like Caleb, my father anticipated the future.

Conclusion

Many things about tomorrow, I don't seem to understand,
But I know who holds tomorrow, and I know who holds my hand.

Ira Stanphill

With this knowledge, you and I can live after the meantime!

SUNDAY EVENING, MAY 1

Title: Look Forward with Concentration

Text: "Brethren ... this one thing I do, forgetting those things which are behind, and reaching forth unto those things which are before, I press toward the mark for the prize of the high calling of God in Christ Jesus" **(Phil. 3:13–14)**.

Scripture Reading: Philippians 3:12–15

Introduction

Paul possessed the unusual ability to soar into spiritual heights one moment and then descend immediately into the valley of the intensely practical. He had made his point concerning the necessity of a personal experience with Jesus Christ as a prerequisite to obtaining a righteous standing before God, being equipped for the problems that arise in the world, and possessing complete confidence and assurance concerning the world to come. The relationship he had with Christ assured his forgiveness, and his daily fellowship with the Lord gave him resources for living each day triumphantly.

This versatile apostle immediately assured his friends at Philippi that he knew that he had not yet "completely arrived" in the business of Christian growth. He also assured them, however, that he was striving every day to reach the goal Christ had for him when he turned him about on the Damascus road and started him in another direction. It is difficult for us to realize the strength Paul possessed as leader of the persecutors of Christianity. Had the battle been merely a human one, Paul and his followers probably would have been successful in stamping out this new movement. But it was not merely a human battle! God was standing within the shadow and keeping watch over his own. When the lion went forth to devour the sheep, God touched the lion and made him a tender lamb. The Lord had a great purpose in mind for Paul when he saved him. Paul was now seeking to reach God's goal for his life. This involved several steps.

I. Forgetting the past.

Paul's sentences are sharp and decisive, especially when writing about the previous experiences of his life. One always has mingled emotions when looking back over things that have gone before and evaluating them in light of present and future opportunities.

How much of the past should we remember? There are many things we want to hold in mind because they serve as didactic elements in facing new situations. Experience often is the best teacher. Indeed, one man said that "in some ways, experience is the only teacher."

On the other hand, some things must be forgotten completely if we are to have mental health and a spiritual dynamic. Paul's determination to forget the past was a part of his resolve as he faced the future. He would not allow any memory of failure to bring depression. He would keep the tense mind of the athlete with his eyes and thoughts fixed on the goal. When we do this, we cannot look backward. Whatever the past has been, God wants us to make certain it will not hinder us. Sometimes our previous sins may have left such a deep mark on our souls that it seems we can never remove them from our memory. But we must do it! Our attitude should be that we have repented of our sins, we have prayed for grace, and we have received God's forgiveness. Robert Louis Stevenson said, "Never allow your mind to dwell on your own misconduct: that is ruin." We should be in prayer constantly that God will give us the courage that enables us never to be cast down and sit lamenting amid the ruins of our happiness or our integrity. If we will surrender to God completely, he will touch us with fire from the altar and enable us to forget our failures. We simply cannot live in the past!

II. Face the future.

We must not live in the past; we must face the reality of the present day. Yet we must do more than this—we must plan wisely for the future. This does not mean that we should ignore the advice of Jesus in the Sermon on the Mount, "Take therefore no thought for the morrow: for the morrow shall take thought for the things of itself" (Matt. 6:34). Jesus was speaking in that context concerning the folly of becoming distracted with material possessions and failing to trust God. Wise people plan for the future and rejoice over every new opportunity for creativity.

Paul pictured his enthusiasm for life as "reaching forth," which is a very interesting phrase. Some translators render it "stretching forward," and the word picture in the original language is very graphic. This is the expression used of a racer as he "goes hard for the tape." He has eyes for nothing but the goal. His arms are clawing the air, his head is forward, and his body is bent toward the goal. He is literally "flat out" for the finish. This is the type of enthusiastic striving that brings flavor to life and motivates others to follow in our steps.

There is always more ahead for the Christian who has a vital experience of living fellowship with God. Spain once stamped all their coins with a picture of the Pillars of Hercules. They took as their motto the Latin phrase *Ne plus ultra,* which means "No more beyond." When Columbus passed beyond that point and on to a new world, Spain changed the slogan. They dropped the *Ne* and left only *Plus ultra*—"More beyond." So it is with the Christian. There is always a better tomorrow. This truth inspires us to find excitement and joy as we anticipate each new day lived in fellowship with our Savior.

III. Keep your eye on the goal.

To attain our goal, we must concentrate all our powers on that which we have adopted as our purpose in life. John Ruskin once wrote, "The law of Nature is that a certain quantity of work is necessary to produce a certain quantity of good, of any kind whatever." When our energy is bent to the utmost and our faculties are working at full speed under high pressure, great gains can be accomplished. We must, however, avoid the tendency to become sidetracked on the insignificant things that do not contribute to the reaching of long-range goals. Do you remember hearing how Michaelangelo worked for a week without taking off his clothes? This is because he was dedicated to his dream. A sculptor was polishing his statue with unwearied repetitions. When asked why he put forth such effort, he replied, "The image in my head is not yet in my hands." At times our hearts grow weary in the struggle. If, however, we can but obtain a glimpse of the diadem of realized ambition, our flagging energies will revive and press forward in faith.

A young man in college had an unusual ability but somehow never could seem to organize himself so as to get his work done effectively. One day, in a science laboratory, he saw the professor take a magnifying glass and concentrate all the energies of the sun in one spot. Suddenly, he spontaneously shouted, "I see it now. That's what I need to do." He realized that he had been spreading himself over too many things and doing none of them well. He saw that he needed to choose priorities and then "zero in" on the most important things with complete dedication and concentration.

Paul had one priority in life. Earlier in this letter to the Philippians, he said, "According to my earnest expectation and my hope, that in nothing I shall be ashamed, but that with all boldness, as always, so now also Christ shall be magnified in my body, whether it be by life, or by death" (1:20). He was seeking to keep this supreme aim clearly before him. If we are to do this, we must keep ourselves close to God and be prepared to surrender much, even our wills, plans, purposes, and eager hopes into his hands. If you want to bore a hole, you do not take a blunt instrument, but one with a sharp point. If we are to advance, we must gather ourselves together and put a point on our lives by concentrating our efforts and energies on the one overarching purpose we have adopted for ourselves.

Conclusion

Have you become self-satisfied in your religious life? Have you relaxed from the diligence that you once showed in Christian living and service? Perhaps you need to put renewed stress on the energizing character of the Christian life. Most of us have not suffered the loss of many things for the privilege of serving Christ. Paul had given up much, and this probably accounts for his greater zeal. Yet we should count it a joy and be eternally grateful that we had the privilege of receiving Christ without suffering the abuses and conflicts of adversity. This should inspire us to greater commitment and motivate us to deeper dedication. We, like Paul, should forget the past—both the failures and the victories of days gone by—and look forward to the future.

Have you found the one thing in life that you believe God has marked out as your particular contribution? It does not have to be a glamorous thing but may be the simple joy of serving others in Jesus' name. Whatever you feel is your mission in life, get busy doing it! Be earnest as you embrace the duties of life and as you enjoy the privileges of serving the Savior. If you are a person of unusual ability, you have an unusual obligation to develop your personality and abilities to the fullest.

Whatever your situation in life, find God's will for it. Then do his will with all your heart. You will be a better and happier person!

WEDNESDAY EVENING, MAY 4

Title: The Christian Character of a Worker

Text: "Teach slaves to be subject to their masters in everything, to try to please them, not to talk back to them, and not to steal from them, but to show that they can be fully trusted, so that in every way they will make the teaching about God our Savior attractive" **(Titus 2:9–10 NIV)**.

Scripture Reading: Titus 2

Introduction

In last week's message, our emphasis was on the Christian character of church workers. Today's message focuses on our work outside of the church. "Slaves" in our text refers to actual slaves in the culture of Paul's day, but Paul's words can also be applied to employees today. "Masters" refers to slave owners in Paul's day, but modern employers, or bosses, can follow Paul's teaching for masters.

I. There are two situations here.

A. When the boss is not a Christian. Here a heavy responsibility lies on a Christian employee. A non-Christian boss seldom, if ever, attends church. Consequently, he or she does not hear the gospel preached. The only way for the message of Christianity to be communicated to him or her is from someone outside the church walls. The employee is to bear a testimony in life and conduct of what Jesus can do for a person.

B. When the boss is a Christian. Christian employees are not to presume on their employers' Christianity and render less than a day's labor. They are to expect no allowances.

II. What are the qualities of a Christian worker?

A. Obedient. Christian workers are to be in subjection to the boss and are to do what they are told to do.

B. Well-pleasing in everything. Christian employees are to do their best to be efficient. They must determine to give satisfaction and never to put less than their best into a task. They are not above taking orders. A proper attitude goes a long way toward avoiding strife.

C. Respectful. They are not to talk back or speak against their employers. They are not to thwart their employers' plans, wishes, or orders.

D. Honest. No Christian in any walk of life is to stoop to petty dishonesties or to steal another's belongings, money, or time. Christians are never to take advantage of the trust placed in them and use it for personal gain.

E. Faithful Christian employees are to be faithful to their employers. They must be trustworthy at all times and under all circumstances. They should prove worthy of their employers' confidence.

III. Paul says that the reason for such conduct is so that "in every way they will make the teaching about God our Savior attractive" (Titus 2:10).

A. This is a legal imperative. When Christians are involved in secular work, they are to conduct themselves in every situation to bring honor to God.

B. The doctrine and teaching of Christians is judged by their conduct. It is shameful when Christians profess to believe the teaching they receive and yet deny it by their life and words. The highest interest of a Christian is always to be for the Word of God.

Conclusion

One of the greatest needs of our day is for Christians to take the principles and conduct of true Christianity into every walk of life.

SUNDAY MORNING, MAY 8

Title: " . . . and Thy Mother"

Text: "Honour thy father and thy mother . . ." **(Ex. 20:12)**.

Scripture Reading: Ephesians 6:1–3

Hymns: "Love Divine, All Loves Excelling," Wesley

"Ask Ye What Great Thing I Know," Schwedler

"Make Me a Blessing," Wilson

Offertory Prayer: Holy Father, we praise you for the gifts of life, salvation, fellowship, and families. We express our worship of you by giving to you a part of all that you have given to us. We thank you for the privilege of sharing with you and your work in return. In the name of Jesus Christ, your greatest gift, we pray. Amen.

Introduction

A simple but profound statement is repeated in the Word several times. It is first spoken in Exodus 20:12 and then repeated for the benefit of the new generation. Jesus quotes these words, and then Paul applies them to everyday life. Ephesians 6:2 says, "Honour thy father and mother."

In 2 Timothy 1:5 Paul reminds Timothy that his genuine faith was first seen in his grandmother and then in his mother.

"Honour thy mother" is the emphasis of this special day for the family. When we honor someone, we evaluate that person accurately and honestly, and treat him or her with the respect, reverence, kindness, and courtesy that this character demands.

Let us honor some special qualities of a mother today as seen in the Bible.

I. Let us honor a mother's sensitive spirit.

Mothers do have a sensitive spirit, as seen in Mary, the mother of Jesus. Luke 2:19 says, "But Mary kept all these things, and pondered them in her heart." Verse 51 says, "But his mother kept all these sayings in her heart." A mother's heart is like a storehouse—she treasures everything that happens to her family. She remembers when the father tends to forget.

A mother is so sensitive that she treasures her children, observes everything they do, rejoices when they show maturity, and grieves when they act foolishly. Proverbs 10:1 says, "A foolish son is the heaviness of his mother." She can tell when something is wrong, and according to Proverbs 29:15 it brings "his mother to shame." This sensitivity to wrong is a God-given capacity, a daily reality. A mother writing to a minister about her son said, "The company he keeps is very bad; I am brokenhearted." A mother especially has the capacity to be brokenhearted. Let us honor that spirit.

And as we recognize this sensitivity in a mother, let the mother not despise it. Rather, let her cultivate it, guard it, share it with her husband, and, most of all, dedicate it to God to be used by the Holy Spirit.

II. Let us honor a mother's sincere faith.

This is seen in 2 Timothy 1:5: "I call to remembrance the unfeigned faith that is in thee, which dwelt first in thy grandmother Lois, and thy mother Eunice; and I am persuaded [is] in thee also." This is faith in two ways.

A. It is the faith a mother lives. It is her daily life and attitudes. It is her influence for good or evil. There is nothing to compare with this. Two illustrations of evil influence found in the Bible are 1 Kings 22:52: "And he did evil in the sight of the Lord, and walked in the way of his father, and in the way of his mother"; and 2 Chronicles 22:3: "He also walked in the ways of the house of Ahab: for his mother was his counsellor to do wickedly." A mother's influence is powerful.

B. It is also the faith a mother teaches. Proverbs 1:8 says, "My son, hear the instruction of thy father, and forsake not the law of thy mother." We are divinely forbidden to forsake the teaching of parents, in which a mother's rules are important. This identical emphasis is repeated and strengthened in Proverbs 6:20. If we are not to forsake her teaching when we are young, neither are we to look with scorn upon a mother in her old age. Proverbs 23:22 says, "Hearken unto thy father that begat thee, and despise not thy mother when she is old." A mother is a part of God's plan to teach her children, and we are to respect her place under him.

III. Let us honor a mother's servant spirit.

This is described in Proverbs 31. Notice the specific description God's Word gives of a mother who possesses the heart of a servant. It is a beautiful picture of an excellent wife and mother whose worth is invaluable, "far above rubies" (v. 10). She is not a threat to her husband or in competition with him (vv. 11–12). Her servant spirit extends to her family. She delights in serving them. She prepares meals diligently. She is not lazy, rising a great while before daylight to provide for the needs of her family (vv. 13–15).

She even has time to consider investments (v. 16). She is physically strong and cares for her health (v. 17), and she is industrious, even working at night (vv. 18–19). She is a servant to the poor and needy (v. 20). She clothes herself and her family with the finest of clothes (vv. 21–22). She assists with family finances (v. 24). Strength and dignity are her qualities, and she is able to smile at the future (v. 25). She thinks not of herself but speaks wisely and kindly to others (v. 26). In such a person there is no idleness; rather, she looks well to the ways of her household (v. 27). No wonder she is praised (vv. 28–31)! Let us honor a mother's servant spirit.

Conclusion

Mothers who have qualities like those of the woman in Proverbs 31 are worthy of honor. And these qualities are possible as the Holy Spirit is allowed freedom to develop them in a mother's life. This challenge rings out to every mother. Then let us as sons and daughters fulfill our responsibility by genuine respect. To do so honors God.

SUNDAY EVENING, MAY 8

Title: Receiving Our Resurrection Bodies

Text: "We look for the Saviour ... who shall change our vile body, that it may be fashioned like unto his glorious body" **(Phil. 3:20–21)**.

Scripture Reading: Philippians 3:15–21

Introduction

Most of us are familiar with Paul's classic passage (1 Thess. 4:13–17) concerning the resurrection of the dead. We are told that the Lord shall descend from heaven with a shout and that the dead in Christ shall rise first. Paul adds immediately that we who are alive and remain shall be caught up together with them in the clouds. In other words, both groups (the living and dead who are in Christ) shall meet the Lord in the air. Paul's last word in this section is that we should comfort one another with this promise.

In Paul's letter to the Philippians, he supplements the truth conveyed to the Christians at Thessalonica. First, we who are living shall be changed at the coming of our Lord. Second, our vile bodies will be made like his glorious body. This latter truth is supplemented further by Paul's words to the church at Corinth (1 Cor. 15:49–54), in which we are told that the "corruptible must put on incorruption." All three of these passages need to be considered together in order to gain the full truth about the Christian's resurrected body.

I. Our citizenship is heavenly, not earthly.

The word "conversation" in the King James Version is rendered "citizenship" by some versions and "commonwealth" by others. Paul uses a strong word here to denote the fact that the Christian's true citizenship is in heaven. Some writers have called heaven our "mother country" because it is there that our Savior lives.

This does not mean that we are exempt from a realistic approach to the duties of citizenship in the country we inhabit on earth. Nothing could be further from the truth. Jesus taught us that we are to "render unto Caesar that which is Caesar's." We are to support the government by paying taxes and rendering other duties that are necessary to support the nation from which we receive many privileges.

Yet our true allegiance is to the "unreachable ideals" of the Christian faith. God's simplest masterpieces are greater than all the creativity of humankind. A wildflower blooming in a remote place is more beautiful than a king or queen dressed up for a function of the state. Earthly wealth stored up is but a temporary stopgap against the insecurities that threaten in this life. But integrity, purity, unselfishness, and redemptive love are rights and privileges that cannot be taken away by worldly powers. Our ultimate citizenship is spiritual and is therefore untouchable by secular hands.

II. We look for the Savior.

Jesus comes to us in a spiritual encounter when we receive him as personal Savior and experience what the Bible calls a new birth. Jesus lives within us. Paul said to the Galatians, "I am crucified with Christ: nevertheless I live; yet not I, but Christ liveth in me" (Gal. 2:20).

But this is not the full story! Jesus has promised to come again in his resurrection body and to receive us to himself. This is the highest reward that God provides to those who serve Jesus. There are many advantages and rewards for serving Jesus in this world. There is a peace that comes to the heart when we surrender ourselves to God's will now in the present life. This, however, cannot be compared to the joy that will be ours when the Savior comes personally and visibly to claim his loved ones and consummate his purposes in this world.

For the Christian, the second coming of Jesus is the "blessed hope." There is absolutely nothing that will purify our attitudes and motivate us for Christian living as the constant expectancy that Jesus may return at any moment. The belief in the imminent coming of Jesus will cause us to evaluate every anticipated action in light of the fact that Jesus may come while we are doing it. We must live in the flesh on this earth, but we can be looking forward constantly to the time when Jesus shall return and put both sin and Satan under his feet.

III. Our bodies shall be changed.

For one to say that Christians believe in immortality does not express the full truth. Greek philosophy, at its highest and best, arrived at this conclusion. Plato presented his famous arguments for immortality. Neither is it sufficient to say that we believe in the continuity of personality beyond the grave. We do believe this, but the Bible teaches more—much more.

Paul taught under divine inspiration that the body will be resurrected when Jesus comes. This refers to the "dead in Christ." They will hear the sound of the trumpet at Christ's coming and arise. Paul also makes it clear, however, that the Christians who are alive at the time of Christ's coming will also receive a new body. He says that Jesus "shall change our vile body, that it may be fashioned like unto his glorious body." This assures us that although the dead in Christ shall rise first, those who are alive at the time of Christ's coming shall receive equal treatment from the Lord.

What kind of body is the resurrection body? This question has baffled students through the centuries. The truth is that we cannot be certain. It will be a body that is not subject to the limitations of time and space—we will have great mobility. Perhaps we will be able to move the body as fast as we can move our mind. This can mean that the entire universe with all of its planets and galaxies will be the dwelling place of the glorified body.

How much will the resurrected and glorified body resemble the present body? Certainly there will be some points of similarity. For instance, Jesus arose with his glorified body. At first the people did not recognize him. Then, as he revealed himself to them and they came to know him better, they realized who he was. Did you ever hear someone say, "You look so much better; I hardly knew you"? Could this be an analogy of the new and glorified body?

Will deformities be gone, or will they still be present? One great Christian theologian says that perhaps we shall see so clearly the true values that a deformity will actually be a beauty. We do know that there will be no pain, sorrow, or disappointment. The resurrected and glorified body will meet our every need. DeWitt Talmadge rejoiced in his faith and exclaimed, "O glorious day of resurrection. Gladly will I fling into the grave this poor, sinful frame, if at thy call I may rise up a body tireless and pure, and glorious and immortal."

Conclusion

What do these truths mean to us today? For one thing, God places a high value on the physical body. Although the flesh has its weaknesses, limitations, and necessities, the Bible nowhere minimizes the value of the human body. It is a dwelling place for his Spirit and is of superlative importance. Yet the continued emphasis of the inspired writers is on our spiritual nature. This is the reason God ultimately will provide a body that can serve as the proper dwelling place for our higher nature. There is, however, no possibility of an eternal life in the world to come unless that life has been begun before death. Thus "eternal life" is not merely quantitative but is qualitative as well. Flesh and blood cannot inherit the kingdom of God. Christ's power within us is what makes us able to share in never-ending fellowship with him.

The resurrection body we will receive will be glorious, but we must be prepared to live within it. This comes by fellowship with Christ now. We are preparing ourselves, during this life, for the kind of life we wish to live in the body we will receive. We can prepare ourselves for becoming like Christ through continuous living in the light of his love and in harmony with his will for us. Then when he appears we shall be like him because we shall see him as he is.

WEDNESDAY EVENING, MAY 11

Title: The Moral Power of the Presence of God

Text: "For the grace of God that bringeth salvation hath appeared to all men, teaching us that denying ungodliness and worldly lusts, we should live soberly, righteously, and godly, in this present world; looking for that blessed hope, and the glorious appearing of the great God and our Saviour Jesus Christ; who gave himself for us, that he might redeem us from all iniquity, and purify unto himself a peculiar people, zealous of good works" **(Titus 2:11–14)**.

Scripture Reading: Titus 2

Introduction

The difference the presence of Jesus makes in one's life is the subject for this message. Our Scripture text refers to Jesus' incarnation but also to his spiritual presence with us today. His realized presence makes a lot of difference in a person's conduct.

I. The thought is introduced by telling of the source and scope of the power.

A. The source is the grace of God. Grace is God acting on behalf of his child when the child does not deserve it. It is the incomprehensible love that God has for fallen people.

B. The scope is for all people. It is for old men and women as well as for young men and women. It is for all people everywhere regardless of race, color, or creed. It applies to all circumstances.

II. The work that the presence of Christ performs is stated negatively and positively.

A. The negative is mentioned first. The grace of God—the presence of Christ—will teach people to deny ungodliness. The word denying means to break with or disown as being abominable. The word worldliness means a lack of piety or reverence toward God. They are the things that will not pass over into heaven but are dissolved with the present world. They are also the things that cannot be shown to God. They are the things of which the sinner is ashamed. The presence of Christ in the hearts of people causes them to do away with everything they know that is contrary to God.

B. The positive is mentioned second. In the presence of Christ, children of God are to live with prudence. The indwelling Holy Spirit enables them to keep everything under control. He allows no passion or desire more than its proper place. Christians are to live "justly." That is, they are to give both God and people what they are due. They are also to live reverently. Christians are to be aware of their collective bodies as the temple of God.

III. The dynamic of this power is further seen in the expectation of the Lord's return (Titus 2:13).

When a royal visit is expected, everything is cleansed and decorated and made fit for the royal eye to see. Few things are more of a challenge to right conduct than the expectation of the Lord's return.

IV. Titus 2:14 is a summary of what the Lord has done.

A. He has redeemed from all iniquity.

B. He has purified unto himself a special people.

Conclusion

All human beings need motivation to do right. Satan is subtle and will entice God's children to do wrong. However, once people realize they are under the constant eye of God and are always in his presence, it is much easier for them to do good and more difficult to do evil.

SUNDAY MORNING, MAY 15

Title: Words for Wives

Text: "Likewise, ye wives, be in subjection to your own husbands; that, if any obey not the word, they also may without the word be won by the conversation of the wives; while they behold your chaste conversation coupled with fear" **(1 Peter 3:1–2)**.

Scripture Reading: 1 Peter 3:1–6

Hymns: "Crown Him with Many Crowns," Bridges

"Break Thou the Bread of Life," Lathbury

"He Leadeth Me!" Gilmore

Offertory Prayer: Heavenly Father, thank you for your unspeakable gift, your Son, Jesus Christ. Thank you for reaching down to earth in him to redeem us to yourself. We acknowledge your riches of grace in salvation and return to you our gifts of material things for your glory and use. Cause our hearts to be committed totally to your purpose for us. In the name of Jesus we pray. Amen.

Introduction

First Peter has three divisions—salvation, submission, and suffering. Today's passage is from the submission division. The one great truth of the morning is the description of a wife's relationship to her husband. In it is God's command to a wife to be in subjection to her husband.

Why is it important to emphasize Scripture that teaches a wife to be submissive to her husband? For one thing, it reveals God's will for wives. So much of what we read and hear today emphasizes only man's point of view and not God's. We need to know what God says in his Word. When we live by the wisdom of God's Word, happiness will result. A second reason is that the truth of this Scripture relates to God's original purpose for husband and wife (Gen. 2:18–24). Third, many wives are frantically searching for true fulfillment in their lives. When wives are told to seek a "role" in life, nothing is more important and fulfilling in life than to do the will of God (Rom. 12:1–2). Fourth, true harmony in a marriage rests on this principle. And fifth, spiritual power can be found in yielding to God's principles.

Look at God's words for wives from three viewpoints.

I. A wife's response.

According to this morning's Scripture, God is calling for a certain response from wives. The word "likewise" (v. 1) points to the preceding paragraph in 1 Peter 2:18–25. In this passage, Jesus' response to suffering is described. He was beaten, whipped, and spit on, yet his response was one of silent suffering. He did not sin, nor was guile found in his mouth. He was reviled but did not revile back; he suffered but did not threaten. He expressed no spirit of anger, resentment, or revenge. Rather, he committed himself and his cause to his heavenly Father. In doing so, he bore our sins in his own body.

On the basis of that example, Peter says, "Likewise, ye wives...." A wife is to have a Christlike manner toward her husband who does not obey the Word of God in his life. He is not a believer in Christ nor is he the spiritual leader in the home that God wants him to be or that she needs him to be. As she treats him in a loving, Christlike manner, she'll make a way for healing in his life.

II. A wife's relationship.

A wife's response is demonstrated in submission to her husband. "Be in subjection" may be translated "be submissive" (v. 1). The verb is in the present tense, calling for continual submission. It is in the imperative mood and therefore is a command to the wife; and it is in the reflexive voice, which expresses a voluntary response. What does submission mean?

A. What submission does not mean.

1. Submission does not mean that a wife is inferior to her husband. Galatians 3:28 refers to the fact that there is neither male nor female in Christ, so spiritually a husband and wife are equal. First Peter 3:7 speaks of both being "heirs together," thus sharing equally in God's inheritance in Christ. As persons in Christ, they are equal, but as partners in marriage, there is a functional difference. God's design for a marriage is that the husband serves as the head of the wife and the wife submits to her husband.

2. Submission does not mean that the wife is to be a slave to her husband. She is related to her husband as the church is to Christ, and that describes a beautiful, meaningful relationship.
3. The wife is not the only one who is to be submissive. Ephesians 5:21 refers to mutual submission of believers. The same applies to husbands and wives. When this principle is ignored, there will be no harmony in the marriage. It is not easy for any of us to be submissive, because our natural inclination is to be independent. But God's Word says that we need each other in every area of life, and this requires mutual submission.

B. What submission means.
1. The word submit means "to arrange under" or "to rank under." When a wife is submissive to her husband, she voluntarily arranges herself under her husband's authority as the one whom God has placed over her. She experiences freedom as she yields to her husband in this divine arrangement. She also experiences his protection and care for her. This every wife deeply desires.
2. Submission involves a spiritual attitude. Ephesians 5:22 says that submission is to be "as unto the Lord." Therefore it is for him, as well as to him. A wife's lack of submission to her husband indicates lack of submission to the Lord, who is over all.
3. Submission is to be "in everything." How submissive is a wife to be? Ephesians 5:24 says "in everything." She is to be completely devoted to her husband. Such a spirit in a wife becomes the spirit of a home. A resentful wife causes a home to reflect a resentful atmosphere. Resistance to a husband cannot be hidden.
4. Submission is to be expressed inwardly as well as outwardly. It is more than action; it is attitude as well. It is both without and within a person. It is not enough to say it; a wife must live it too. There is nothing more powerful in a marriage than the submissive attitude of a wife toward her husband. How is that power expressed?

III. A wife's rewards.

Is submission worth it to a wife? The highest example of all submission is seen in the life of Jesus, as seen in Philippians 2:5–11. After his submission came his exaltation. Rewards come to the wife who is submissive.

A. God works in a wife's life. She becomes a beautiful person, as seen in verses 2–6. Beauty is not one's outward appearance primarily; it is related to the inward qualities of a quiet and gentle spirit. A wife who so fulfills these words becomes a grateful and appreciative wife because she is trusting in the Lord to meet her needs through her husband.

B. God works in the atmosphere of the home. The atmosphere begins to change to one in which the influence of the Lord is deeply felt. Faith is genuinely expressed (v. 5) and spreads to future generations.

C. God works in the heart of the husband. Her husband is won to the Lord. How? Not by a wife's pressure of words, but rather by the fact that "without a word" she demonstrates a quiet and grateful spirit. One word of nagging is like a whole volume of pressure and drives away the husband from opening his heart to the Lord.

Conclusion

God's plans—whether for salvation, marriage, or something else—work whenever they are followed in a true spirit of trust. He is waiting to demonstrate his divine arrangement in those families that will respond.

SUNDAY EVENING, MAY 15

Title: Do Not Be Anxious ... Pray and Find Peace

Text: "Be careful for nothing ... let your requests be known unto God. And the peace of God, which passeth all understanding, shall keep your hearts and minds through Christ Jesus" **(Phil. 4:6–7)**.

Scripture Reading: Philippians 4:1–7

Introduction

As Paul comes to the last section of his letter, he deals with personal matters. He begins by urging two members of the congregation who seemingly have become "miffed" to think alike and try to work together. He prefaces his remarks, however, with words of endearment to the congregation. They are his "dearly beloved and longed for" and his "joy and crown." His characteristic word in this letter is emphasized also in this section. He calls on the Christians at Philippi to rejoice.

The word translated "moderation" in the King James Version is perhaps best rendered as "self-control." There does not seem to be any evidence that the Philippians were excessive in their indulgences. This caution of Paul in verse 5 may have been merely "preventive maintenance" that he felt they needed. The heart of this section is the plea by Paul that the people refrain from becoming so "uptight" in everyday living that they fail to realize the calmness and serenity that can come to one who has placed unqualified trust in the Lord. Only in complete surrender does perfect peace come to a Christian.

I. "Be anxious about nothing."

Let it be firmly understood that Paul nowhere advocated a careless and flippant attitude toward providing for the necessities of life. Paul was a realist. He expected a man to work in order to provide for himself and his loved ones. He wrote to Timothy, "But if any provide not for his own, and specially for those of his own house, he hath denied the faith, and is worse than an infidel" (1 Tim. 5:8).

On the other hand, Paul always cautioned the people with whom he ministered that spiritual values should be placed ahead of material desires. Paul must have been thinking of the words Jesus spoke in the Sermon on the Mount as he exhorted the Philippian Christians to refrain from too much concern for the necessities of life. Jesus said, "Therefore take no thought, saying, What shall we eat? or, What shall we drink? or, Wherewithal shall we be clothed?" (Matt. 6:31). Jesus insisted that it is pagan people who make this their aim in life, and he assured his listeners that their heavenly Father was aware of their needs. The expression "take no thought" probably is best rendered "Do not become overly anxious" and should never be interpreted to mean that we should pay no attention to the essential duty of making a living. It is rather that we should give more attention to making a life. We can find great wisdom in the "conversation overheard in an orchard" as two birds chatted with each other:

Said the robin to the sparrow,
"I should really like to know
Why these anxious human beings
Rush about and worry so."
Said the sparrow to the robin,
"Friend, I think that it must be
That they have no heavenly Father
Such as cares for you and me."

—*Elizabeth Cheney*

Prudence is the duty of every person. Anxiety, however, is the great foe of prudence. Becoming distracted is to the mind and soul what friction is in the working of a machine. Our effectiveness is diminished in direct proportion to its presence.

II. "Pray with thanksgiving."

Prayer is not a pious excuse for laziness. A person who is unwise and lazy cannot expect God to "work magic" merely because he or she utters a few pious words of entreaty under great emotional stress. Paul is speaking of an attitude toward life. Indeed, prayer is a way of thinking and living as much as it is specific requests at definite times and places. Paul said to the Thessalonian Christians, "Pray without ceasing" (1 Thess. 5:17). This does not mean that you must remain on your knees all your life, but rather that you should go about your daily business with your heart and mind turned toward God. Prayer is unreserved confiding in God. The words "in everything" are important. God made us and knows our nature. He knows his will for our lives, and he knows all of the circumstances we face. There is no anxiety from which our Creator is barred, and nothing is hidden from him. God sees all of our difficulties—our probable losses, our dread of certain contingencies, and every difficulty and struggle we must face. God is great enough to care for small things as well as for great ones. The wonders revealed by a microscope are as much God's work as the objects we see through telescopes. God's providence is real and operates in every part of our universe.

The prayer life of a Christian should be filled with thanksgiving. Someone has said that ingratitude is not only the greatest of sins but the mother of all the rest. Paul is not advocating the "Pollyanna philosophy" toward life that everything is bright and sunny. This is, of course, a one-sided philosophy and is practiced by those who refuse to face up to the realistic things of life that are discouraging and gloomy. Paul is, however, urging us to realize how many good things there are in the world and to recognize that God is the one who has given them to us. The more grateful Paul was, the more eager he became to consider his entire life a stewardship, an obligation to serve God and all of God's creation. Nothing gives more flavor to life and makes our goals more meaningful than to live constantly as a humble and grateful Christian.

III. "Peace that passeth all understanding."

Paul mentions two kinds of peace. First, there is the "peace with God" that comes in the initial experience of conversion or, as Jesus called it, the "new birth." We find peace with God when we confess our sins to Jesus Christ and trust him completely for our salvation. Jesus died on the cross for our justification. What we could not do because of our sinfulness, Jesus Christ has done. He redeemed us from the penalty of our sins. He paid the price for our iniquities when he died on Calvary. He was and is the Lamb of God who takes away the sin of the world (John 1:29). When we come to him as personal Savior, we have peace with God. Our guilt is dealt with once and for all. We have peace concerning our eternal destiny.

The other kind of peace that Christians can experience is what Paul refers to as the "peace that passeth all understanding." This has been called a "postgraduate" peace. It comes as we grow in the Christian life. None of us attains this peace completely, but it is the goal toward which we constantly should be striving in our Christian pilgrimage. The more surrendered we are to things of the Spirit and the more we depend on Christ for leadership in our personal lives, the more of this peace we will realize.

Conclusion

The quest for peace is humankind's major concern in our day. The world's peace always is linked with the self-interest of people. Each person views life from his or her own perspective. To see the whole view is difficult. When we are centered on our selfish interests, it is easy for our relationships to deteriorate and to eventually result in conflict. The answer to humanity's age-long search for peace is to be found in serenity within individual human hearts.

Although all Christians should cooperate, without compromising their consciences, with every good agency seeking to promote peace, truly born-again persons know deep within that universal peace can come only when the Prince of Peace reigns within the hearts of people in this world. Jesus said, "Blessed are the peacemakers." The true peacemaker is the one leading others to the Savior who gives inward peace.

Do you have both kinds of peace that God offers? Have you been born again by God's Spirit? Are you growing toward the "peace that passeth all understanding" that will guard your mind and bring contentment in every area of your personality?

WEDNESDAY EVENING, MAY 18

Title: The Expectancy of Jesus' Coming

Text: "Looking for that blessed hope, and the glorious appearing of the great God and our Saviour Jesus Christ" **(Titus 2:13)**.

Scripture Reading: Titus 2

Introduction

In last week's message, we emphasized the theme "The Moral Power of the Presence of God." We discovered that a realization of God's presence provokes people to right living. In this message, the emphasis is on an expectancy of the Lord's return, which also makes for right living. The Scriptures are emphatic in telling of Jesus' coming, but how he is coming is debatable and when is unknown.

I. To better grasp the expectancy of Christ's coming, we must understand some terms.

A. The first of these terms is "looking." It means to receive to oneself, to admit, give access to oneself. The verb has an atmosphere of expectancy about it and a readiness to welcome the person for whom one is looking. Thus, when we attach the word looking to the second coming of the Lord, it means that the one looking with expectancy will receive Jesus to himself.

B. The second term is "blessed." Most of the time this word is associated with happiness. The person who looks for the return of the Lord will be happy. The word also conveys the concept of prosperities, filled with benefits and good things.

C. The third term is "hope." This is when all equalities will be adjusted. All wrongs will then be redressed. Also, all the faithful service will be rewarded. At the same time, all true character will be revealed.

The average Christian lives in a world of confusion and at his best does not understand many things that go on around him. The Lord's return will shed light on these.

II. Consider why it is that the expectancy will provoke right living.

A. The expectancy of a royal visit always brings about preparation. When the president or queen or some other high official visits a country other than his or her own, much preparation is given in the form of protection, welcome, and comfort. Surely, when people have been saved by the blood of Jesus and they expect the return of the one who has done so much for them, they will live righteous lives.

B. This expectancy will cause people to have self-control. They are determined to be ready for their Savior and will live as clean and pure lives as possible in order to welcome their Savior unashamedly.

III. This character in the present is one of attitude.

A. The second coming of Christ completes the redemption of believers. Many followers of Jesus have already been taken from their earthly home in death. At the return of Christ, the dead in Christ will be resurrected. The ones who are alive at his return will be caught up to be with him.

B. The second coming of Christ marks real victory. To many struggling Christians in this earthly life, life seems to be dominated with evil and sin. When Jesus comes back, we will have the ultimate victory over Satan and sin.

The seeming finality of death and the grave constantly casts a shadow over all believers. But thanks be to God, Jesus has conquered these, and at his return this truth will be realized more fully.

C. The second coming of Christ will mean a face-to-face encounter with the wonderful Lord who came, lived, died, arose, and returned to heaven.

Conclusion

For the Christian, nothing can compare with seeing the Lord in person. And when he appears, we shall see him face-to-face.

SUNDAY MORNING, MAY 22

Title: As for Me and My House

Text: "And if it seem evil unto you to serve the Lord, choose you this day whom ye will serve; whether the gods which your fathers served that were on the other side of the flood, or the gods of the Amorites, in whose land ye dwell: but as for me and my house, we will serve the Lord" **(Josh. 24:15)**.

Scripture Reading: Joshua 24:14–18

Hymns: "Crown Him with Many Crowns," Bridges

"Word of God, across the Ages," Blanchard

"God, Give Us Christian Homes" McKinney

Offertory Prayer: Heavenly Father, hallowed be your name in our hearts this morning. We lift up our hearts in thankfulness for your perfect gifts to us. We praise you with word and song. We humble ourselves before you, the source of every blessing, the Lord of all the universe. We offer up to you our gifts in recognition of your ownership of our lives. How we do thank you for the privilege of giving unto you! We trust you to bless these tithes and offerings to the needs of your work here and throughout the world. In the name of Jesus Christ we pray. Amen.

Introduction

How are things with you and your family? There is something special about the family—so special that our families are our dearest earthly relationships. As far as institutions are concerned, the family is the oldest on the earth, before government or church. Family life is the foundation of society. So when I speak of the family, I touch the tenderest spot in your heart and mine.

Joshua's statement in today's Scripture text is one of the most important statements in the Old Testament. He spoke it to the Israelites whom he was leading. They are the words of a man committed to the task of leadership. More personally, they are the words of a determined father, whose spiritual dedication affected not only himself, but also his family. Joshua recognized the stewardship of a family.

I. Parents have a stewardship to the family.

Parents are responsible for the attitude and direction of the family. They also are responsible for the support of its needs. These are not optional; rather, they are urgent necessities when we think of the indescribable pressures that are being applied to the home today. Basically, there are two Scripture passages that teach this responsibility.

One is Deuteronomy 6:2–7: "And thou shalt teach them diligently unto thy children, and shalt talk of them when thou sittest in thine house, and when thou walkest by the way, and when thou liest down, and when thou risest up" (v. 7). God's ways are to be taught to children at home; they are to be the theme of conversation in all of our activities.

By teaching we pass God's truth to future generations (v. 6). The attitude in which the teaching is to be done is in total love for the Lord (v. 5).

The second passage is Ephesians 6:4: "And, ye fathers, provoke not your children to wrath: but bring them up in the nurture and admonition of the Lord." Fathers are to accept ultimate responsibility for teaching and leading the children, but not without the assistance of the mother. Authority is not to be exercised in unkindness and harshness; rather, it is to be done positively. "Bring up" speaks of developing character; "nurture" refers to imparting general training for a controlled life; "admonition" describes correction and warning; and the phrase, "of the Lord," means that it all is to be done in a thoroughly Christian manner. Anything less than this is a rebuke to us as careless parents who are failing to give the Bread of Life to our children. We can see Joshua's determination to fulfill God's Word in his family.

II. Children have a stewardship to the family.

Children's roles as stewards are best described in Ephesians 6:1–3, where two words are emphasized. The first word is "obey" (v. 1). Obey is from two Greek words that mean "to hear submissively." It means there is a readiness to listen and carry out the will of parents. This is a Christian duty, being done "in the Lord." Such requires a cheerful, prompt, habitual response. But it also is a moral duty, "for this is right." It is the only right thing to do as the nature of the relationship between parents and children suggests.

The second word is "honor" (vv. 2–3). This is the disposition that makes obedience possible. Fulfilling this results in divine blessings; rejecting it results in rebellion against God, as well as against one's parents. Children can either break the hearts of their parents or bless them. There need be no communication gap if both parents and children are submissive to the Lord's directions.

III. The family has a stewardship to destiny.

In 2 Kings 20:1 Isaiah the prophet spoke to Hezekiah the king, "Thus saith the Lord, Set thine house in order; for thou shalt die, and not live." He was saying to him, "Prepare for your destiny, and your destiny will be the destiny of your family." We have not only a stewardship for life, but also for death; not only for time now, but for eternity. We fathers have a heavy responsibility to lead our families to a destiny that suffices the tests of eternity.

Another illustration is seen in Acts 16:34, in the experience of the Philippian jailer finding Christ: "And when he had brought them into his house, he set meat before them, and rejoiced, believing in God with all his house." Not only was the jailer converted to Christ, but all his house was also saved. What a testimony of the saving grace of God—that a whole household could come to him. God is reaching out to many families today, possibly yours, to call to salvation and abundant life. He is waiting for some fathers who will become desperate enough to humble themselves before him for salvation and leadership of the family.

Conclusion

Joshua had arrived at that point in his life. He said, "As for me and my house, we will serve the Lord." He led the way with the dedication of himself. God is calling to your heart and home for your decision to receive Christ as Savior and Lord or to make that commitment that will allow him to mold your family into what he wants it to be.

SUNDAY EVENING, MAY 22

Title: In Jesus We Are Able for Anything

Text: "I can do all things through Christ which strengtheneth me" **(Phil. 4:13)**.

Scripture Reading: Philippians 4:8–13

Introduction

Paul did not share the philosophy of the man who said, "Don't do as I do; do as I say." He realized that his example was of utmost importance and thus sought, in every way, to live in such a manner that if people followed his lifestyle they would be pleasing to God. Yet Paul recognized that he was not sufficient within himself to do the things necessary either for growth in his own life or to serve as an example for others. It had been necessary, therefore, for him to make many adjustments along the way. Often he needed material assistance when none was available. The Christians at Philippi had given financial support to him in his missionary work a number of times, but they had lost contact with him at a late period of his ministry. Paul assured them that he had learned how to adjust to any environment and become superior to his circumstances.

How had he done it? He had learned that his power and strength came because of his personal relationship and his growing fellowship with Christ. No one other than the one who had saved him and continued to be his Master and Friend could "pour power" into him and make him strong for every occasion. Our text could be read as saying, "In him who strengthens me, I am able for anything."

I. We are able for life's sufferings.

The adversities of life are real! We all have difficulties that crush us and bring sorrow. Sometimes our sufferings seem more than we can bear. But in Jesus we learn some great lessons about suffering. Our Savior did not try to avoid the greatest suffering of his life—going to Calvary. He faced his death realistically and used it as an instrument by which he brought redemption to the world. In the same way, we can find victory in suffering.

How do you face your suffering? Does it make you bitter or better? If we use suffering creatively, it can be the means by which our character is deepened and our life made more meaningful. One of the greatest examples of suffering in the Old Testament was that of Hosea. His wife left him for another lover, and his heart was broken. Yet Hosea used this experience as a means of discovering God's great love for his bride, Israel.

In the strength of Christ, we are able to face suffering. With his inward presence, we can understand that suffering gives identification and compassion. It makes our life more beautiful. A traveler in Africa saw the large butterflies of the tropics as they struggled to free themselves from their cocoons. He took pity on one of them and, with his knife, cut the cords at which it was straining. It came out safely and easily. There was, however, a great tragedy: all the brilliant coloring was gone! The anguish of the struggle was necessary for that. So the beautiful colors of the soul are won, not in times of ease and prosperity, but in the struggle with and the victory over trials and adversity.

II. We are able for temptation.

We should candidly face the fact that it is not a sin to be tempted. There is a great difference between being tempted and yielding to the temptation by committing the overt act. It is true that Jesus said that he who lusts after a woman has committed adultery with her already in his heart (Matt. 5:28). Jesus, however, certainly did not mean that to be tempted is to be guilty of the act. If so, we would all throw up our hands in despair. To have Jesus present in our heart is the best, and indeed the only, assurance that we have the power to overcome temptation. Do you remember how Jesus fought temptation when he was led in the wilderness for his testing? The devil sought three times to lead Jesus to a compromise. After each proposal, Jesus replied by quoting from God's Word. He had so stored up into his mind and heart the Old Testament Scriptures that he could call on them at a moment's notice to serve as a resource in time of need.

Today we have not only the Old Testament, but the New Testament as well—especially the words of Jesus in the gospel. With the aid of the Holy Spirit, we can summon all the wisdom that Jesus taught us, plus the redemptive power from our personal experience with him in salvation. A pilot flying alone heard the gnawing of a rat in the cockpit. It was too late to turn back. He remembered that a rodent cannot live in high atmosphere. He sent his plane as high into the sky as he could. After a while, the gnawing ceased. When he landed, there was a dead rat in the cockpit. Similarly, temptations cannot live in spiritual environments. As we love Jesus, admire his way of life, and live in intimate fellowship with him, temptations will cease to have attraction. In Christ we have the power for dealing with the testing times of life.

III. We are able to face death and eternity.

Christianity is more than a "fire escape" from an eternal hell. Being a follower of Jesus gives purpose and direction to life now. With Christ living in our hearts, we can enjoy an inward peace that comes closer to a "heaven on earth."

On the other hand, we should never minimize the fact that salvation is, first of all, a deliverance from the penalty of sin—we are saved from hell and for heaven. Jesus made it plain a number of times that there is a place of punishment awaiting the person who rejects the call to salvation. There is also a heaven to be gained. Jesus said to his disciples, "In my Father's house are many mansions: if it were not so, I would have told you. I go to prepare a place for you" (John 14:2).

With Jesus as Savior, we can face the matter of our eternal destiny with complete assurance. Our sins are under the blood of Jesus. We have been justified from the guilt of our sins and shall never come into condemnation. An old story tells how a man dreamed he died and faced judgment. In the dream, he saw Satan bring before him a large armful of books. He asked what they were and was told they were a record of his sins. He asked if that were all. The devil replied that there were still more. The man asked the devil to bring all of them. After all had been brought before the man, he replied, "Now write over every one of my transgressions these words, 'The blood of Jesus Christ cleanseth us from all sin.' "

Conclusion

How real is the indwelling presence of Jesus in your life? A great Christian of another generation said, "I link my earthly feebleness to thine almighty power." Many witnesses in every age have found that out of personal weakness they can become strong through the living Christ.

What is Christian power? Humans are the highest order of beings in the universe and yet when left to themselves, can sink deeper in depravity and wrongdoing than any of God's creation. They find their true worth by linking themselves with their Creator in personal fellowship. The greatest personal power comes when we are willing to be entirely selfless and lose ourselves and our own ambitions in doing God's will.

On the human level, this is unexplainable. Yet there are some evidences of parallels. In the material universe, power is not originated by humans but is always given to them. People do not create power; they find it and convert it into other forms of power. So, in our spiritual lives we do not create our own power; we find it in our Savior and channel it into useful living and worthwhile deeds.

True power is in the divine personality who is able to control and utilize our hearts and will do so even as the wind is able to fill the sail of a ship. However, this power can come only when we supply the means—we stretch out the hand of faith even as the seaman hoists the sail. Because God is present in the world, faith succeeds and thus confirms itself. Our faith passes into a personal experience with the Savior.

Do you have this power in your life? If not, surrender to the Savior!

WEDNESDAY EVENING, MAY 25

Title: A Peculiar People

Text: "Who gave himself for us, that he might redeem us from all iniquity, and purify unto himself a peculiar people, zealous of good works. These things speak, and exhort, and rebuke with all authority. Let no man despise thee" **(Titus 2:14–15).**

Scripture Reading: Titus 2

Introduction

The passage of Scripture used in this message is a kind of summary of the several verses preceding it. It is good to review them. Verse 13 deals with Jesus' second coming and how it affects one's moral conduct. Verses 11 and 12 deal with the moral power of God's presence. The verses prior to these deal with the Christian character of different ages and of both sexes. In these two verses, Paul sums up all of these ideas by calling God's children "a peculiar people."

I. First, consider some significant words as they relate to this passage.

A. The word "for" in verse 14 is the first to be considered. This word identifies Jesus with all of his atoning work. This includes his incarnation, life, death, resurrection, ascension, intercession, and second coming. Thus it identifies him with the sinner and his sin. For contemporary use, it would be better understood as "instead of" or "on behalf of." Note two different passages of Scripture where it is used other than this text (John 11:50 and Gal. 3:13).

B. The word "redeem" in verse 14 is the second word to be considered. This word tells the story and purpose of the cross. It is why 1 Corinthians 6:20 uses a word translated "redeemed." It means to buy a slave in the marketplace. All unsaved people are slaves of sin and of Satan. When they are bought by the blood of Jesus, they become the possession of God. They are the redeemed.

Galatians 3:13–14 uses the term bought "out" of the slave market, and in Titus 2:14 one can see that the word is translated "from."

II. The special word in this text is the word peculiar (2:14).

A. This is a suggestion that the redeemed are the private possessions of God. Each person is distinct from the family as a whole.

B. How does this come about? What makes God's people peculiar?

1. They have been purified. The word purify means to make clean. The blood of Jesus applied to the sin of the sinner washes all the sin away and the sinner stands clean before God.
2. After the purification, the sinner becomes zealous for good works. Anyone who experiences this redemption has a motivation that will give him or her the kind of character mentioned in the verses immediately prior to these.

Conclusion

Paul tells Titus to speak of these things (Titus 2:15) and to live a clean life. Paul further tells Titus to exhort others to live this kind of life and to rebuke those who do not.

SUNDAY MORNING, MAY 29

Title: God Has a Plan for the Home

Text: "Hear, O Israel: The Lord our God is one Lord: And thou shalt love the Lord thy God with all thine heart, and with all thy soul, and with all thy might" **(Deut. 6:4–5).**

Scripture Reading: Deuteronomy 6:1–9

Hymns: "He Leadeth Me!" Gilmore

"Forward through the Ages," Hosmer

"Purer in Heart, O God," Davison

Offertory Prayer: O Lord God, how great you are! Eternal God, heavenly Father, Father of mercies, and God of all grace! I praise you and worship you for all your goodness and mercy to your people throughout the ages. We thank you for our health and our lives and for providing our needs. We acknowledge that we need you in our personal lives and in our families. We need you in our country and in your church. We are nothing within ourselves, but we are everything through you. Receive our offerings today for your use and glory. We gratefully give them to you through Jesus Christ our Lord. Amen.

Introduction

The home is battling for its life today. People are searching for fulfillment outside the home because their homes are unstable, lacking the foundation of principles that will guide the affairs of a family. More than half of all marriages end in divorce, and as a result, single parents are overburdened with the tasks of raising a family and working to provide for the family. This is not God's will for the home. God has a plan for the home just as he has a plan of redemption and a plan for every person's life. Let us discover some aspects of God's plan for the home. Deuteronomy 6 is one passage that reveals God's plan for our homes.

I. A place of spiritual strength.

God intends for the home to be a place of spiritual strength. Deuteronomy 6:4–5 tells us that we are to found our families on love for God and a spiritual relationship to him. God loves us, and we return his love toward us obediently. This is truly the beginning place, yet many forget, reject, or ignore God in their lives and homes.

A pastor recalls that one summer in England he visited the house of a lovely English couple. The husband was a pastor in the East End of London. All around their house and church was evidence of the destruction of war, but the couple themselves revealed the peace and assurance of a deep faith and devotion and love. The motto over the entrance to the house was "Lord, make my house Thine until Thine shall be mine."

In contrast, he described another house—a beautiful, modern dwelling with lovely landscaping in a fine residential section. To look at it, you would think it must surely be the dwelling place of a happy family. But he remembered that he had seen two unhappy couples live in that home, and he had watched both couples break up. What was the difference between the two homes? The family in the war-torn neighborhood had a personal relationship with the Lord that resulted in fellowship and great spiritual strength.

II. A place for divine truth.

All of the commandments, statutes, and judgments of the Lord are to be observed and taught to each generation. Verse 6 refers to the "words" that are so important, and verse 7 says that we are to "teach" them to our children. Not only is God to be loved and worshiped, but his words and commandments and faith are to be taught in our homes. At stake is the faith of the living God in the lives and homes of our nation.

The word "teach" means to whet, to sharpen. As a man sharpens a knife to make it more effective, so teaching sharpens the minds, hearts, and character of our children with divine truth.

We parents must accept this responsibility! It cannot be shifted to another without serious trouble. Someone has said, "Modern parents have become adept at the art of delegating. We send our children to a school to get their education, to the library to get their books, to the park to get their recreation, to the movies for their entertainment, and to the church for their religion. But there are some responsibilities that cannot be delegated. These belong fairly and squarely on the shoulders of the parents. The teaching of religion is one such responsibility." It is our responsibility to teach God's Word consistently for our children's spiritual awareness.

III. A place for Christian character.

God intends for the home to be a place to develop Christian character, as seen in Ephesians 6:4, "Bring them up in the nurture and admonition of the Lord."

Character development demands training, and the home provides it from infancy to maturity. I understand now why my dad sent me to the garden regularly. It was not just to hoe potatoes; rather, it was to build in me a sense of responsibility. I fussed and fumed within myself, but I learned something of character I could have learned in no other way.

Character development demands discipline. Verse 4 includes the idea of correction as well as instruction, and this is vitally important to a family. There can be no sense of direction for a child unless discipline is practiced. This is where respect for authority is learned; and this is where we learn to accept and understand one another and how to get along with one another.

God's Word is clear about the need to practice discipline. Proverbs 13:24 says, "He that spareth his rod hateth his son: but he that loveth him chasteneth him betimes." Proverbs 29:15 says, "The rod and reproof give wisdom: but a child left to himself bringeth his mother to shame." Verse 17 says, "Correct thy son, and he shall give thee rest; yea, he shall give delight unto thy soul."

Children need the security that discipline gives, and parents need the fulfillment that such leadership provides.

IV. A center of creative fellowship.

God intends the home to be a center of creative fellowship. When we talk about fellowship and, specifically, Christian fellowship, it is best described as "family spirit." Where such exists, there is love and forgiveness and understanding. It is a place where patience and kindness and courtesy thrive. It is the place of warmth and oneness of spirit. It is the oasis of fellowship in a world that starves for someone to care.

Conclusion

If we respond to God's Word as he calls to and leads our families in the light of his love and Word, we will experience the joy of God's plan.

A pair of farm parents were thrilled over their son graduating from a university. Uneducated themselves, they had sacrificed much to keep the boy in college for four years. At commencement time they were privileged to attend. Although the parents were poorly clothed and unlettered in education, the son welcomed them gladly and proudly presented them to the faculty and his classmates. On commencement day, the son gave the class address, and his listeners were moved by his message. As the boy returned to his seat, his father wiped a tear from an eye, and leaning toward his wife, he whispered, "Ma, that's the best crop we ever raised."

God does have a plan for your home if you will let him help you find it.

SUNDAY EVENING, MAY 29

Title: Being a Christian—Regardless

Text: "All the saints salute you, chiefly they that are of Caesar's household" **(Phil. 4:22).**

Scripture Reading: Philippians 4:14–23

Introduction

The concluding section of Paul's letters are always interesting. He almost invariably adds personal touches and often includes the names of people to whom he sends personal greetings. The last words of Paul in his letter to the Philippians are tender and intimate. He mentions the matter of their financial support and reminds them that it is more important for them to give than it is for him to receive. He assures them of his personal comfort and expresses thanks again for the things they have sent to him by Epaphroditus. He makes certain they understand that God is sufficient to meet all their needs.

Paul's final words to the Philippians are unique. He speaks of something he has never before experienced. After expressing the greeting of his fellow Christians, whom he calls "saints," he adds a unique phrase. He says that the "saints in Caesar's household" have a special word of greeting for the Christians at Philippi.

I. What is a saint?

Perhaps no word is more misunderstood within the framework of Christian terminologies than saint. Unfortunately, through the years a saint has come to be understood as a person who possesses a superabundance of virtue and piety. Because this meaning has become attached to the word, some people have shied away from using the term except in the context of mockery and criticism as though one who claims to be a saint is actually a hypocrite. In extreme abuse of the word, some religious groups have suggested that our prayers can be more effective if they are made through one of these "saints," who, because of their virtue, can get through to God where normal Christians fail.

The true meaning of saint in the New Testament, however, is far from these false conceptions. To put it simply, a saint is one who is a Christian. Every Christian is a saint. There are, of course, stages in our Christian growth, but this does not mean that the ones who have reached a certain stage of sanctification are saints while others are sinners. All people are sinners, but some are saved and some are lost. All who are saved are saints.

The words used in the original language, both in the Old Testament and the New Testament, for "saint" have the idea of purity, but even more is involved. The basic idea of both the Hebrew and Greek words has to do with being set apart. Purity comes when one is single-minded and is set apart for a special purpose. Thus, a saint is one who has been set apart by God for growth as a Christian. The word has nothing to do with a person's stage of growth. Thus the word saint may be applied to anyone who is truly a born-again believer.

II. What was "Caesar's household"?

To begin with, we can be sure that the phrase "Caesar's household" included more than members of the imperial family such as princes, princesses, courtiers, and nobles. In a broader sense, it included the thousand subordinates who served in various capacities for the benefit of the emperor, including slaves, freedmen, soldiers—anyone in the emperor's service. These people fulfilled various duties from menial domestic chores to supervisory positions. They literally belonged to Caesar's world and were at his beck and call to run his errands and humor his caprices. Archaeologists have uncovered tombs with inscriptions as to whom many of these men and women were and what they did. Caesar's household was indeed a strange and unlikely field for the cultivation of a Christlike life.

As Paul was a prisoner in his own hired house when he wrote the Philippian letter, he was in contact with various people who were dedicated to the service of the emperor. He had, no doubt, been able to lead many of them to faith in Christ. They maintained a perfunctory loyalty to Caesar as their emperor, but their higher loyalty was to Jesus Christ. They continued to serve faithfully the needs of their emperor, but if the choice came between loyalties, they were ready to give themselves, if need be, as martyrs to the Christian faith.

III. How can one be a saint in Caesar's household?

The history of Christianity through the centuries has been that of people seeking to be victorious over their environment. It is easy for us to fall into the habit of blaming "Caesar's household" for all that is non-Christian and second rate in our lives. When we do this, we are unfair to Christ, and we misinterpret the laws that operate in the realm of his Spirit. Also, we ignore our most precious emotional possession—freedom of will. When people say they cannot break with social customs and unworthy traditions, they are forgetting the greeting that came to the Christians at Philippi from the saints in Caesar's household.

A dedicated life is possible regardless of the circumstances, but it is never easy even among the most favorable environments. In the days of Paul, it cost some of the saints their lives. The martyrs were made living torches to illuminate the gardens of Nero. Others were made food for the lions or sport for the cheering crowds when Rome had a celebration.

There is only one way to be a "saint in Caesar's household." We must have a desire to please God whatever conditions exist and whatever the cost may be. We can find sympathetic fellowship among dedicated friends, but usually we find far more people hindering us in Christian living than seeking to aid and encourage us. When the world is at its worst, followers of Jesus need to be at their best.

Christians always have been called on to live godly lives in an ungodly world. Flawless honesty amid shady practices, and crystal purity of thought and deed in the midst of sensual and unclean things in social life are two of the main things that it takes to be a saint in Caesar's household.

If we have to apologize for our religious faith, we should discard it. God never intended for Christians to have a "hope I don't intrude" attitude. Christians should intrude. Jesus intruded. Christianity is a powerful and splendid intrusion into the selfishness and immorality of the world. We cannot wear the pearl of great price beneath a thin veil of compromise. If we try, we will lose the pearl!

In a stained world, we need pure hearts. We must keep a sweet spirit but maintain firm convictions.

Conclusion

How long has it been since your Christian faith called on you to make a tough decision? Did you make that decision to God's glory?

Our religion must be lived "in the marketplace" if it is to be effective. We cannot seclude ourselves from the rush and hurry of everyday living. Regardless of where we are and with whom we associate, Christ must be honored in our everyday living. We can be saints in Caesar's household if we wish to be, and we should earnestly desire to attain that goal!

SUGGESTED PREACHING PROGRAM FOR THE MONTH OF

JUNE

■ Sunday Mornings

Continue with the theme "Christ, the Church, and the Enrichment of Family Life" through Father's Day.

Then take up the theme "A Celebration of Freedom." This theme will run through July 24.

■ Sunday Evenings

The suggested theme for Sunday evenings is "Messages from the Past to the Present." Some mighty men of God who lived in the past can communicate God's message to us in the present.

■ Wednesday Evenings

Conclude the series of messages based on the book of Titus with an emphasis on the responsibilities of Christian citizenship (see July 6 entry), or use the "What Makes a Nation Great?" message on the last Wednesday of the month and complete the series on the first Wednesday in July.

WEDNESDAY EVENING, JUNE 1

Title: The Christian Citizen

Text: "Put them in mind to be subject to principalities and powers, to obey magistrates, to be ready to every good work, to speak evil of no man, to be no brawlers, but gentle, shewing all meekness unto all men" **(Titus 3:1–2)**.

Scripture Reading: Titus 3

Introduction

If there was ever an up-to-date message in Scripture, it is the Scripture for this message. The circumstances when it was written are similar to those that exist in the present era.

The Cretans were notoriously turbulent, quarrelsome, and impatient of all authority. So are the people of the world today. The Cretans were constantly involved in insurrections, murders, and internecine wars, and this reads like a modern newspaper.

The Scripture passage lays down six qualifications for the Christian citizen. All present-day citizens would do well to follow them.

I. The good citizen is to be law-abiding.

A. Unless laws are kept, life becomes chaotic. This is true in every respect. The Christian is to set the example of giving proper respect to those in authority.

B. This respect is true irrespective of the particular form or of the person in whom it is invested.

1. The government during the New Testament days left much to be desired. Pilate and Felix detained Paul, hoping to receive a bribe. Festus obstructed justice in regard to Paul. Pilate admitted he found no wrong in Jesus, yet he had him crucified.
2. The religious corruption of the Sanhedrin and the treatment of Jesus is almost unbelievable. So it was with Stephen. Our government today is corrupt from the top down.

II. The good citizen is active in service.

A. Interest of life lies in service. A modern disease is boredom, and this comes from selfishness. It is the principle, "Why should I do it? Let someone else!"

B. The motive as found in this text is purely Christian. It applies to all religious activities. Be ready to serve. It also applies to the secular. A citizen is to serve one's country with Christian principles.

III. A good citizen is to be careful in speech.

A. The Christian does not give way to an ugly temper and to sinful language. Christians are not to use cursing and foul language to denounce some person in authority. They are not to say about others what they would not like said about themselves.

B. The Greek word translated "evil" in the King James Version is "blaspheme." It means cursing or reviling God or the king who is God's representative. It means pronouncing the forbidden name of God and also irreverence toward anything that is sacred.

IV. The good citizen is to be tolerant, not contentious or a fighter.

A. This is not advocating compromise. There is a close relationship between standing on a principle that one believes to be right and guarding against being so opinionated that one cannot accept another.

B. The idea is that of always being an agitator. Christians are not to stir up trouble and cause disharmony.

V. The good citizen is to be gentle.

A. A good citizen is ever ready to temper justice with mercy.

B. A good citizen does not push legal rights to a moral wrong and is satisfied with less than is due.

VI. The good citizen is to be meek.

A. This is characteristic of the inner person and not just an outward behavior.
B. This is a person who has temper under control.
C. This is a person who patiently bears wrongs done to him or her.

Conclusion

No person can fulfill the qualifications of the Christian citizen apart from being a Christian. It takes the indwelling of the Holy Spirit to supply the characteristics Paul mentions to Titus in this passage.

SUNDAY MORNING, JUNE 5

Title: Trouble and Triumph in the Home

Text: "He that troubleth his own house shall inherit the wind: and the fool shall be servant to the wise of heart" **(Prov. 11:29)**.

Scripture Reading: Proverbs 11

Hymns: "All Hail the Power of Jesus' Name," Perronet
"Yield Not to Temptation," Palmer
"Amazing Grace," Newton

Offertory Prayer: Heavenly Father, we receive your love into our hearts this moment and return that love to you with thanksgiving in our hearts and praise on our lips. We also return it to you by giving our tithes and offerings to be used for the needs of others in the world. Thank you for the privilege of giving and for the joy of seeing you abundantly provide for our needs. Release those who are selfish and stingy from that kind of bondage. Grant that our hearts may be clean and pure as we place our offerings on your altar. In the name of him who is Lord of all, we pray. Amen.

Introduction

Our text is an unusual proverb that has a warning against troubling one's home. It is a message to all members of a household and is a plea for true harmony and happiness in the home. When we create disturbances in the home, we can expect to lose everything or, in other words, to inherit the wind.

There is no more needed message in America than the one concerning the home. Someone has said that what is wrong with America begins and ends with the family. But I hasten to say that there is hope for homes that find spiritual direction. Let us look at both the troubles and triumphs of the home today.

I. Troubles in the home.

What troubles the home today?

A. The home is troubled by the relative morals of the times. Popular ideas going around are "What I do is nobody's business except mine" and

"Anything goes as long as no one gets hurt." These ideas are based on the philosophy that there are no absolutes in life, that all of life is relative. It is openly declared today that lies, adultery, fornication, theft, promise-breaking, and killing are sometimes permissible, depending on the situation. But let us remember the words of Galatians 6:7: "Whatsoever a man soweth, that shall he also reap."

B. The home is troubled by social pressures, as seen in financial stresses, moral needs, and social demands. If permitted, social pressures will create disturbances in the home. Conformity to society is a powerful force.

C. The home is troubled by moral inconsistencies. Parents often have a double standard for what is permissible for themselves and their children. But children see the sins of their parents and are apt to copy them. What parents are surely is reflected in their children.

D. The home is troubled by spiritual indifference, as seen in the crumbling foundations of faith and in the uprooting of spiritual relationships. Studies in human behavior say that formal religion is one of the strongest influences of a happy home. Where husbands and wives actively participate in the life of a church, they tend to have lasting marriages. It takes much more than just a "church connection," however, for a home to know triumph. What will make our homes victorious?

II. Triumphs in the home.

A. The home needs leadership. God has willed that parents are the leaders in the home. Deuteronomy 6:4–9 is a command to parents to lead their children in the worship of God and the teaching of the Word in the home. God's Word is to be kept in our hearts, taught and talked about, and remembered in our daily lives. God's Word to children is in the fifth commandment, "Honour thy father and thy mother" (Ex. 20:12). These two ideas relating to parents and children dwell side by side in life. They create harmonious relations in the home.

B. The home needs love.

1. Love between husbands and wives, as seen in Ephesians 5:22–23. This is God's kind of love—real, deep, and meaningful.
2. Love that transforms a home from frustration and fussing to harmony and a healthy spirit.
3. Love that communicates itself, rather than nursing itself and the wrongs done to it.
4. Love that practices faithfulness to the marriage vows made at the marriage altar.
5. Love that expresses itself in the Christlike spirit of respect and thoughtfulness in the home.
6. Love that forgives one another. This is the key to solving many family conflicts.
7. Love that is positive-minded, that strives to be an answer rather than a problem.

8. Love that is growing, realizing that none of us are full-grown. God is not finished with us yet, so let us not only be patient with him, but also with ourselves and with one another.
9. Love that shares with others in all relationships.

III. The home needs a Lord.

Most of all, the home needs a Lord, Jesus Christ, to whom the family can look for direction and power. Just as he gives abundant life to individuals, he does also to families. He gives us direction and shares his presence with us daily.

In Acts 16 a man in deep spiritual need sought help for his life spiritually. He was saved, and in the experience made Christ Lord of his home. Is Jesus Christ Lord of your life? Is he Lord of your family?

Conclusion

Life's crises are too many and too deep to try to live without leadership, love, and Christ's lordship in your home. Will you open your heart to his triumphs? Anything less means trouble.

SUNDAY EVENING, JUNE 5

Title: The Man Who Led His People to God—Moses

Text: "Now therefore, if ye will obey my voice indeed, and keep my covenant, then ye shall be a peculiar treasure unto me above all people" **(Ex. 19:5)**.

Scripture Reading: Exodus 19:16–25; 35:4–5, 21

Introduction

When God reveals himself, it is in a manner suitable to the occasion. No revelation that God has made of himself has ever been so terrible as at Mount Sinai. No occasion in the history of the world demanded a more startling revelation than the circumstances surrounding this experience.

The Israelites gathered at the base of Sinai were sinful and debased by slavery. They were immoral and careless with freedom and were inclined to idolatry. This was God's prospect as he considered a plan to elevate them to the highest level of witness among the nations for ages to come. He decided to impress the Israelites with a divine revelation of his law and with the knowledge that dreadful consequences would follow their failure to obey his admonitions, hence God's use of thunder and other terrors at Sinai.

At other times and in other places, God followed quite different means in making himself known. To Elijah, he spoke in a still, small voice. To Isaiah and John, he revealed himself in visions. To the apostles in general, he spoke in words that magnified the teachings of his Son. To the apostle Paul, his revelation came through ecstasies, wherein Paul received unspeakable truths.

God's people must take advantage of every manifestation of God's presence, listen when he speaks, obey when he calls, and respond to every occasion when the Lord reveals himself in his own way. Let us notice the response of Moses to God's presence in this eventful hour of his life.

I. God's purpose expressed.

The events that transpired at Mount Sinai were truly providential. God intended that all the people should see and hear what came to pass at this place. What happened was the fulfillment of the divine plan to establish Moses as the permanent authority and messenger of all that God would reveal through him in the future. Earlier when God had met Moses at Sinai and had entrusted Moses with his message to Israel, Moses had pointed out that one of the difficulties was that Israel would not believe him. "They will not believe me, nor hearken unto my voice: for they will say, The Lord hath not appeared unto thee" (Ex. 4:1).

Without question, it was God's purpose to establish the position of Moses. The people had an inadequate sense of who God was and knew little or nothing about God's holiness. Therefore, in the midst of gracious and unfailing providences, they must be made to feel that it is a fearful thing to fall into the hands of the living God (Heb. 10:31). By the terrors of Mount Sinai, the Lord intimated to his people, once for all, that he was not a God to be trifled with but demanded careful and humble attention at all times.

God's concern has not changed through the years. His message of redemption is simple and clear so that all can understand. The writer of Hebrews encourages all people "to give the more earnest heed to things which we have heard, lest at any time we should let them slip" (Heb. 2:1). People are lost because they choose to be lost; they neglect the great salvation that God has to offer. To use a modern analogy, a businessman does not need to burn his store to ruin himself; all he has to do is neglect his business. Neglect will guarantee ruin in all areas of life.

II. The days of preparation.

Moses found it necessary to prepare the people for the Sinai experience. The manifestations were not to come all at once. The people had to wait for them, and the waiting period made it possible for them to make sufficient use of the time for preparation. This time of waiting must have produced a state of mind full of expectation and suspense. God fixed the day of his appearing (Ex. 40:34–38).

God has also set another day—the Day of the Lord. The precise moment of this event in time no one can tell. It was in mercy that the date of the visitation on Mount Sinai was made known to Israel. It will be in equal mercy that the great Day of the Lord will be unveiled. God is giving us adequate time to prepare for the experiences of this great day, and the Bible gives clear teaching on how to prepare. Jesus says, "Therefore be ye also ready: for in such an hour as ye think not the Son of man cometh" (Matt. 24:44).

We must learn from Jesus to work as well as wait. A large part of life is preparatory. At the moment Jesus felt impelled to begin his life work, he was called aside. And for the next eighteen years, his life was spent in the solitude of a humble home and in the daily round of humble toil. Paul retired to Arabia after his conversion to prepare for his work. The right kind of waiting always is followed by the right kind of working.

III. A new beginning.

It was a new day for the people of Israel when they "saw that great work which the Lord did upon the Egyptians: and the people feared the Lord, and believed the Lord, and his servant Moses" (Ex. 14:31).

Israel had learned a lesson. No longer would they waste their time in courting the favor of material gods. The people had become sick of false gods of silver and gold. They were too frightened at what had happened to seek out new inventions. They were penitent. When the good news came that God had forgiven them, their zeal for service knew no bounds. With a new determination to serve God, they discovered that God brings good out of evil. They learned that a revival is best revealed by the effect it produces in the life and conduct of the people. Now they were willing to hear. Now they were willing to give. Now they were willing to work.

The joy of salvation cannot better express itself than in the complete dedication to the work that God wants done in this world. It follows as the night the day; first there is the open heart and then the open hand. Obedience still is the key to every successful spiritual experience.

Conclusion

A study of the book of Exodus will serve as a genuine inspiration in spurring us on to serve God. We will see that God can remove difficulties that seem impossible to surmount or can empower us to conquer them. Two facts stand out as we examine the message of this great Old Testament book.

First, God does for us what we cannot do for ourselves. When trial and hardship confront us and it seems impossible to overcome them, he takes a hand. When difficulties appear with which we cannot cope, he interposes on our behalf. When we are bowed with the heavy load of dead hopes, he is working out our deliverance. When Israel was hemmed in at the Red Sea, and on their right was the wilderness and on their left great rock crags, before them the giant billows of the sea and behind them the pursuing Egyptians, the divine command rang out, "Speak unto the children of Israel, that they go forward" (Ex. 14:15).

Second, God never does for us what we can do for ourselves. He often requires cooperation before exercising power on our behalf. Many instances in Scripture show the blending of human and divine activity. God told Moses to stretch forth his rod and smite the waters. Before the walls of Jericho fell, the people obeyed God by marching around them for seven days. Jesus told the blind man whose eyes he anointed with clay to wash in the pool of Siloam that the cure might be completed.

Just as Moses led his people to God, so today the Holy Spirit leads us to serve our Lord Jesus Christ each day.

WEDNESDAY EVENING, JUNE 8

Title: A Look at the Past and a Warning for the Present

Text: "For we ourselves also were sometimes foolish, disobedient, deceived, serving divers lusts and pleasures, living in malice and envy, hateful, and hating one another" **(Titus 3:3)**.

Scripture Reading: Titus 3

Introduction

Titus 3:1–2 tells about Christian citizenship. This is followed closely by a presentation of what we were like before our redemption. This contrast reminds of what we were before we were saved and what it is still like for those who are unsaved.

I. Paul says, "We ourselves also were sometimes foolish."

A. Two words in this phrase demand attention. The word ourselves here is all-inclusive. The word sometimes means "once." At one time, all Christians everywhere were foolish.

B. Study the word foolish. It means without an understanding of spiritual things. Proverbs 17:28 says, "Even a fool who keeps silent is considered wise; when he closes his lips, he is deemed intelligent" (RSV). This word is a description of a mind that is unable to perceive a higher law.

II. Paul says, "We ourselves ... were ... disobedient."

A. A lack of understanding leads to disobedience. It is the opposite of submission, as is found in Titus 3:1. Prior to our conversion experience, this is our condition.

B. It is the opposite of what the mind under the Holy Spirit's control would dictate. It does not have proper reason, motive, experience, and conscience.

III. Paul says, "We ourselves ... were ... deceived"—that is, led astray.

A. A person who is ignorant of the Way is at the mercy of false guides. Before we can do God's work right, we must have perception. Apart from perception, we will sooner or later get on the wrong path.

B. The term "deceived" suggests the idea that we were caused to wander from the true path. We were persuaded in the wrong direction. When headed in the wrong direction, there is no way we can arrive at the proper destination. There is only one solution—to turn around and get on the right course.

IV. Paul says, "We ourselves ... were ... serving divers lusts and pleasures."

A. In the unconverted state, we were slaves to various passions and pleasures. We were helpless against them; they pulled us in all directions.

B. When these passions and desires dictate our minds, we become blind to what will be the result.

V. Paul says, "We ourselves ... were ... living in malice and envy."

A. Webster defines malice as "enmity of heart; ill will ... the state of mind shown by an intent to commit an unlawful act." All who are Christians know this to be their state prior to becoming Christians.

B. Envy is discontent at the sight of another's excellence or success. It is to begrudge or to desire to have an equal advantage.

VI. Paul says, "We ourselves ... were ... hateful and hating one another."

The idea of hating one another is totally unchristian. This is a contrast of the love Christians are to have for everyone. How God changes the heart of a person when he or she is saved is amazing.

Conclusion

One of the most glaring weaknesses in modern-day Christianity is that there is very little, if any, difference between many so-called Christians and the unregenerate. Let us make sure that others know we are Christians by the love of God and change of heart manifested in us.

SUNDAY MORNING, JUNE 12

Title: I Believe in a Christian Home

Text: "I call to remembrance the unfeigned faith that is in thee, which dwelt first in thy grandmother Lois, and thy mother Eunice; and I am persuaded that in thee also" **(2 Tim. 1:5)**.

Scripture Reading: 2 Timothy 1:1–7

Hymns: "O God, Our Help in Ages Past," Watts

"O Master, Let Me Walk with Thee," Gladden

"Must Jesus Bear the Cross Alone?" Shepherd

Offertory Prayer: O God, our heavenly Father, we praise you for your grace that saves and sustains; we praise you for your tender mercies to forgive us of our sins; we praise you for your faithfulness to keep your promises to provide for our needs; we praise you for who you are now and forever.

We lay our lives on your altar of dedication; we present our gifts of tithes and offerings as worship of your holy name. Bless them to their use in spreading the gospel and shedding the light of your Holy Word. In Jesus' name. Amen.

Introduction

More than a half century ago, a boy got into a terrible argument with his father. The father lost his temper and slapped the boy across the face. The boy ran out of the house and climbed upon some rocks above a lake. He said he was going to drown himself. Everyone knew he meant it. The father ran after him, still screaming. All the family and half the town became involved. Finally, they got the boy to come back home, but awful bitterness remained between father and son. The bitter son grew into a surly man. In fact, he reached a point where he was considered one of the most dangerous men in the world. His name was Mao Tse-tung, the former Communist leader of Red China.

Would a Christian home have made any difference? It made a difference in Timothy's life. He was born, reared, and instructed in a godly home. His grandmother's and mother's faith became his personal faith. It was not a proxy, impersonal, meaningless faith; it was so vital that it overflowed his life. One of my deepest convictions is that I believe in a Christian home. Let me say why.

I. I believe in the distinctiveness of a Christian home.

Something is distinctively different about a Christian home. One difference is love! Not a sentimental, selfish love, but a maturing attitude of thoughtfulness and consideration for others. It is the love that seeks to give to another's basic needs without looking for anything in return. This is God's kind of love; it is Christian love; it is the Bible's description of love; and it is the love of 1 Corinthians 13, where love is personal, patient, selfless, and lasting.

Another distinction is happiness. Joy is a mark of the Christian life. Jesus said, "These things have I spoken unto you, that my joy might remain in you, and that your joy might be full" (John 15:11). The Christian home thrills with joy and laughter. Those who live there know the meaning and ministry of a smile and practice it. The happiest homes I know are Christian homes.

A third distinction is forgiveness. Some homes know much about quarrels, fusses, feuds, and friction—strife and selfishness—but the members of a Christian home practice forgiveness. Sometimes unkind words are said in haste. Later forgiveness is asked for and received and fellowship resumes. That is the spirit of Jesus Christ in a home! We cannot exist joyfully without it.

II. I believe in the dynamic of a Christian home.

In our times, when the home is attacked by improper emphasis on such things as wealth, status, and sex, there is an inner dynamic that will save the home—the dynamic of faith, a believing relationship toward Jesus Christ. He is the Way, the Truth, and the Life; we cannot possibly experience a dynamic relationship with God apart from him (John 14:6). In him is life—abundant, overflowing, dynamic life (John 10:10).

For Mary and Martha, sisters of Lazarus, Jesus was the dynamic of their lives (John 11). At the time of Lazarus's death, Jesus came to them, knowing what he would do, with the question, "Do you believe?" (v. 26 RSV). The answer was,

"Lord, I believe" (v. 27 RSV). In that relationship there was power and light and life! Jesus is the source of hope, and he makes the difference for life and home.

Accompanying that dynamic faith is dynamic worship. I do not mean that dead, formal, unmoving type of worship that makes no difference to a person. I mean an awesome, personal, living, daily relationship with the Lord—life filled with praise and victory. I am not referring only to corporate worship, but also to worship that sets a joyful example for children in the home. Such worship molds and builds the spirit of the home. Children need to experience the power of God's Word and prayer at home. Homes that have this kind of worship know it and show it by the lives of the occupants.

III. I believe in the dividends of a Christian home.

A Christian home is a long-term investment that pays. Its dividends are assured. Its market value is always appreciating rather than depreciating.

Not everyone can become president or an all-American athlete or financially rich, but all young people who marry can do something creative about building a Christian home. It is questionable whether there is any other field in which so many can make a contribution and whose contribution will bear such great dividends.

Some years ago, there was a humble Christian home in England, a home that had few of the luxuries and comforts of life but that stayed close to the church and welcomed the church into all its relationships.

Three daughters were born to the parents of the home. These three daughters grew to young womanhood and were married. One of these girls became the mother of Edward Burne-Jones, the celebrated artist whose pictures we enjoy. Another became the mother of Rudyard Kipling, the famous author whose writings thrill us. The third girl became the mother of Stanley Baldwin, former prime minister of England. The parents kept the home in the church and the church in the home. In return, God gave beauty to inspire us, books to thrill us, and freedom that liberates us.

Conclusion

We can have Christian homes if we really desire them. We can have Christ in our hearts and homes if we invite him. We can have his daily leadership, life, and love as we make ourselves available to him. But we must make up our minds to do so!

SUNDAY EVENING, JUNE 12

Title: Worship That Pleases God—A Message from Amos

Text: "Let judgment run down as waters, and righteousness as a mighty stream" **(Amos 5:24)**.

Scripture Reading: Amos 5:4–9, 14–15, 21–24

Introduction

There has never been a time when people did not worship. Since the beginning of time, people have sought to have fellowship with the infinite. Thus people have worshiped the sun, moon, and stars. People have worshiped nature, bowing down to mountains, rivers, and various material objects that have attracted their allegiance. If suitable objects of worship could not be found, people created and still create these idols with their hands—idols of wood, silver, and gold.

Yet all such worship, past or present, serves only as an end in itself. Jesus condemned the Pharisees for overemphasizing the externals of formal worship. His constant invitation was for them to worship God in spirit and in truth. He called people to a worship that would transform the inner life, the only foundation on which successful character building takes place. Let us hear the word of Amos as he calls his people to discover the kind of worship that pleases God.

I. Moral corruption and religious zeal.

The prophet Amos observed that the religious forms of the Israelites involved nothing in the way of spirituality. "Yet have ye not returned unto me, saith the Lord" (Amos 4:4–6). They enjoyed their formal act of worship entirely apart from spirituality. They had a sensuous delight in music, oratory, and other ecclesiastical appointments, but their souls were insensitive to God's presence.

Today many confess that they attend the house of God exclusively for the music and singing, never waiting for the Word of God to be brought home to their hearts through the message declared from the pulpit. So often, the appeal that produces soul satisfaction and spiritual security is left out in the cold and the deeper senses are not moved. Going to church has no more bearing on the spiritual life than club-going, theater-going, or any other activity that would cause a temporary stirring of emotions.

External religious observances may quiet the conscience and smooth the pathway of the self-indulgent, but they fail to provide a release from the grasp of sin on the human heart. It is much easier to salve the conscience with some form of religious exercise than it is to crucify the flesh and to be separate from sin.

One of the greatest tragedies of our day is to witness the churches that are dying spiritually for the want of a spiritual dynamic that can move the conscience and the heart. Drawing near to God with our lips is a dangerous practice when the heart does not respond to his divine presence. God is still speaking, "Awake thou that sleepest, and arise from the dead, and Christ shall give thee light" (Eph. 5:14).

II. The emptiness of formality.

People who rest in forms are prone to multiply them. This is a logical necessity. If the form is everything, then the more of it the better. Besides, the sensation produced by it gets dull after a time, and to keep it fresh and full of strength, the dose must be continually increased.

Israel illustrated this principle in two degrees. They were particular about ceremonial observance. They offered the slain sacrifices, the praise offerings, the free offerings, and the tithes at their appointed times, but there was one glaring exception—they did not bring the sin and trespass offerings. That is, they had no consciousness of sin. They conducted themselves as people who had praise to offer and gifts to bestow but no sin to be atoned for or confessed. To a formalist, an adequate idea of sin is impossible, and in his worship the question is not raised. He believes that strict obedience to the letter of the law releases him from any sense of moral responsibility.

In this present day, when the individual is being lost in the whirl of modern society, we need a revival of personal responsibility. There is something for each person to do, and to do now. What our duty will be in the by-and-by is at best a matter of conjecture. With that we need not concern ourselves at present. Thomas Carlyle said, "Our grand business is not to see what lies dimly in the distance, but to do what lies clearly at hand." The Bible says, "Whatsoever thy hand findeth to do, do it with thy might; for there is no work, nor device, nor knowledge, nor wisdom, in the grave, whither thou goest" (Eccl. 9:10).

Let us dedicate all of our resources to serving our Lord acceptably so that our hearts might know the joy and the fullness of the life that worships him in sincerity and truth.

III. The consecrated life.

"Let judgment run down as waters, and righteousness as a mighty stream" (Amos 5:24). God demands morality in life and conduct. The way to worship God acceptably is not by ceremonial observances, not by religious contributions, but in daily confession of sin and daily renewal of the vow to do God's will in all relationships of life, with the express determination to take up the cross each day and follow Jesus Christ as Lord.

The end result of all true worship that pleases God is found in lives that are consecrated to the doing of God's work in God's way for God's glory. True consecration begins with the surrender of self. Speaking of the Macedonian churches, Paul wrote, "They gave themselves first to the Lord, and then by the will of God also to us" (2 Cor. 8:5 NIV). Paul caught the spirit of King David as he challenged the people of Israel to build the most magnificent temple that was ever erected by humans. David asked, " 'Who is willing to consecrate themselves to the Lord today?' ... The people rejoiced ... for they had given freely and wholeheartedly to the Lord. David the king also rejoiced greatly" (1 Chron. 29:5–9 NIV).

Conclusion

The prophet Amos was using every possible influence to awaken his people to the meaning and significance of genuine worship of the living God. He cried, "Seek the Lord, and ye shall live" (Amos 5:6). Amos believed that devotion to a grand aim gives glory and success to life. Consecrated people are strong because their activities are centered on one objective. The motto of such a life is, "This one thing I do" (Phil. 3:13). All people need to have aims outside the circle of their personal interests in order to save life from spiritual barrenness. They need to consecrate their service to some worthy goal in a wholehearted way to know what a blessed thing life can be.

The most joyful experience that can come to Christians is in worship when they set their affections on things above. The apostle Paul said, "Set your affection on things above, not on things on the earth" (Col. 3:2). Life becomes more meaningful when with consistent regularity people come to seek resources of spiritual power for life's duties. The smile and blessing of God will be on the person who confesses a need for divine wisdom and strength and yields to the Holy Spirit's guidance in witnessing to Christ's redeeming and saving message to a weary world.

"Seek the Lord and live," was the message of Amos for the people of his day. This challenge has not changed with the passing of the centuries.

WEDNESDAY EVENING, JUNE 15

Title: The Dynamic of the Christian Life

Text: "But after that the kindness and love of God our Saviour toward man appeared, not by works of righteousness which we have done, but according to his mercy he saved us, by the washing of regeneration, and renewing of the Holy Ghost; which he shed on us abundantly through Jesus Christ our Saviour; that being justified by his grace, we should be made heirs according to the hope of eternal life" **(Titus 3:4–7)**.

Scripture Reading: Titus 3

Introduction

Being a Christian is the most thrilling, rewarding, and happy life a human being can experience. It is amazing that many people who call themselves Christians live such drab lives. Our Scripture text tells about the dynamic life of the Christian.

I. This dynamic comes from a realization of what God has done for a person.

It comes from love and grace that no one can earn or achieve but can have only by faith.

A. This is the kindness of God (3:4). God's kindness is his goodness. Sometimes the word translated here as "kindness" is translated "goodness." It means being always ready and eager to give what is necessary. God is ready to give forgiveness and blessings as required. His is an all-embracing kindness that is issued in generous acts at all times.

B. This is the love of God (3:4). The word used here is not the word that is ordinarily thought of as God's love. It is kindliness to one's equal. It is that of a good king being good to his subjects. It is a generous man's compassion for those in trouble or distress.

C. This is the mercy of God (3:5). Nothing the Lord does for people is according to merit. Rather, "mercy" implies a wretched condition. It is not according to a person's works or goodness.

II. The means or process by which this salvation is communicated to people.

A. The washing of regeneration (3:5). This washing comes only from the blood of Jesus Christ. There is nothing in the form of works or acts that people can do to make themselves righteous before God. It all comes from the atoning work of Jesus on the cross. "Regeneration" means to become again. It is the imparting of divine life to the believing sinner.

B. The renewing of the Holy Spirit (3:5). When the life is worn-out and rundown, and the person takes Christ as Savior, he or she becomes a new person. This is the work of the Holy Spirit through Jesus Christ.

III. The effect of this dynamic life is threefold.

A. It brings forgiveness of past sins. The sinner is justified (3:7). In his mercy, God does not hold our sins against us. We are not to bemoan our sins but to look away from them and look to God.

B. It brings quality to present life. This concept is conveyed in the word "heirs" in verse 7. We do not really begin to live until Christ enters our lives.

C. It brings hope of greater things. Christians believe the better life is yet to come. Eternal life is the property of Christians now, but the consummation of that eternal life is even greater.

Conclusion

If anyone hearing these words does not have the dynamic life found in Jesus, I urge you to open your heart and let Jesus save you. This will be the beginning of real living for you, and you will have a truly dynamic life.

SUNDAY MORNING, JUNE 19

Title: A Father's Biggest Test

Text: "And it came to pass after these things, that God did tempt Abraham, and said unto him, Abraham: and he said, Behold, here I am. And he said, Take now thy son, thine only son Isaac, whom thou lovest, and get thee unto the land of Moriah; and offer him there for a burnt offering upon one of the mountains which I will tell thee of" **(Gen. 22:1–2)**.

Scripture Reading: Genesis 22:1–14

Hymns: "This Is My Father's World," Babcock

"Have Faith in God," McKinney

"Trust and Obey," Sammis

Offertory Prayer: Heavenly Father, we lift up our eyes unto the hills, from whence comes our help. Our help comes from the Lord, who made heaven and earth. We acknowledge that you are the Giver of every good and perfect gift, the source of every blessing.

We praise you that you are the Father of our Lord Jesus Christ and that you have blessed us with every spiritual blessing in heavenly places in Christ Jesus.

We acknowledge your command to us to give, and we confess our selfish desires to get rather than give. Forgive us, and put within us the grace to give generously as you have prospered us. We gratefully commit ourselves and our gifts to you for Christ's glory. Amen.

Introduction

Genesis 22 contains a beautiful picture of a father and son relationship. It is one of the most moving stories in all the Bible. It has a message for fathers that will give powerful direction. There are two beautiful pictures in this story.

I. The picture of the submission of a father to God.

Abraham becomes an object lesson for fathers as Israel is an object lesson for nations. The submission of Abraham is an awesome thing to behold. In Genesis 12 God calls Abraham to fulfill his plan. He promises him the land, an heir, and his blessings. In order for all this to be fulfilled, Abraham had to have a son. In an effort to hurry God's plan, Abraham had a son by Hagar as a result of Sarah's counsel. The son, Ishmael, however, was not the heir God intended, and much trouble has resulted ever since as a result of his birth. Finally, Isaac was born to Abraham and Sarah in their old age. He was known as the son of promise and was loved devotedly by Abraham.

One day God came to Abraham and commanded him to offer up as a sacrifice his only son, Isaac, the son of promise, the one through whom the nations of the earth were to be blessed. Abraham's response was immediate and full in that he yielded himself to God's direction. This was the biggest test of his life as a father.

A. It was a test of obedience to God's command. It related to his life, family, and future, but his response was complete. This is a father's deepest test, to commit himself and his family to God. Abraham obeyed God because he wanted God's best for his life and family. Is this what you want for yourself, your wife, and your children? Well, know then that obedience to God and his Word will bring it.

B. It was a test of faith. Abraham accepted God's will, believing God's promise. Romans 4:20–21 says, "He staggered not at the promise of God through unbelief; but was strong in faith, giving glory to God; and being fully persuaded that, what he had promised, he was able also to perform."

A Father's power rests in submitting to God and his principles, obeying him daily, trusting him to fulfill all that he promises to do, and submitting to his leadership.

The key to family harmony and direction is for fathers to become responsible for leading their families. A father is responsible to God and to his family to provide for their needs, to protect them in all types of situations, and to serve as a priest for them. Spiritual leadership in the home rests with the father.

How does a father exercise spiritual leadership? He is responsible directly to God for teaching, instructing, warning, and providing the basis for discipline in the family (Deut. 6:1–7; Prov. 4:1, 4–7; 6:20). He gives kind leadership to his children (Ps. 103:13) and guards against wounding their spirit by harshness and overcorrection (Col. 3:21; Heb. 12:9). Of the things that teenagers want from their fathers, these two come near the top of the list: they wish they would not lose their tempers so quickly, and they wish they would acknowledge when they are wrong. Wise spiritual leadership will take those things into consideration. A father also stimulates the faith of and gives encouragement to his children (1 Thess. 2:11). He takes time to give them personal attention.

II. The picture of the submission of a son to his father.

Every step of the story indicates that Abraham and Isaac had a close relationship. They traveled together to the spot where the sacrifice was to be made. Abraham must have tenderly told his son God's message, and with total yieldedness Isaac allowed his father to bind him to the altar. How like Christ he really was! Isaac was submissive to his father's will and authority, and in being so, he was beautifully submissive to God, who was responsible for the whole experience.

The amazing truth is that God works through fathers and mothers! Both are tools God uses to develop mature attitudes in the lives of sons and daughters. If a father fails to exercise his responsibility, a family is deprived of God's best. Extra pressure is put on the mother and children. Protection is removed from the family like an umbrella that is removed from over our heads during a rain. The father has a sense of guilt in his life—he knows something is missing, and it affects his relationship with his wife and children.

When fathers (and mothers) accept their responsibilities, it gives the children something to be submissive to. It is that submission of Isaac that is so beautifully described. Anything less has the ring of rebellion to it and is displeasing both to parents and to God.

A father is free not to accept the responsibility of spiritual leadership of his family, but he is not free to escape the consequences of doing so.

Conclusion

How can you as a father begin to be the spiritual leader of your home? First, you must acknowledge to God your lack of leadership. Second, ask your wife and your children to forgive you for your lack of leadership. Third, rearrange your priorities so that this new relationship will become a permanent one. Your priorities are in this order: your own personal spiritual growth and development, your wife and children, and then your work and ministry. Fourth, set a personal spiritual example. Let the family see you reading God's Word and hear you pray.

Fifth, begin to lead the family in Bible reading, prayer, and sharing. Sixth, give personal time to your children regularly for Scripture study, prayer, teaching, and sharing. Seventh, have a regular time with your wife for prayer and spiritual fellowship. Eighth, develop attitudes that encourage the family, such as love, patience, and faith. May God guide you to the highest mountain of his best for you and your family.

SUNDAY EVENING, JUNE 19

Title: A Courageous Scribe—A Message from Jeremiah

Text: "And Baruch wrote from the mouth of Jeremiah all the words of the Lord, which he had spoken unto him, upon a roll of a book" **(Jer. 36:4)**.

Scripture Reading: Jeremiah 36:4–8, 17–24, 32

Introduction

People who set themselves against divine truth and divine purpose are bucking the universe. It is vanity for people to attempt to hinder the declaration of God's truth. Truth is eternal. Kill all the prophets, and other prophets will be raised up. Destroy the prophets' writings, and more will be produced. Truth cannot be destroyed; it will survive all enmity.

God is persistent. Scheming and violence cannot stop God's will from being carried out. God does not change his plans to suit our desires. Scripture is clear on this point.

I. Reading the roll.

Baruch, secretary to Jeremiah, was sent to read this roll. Nothing is recorded here as to the reason why the prophet was detained. He often had made bold utterances in public before, but on this occasion we find that it was necessary for another to speak for him.

Truth is far more important than the speaker. The real importance is the message itself. People forget this today when they run after a Jeremiah and neglect a Baruch. With deep regard for the character of the person who proclaims the message, we must not forget that the gospel is far more important than the person who preaches it. Baruch did his work bravely and modestly. His duty was to read the roll. It was God's business to take care of the consequences.

The Bible is filled with references to the power of God's Word. Isaiah, prince of the prophets, magnifies the significance of the Lord's Word at work. He says, "So shall my word be that goeth forth out of my mouth: it shall not return unto me void, but it shall accomplish that which I please, and it shall prosper in the thing whereto I sent it" (Isa. 55:11). The Word of the Lord is lifted high as the prophet says, "For my thoughts are not your thoughts, neither are your ways my ways, saith the Lord. For as the heavens are higher than the earth, so are my ways higher than your ways, and my thoughts than your thoughts" (vv. 8–9). One of the most profitable and encouraging exercises for the believer is a study of Psalm 119, which can be summed up by the psalmist's words in verse 11: "Thy word have I hid in mine heart, that I might not sin against thee."

In all of our churches, there needs to be a revival of listening to what God says through his inspired Word. Unmeasurable blessing will come to God's people as they rededicate themselves to the reading of his inspired Word.

II. Burning the roll.

When the princes informed Jehoiakim of the circumstances connected with the reading of Jeremiah's prophecies, the king sent Jehudi, an attendant, to bring the roll and read it to him. The king showed contempt for the Word of God by permitting a servant to read it instead of sending for Baruch. As the roll was read, the king cut it up and flung it into the fire. He carried out this act of rage and folly until all of the roll was destroyed. He did not have the courage to face the demanding words the prophet had spoken concerning him. He tried to prevent this word from having any influence on others. Though he could vent his rage on the records, he could not touch the truth contained in them.

Are there not many people today who inwardly sympathize with the violence of Jehoiakim? They do not dare to say that they wish the Bible would be destroyed, but because there are things in it that strongly testify against them, they keep his Word out of their sight. The burning of the roll was a great loss to the king, for it contained the only prescriptions for the healing of the distresses in his personal life and in the lives of his subjects.

The Bible is sent for the good of the worst of people. Their rejection of it results in their own personal loss. The Bible says, "Taste and see that the Lord is good" (Ps. 34:8). A person can know more about honey in one minute by tasting it than in two hours by hearing a lecture on its delicious qualities. Thank God for the message of salvation so gloriously proclaimed in the Bible. A person can know more about salvation and God's redeeming love in one minute after being saved than could be told in a day.

An intelligent man of unusual ability was sincere in seeking to find God's plan for his salvation. He could not understand the simplicity of the gospel message. He questioned, "How can a person who has lived an ungodly life be saved all at once? It is not reasonable." Yet the Lord's answer comes most clearly. It may not be reasonable, but it is true, and that is the most important thing. God hates sin, but he loves the sinner. And God is willing to save the sinner at once. No matter how unfit a person may be, God's salvation guarantees that that person will survive. The Lord does not accept a person because of personal merit or good works. The Bible says, "If thou shalt confess with thy mouth the Lord Jesus, and shalt believe in thine heart that God hath raised him from the dead, thou shalt be saved. For with the heart man believeth unto righteousness; and with the mouth confession is made unto salvation" (Rom. 10:9–10).

Destroying the Bible would not destroy truth. People would still need to be saved. "Believe on the Lord Jesus Christ, and thou shalt be saved" is forever the message of the Bible as it is recorded in Acts 16:31.

III. Rewriting the roll.

Under the inspiration of God, Jeremiah required Baruch to write another roll containing all that was in the roll that had been burned, along with additional words that were pertinent to the hour. When God speaks, people cannot prevent the sacred record from being recorded. There is nothing to be gained by opposing the eternal will of God.

Why should the roll be rewritten? The words it contained could be executed within any reissue of them. Yet, out of a great loving heart and his long-suffering grace, God issued his warning afresh. Once more God sent his written message to move and impress the same people. The continuance of revelation to us is a constant reminder of God's forbearing mercy.

In our day, we do not believe that the Bible needs to be rewritten. It needs to be reread. Our hearts need to be reminded that the central message of the Bible is that Jesus Christ came into the world to save sinners. His mission was proclaimed with boldness and calmness. In proposing to reconstruct the entire human race, he saw no possibility of failure. He looked confidently forward to the conquest of the world. He founded a church that has continued to this present day to witness for him and to tell the story of his power to bring people into that fellowship that endures for time and eternity. He is the wonder of the past, the most potent power for good in the present, and the only hope for the future.

Conclusion

The message we proclaim has its origin in the Bible. We still believe that this message is the power of God unto salvation. Christ is a practical force in our world today. Let us rededicate our resources to him whose purpose is still to save the world from the power, the penalty, and the curse of sin.

WEDNESDAY EVENING, JUNE 22

Title: Action and Discussion

Text: "This is a faithful saying, and these things I will that thou affirm constantly, that they which have believed in God might be careful to maintain good works. These things are good and profitable unto men. But avoid foolish questions, and genealogies, and contentions, and strivings about the law; for they are unprofitable and vain. A man that is an heretick after the first and second admonition reject; knowing that he that is such is subverted, and sinneth, being condemned of himself" **(Titus 3:8–11)**.

Scripture Reading: Titus 3

Introduction

If one reduces this passage to its bare statement, it says there are times when discussion is superfluous and bad, and there are times when action is needed.

By implication, then, one can say that discussion is bad when it is at the expense of action. At times a matter can be discussed to death while action is desperately waiting.

I. This passage stresses the need for Christian action.

A. Titus 3:8 says, "Be careful to maintain good works. "The word "maintain" as it is used in this verse is to stand in front. It is a picture of a shopkeeper standing in front of his shop. The time comes when we are not to lag or drag but are to take our place in the front ranks. We are to continue to devote thought and care to excellent works.

B. "Good works" has more than one meaning. Christians are to be engaged in work that is respectful and useful. They are not to be employed in dishonorable work or that which would be contrary to God's will. Another meaning is that Christians are to practice good deeds and deeds that are helpful to humankind.

II. This passage warns against discussion.

By "useless" is meant the things that are foolish, dull, or stupid.

A. The things Paul mentions in verse 9 had real meaning in that day and especially to those with whom Titus was dealing. A discussion of them in contemporary society has less meaning.

It is much easier to get into a big discussion and spend much time in the discussion than it is to be kind, considerate, and helpful. There is no particular virtue in sitting around and discussing a matter when there is a task to be done. Of course, there are times when discussion results in action or when discussion is necessary before action is taken.

B. Paul says contentious and opinionated people should be avoided. This concept applies to the church and to individuals. The church should avoid these kinds of people. They are troublemakers rather than helpers. But individuals should also avoid people who create problems. They are called heretics (Titus 3:10). This word comes from two words—one meaning "to choose," and the other, "a party." Heretics foster division. Trouble creeps in when a person sets private opinion against the Word of God and tries to influence others. A heretic is one who has falsely determined that he or she is right and everyone else is wrong (v. 11). Such a person is subverted—turned or twisted away from the path of right.

Conclusion

A current danger in many churches is that people are spouting their own opinions rather than resting in what the Word of God says. As a result, there is a lot of discussion that leads to division. When division happens, Satan is the winner and the church loses. It is time for the church to recognize the work of the enemy and stand together on the Word of God.

SUNDAY MORNING, JUNE 26

Title: The Cultivation of a Christian Conscience

Text: "Thus, sinning against your brethren and wounding their conscience when it is weak, you sin against Christ" **(1 Cor. 8:12 RSV)**.

Scripture Reading: 1 Corinthians 8:1–13

Hymns: "Take Time to Be Holy," Longstaff
"Let Others See Jesus in You," McKinney
"More Like the Master," Gabriel

Offertory Prayer: For the warmth of the sun and the beauty of the day and the productivity of the soil, we thank you, heavenly Father. Thank you for every indication of your grace in your provisions for our continued well-being. Today we praise you with our spirits, souls, and bodies. We give the testimony of our lips and the treasure of our hands that your kingdom might advance and that people might come to know the healing power of the help that comes from Jesus Christ. Bless these gifts and those who receive special benefits from them. In Jesus' name. Amen.

Introduction

We often have heard people say, "I always follow my conscience. If you follow your conscience, you will never go wrong." Is this necessarily so? The word conscience needs careful definition and a proper understanding.

Some consider their conscience to be "the voice of God within," which will guide them unerringly to that which is right. These people are disillusioned when they later discover that they have been wrong or have done that which is harmful to themselves or to someone else.

Conscience has been defined as "a God-given sense of oughtness." Conscience is an inward conviction that there is such a thing as right and wrong. People have an inborn sense of "oughtness." This inborn sense of obligation to do what is right and to avoid what is wrong is the common possession of Christians and non-Christians alike.

The Bible speaks of many different kinds of conscience. One can have a weak conscience, a good conscience, a pure conscience, an uneasy conscience, or a guilty conscience; the conscience also can be ignorant. Paul confesses that he persecuted the church without any qualms of conscience at all (Acts 26:9–11). It was not enough for him to merely be sincere in what he was doing. Paul speaks of those who have a seared conscience (1 Tim. 4:1–2). He also speaks of a defiled or corrupt conscience (Titus 1:15).

These passages of Scripture and these illustrations demonstrate that the conscience cannot always be treated as if it is the voice of God within.

I. The content of conscience.

A. We need to recognize that the content of our conscience is the result of the education we have and the decisions we have made concerning right conduct.

1. The teaching received from parents, be it good or bad, forms a part of the content of one's conscience.
2. The customs of the community form a part of the content.
3. The thoughts, habits, and ideals of one's peer group form a part of a person's conscience.
4. The content of one's conscience can be formed by books read, television programs and films watched, and music listened to.

B. We need to recognize that one's conscience is not an inerrant guide.

1. One can be mistaught by parents or teachers.
2. One can choose a peer group whose ideals and philosophy are diametrically opposed to what is good for the individual or the community.
3. One can come to a faulty conclusion as a result of thinking that is not straight and fully informed.

II. The authority of conscience.

A. While the conscience may not be inerrant, one is wise to follow the dictates of his or her best conscience.

1. Not to do so is to create a guilty conscience.
2. Not to do so is to deprive oneself of a better conscience.

B. A conscience that is continually violated will cause one to lose a sense of God's presence.

C. Only when the conscience is filled with the mind of Jesus Christ and led by the Holy Spirit can we have the assurance we are hearing the voice of God within.

III. Guidelines for the Christian conscience.

In seeking to do what is right and to know what is the highest and the best, we should ask several questions.

A. Questions concerning the effect of a course of conduct.

1. What effect will this have on me personally—both short-term and long-term?
2. What effect will this have on others?
3. What effect will this have on the cause of Christ?
4. What effect will this have on the non-Christian?

B. Four tests concerning moral decisions we face.

1. The test of secrecy. Do we want to keep this secret? If so, it is doubtful.
2. The test of publicity? Would we be willing for the public to learn fully of our decision at this point?
3. The test of universality. Would the entire community be uplifted if each person arrived at the same decision?

4. The test of prayer. Can I truly ask God's blessings on this decision and this course of conduct?

IV. Cultivating the Christian conscience.

We must not assume that our conscience is fully Christian merely because we have trusted Jesus Christ as Lord and Savior. The Christian life should be looked upon as a journey from the mind of the flesh to the mind of the Spirit. We should seek daily to be more like Jesus Christ in both thought and conduct.

A. The conscience must be educated and disciplined by the renewal of the mind (Rom. 12:1–2).

B. Our conscience should always be subjected to the will of God for our life and for others. Instead of merely following the dictates of our conscience, we should seek to know the will of our loving Lord.

C. We should walk in the Spirit (Gal. 5:16). Our daily walk should be one of faith in the leadership of the Holy Spirit as we seek to let the Spirit guide our thinking and determine our attitudes and actions.

D. We can develop a Christian conscience by studying the Word of God and letting the great truths of the Scriptures determine the content of our conscience.

Conclusion

Do you have a guilty conscience that accuses you of some evil, some failure, some shortcoming, some mistake? Congratulations if you do. There is hope for you if you will follow the leadings of this conscience to make confession and, where possible, restitution. A conscience that hurts is indicative of the fact that your conscience is not corrupted and seared. A conscience that hurts is God's way of telling you that he wants to help you and that he will help you.

Recognize a guilty conscience as God's call to a nobler way of life. It is not necessary that you continue to suffer from a guilty conscience. Come to the Father God in confession and repentance, and experience his cleansing and forgiving grace (1 John 1:9).

SUNDAY EVENING, JUNE 26

Title: A Preacher of Repentance—John the Baptist

Text: "Bring forth therefore fruits worthy of repentance" **(Luke 3:8)**.

Scripture Reading: Luke 3:7–10

Introduction

John the Baptist was the son of a well-known priestly family. Thus his reputation probably preceded his divine summons to proclaim the gospel of repentance. His family, the marvelous circumstances attendant on his birth, and his ascetic manner of life all contributed to making him a marked person. So when John left his solitude and time of preparation, multitudes flocked to hear the burning message and the divine eloquence of one long looked upon by the people as set apart for a great work.

John ministered mainly to the people of the villages in the Jordan Valley, making it convenient for his baptismal candidates. He did not confine his preaching to one area. The expectation of the Messiah had been the root of all true life in Israel for centuries. Because of so many mistaken notions about the Messiah, the misconceptions about his character and his reign, it became necessary for God to raise up a prophet like John who would have the assignment of preparing the way of the Lord. We can still hear him saying, "I indeed baptize you with water; but one mightier than I cometh, the latchet of whose shoes I am not worthy to unloose: he shall baptize you with the Holy Ghost and with fire" (Luke 3:16). He called them to turn from their old thoughts, from their state of satisfaction, and to mend their ways.

Let us give careful study to the life and work of a man so aptly known as John the Baptist.

I. A day of decay.

Glory and honor were passing rapidly from the Jewish kingdom. The ancient glory of the Israelitish monarchy only made the present decline more impressive. The kingdom needed to be revived, and it needed a new leader. The fullness of time surely had come.

The Jewish religion was decaying, becoming traditional rather than experiential. The letter of the law had become a burden rather than a blessing. People were mumbling meaningless holy words, thinking that this was the stuff out of which religion was made. They were closing their eyes to the sore spots of civilization and hiding themselves in the vast recesses of the temple.

Reformation, therefore, was sadly needed. The hour struck. God appointed and commissioned his man. Moral decay called for radical surgery. Repentance was the only means by which spiritual health could be restored.

God's remedy for the helpless, sin sick soul has never changed with the passing of the years. "Wilt thou be made whole?" is still the question the Lord puts to the hearts of wandering humanity. God's appeal to apply this remedy is still the same. "Believe on the Lord Jesus Christ, and thou shalt be saved" (Acts 16:31).

II. A pioneer of the Lord.

John, like a pioneer, was to make a smooth pathway for the Prince of Peace. But the valleys to be raised, the mountains to be laid low, the crooked to be made straight, and the rough way to be made smooth were not outward or physical obstacles. It was not by force that they were to be overcome, but by a voice, by a cry. The valleys represented the depressed and the despairing. The mountains represented the exalted and the proud. The crooked represented the twisted in sin. The rough ways spoke of the rugged and uncouth in nature. All these classes, through John's preaching, were to be prepared for God's salvation in the person of the Messiah.

This pioneer proclaimed that reformation was needed in order to have better times, and reformation had to begin in a person's heart by the grace of God. Repentance has been defined as a taking of God's side against ourselves. This was the spirit of John's reformation. It was a call to arms against self, not against one's neighbors. And it is here that all true reformation must begin. We must be transformed in heart by the grace of God in order for there to be reformation in the world.

Pioneers for God still have a place in our modern world to make known God's eternal plan of salvation. Determining to be a witness for the Lord is the most meaningful decision a believer can ever make. Our testimonies in word and deed can bring people to the knowledge of the hope that lasts for all eternity.

III. Preaching plain and practical.

John did not mince matters. The vast multitudes that came to hear him were of the Pharisaic class. Proud to be children of Abraham according to the flesh, they imagined that this was sufficient to secure their acceptance with God. In spite of their good pedigree, they possessed poisonous hearts, stung neighbors like vipers, and did unbrotherly things. As a faithful messenger of God, John told his hearers what they were—a "generation of vipers" (Luke 3:7). Thus he warned them to flee from the wrath to come, to repent. If sorrow for sin is genuine with us, God will work out the transformation in our conduct.

Jesus can read the human heart. Our Lord is a heart specialist of the first magnitude. Notice what he has to say about it as the Great Physician: "Out of the heart of men, proceed evil thoughts, adulteries, fornications, murders, thefts, covetousness, wickedness, deceit, lasciviousness, an evil eye, blasphemy, pride, foolishness" (Mark 7:21–23). These thirteen specifications show us the blueprint of the human heart. The observation is not very flattering. But unless this matter of sin in the human heart is dealt with by the blood of Jesus Christ, it is only a question of time until we incur God's eternal punishment for sin. What a tragic moment it is when unbelievers move out into a darkness from which they will never return.

Conclusion

People cannot escape the moment when they must give an account of themselves to God. Are you living in the midst of unhallowed pleasures? God knows about it. Are you immersed in worldliness? God knows about it. Are you living in secret sin? God knows about it. Every person needs to know where he or she stands before God. Pause and take your bearings. Find out your spiritual latitude and longitude. If you are in the wrong place, you need to know it. Self-ignorance at this point is fatal, and those who are out of harmony with God are on the way to ruin.

There was a certain man whose one ambition in life was to make a fortune—and he made it. As the years went by, he began to reflect on the fact that he would not always stay in this world. Day after day he thought of many ways by which he might secure his hope of heaven as his eternal home. He came to the conclusion that the giving away of his money to help unfortunate people would guarantee his entrance through the portals of heaven. One night he dreamed he saw a ladder reaching to the very door of heaven. He noticed that with the giving away of each gift, he mounted round after round on the ladder. So he said good-bye to his friends and started to climb. On and on he climbed past clouds, past the moon, past the stars. Suddenly his ladder came to an end. He was awakened with a start with the awareness that his ladder was extended out into the immensity of space. Then he realized that even though he had given away his money to help others and had performed many good works of love and charity, without Jesus Christ he was lost.

The lifeline of the gospel is thrown out to you in these moments. Grasp it by faith in Christ and make the angels of heaven happy now. Join the millions of redeemed who sing the glorious hymn of security, "I know whom I have believed, and am persuaded that he is able to keep that which I have committed unto him against that day" (2 Tim. 1:12).

WEDNESDAY EVENING, JUNE 29

Title: What Makes a Nation Great?

Text: "Righteousness exalteth a nation: but sin is a reproach to any people" **(Prov. 14:34)**.

Scripture Reading: Proverbs 14:12–34

Introduction

Note: You may want to begin this service by singing some patriotic hymns, such as "My Country, 'Tis of Thee," "America the Beautiful," or "God Bless America."

The United States of America is a great nation. We have been preserved these many years by God. We have grown in numbers, wealth, and power. America has a surplus of the necessities of life and offers the freedom of opportunity. Truly we are a God-blessed nation. What has made America great?

I. A nation becomes great when that nation has the right kind of citizens.

The people of America have helped make America great.

A. God-fearing citizens make a nation great. Dr. J. D. Grey said in an address before a Kiwanis International Convention in Seattle, Washington, June 15, 1952:

> The founders of our nation were, in the main, a God-fearing, God-honoring people. They were not the renegades, the backwash, the off-scourings of the nations of Europe. Among the fifty-six signers of the Declaration of Independence, forty-seven

of them were graduates of Christian colleges, eight of which were functioning in our land before 1776. But even prior to this, when the Pilgrims were about to land at Plymouth Rock, they bowed their knees before almighty God in grateful recognition of his blessings upon them in bringing them to a safe harbor, and in that spirit they dedicated to him their endeavors in this new land.

B. Freedom-loving citizens make a nation great. The people who came to the shores of America were people seeking freedom. The framers of the Constitution of the United States were freedom-loving people. America's name has been made glorious because her citizens are people who love freedom and want freedom for all people.

C. Sacrificial-living citizens make a nation great. In moments of crises, Americans have shed precious blood to protect America.

II. A nation becomes great when the citizens establish the right kind of institutions.

A. Homes.

B. Churches.

C. Schools.

D. Businesses.

All of these great institutions have contributed to America's greatness.

III. A nation becomes great when the citizens are righteous.

The writer of Proverbs said, "Righteousness exalteth a nation: but sin is a reproach to any people" (14:34).

A. What are some of the evils that threaten America today?

1. Atheism. Atheism manifests itself in many ways. Millions in America do not believe in God at all. Millions more claim they believe in God and Christ but live like pagans, ignoring God in their thinking, planning, and living.
2. Materialism. Many Americans have made materialistic objectives their goal. They spend their lives getting things.
3. Socialism. The equal distribution of the wealth of America is the *summum bonum* to the socialist. Equal rights before the law and a fair opportunity are not enough. Under socialism, thrift is penalized and laziness is rewarded.
4. Alcoholism and drug abuse. Substance abuse in America has become a major problem. Social pressure, business pressure, and spiritual emptiness have driven many to become slaves of alcohol and other drugs.
5. Secularism. In America there has been a concerted effort to take God out of schools and government. One of the enemies of America is secularism.
6. Violence. Dr. H. H. Hobbs tells the following story:

> A newspaper writer tells of going to a crowded theater in New York the night after Senator Ted Kennedy died. The movie glorified a man who delighted in shooting people in the head while they were on their knees pleading for life. As he put his gun to a horrified victim's head and pulled the trigger, the audience laughed. After killing a priest, someone in the film remarked, "I don't like that. It is bad luck to kill a priest." The audience laughed heartily as though it was viewing a comedy rather than a tragedy. What is happening to our world? We want blood, blood, and more blood.

We live in days of violence that threaten our nation.

7. Evil forces, demon forces, threaten America. Paul said, "Now the Spirit speaketh expressly, that in the latter times some shall depart from the faith, giving heed to seducing spirits, and doctrines of devils" (1 Tim. 4:1). It seems as if satanic forces have invaded our nation.
8. Humanism threatens America. Public schools and colleges and the media are propagating the idea that oneself is one's god. From this false teaching stem other evils such as abortion and euthanasia.

B. What will save America from these evils and make our country strong and great? The writer of Proverbs has the answer for us—righteousness!

1. Righteousness is required by God. A nation will be punished for its sins. America must repent of its sins because God requires righteousness.
2. Righteousness will bless a nation.
3. Righteousness is found in following Christ. National righteousness will follow where there is submission to Christ. We must repent of our sins and put our faith in Jesus Christ if we want to be righteous.

Conclusion

God will bless America if we turn to Christ, our only hope, our sufficient Savior.

SUGGESTED PREACHING PROGRAM FOR THE MONTH OF JULY

■ Sunday Mornings

Continue with the theme "A Celebration of Freedom" for the first four Sunday mornings of the month.

On the last Sunday morning of the month, begin a new nine-part series titled "Qualities of Discipleship." If disciples are to make a quantitative impression on the unbelieving world, they must do so in a qualitative manner. The parables used in these sermons focus on some essential qualities of heart.

■ Sunday Evenings

"Relevant Questions Facing Americans" is the theme for the first four Sunday evenings in July. Every question should be faced with honesty and with a desire for divine leadership for ourselves and our country.

On the last Sunday evening of the month, begin the series "Knowing the Character of God," which focuses on five of the great parables of our Lord that highlight God's character. Our concept of God affects our response to him and to others.

■ Wednesday Evenings

Finish the series from Titus on the first Wednesday of the month or use the "What Makes a Nation Great?" message (see June 29 entry).

On the following Wednesday, begin a series of expository studies from Jude on problems facing the church. The suggested theme is "A Big Message from a Little Book."

SUNDAY MORNING, JULY 3

Title: Forms of Freedom

Text: "Stand fast ... in the liberty wherewith Christ hath made us free, and be not entangled again with the yoke of bondage ... ye have been called unto liberty; only use not liberty for an occasion to the flesh, but by love serve one another" **(Gal. 5:1, 13)**.

Scripture Reading: Galatians 5:1–3, 13–16

Hymns: "A Mighty Fortress Is Our God," Luther

"America the Beautiful," Bates

"Mine Eyes Have Seen the Glory," Howe

Offertory Prayer: Our Father, we thank you for the freedom for which others sacrificially gave themselves, which demands our constant vigilance and consistent practice, which all people aspire to enjoy, and which is fully found only in and through your Son, Jesus Christ, in whose name we pray. Amen.

Introduction

Over two centuries ago a few men assembled in Philadelphia endorsed the words of Thomas Jefferson that prefaced one of the major political revolutions in human history, words that stir the feelings of persons who seek and value freedom: "We hold these truths to be self-evident, that all men are created equal, that they are endowed by their Creator with certain unalienable Rights, that among these are Life, Liberty, and the pursuit of Happiness."

Freedom—the ideal in every age. Where do we seek it? How do we exercise it? Let's consider some forms that peoples' quest for liberty take.

I. Some seek freedom by force.

A. People who want freedom for themselves seek it through force. What they want, they take. They respect neither the person nor the property of others. Their sole intent is to satisfy their own lusts, whatever their nature.

B. The philosophy of this quest is that "might makes right." It is the philosophy of the bully who demands that others give in to his wishes. He uses verbal force or threats when possible, physical force or violence when necessary.

Force cannot bring freedom. When people get on top by force, they become the victims of two forces against which they have no protection—a lust for more power and a fear of those below them who aspire for freedom through the overthrow of their freedom. Lust and paranoia become the bully's captors. They gain deliverance from them only as they succumb to another bully. As Jesus said: "All they that take [or live by] the sword shall perish with the sword" (Matt. 26:52). The "fastest gun in the West" was a wanted man—wanted by each gunman who wanted the reputation of being the fastest. The team that brags about being number one is the one other teams want to beat.

C. The exercise of raw force inspires in its victims a yearning for real freedom. When English officials used imprisonment in 1667 in an effort to force William Penn to give up Quaker views, he said, "The jail will be my grave before I'll change one jot.... The Tower was the worst argument to use against me; for whoever may be right or wrong, those who use force can never be right."

II. Most seek freedom through law.

A. Civilized society cannot exist where each does what is right in his or her own eyes (Judg. 21:25), where personal whim and force are the only guides to social conduct. One theme of human history is the futility of force, the law of the jungle. Another is the quest for rules or laws for ordering society.

B. The Declaration of Independence is history's best-known statement of this quest; the US Constitution and its Bill of Rights are the most celebrated expressions of its achievement. One states, the other assumes, that "the Laws of Nature and of Nature's God entitle" people to the equality to which all people are created; that government's purpose is to secure human rights; that government derives its just or lawful powers "from the consent of the governed"; that public officialdom, which is insensitive to human rights and humane laws—in 1776, a king—is a threat to freedom, as a train of twenty-seven abuses and usurpations proves; and that lovers of freedom through law look "to the Supreme Judge of the world for the rectitude of ... intentions," rely "on the protection of divine Providence," and "pledge to each other ... Lives ... Fortune and ... sacred Honor." The Constitution rests on the premise that government's powers are dangerous when concentrated, so it distributes them: the legislature has the power to make laws; the executive, to administer them; and the judiciary, to interpret them. The Bill of Rights rests on the premise that some rights are beyond the reach of government's power.

C. The philosophy of freedom through law is, as President Gerald R. Ford phrased it in his inaugural address, that "right makes might"—that is, right laws are a beneficent force, essential to civil tranquility, domestic peace, and social harmony.

D. Law provides limited freedom at best. It marks the boundaries within which one can operate freely but beyond which one cannot go. Often it appears in the negative, "Thou shalt not...." For law to work, all must be equally subject to it; also, officials must administer it even-handedly. We are not free to obey the laws we like and transgress those we dislike. Whoever seeks freedom under law—whether it be the Jewish law, which Paul, in Galatians, contrasted with the gospel and viewed as a tutor preparing for the gospel, or some other law—"he is a debtor to do the whole law" (Gal. 5:3). Sometimes we yearn for more freedom than law can provide, and we feel like applying to law what the song applies to other things—"Don't Fence Me In."

E. Anyone acquainted with the changing concept and practice of law in the last two centuries cannot avoid the conclusion that law is capable of abuse and that it can be a force that tyrannizes peoples' persons and spirits. Law is no better than those who make, execute, and interpret it, supported by people who have confidence both in the laws and in public officials. The US system rests on the view that God implanted a law in nature and that government's laws are to be consistent with it. In the mid–1800s, the "historical school" viewed law as the expression of folk custom, a view that served nationalism—one law for the Englishmen, another law for Germans, another law for Frenchmen, another law for Americans, and so on. Later the "analytical school" viewed law as something consciously created by lawyers, the state as the entity with sole power to create law, individual "rights" as nothing more than concessions granted by the state, and compulsion, not justice, as the criterion of law. Still later, the "pure theory" school emphasized the procedure by which the state enacts law, not the substance of law, as the clue to law; if lawmakers employ the "pure" procedure or form, law is valid, whatever its nature. Such a view of law provided the basis for several twentieth-century dictatorships, one of them being Adolf Hitler's Third Reich, which acted according to positive or government-made law in all matters but violated elemental laws of nature.

F. However essential good laws, applied equally to all and administered even-handedly, are to ordered society, law cannot give people the full freedom for which they yearn. So one prays as Katharine Lee Bates prayed for America: "God mend thine every flaw, confirm thy soul in self-control, thy liberty in law."

III. Anyone can find freedom in grace, available through faith and expressing itself in love.

A. Freedom is available to anyone who believes in the gospel of Jesus Christ. This is the theme of Galatians, a letter written in the heat of controversy between those who tried to make Gentile Christians observe Jewish levitical and ceremonial laws (Judaizers) and those who insisted that God's grace, which leads one to believe in Jesus Christ, frees one from law's tyranny and liberates the spirit so that he or she can voluntarily accomplish only what law cannot achieve because of compulsion (Paul's party).

B. Spiritual freedom can exist even when human law constricts. When Paul wrote in prison, "I have learned, in whatsoever state I am [abasement or abundance], therewith to be content" (Phil. 4:11), he was a freer man than Emperor Nero, who was torn between his own ego drives and his fear of enemies. Madame Guyon, imprisoned by Louis XIV for ten years (1695–1705), said it well:

My cage confines me round;
Abroad I cannot fly;
But though my wing is closely bound,
My heart's at liberty.
My prison walls cannot control the flight,
The freedom of the soul.

Stone walls do not a prison make,
Nor iron bars a cage;
Minds innocent and quiet take
These for a hermitage;
When I am free within my heart
And in my soul am free,

Angels alone that soar above
Enjoy such liberty.

C. Love is the companion of faith. "There is no fear in love; but perfect love casteth out fear" (1 John 4:18). Where there is no fear, there is freedom.
D. Love fulfills what law at its best can only aim at. Law and officials are a terror to evil works, not to good works (Rom. 13:3). The ideal, which the best of laws seeks to attain by observing negative prohibitions ("Thou shalt not . . ."), is attained only by observing the positive demands of love: "Thou shalt love thy neighbor as thyself" (Gal. 5:14; Rom. 13:9).
E. If the Son of God makes us free, we are free indeed (John 8:36)! And from that time on, we are never the same. For, like our Master, we then minister as servants to others (Matt. 20:28).

Conclusion

If you want freedom, seek it where it can be found—not in force, however strong; not in law, however good; but in faith, which expresses itself in love.

SUNDAY EVENING, JULY 3

Title: Patriotism or Civil Religion—Which?

Text: "Live as free people, but do not use your freedom as a cover-up for evil; live as God's slaves. Show proper respect to everyone, love the family of believers, fear God, honor the emperor" **(1 Peter 2:16–17 NIV).**

Scripture Reading: 1 Peter 2:11–17

Introduction

In 1976 the bicentennial celebration that marked the two-hundredth anniversary of the signing of the Declaration of Independence sparked a great wave of patriotism and great interest in our nation's history. Much of this patriotism, however, was an idolatry that paralleled the sins of the past.

We need a Christian patriotism as never before. We do not need a blind loyalty to our nation's political government that will give blanket approval to every policy of every administration. Stephen Decatur once said, "My country, may she ever be right. But, right or wrong, my country." Some people today, far from echoing the words "My country, right or wrong," are even refusing to say, "My country when she is right."

Sir Walter Scott once wrote, "Breathes there a man with soul so dead, who never to himself has said, 'This is my own, my native land.' " Contrast that statement with the words of Samuel Johnson in the eighteenth century, "Patriotism is the last refuge of a scoundrel." We thank God that we live in a land where we may say, "My country, may she ever be right. But if she is wrong, she will hear from me." This is freedom in its highest measure.

To many people today, patriotism is corny and out of date. They ignore what is right with our country. They emphasize what is wrong—and much is wrong. America is not perfect because it is made up of people, and people are not perfect. The reason the world knows much about our imperfections is that we have a free press that publicizes our faults and our sins.

A missionary to Africa once said that it was only when he was at home in the United States that he heard the statement "America is a Christian nation." Many of the founders of our country were Christians. There are many wonderful Christians in our land today. But we are far from living up to the title of "Christian nation."

I. To be a patriot means more than saluting the flag.

Saluting the flag is an inspiring expression of patriotism to many of us. But there are people who would betray our country yet salute the flag just to put up a front. It is possible to pledge allegiance to the flag and never even think of the solemn words that are spoken. Jehovah's Witnesses are zealous and sincere people who believe that saluting the flag is idolatry. Can we say that they are not patriotic just because they follow their conscience and do not participate in this formal tradition?

II. To be a patriot means more than fighting for our country.

Many people have died on the battlefield. We honor these as our patriotic dead. But what about those who live for their country as well as those who die for it? What about those who vote faithfully and conscientiously? What about those responsible citizens who offer themselves for public office?

Conclusion

God had a special purpose in bringing our nation into being. Like Israel, we, too, have escaped tyranny and crossed stormy seas and trackless wilderness. God has truly given us a promised land, flowing with milk and honey. This gives us an awesome stewardship. We must not fall into the same trap of rejecting God that caused the downfall of ancient Israel. We are responsible to build a better world.

Long may our land be bright
With freedom's holy light;
Protect us by Thy might,
Great God, our King!

WEDNESDAY EVENING, JULY 6

Title: Final Greetings

Text: "When I shall send Artemas unto thee, or Tychicus, be diligent to come unto me to Nicopolis: for I have determined there to winter. Bring Zenas the lawyer and Apollos on their journey diligently, that nothing be wanting unto them. And let ours also learn to maintain good works for necessary uses, that they be not unfruitful. All that are with me salute thee. Greet them that love us in the faith. Grace be with you all. Amen" **(Titus 3:12–15)**.

Scripture Reading: Titus 3

Introduction

This is the final message in our series on Paul's epistle to Titus, and it is fitting that the closing message be "Final Greetings."

I. Paul mentions the names of friends.

A. Artemas is mentioned in 3:12. Little is known about Artemas, but it is evident that he is a person who can be trusted. Possibly he was to take Titus's place, for Paul said, "I shall send Artemas unto thee."

B. Tychicus also is mentioned in 3:12. This man was one of Paul's most trusted friends. Paul referred to him in Colossians 4:7 as "a beloved brother," which means a much-loved Christian; "a faithful minister," or a loyal servant of Christ; and a "fellow servant," or a bond slave of Jesus Christ—a term Paul gave himself (Titus 1:1).

C. Titus is the main character. He was Paul's friend at an awkward and difficult time. Many will stick by a person when things are going well, but Titus was a friend in hard times. He was a man for a tough assignment (2 Cor. 8:16). Titus also had the gift of administration. This type of person always is needed in the church. Paul gave Titus some affectionate names, such as "true child" and "brother."

II. Paul makes an appeal for help (3:13).

A. Paul says to bring Zenas the lawyer. Zenas is called nomikos. Nomikos has two different meanings. One meaning is "scribe," and if that is the meaning here, it would mean that Zenas was a converted rabbi. The other meaning is "lawyer," which seems to be the most likely use.

B. Paul says to bring Apollos on their journey. Apollos was well known. Acts 18:24 tells that he was born in Alexandria, was an eloquent man, and was mighty in the Scriptures. Acts 18:25 says that he was well instructed in the law, fervent in the Spirit, and a diligent teacher. It is obvious why Paul thought so much of this man.

III. Paul points out that Christians should practice good deeds and be engaged in honest occupations.

A. Working people were to supply their own needs. This is an important admonition in a day when many people are seeking to sponge off others.

B. Workers are able to help those who cannot help themselves. One great Christian trait is compassion. We want to help those who cannot help themselves, but before we can do so, we must be employed.

IV. The last word is "grace."

A. Grace is defined as the favor of God and is related to joy. The grace of God brings joy to the heart of the believer.

B. Grace is freely given by God and cannot be achieved within oneself.

Conclusion

A study of Bible characters is of great help to a student of God's Word. The people named in this passage are no exception.

SUNDAY MORNING, JULY 10

Title: The Priesthood of Each Believer: Spiritual Freedom and Equality in Christ

Text: "Ye also, as lively stones, are built up a spiritual house, an holy priesthood, to offer up spiritual sacrifices, acceptable to God by Jesus Christ" **(1 Peter 2:5)**.

Scripture Reading: 1 Peter 2:1–17

Hymns: "Come, Thou Almighty King," Anonymous

"The Master Hath Come," Doudney

"In Christ There Is No East or West," Oxenham

Offertory Prayer: Our Father, we have been taught, and we believe, that the ground at the foot of Christ's cross is level, that your salvation is for all people, and that your holy purposes are equally the duty of all Christians. Help us to act in such a way as to demonstrate in the church and in the world that in Christ there is both freedom and equality. In his name. Amen.

Introduction

The notion that some people are superior to others is very popular. It has advocates wherever elitism or snobbery flourishes. Sometimes it creeps out in bizarre forms. For example, a layman once wrote a letter trying to explain some difficulties he had with a church; with twisted, paranoid pride, he repeatedly referred to himself as "Brother Inferior," insinuating that he was superior because he viewed himself as inferior!

Thomas Paine (1737–1809), an Englishman who moved to America and perhaps was the most influential political propagandist in behalf of the Revolution, used to say that God did not create some persons with saddles and others with spurs; some to be ridden, others to ride them. With this colorful analogy, he voiced a sentiment that helped to produce the American Revolution and a new nation—namely, that all men are created equal.

People are also re-created equal. This re-creation, which we call regeneration, breaks down the class structure that people erect on such foundations as heritage, wealth, position, profession, and power.

Freedom and equality in religion are what the doctrine of the priesthood of each believer is all about.

I. The doctrine of the priesthood of each believer is an antidote to the view that the church's professional ministry is a favored, privileged class among Christians.

A. Thc Christian community is a spiritual house or temple made up of living stones, Jesus himself being the chief cornerstone. Even if the stones vary in size, they still share the same characteristic. Christians are living stones because they have come to the living chief stone, Jesus Christ, and have taken on his character (1 Peter 2:4).

B. The Christian community is a holy priesthood. It, therefore, is not proper to say that the church has a priesthood. It is a priesthood! (1 Peter 2:5). It is a holy nation; that is, it consists of holy people (v. 9).

C. The church's function is to offer spiritual sacrifices through Christ, sacrifices that God is pleased to accept (1 Peter 2:5). These sacrifices are not reserved for the mysterious inner sanctum that only the church's official priesthood can enter or are observable only by the faithful who withdraw from the world. Rather, these sacrifices have a distinctive role toward non-Christians; they praise or glorify God who, through Christ, calls believers out of darkness into God's marvelous light (v. 9). The movement from darkness to light is visible because of the higher ethics believers manifest (vv. 11–12).

D. In the Christian community there is equality among believers. Each believer is a priest because he or she helps to make up the total priesthood which the church is.

E. The recovery of this concept of the entire church as a priesthood and of each believer as a Christian was a distinctive contribution of the historical movement variously called the Protestant Reformation or evangelicalism. A review of this historical recovery helps in understanding what the doctrine of the priesthood of each believer means.

1. Though factors leading to the view that the official priesthood is a special class appear early in Christian history, the plainest expression of this view became fixed in the Middle Ages.

   According to the medieval view, the church's priests stand between God and man; they are custodians of the sacraments or means of grace; God has chosen to convey grace to sinners through sacraments. Whereas a couple of sacraments may be administered by laypersons, all should be administered, and five must be administered, by priests. Thus priests occupy a privileged status—above man but under God. In fact, a church may use the name "vicar" when referring to a local priest. A vicar is one who stands in the place of another. The idea of the priest as a vicar is this: the priest stands in the place of God or Christ.

2. One feature of the Reformation was a reaction to the medieval view that the church's official priesthood stands between God and man, administering divine grace. The three cardinal principles of the Reformation are justification by grace through faith, the supremacy of Scripture, and the priesthood of each believer.

Credit is due Martin Luther (1483–1546) for developing the basic rationale of the priesthood of each believer. The root of this principle appears in the doctrine of justification by grace through faith. Rejecting the traditional view of salvation through observance of the sacraments, and appealing to Paul's reasoning in Romans, Luther held that one gets right with God by believing in Jesus Christ. There is only one way to get right with God, and it is through faith in Christ's atoning work. Not only is there only one way to get right with God, but there also is only one level of satisfaction. One is either saved or unsaved. There are no degrees to salvation.

Luther did not reject the idea that there should be no ministers or priests in the church. He insisted that a church have ministers. However, the difference between ministers and laypersons, Luther held, is one of function, not status. In status, they are equal. In function, they are different. Though the minister has distinctive functions in the church, these functions do not make the minister a superior Christian. The minister's functions are necessary for order.

Thus the doctrine of the priesthood of each believer is an antidote to the notion that the real priesthood consists of those few persons whom the church singles out for leadership in worship, teaching, and pastoral care. This notion is unfair to the essential character Christians share in common; it has a harmful effect in the church, for it deprives the church of some of the resources spread among believers.

In respect to basic character, all Christians are in charge. Therefore, it is proper to refer to all Christians as a royal priesthood (1 Peter 2:9).

II. As a priest, each believer has direct access to God.

A. By virtue of faith, said Luther in *On Christian Liberty* (1520), each Christian person is a free, sovereign lord and subject to none.

B. The meaning of Luther's point is that faith liberates people and sets them in a lofty position, beyond the spiritual rule of any person. To understand this point, it is helpful to understand the idiom Luther used. It is the idiom of feudal society. A feudatory was a structured society in which one was a lord and others were his subjects, though the status of all subjects was not the same. The feudal system was like a giant pyramid—pointed at the top, broad and flat at the bottom. The numerous castles sprinkled throughout Western Europe are relics of this pyramidal structure, which placed one person in a given territory at the top of the heap and distributed others among various levels of authority and privilege, the lowest level consisting of serfs or servants.

C. Luther said, in effect, that faith places the Christian in a lofty position. In *On Christian Liberty*, he differentiated between the inner, spiritual man and the outer, physical, social man. He emphasized that each Christian is a priest in the inner person and that faith does not affect one's outer station in society. Some in the twentieth century may be inclined to criticize Luther for being too mindful of the status quo and for interpreting the liberty of the Christian believer in spiritual terms only. However, we need to recognize the revolutionary nature of Luther's emphasis on the spiritual equality of believers before God. Luther understood that this principle called for a reordering of the church, and the Protestant Reformation produced several new forms of worship and church government.

D. The believer does not have to go through some ecclesiastical middle man. Christ is the only intermediary one needs (Heb. 4:14–16). The believer has direct access to God through Christ.

III. As a priest, the believer has responsibility for others.

A. By virtue of love, Luther said, each Christian is a dutiful servant and is subject to all. Faith liberates one from the tyranny of sin and from ecclesiastical overlords, and gives one free, direct access to God; love subjects a person to others.

B. In the biblical sense, a priest never represents himself alone. He has responsibility for others. Aaron symbolized his corporate role as a priest by bearing the names of Israelite tribes when he went into the Holy Place (Ex. 28:29). The priest made sacrifices for others as well as for himself (Heb. 5:3). The high priest entered the Most Holy Place once each year to intercede for himself and for the people (Lev. 16:29–34). Thus the priest is a public, not a private, person.

C. In the New Testament, the concept of the priest's responsibility is a high view, indeed. Jesus Christ is the great High Priest, excelling any high priest of the levitical system. The high priest of the Old Testament was himself a man, subject to human infirmities. When he offered sacrifices, he offered both for others and for himself (Heb. 5:1–3). Jesus, however, is the Priest, who, while being tempted, did not yield to temptation and thus opened the way to the throne of grace, to which believers have unrestricted access.

D. Jesus discharged his ministry in the world, in service to others. He said that he came, not to be deaconed (to be ministered to), but to deacon (to minister), and to give himself in the place of others (Mark 10:45). This he said as a corrective to the notion, esteemed by the world then and now, that the greatest are those who exercise lordship over others. The ministering or priestly function in Christianity is such that the chiefest is the one who is the servant of others.

The priesthood of each believer has two dimensions. Vertically, the Christian stands directly under God; no person can usurp God's place; to give to man the adoration that belongs only to God is a form of idolatry, however subtle its attractiveness or however common its practice in organized religion. Horizontally, the Christian's responsibility reaches out to embrace others.

Where the priesthood of believers is genuine, it overcomes the structured levels that society erects. My family once held membership in a church in which the members ranged from the very wealthy to the very poor, from the very learned to the poorly schooled. But there was rich fellowship in the church. Explaining this fellowship, one woman said, "What we have in common is faith in one Lord." Christ breaks down those walls of partition that men erect, so that there are neither bond nor free, neither male nor female (Gal. 3:28).

E. During the days of slavery, the Six Mile Baptist Church, Jackson County, Missouri, founded in 1824, experienced the drama of this radical priesthood that Christ requires. Deacon Peace was a slaveholder. It was the practice for deacons to wash members' feet in connection with the observance of the Lord's Supper. One day Deacon Peace was washing members' feet. Before him appeared the feet of a black man. Deacon Peace hesitated for a moment, which, to observers, seemed like a long time. Then he proceeded to wash and wipe the black man's feet. The congregation burst into singing, "Washed in the Blood." The feet were those of Deacon Peace's slave.

Conclusion

The church cannot make it if it relies only on a professional ministry, whether the office be priest, pastor, minister, or something else. The church is a priesthood, and each member is a priest—with direct access to God, with direct responsibility for others.

In a sense, therefore, every Christian is in charge.

SUNDAY EVENING, JULY 10

Title: Has the Supreme Court Outlawed God?

Text: "Ye have condemned and killed the just; and he doth not resist you" **(James 5:6)**.

Scripture Reading: Matthew 6:5–13

Introduction

In 1962, just before Independence Sunday, the Supreme Court announced its decision that a prayer composed by the New York Regents in Public Education was illegal. They concluded that a prayer composed by agents of the state (the regents), and enforced by other agents of the state (public school teachers), violated the provisions of the First Amendment.

The justices of the court were not prepared for the emotional explosion that rang throughout our country. Political and religious demagogues had a field day prophesying that America was on the road to total paganism and atheism.

The court did not rule against prayer but against compulsory prayer. It did not make God illegal. There is no constitutional restriction against voluntary prayer in the schools (although the law is often misinterpreted and students are wrongfully persecuted for or banned from voluntarily praying and reading their Bibles). The court said, "No government agent, no school board, no school administrator, no school teacher has a right to tell a school child when to pray or where to pray or what to pray." Do you not agree with this principle?

In 1963 the Supreme Court decreed that no government agent could require Bible reading in public schools. The court said further that no public official could require the recitation of the Lord's Prayer in public schools. The Constitution says that Congress has no right to prohibit the free exercise of religion. Compulsory prayer is not the free exercise of religion. Required Bible reading is not the free exercise of religion. The recitation of the Lord's Prayer, a Christian prayer, by the mandate of the state, is not the free exercise of religion.

For several decades there has been a concerted effort to amend the First Amendment. The zealous leaders of this movement are sincere but misguided Christians who have misunderstood the decision of the Supreme Court. They believe that an amendment will restore prayer to its proper place and will reintroduce God to public life. I believe that a revision of the First Amendment would actually weaken the practice of prayer in public places.

A sample of these Congressional resolutions is: "Nothing contained in this Constitution shall abridge the right of persons lawfully assembled in any public building that is supported in whole or in part through the expenditure of public funds, to participate in nondenominational prayer."

We should oppose any amendment to the First Amendment for the following reasons:

I. This amendment would add nothing to the liberties we already enjoy.

The First Amendment has worked to keep the state and the church separate in the practice of religion for more than two hundred years. There is no threat of the state adopting or forming a state church. No other nation on earth enjoys the freedom of religion that the United States affords.

II. This amendment would actually weaken the Constitution.

When we tamper with an amendment, we open the door for further tampering in the future. The First Amendment says, "Congress shall make no law respecting an establishment of religion, or prohibiting the free exercise thereof." If we amend this statute, we would be saying, "Congress shall not interfere with the free exercise of religion except in the area of prayer in public assembly, where the prayer must be a nondenominational prayer."

What is a nondenominational prayer? Who determines if it is nondenominational? According to this amendment, it would be the state officials and the courts who would make this decision. This would make the government the judge of theology and the administrator of religious practices. Would this increase our freedom? Would this enhance our constitutional right to the free exercise of our religion?

Conclusion

Let us fight every effort to tamper with the First Amendment. Let us resist any attempt to impose an innocuous, so-called nondenominational prayer on our public life. Prayer is an intensely personal practice. The Constitution protects our right to keep it so. We need to heed the words of Kierkegaard, "There is that which is more contrary to Christianity ... than any heresy, any schism ... and that is to play Christianity."

WEDNESDAY EVENING, JULY 13

Title: A Call to the Called

Text: "Jude, the servant of Jesus Christ, and brother of James, to them that are sanctified by God the Father, and preserved in Jesus Christ, and called" **(Jude 1)**.

Scripture Reading: Jude

Introduction

This is the first of nine studies in the little book of Jude. This first study contains some introductory material that will serve as a background for all the lessons in this series.

I. The servant (Jude 1).

A. Jude, or Judas, was a popular name in New Testament times. Today not many people are named Judas. It is because the betrayer of our Lord brought a meaning to the name that makes it unwelcome to us. But it was not always so. There are several Judes or Judases named in the Scriptures.
   1. Judas, the son of Jacob (Matt. 1:2–3).
   2. Judas, ancestor of Jesus (Luke 3:30).
   3. Judas of Galilee, who instigated a revolt and was slain (Acts 5:37).
   4. Judas Iscariot, who betrayed Jesus (Matt. 26:14–17; 27:3).
   5. An apostle distinguished from Judas Iscariot (Luke 4:16).
   6. One of the four brothers of Jesus (Matt. 13:55; Mark 6:3).
   7. A man of Damascus with whom Paul remained after his conversion (Acts 9:11).
   8. Judas, surnamed Barsabas, a prominent man in the Jerusalem church (Acts 15:22, 27, 32).

B. "Jude, the servant" means Jude the bond slave.

C. Jude identifies himself as the bond slave of Jesus Christ, and this relationship gives meaning to all that is reflected in the letter.

II. The saints (Jude 1).

A. They are "called of God."
   1. The expression was used to denote being called to an office; therefore there was a responsibility, a serious duty.

2. The expression was used to call people to a feast. Hence, there is great joy in responding to the call to be a Christian.
3. The expression was used to call people to judgment, to a trial, or to a court. Because it is a subpoena, Christians are engaged in serious business when they answer the call.

B. They are "preserved in Jesus Christ." Here is the perfect tense. This means that the Christian's preservation has already happened, it is happening, and it will continue to keep on happening. This is complete preservation.

C. They are sanctified. This is a reference not so much to the excellence of their spiritual attainment as to their position. It means that love has placed them where they are.

III. The salutation (Jude 2).

We are reminded in verse 2 that Jude is fond of triplets. Here is a beautiful example:

A. Mercy. "Mercy is God's love in action."

B. Peace. The peace here described comes from being joined to a strong ally. D. L. Moody was so right when he said, "[Peace] is ours when we worry about nothing, pray about everything, and thank God for anything."

C. Love. This agape love, the highest form, is abundant in quantity. Mercy, peace, and love—all three overflow in gracious abundance.

IV. The salvation (Jude 3).

A. It is said to be a "common salvation," not commonplace. It is for everyone, and it is adequate for all.

B. Here is the starting place for all the Christian conquest.

V. The switch (Jude 3).

Jude says that he would prefer in "all diligence" to stick to the subject of this great salvation. But necessity thrusts on him the primary focus of another matter. It is that they "earnestly contend for the faith which was once delivered unto the saints." To refocus is not to retreat. What we prefer to say is not always what we ought to say. God's will is to have priority over our inclination.

VI. The struggle (Jude 3).

Christians are at war, and it is not a cold war. To contend here means to agonize, and the object of our spiritual agony is the entire Christian enterprise.

Conclusion

We, too, are favored bond slaves of Jesus Christ. As such, we are called, kept, and forever loved. Mercy, peace, and love are God's strong trilogy for us.

SUNDAY MORNING, JULY 17

Title: Liberty of Conscience: Each Person under God

Text: "For when the Gentiles, which have not the law, do by nature the things contained in the law, these, having not the law, are a law unto themselves: which shew the work of the law written in their hearts, their conscience also bearing witness, and their thoughts the mean while accusing or else excusing one another" **(Rom. 2:14–15)**.

Scripture Reading: Romans 1:16–20; 2:1–3, 11–16

Hymns: "Immortal, Invisible," Smith

"Ye Servants of God," Wesley

"Holy Ghost, with Light Divine," Reed

Offertory Prayer: O God, our Maker, there is a restlessness in our hearts when we act contrary to the standard that you implanted in us when you made us in your own image. And we find rest only when we recognize that, though we deserve your displeasure, judgment, and punishment, we have One who has made things right in your sight and reconciled us to you, your Son and our Redeemer, Jesus Christ. Amen.

Introduction

To those closest to King James I, king of England (1603–25), the words with which Thomas Helwys inscribed a copy of his book seemed heretical in theology and anarchistic in politics:

> The king is a mortal man, and not God, therefore he hath no power over the mortal soul of the subjects to make laws and ordinances for them and to set spiritual lords over them. If the king has authority to make spiritual lords and laws, then he is an immortal god and not a mortal man.

These words were revolutionary indeed! They signaled the introduction of a new teaching that, because God is the Creator of each person, the conscience of each person is, and must be, free from any human institution that would tyrannize the conscience or usurp God's rightful place on the throne of each person's conscience.

Helwys was an English nobleman with legal training. He had broken with the official church in England. Breaking the law, he and others organized in 1606 an illegal Separatist or Congregational church by means of a covenant. Shortly thereafter, they divided their group into two churches—at Gainsborough and Scrooby in England—to avoid detection. They soon fled to Holland to escape persecution. The Scrooby group eventually settled in Leyden, and in 1620 more than thirty persons related to it went with other Englishmen to the New World and planted a colony at Plymouth, Massachusetts. The Gainsborough group settled at Amsterdam; by 1609 this group instituted the practice of believer's baptism. In 1611 several of them, led by Helwys, decided that they had erred when they fled England to escape persecution, that they had a responsibility to exercise the religion that Scripture teaches and that their consciences confirmed to be right, and that their devotion to God and their love for their English kinsmen and friends required them to go back to England, whatever the cost to them personally. Preparing for their return, Helwys wrote *A Short Declaration of the Mystery of Iniquity* about the same time that the King James Version of the Bible was published. He took copies of his book, dated 1612, back to England and sent an autographed copy to James I, inscribed with the words quoted earlier. Within a short time, Helwys was jailed, and he was dead three or four years later.

But the principle that Helwys enunciated survived and is now the law of the United States. Known as liberty of conscience, it affirms that each person is under God and directly accountable to him.

I. Liberty of conscience is an antidote to the notion that civil officialdom can stand between God and people in religious matters.

A. The theory of the "divine right of kings," a theory that historians of political science attribute to James I, was the immediate evil that the concept of liberty of conscience redressed. James regarded monarchy as the form of government that God instituted. Once monarchy is established, the king represents God. Indeed, according to James I, "Kings are breathing images of God upon earth." He declared that just as it is blasphemous to dispute God's power, it is contemptuous to dispute the king's power. The king occupies his position by divine right. To obey the king is to obey God; to disobey the king is to disobey God. A subject must submit to a good king as to God. One also must submit to a wicked king, for the wicked king is God's agent in punishing unrighteous people; patience, prayers, and penitent amendment of conduct are the only God-appointed means for relieving the curse of a wicked king, James I held.

Soon after becoming king of England, James I undertook to enforce religious uniformity. When Puritans complained about imperfections in the state religion, Anglicanism, James took the side of the religious establishment. His policy was to make his subjects conform in religious matters to the Anglican system or to harry them out of the land.

B. Helwys challenged James I's theory head-on. While conceding that subjects should obey the king with body, life, and goods, Helwys contended that they could not surrender their consciences to the king—for several reasons. First, the king is mortal like his subjects are. Second, if the king be a Christian, he is obliged to obey and honor Christ, just as his subjects are to obey and honor him. Third, if each king holds office by divine right and if each king can determine the religion of his realm, there would then be as many valid religions as valid kings; this notion runs counter to the truism that, since God is one and God alone is the author of true religion, there can be only one true religion. Fourth, in the Great Judgment (see

Matt. 25) all people will have to give an account of their religious belief and practice; since they cannot throw responsibility on anyone else for religious error, they must be faithful to what they understand to be right, regardless of temporal consequences.

C. Civil officialdom cannot interpose itself between God and humans. Civil authority, Helwys held, is to be obeyed in civil, temporal matters essential to good order. Civil authority has no power to produce faith; only God can do this. Therefore, government is to stick to its precincts and not to invade the precincts of conscience where God alone is the authority.

D. After generations, the principle of liberty of conscience became a fixture of American law. Thomas Jefferson introduced the will that established this principle in Virginia's law. Jefferson asked that his tombstone attest to only three of his contributions: writing the Declaration of Independence, founding the University of Virginia, and drafting the bill that guarantees liberty of conscience. The constitution of the state of Missouri (art. 1., sec. 5) expresses liberty of conscience in these words: "That all men have a natural and indefeasible right to worship Almighty God according to the dictates of their own consciences; that no human authority can control or interfere with the rights of conscience; that no person shall, on account of his religious persuasion or belief, be rendered ineligible to any public office of trust or profit in this state."

II. Creation is the basis of liberty of conscience.

A. In the doctrine of the priesthood of each believer, it is the Christian who enjoys free access to God—by virtue of faith, or the second birth.

B. In the doctrine of liberty of conscience, it is each person—every person—who has a right to enjoy liberty under God—by virtue of creation, or the first birth.

C. Each person sustains the same natural relationship to God. When God created man male and female, he implanted in them the divine image and likeness (Gen. 1:26–27). Even after humans sinned, all people sustained the same relationship to God; all sinned and fell short of God's glory (Rom. 3:23). There is none righteous, none good, in his or her own right. All are estranged from God; they do not understand God (Rom. 3:10–11). Even when people know what is right, they fail to perform it and experience the frightful tension between what they ought to do and what they do (Rom. 7:21–24).

D. This inner tension caused by conflict between what people ought to do and what they actually do is an index to the indelible effect of the Creator on the creature. However depraved human conduct may be—and Paul's review (Rom. 1:20–32) is enough to make the fearless wince—people cannot get away from God's witness in their consciences. Thus they stand before God without excuse.

E. Because people are responsible to God, they cannot be indifferent to their relation to God. They cannot afford to let anyone else tamper with this relationship. Even at best, humans know only in part; they are fallible; their understanding is imperfect. Nevertheless, people are directly responsible, and they cannot abdicate their religious obligations to either ecclesiastical or civil authority.

F. Insofar as other persons are concerned, each person—whether Baptist, Congregationalist, Presbyterian, Anglican, Catholic, Jewish, Muslim, Hindu, or even atheist, according to Helwys—must preserve and exercise the liberty of his or her own conscience.

III. Liberty of conscience is indispensable for true evangelism.

A. The easy thing is for one to let someone else make his or her religious decisions. This is why so many look to priests and pastors. Where such practice is common, it is also common for religion to be superficial and for persons to maintain only a nominal relationship. If we take priest or pastor too seriously, we find our security in churchism, not in Christ. This easy way is a broad way, and many walk in it. But this way does not lead to God.

B. The hard but safest thing is for one to assume direct responsibility for religious belief and practice. This is what faith is all about. People must believe for themselves; no one else can do it for them.

C. Liberty of conscience places on individuals the heavy responsibility of their own religious belief, making them realize that only they can believe. When people reach this position, they are fit prospects for genuine evangelism, for they know that they cannot depend on any other person to make themselves right with God.

Evangelism is the serious telling and the serious hearing of the gospel. When people acknowledge that liberty of conscience places on themselves responsibility for religious decisions, they have to sift out religious views and reach their own conclusions. And this is the point to which evangelism leads hearers of the gospel.

Conclusion

God created each person and has implanted in the creature an instinct for the Creator. Each is responsible to God. Neither ecclesiastical nor civil authority can usurp the position reserved for God alone. Once we realize that our native liberty of conscience intensifies our responsibility under God, we must be sure that we know and believe the truth and act accordingly.

SUNDAY EVENING, JULY 17

Title: Is There a Tomorrow?

Text: "Seeing then that all these things shall be dissolved, what manner of persons ought ye to be in all holy conversation and godliness, looking for and hastening unto the coming of the day of God, wherein the heavens being on fire shall be dissolved, and the elements shall melt with fervent heat?" **(2 Peter 3:11–12)**.

Scripture Reading: 2 Peter 3:1–13

Introduction

The *Bulletin of the Atomic Scientists* has for many years pictured a clock on its cover. The position of its hands shows the minutes before midnight. According to this symbolism, when the hands reach midnight, humankind will have brought about its own end. Will there be a tomorrow?

A young couple looks with pride at their new baby who has just been born. But with their pride in her life there is also a haunting question about her future. What kind of world will this lovely child grow up to inherit? Will there even be a tomorrow?

Many people fear economic collapse or nuclear war or killer diseases. As Christians we need not fear anything. We know that no matter what happens in our world, God is still in control. We also know that there will come a time when the world as we know it will be brought to an end. This will occur at the return of Christ.

Second Peter 3 sounds very contemporary. In the day of the Lord's return, Peter said, the heavens will pass away with a great noise. The earth and everything in it will be burned as the elements melt in fervent heat. As the ancient world perished by means of the flood, this present one will be destroyed by fire. In place of that which is destroyed, there will be new heavens and a new earth in which righteousness will dwell. The word translated "new" means "new in kind." There will be a new kind of heaven and earth, one marked by righteousness.

Knowing that the present world order would not last forever, Peter asked a significant question: "Seeing then that all these things shall be dissolved, what manner of persons ought ye to be?"

I. When we ask, "Will there be a tomorrow?" there is an anticipation.

A. We anticipate the second coming of Christ.

1. Some people may scoff at Christians' belief in the Lord's imminent return. In Peter's day, scoffers looked at the world around them and could detect no outward change. They were sure that the belief that Christ would return and that the world would end had no substance.
2. A historical reminder. To scoff at the belief in the second coming of Christ is to ignore at least one historical fact: God destroyed the world once before.

B. We live as citizens of two worlds. Christians have never centered their lives in this world alone. We have always known that we are citizens of two worlds. Our belief in God is that even when this world is brought to an end, we still have a greater world in which to live eternally. This world is not our home; heaven is our eternal home.

II. Will there be a tomorrow? The return of Christ is an actuality.

A. Sometimes the return of Christ seems distant. Even so, it will happen. We are reminded that God does not reckon time as we do. For the Lord, a day is as a thousand years and a thousand years is as a day. Removed from the time and space limitations of the earth, time is reckoned differently.

B. The delay in Christ's return is an act of mercy. While we may wonder at the apparent postponement of Christ's return, Scripture says that this is an indication of God's mercy rather than an oversight. The longer he delays his return, the greater the opportunity for people to turn to him in repentance and faith.

C. The Lord will return suddenly and unexpectedly. We cannot ignore or escape the Lord's return. It will be sudden and unexpected. While life goes on as usual, suddenly as a thief in the night, Christ will return and our world will end.

III. Will there be a tomorrow? Consider our attitudes.

A. Holiness. We are to live wholesome Christian lives in anticipation of Christ's coming. This is not the time for one last fling or for sowing wild oats while we can. If anything is an incentive for Christian living, it ought to be this.

B. Hope. We are to have an attitude of hope. While the end of the world carries a threat, it also carries a hope. We know that God will institute his eternal kingdom.

C. Witness. We are to use Christ's imminent return as an opportunity for Christian witness. In more than one place (vv. 9, 15), we are told that the delay of Christ's return is for our good. It gives us an opportunity to witness of his grace and others an opportunity to accept his grace.

Conclusion

Jesus repeated the warning many times that we should be prepared for his return. One day he will return. At that time, we will either meet him with joy or with sadness, depending on the preparation we have made. What will it be for you? Will there be a tomorrow? There can be an eternity of tomorrows in Christ's presence.

WEDNESDAY EVENING, JULY 20

Title: Contents Dangerous!

Text: "For there are certain men crept in unawares, who were before of old ordained to this condemnation, ungodly men, turning the grace of our God into lasciviousness, and denying the only Lord God, and our Lord Jesus Christ" **(Jude 4).**

Scripture Reading: Jude 1–4

Introduction

Our text comes from Jude 4. Jude says that certain men who have joined the church are not worthy of the fellowship of the church. They have sneaked in, and their presence is deplorable. Their character and conduct qualify them to be labeled "Contents Dangerous!"

I. The crowd.

A. Shakespeare has a line in *Macbeth* that describes them:

> *To beguile the time,*
> *Look like the time, bear welcome in your eye,*
> *Your hand, your tongue; look like the innocent flower,*
> *But be serpent under't.* (Act 1, Scene 5)

B. These are stable mates of the proverbial Trojan horse.

C. Three enemies within the church threaten it: heresy, schism, and wickedness. These are in sharp focus in our text.

D. It may well be that our own dangers lie not so much in attack from without as from apathy within, bombardment from without as from blight within, conquest from without as from collapse within, destruction from without as from decay within, or enemies from without as from emptiness within.

II. The corruption.

A. Theirs was an ungodly character. The expression "ungodly" is loaded with the idea that their entire spirit was lacking in fundamental reverence. They are members of the church but have no spiritual atmosphere appropriate for a church. They belong because it is the decent thing to do, or because of the family, or for business reasons.

Not in our century has there been such an inside job of church demolition as is evident today. Evil forces are not lining up against the church: they are forming a church. A church filled with unregenerate people is the most deplorable of sights. It is a living contradiction. Such were these long ago, and such are these today. They are appropriately labeled "Contents Dangerous!"

B. Theirs was an unthinkable attempt. They were guilty of "turning the grace of God into lasciviousness," or, as Weymouth puts it, "pervert[ing] the grace of God into immorality." They counted God's patience and mercy as softness and weakness. They mistook his longsuffering for impotence. But they did not stop there. They went so far as to try to utilize the characteristics of God for their own selfish ends. If they recognized him at all, they interpreted the delay of his judgment as being the approval of their wickedness.

C. Theirs was an unpardonable sin. They went on "denying the only Lord God, and our Lord Jesus Christ." The unpardonable sin is the complete and final rejection of Jesus Christ as Savior and Lord. For such sin in its finality there is no remedy, no pardon, no forgiveness.

III. The condemnation.

The text describes this corrupt crowd as those "who were before of old ordained to this condemnation." Perhaps "marked" is a better translation than "ordained." Verse 13 describes this condemnation as "the blackness of darkness for ever." They are going on a journey. Their reservations are made. The time of their arrival is not definite, but the reservations are guaranteed. The judgment of God is upon them, sealed and irrevocable.

Conclusion

Church membership and salvation are not the same. Across the centuries, some wicked people have always belonged to the church. Corruption in our churches today is not new, nor is it likely more pronounced than in other generations. We can leave the matter of judgment safely in the hands of a just God and can devote our time to witnessing in a triumphant way.

SUNDAY MORNING, JULY 24

Title: Separation of Church and State: A Free Church in a Free State

Text: "Then saith he unto them, Render therefore unto Caesar the things which are Caesar's; and unto God the things that are God's" **(Matt. 22:21)**.

Scripture Reading: Romans 13:1–10

Hymns: "Glorious Things of Thee Are Spoken," Newton

"The Church's One Foundation," Stone

"America the Beautiful," Bates

Offertory Prayer: O God of all people, we thank you that we live in a land of the free and that freedom is most visible in the religious liberty we all enjoy, in the freedom of the church from state control, and in the freedom of the state from church control. Help us to value these freedoms, to teach them to our children, and to observe them in such fashion as to commend them to all people, through Jesus Christ our Lord. Amen.

Introduction

"Congress shall make no law respecting an establishment of religion or prohibiting the free exercise thereof." So read the first clauses of the First Amendment of the US Constitution. Courts refer to them as the Establishment Clause (actually, it could more accurately bear the title No Establishment Clause) and the Free Exercise Clause.

The United States was the first nation to establish the constitutional principles of religious liberty and no establishment of religious principles, usually presented under the slogan "separation of church and state." This slogan was inspired by Thomas Jefferson's comment that the First Amendment erected a wall of separation between church and state.

In 1663 Rhode Island, due to the labors of Roger Williams and John Clarke, obtained a charter from King Charles II of England, guaranteeing religious liberty. But Rhode Island was a small colony, not a nation. Charles II may have granted a charter for Rhode Island's "lively experiment," fully expecting the experiment to fail, thus proving that stable society requires a union of church and state and a uniformity of religion. Rhode Island's policy succeeded, and its underlying principles became increasingly popular. As American colonists struggled for political and civil freedom during the American Revolution, some, especially those affiliated with minority religious groups, contended for religious freedom also. And they succeeded.

I. The principle of separation of church and state developed as an antidote to church control over the state and to state control over the church.

The religion clauses of the First Amendment are a corrective of former arrangements between church and state stretching over several centuries.

A. When the Roman emperor Constantine (d. 337) adopted Christianity as the official religion of the empire, government began to intervene in religious matters. Civil authorities called and exerted influence—and, in some cases, pressures—in the first seven so-called ecumenical councils (325–787). In Eastern Orthodoxy, the church became subservient to government. Religion emphasized right doctrine (orthodoxy) and observed a fixed liturgy, but its prophetic voice became quiet, and the ethical teachings of Jesus received little attention. The church was under the state.

B. In Western Europe the Roman church became increasingly strong during the early (500–1100) and high (1100–1300) Middle Ages. As barbarian tribes overran Western Europe, government lost its force, and the church stood as the stablest institution in a society of radical changes. Only slowly did government recover impressive power—first, during the reign of Charlemagne (769–814) and, second, following the founding of the Holy Roman Empire (962). Over several centuries, the bishop of Rome acquired more and more power. During the 1070s there was a head-on conflict between the pope (Gregory VII) and the emperor (Henry IV), each of whom claimed highest power.

In this context, the doctrine of papal primacy emerged, advanced by Gregory VII. For centuries Roman bishops had asserted, and with rare exceptions other churchmen had conceded, that the pope is the highest ecclesiastical official, at the top of the priestly or clerical class. Gregory VII contended that he was God's vicar with absolute authority in both spiritual (churchly) and temporal (civil) matters. He asserted that the pope can control the church hierarchy, that he can approve and depose emperors, that he cannot err, and that all persons, clerical and lay, owe obedience to the pope because he represents God.

The view of Gregory VII was that the church is over the state. The emperor did not acquiesce. Civil war broke out. For generations the conflict between church and state persisted. Pope and emperor agreed in 1122 that the emperor would defer to the pope in spiritual matters and that the pope would defer to the emperor in civil matters. This compromise pleased neither pope nor emperor, but it set the precedent for treaty arrangements, called concordats, between the Roman church and various states. The church's official teaching became that, because spiritual matters are superior to temporal matters, the church is superior to the state. Pope Innocent III (1198–1216) advanced this view under the analogy of sun and moon. The church represents the sun; the state, the moon. The sun radiates light; the state reflects it, Innocent stated.

C. The English Reformation began with a law desired by Henry VIII and adopted by Parliament that the king is the supreme head of the church in England (1534). This law implies that civil authority is dominant in religious matters. It was civil authority—specifically, Queen Elizabeth (1559–1603)—which established the Church of England, or Anglicanism, as the official religion. Except for a brief period (1642–60), Anglicanism remained the state religion.

With the restoration of monarchy in 1660, the Church of England intensified pressures to strengthen its position. Within a dozen years, Parliament passed laws to limit high civil office to Anglicans (1661), to require complete conformity to the Anglican system and to remove all ministers who objected to any part of it (1662), to forbid meetings for religious purposes other than in Anglican settings (1664), to prohibit non-Anglican ministers from returning to communities where they had served, to increase penalties for illegal religious meetings within given miles of a parish church house (1665), and to condition civil offices and some government services (for example, university training) on conformity to the Anglican system (1673). Thus, the state used its powers to establish one religious group and to penalize all others. Even when the king relaxed the enforcement of these laws, he required Nonconformists to register their leaders and meeting places. Many complied in good faith with the king's indulgence, but information submitted with registration later hurt Nonconformists, for the state used it during periods of renewed persecution. In 1689 the state granted toleration to Nonconformists under certain conditions; Anglicanism remained the favored religion, and Nonconformists labored under legal and social handicaps.

D. The English laws on religion prevailed in several American colonies until the Revolution, when their inequities came under attack. In Virginia in particular, some patriots worked hard during and immediately after the Revolution to replace toleration with liberty, to make all religions equal under law, to disestablish the state church, and to prevent taxation for education conducted by churchmen. Reacting to laws that established religious tests and conferred special benefits on Anglicanism in some southern states and on Congregationalism in some states in New England, Americans adopted the US Constitution, which stated that "no religious test shall ever be required as a qualification to any office or public trust under the United States" (art. 6). They demanded and got amendments to protect certain rights against governmental action.

The first of these amendments contains the religion clauses previously quoted. It also guarantees freedom of speech, freedom of the press, and freedom of assembly, all of which are essential to religious liberty. If government can decide what religionists can say or write or when and under what conditions they can assemble, it can prohibit the free exercise of religion, and conversely, it can establish whatever religion satisfies public officialdom.

Thus, the principle of separation of church and state developed as an antidote to former practices under which state controlled church, church controlled state, or church and state worked in union to suppress those who did not accept state-approved religion.

II. The constitutional principle of separation of church and state stands as a safeguard against coercion in religion and against government-sponsored religion.

A. The US Supreme Court has said that the Free Exercise Clause withholds from government any power to interfere with religious liberty or to coerce one to violate his or her religious conscience.

The test to be applied in Free Exercise cases is coercion. "If there is any fixed star in our constitutional constellation" the Court said in Barnette, "it is that no [government] official, high or petty, can prescribe what shall be orthodox in politics, nationalism, religion, or other matters of opinion or force citizens to confess by word or act their faith therein." Government has no power whatever to coerce people to engage in any religious exercise. For more than three decades there have been persistent attacks on the Supreme Court's rulings in the so-called prayer and Bible reading cases. Opponents misrepresent the court's decisions, alleging that the court threw God, prayer, and the Bible out of public schools. No public official has power to throw the God in whom I believe out of any setting! The court overthrew only compulsory praying and compulsory Bible reading; it ruled that government cannot coerce anyone, especially children who attend public schools pursuant to compulsory attendance laws, to engage in religious exercises. The court ruled rightly! Anyone who believes that genuine faith is in response to divine grace cannot accept the notion that government can force one to believe or that government-coerced religious exercises will produce faith.

B. The court has ruled that the Establishment Clause was designed to prevent three evils: government's sponsorship of religion, government's financial support of religion, and government's active involvement or entanglement with religion (Walz, 1970).

The purpose of the no-entanglement test is to keep church and state out of the other's precincts insofar as feasible; it calls for a close scrutiny of any entanglement, whether administrative or political (Lemon, 1971).

The Establishment Clause creates a dilemma. If a law provides public aid without administrative controls, its effect is to advance religion; if it imposes controls, it may involve the government in excessive, continuing entanglement. Rulings since 1970 have tended toward a clear conclusion: It will be difficult for any form of public aid to education in church schools to course between the Charybdis of aid to sectarian purposes and the Scylla of excessive entanglement between agents of church and state. Moreover, any form of aid benefiting a limited class intensifies the potential of political division along religious lines, one of the evils against which the Establishment Clause affords protection (Lemon, 1971).

III. It is compatible with separation of church and state for a person to be active both in state and in church.

A. American law requires no one to choose between church and state. Some may think that a Christian is to have as little contact as possible with the state and with nonreligious society; but this is a view not advanced by American law. The American legal principle is that one can participate in affairs of both church and state. One does not have to abdicate civil rights in order to be a church leader; one does not have to forgo religious activity in order to qualify for public office or public services. If one chooses to forgo public services (for example, public education), he or she does it voluntarily; the state takes no action toward this end.

B. Some improperly interpret separation of church and state to mean separation of religion and politics. Church is the institution of religion; state is the institution of government. And they are to be separate. But the American system does not require one to choose between religion and politics. Too many religionists view politics as dirty and distrust those who take an interest in public affairs; the effect of this hands-off attitude would be to turn government over to those who have no religious sensibilities.

C. Christ told his disciples to render to Caesar (symbolically, government) what belongs to Caesar and to God what belongs to him. The reasonable inference from this commandment is that the Christian should discharge both civil and religious obligations. To render all to Caesar is to deprive God of what one rightly owes him. To withhold all from Caesar is to deny what one rightly owes to government.

D. Government is essential to society's well-being. God ordained civil authority for society's good and, specifically, for the restraint of evil (Rom. 13:1–3). It is proper to give due deference to government in areas where it has competence, and it is proper to pay taxes (vv. 4–6). In the American system, each citizen, including the Christian, has an opportunity to take part in shaping governmental policy. If early Christians were obligated, in keeping with religious conscience, to honor the Roman government, how much more are present-day Christians obligated to take part in improving government?

E. Christianity takes one beyond law's bounds. Christians are to go further than government can lead them. Law may prohibit acts deemed criminal or harmful to society, but law is not self-enforcing; for this reason, law carries penalties for violations. The key to compliance with law is the will of citizens. Equitable law calls for one to grant to others the benefits he or she claims for self, and Christian love cannot be satisfied with less than equity. Paul expressed it like this: "All the law is fulfilled in one word, even in this; Thou shalt love thy neighbour as thyself" (Gal. 5:14). "Love worketh no ill to his neighbour: therefore love is the fulfilling of the law" (Rom. 13:10). Of all people, Christians should be exemplary citizens.

Conclusion

If there is to be a free church in a free state, Christians must be active in both church and state. To limit one's interest to the church is to leave public affairs to non-Christians. To limit one's interest to public affairs is to undermine the church. The Christian has a twofold obligation: To render to the state what properly belongs to it and to render to God what properly belongs to him. If Christians continue to discharge this obligation, there will continue to be a free state in which justice prevails and in which free churches thrive, and free churches that engage in genuine worship of God and inculcate high ethical ideals for humanity's social betterment.

SUNDAY EVENING, JULY 24

Title: Do You Drive Like a Christian?

Text: "Then the Lord said to Cain, 'Where is your brother Abel?' 'I don't know,' he replied. 'Am I my brother's keeper?' The Lord said, 'What have you done? Listen! Your brother's blood cries out to me from the ground'" **(Gen. 4:9–10 NIV)**.

Scripture Reading: Romans 13:1–6

Introduction

George Dolan, in a column in the Fort Worth Star-Telegram, once told of a woman from out of town who came to Fort Worth to shop. She was delighted to find a parking space adjacent to her favorite department store. She stopped parallel with the car in front of the space and began to back in. A woman in a car behind her, seeing the space, angled into the opposite end of the space and stopped, thus blocking the first driver from backing the rest of the way into the space. There they both sat, and neither would yield to the other.

Finally, the woman from out of town got out of her car and walked back to converse with her adversary. The woman in the second car placed her fingers in her ears and would not roll down the window or even look at her. Finally, the first woman got back in her car and drove away. She found another parking space a few blocks away. She parked and then entered a variety store nearby. There she purchased a cheap tube of lipstick. Returning to the former place of conflict, she proceeded to use the whole stick in circular motions on the windshield of the other woman's car.

As I chuckled at the emotional immaturity of both of these women, I speculated that both of them were probably in their churches the next Sunday. Perhaps they were leaders in their missionary organizations. But in this particular incident, neither one acted like a Christian. One would not even go the first mile, and the other flunked the test on the second mile.

As I sought to prepare this sermon on highway safety, I searched my library. I did not find a single sermon on the subject. As I searched my own memory and my own sermon file, I realized that I had never preached a sermon on this area of life.

Is a minister justified to take the time of an entire sermon to preach on this subject? I believe that he or she is. Driving an automobile is a privilege, a stewardship, a trust. It is not a basic right. People are licensed to drive. They are tested and issued a license to entitle them to a responsible privilege. They sit behind the wheel of a ton of steel with power over their own lives and the lives of others.

I. A matter of Christian concern.

Christians believe that human life is precious, that people are created in the image of God, and that God loved them so much that he gave his Son to die for their sins. Therefore Christians must be concerned about the thousands who are injured and killed on US highways every year.

During World War II, famed political cartoonist Bill Mauldin featured two G.I. characters he called "Willie and Joe." One of his cartoons pictured these two odd characters cowering behind the rubble of a destroyed German village. Shells were bursting all around them. The caption beneath read, "I feel like a fugitive from the law—of averages." When we get in our cars today, we feel the same way. Recently I returned home on a plane. As I entered my car at the parking lot to drive the last forty miles home, I said to myself, "And now for the most perilous leg of the journey!"

Let me come back to my original question: "Do you drive like a Christian?" Many of us try to behave like Christians when we are with other people. But when we get behind the wheel of an automobile our character changes. We become victims of our moods. We are normally patient and courteous in society, but we become impatient and aggressive when we drive our cars. I would not think of racing a woman out of a door of the church, but I must confess that I have been guilty of racing a woman driver away from a four-way-stop intersection.

I remember coming to one of those intersections once on the way to church. The car to my left stopped a split second before I arrived. But the woman driver was unsure, and she hesitated. I used that as the occasion to accelerate into the intersection. As I crossed over, I glanced to my left, and, to my horror and humiliation, I recognized the driver as a charming member of our church. From the pulpit, I said, "If you are here today, please accept my abject apology!" And after the sermon, seven different women came up and said, "I accept your apology."

Do you drive like a Christian? Do you get furious when someone almost hits your car or gently bumps your rear bumper, or honks impatiently? There have been times when I was glad I wasn't a lip reader, as both myself and an oncoming driver slammed on our brakes to avoid a collision. Do you honk your horn in the hope of saving a few seconds of driving time?

Do you dim your lights for an approaching car even when the driver of the car refuses to dim his or her lights? Do you tailgate? What emotions erupt when a car in another lane slips in front of you when you do leave space ahead of you? Do you cross the yellow line in your lane and pass a car on a hill or around a curve? Nine out of ten accidents involve breaking the law.

II. Driving too fast.

In the remaining moments of this sermon, I wish to speak about the two major causes of highway accidents. The second greatest cause is speeding. Do you drive like a Christian? Do you knowingly speed? Our children watch us inch up above the speed limit. They observe us watching through the rearview mirror for police cars, and they note that we slow down as we top a hill lest there be a radar trap on the other side. Then we wonder why the police call us in the middle of the night to come and face our child in the city jail. They say, "If Dad or Mom can break laws, so can I."

III. Drinking and driving.

The greatest traffic problem is the drinking driver. Around eleven thousand people are killed on US highways each year as a result of alcohol-related crashes. Two out of every five Americans will be involved in an alcohol- or other drug-related crash during their lives. And, according to the Pacific Institute for Research and Evaluation, along with the human toll in destroyed lives, drunk driving costs the United States $132 billion every year in direct expenses (http://www.lifesaver.com/blog/real-cost-drunk-driving).

Conclusion

In our Scripture passage, Cain rather contemptuously asks, "Am I my brother's keeper?" Have you ever noticed that God did not answer him, except by inference? Perhaps it was because he was to reveal to humanity when they were ready to receive it, "You are your brother's brother."

Because I am my brother's brother, I shall drive like a Christian. For my family's sake, for other motorists' sake, for my own sake, and, most of all, for Jesus' sake, I shall be a good and careful steward of the license to drive an automobile.

WEDNESDAY EVENING, JULY 27

Title: Revival through Remembrance

Text: "I will therefore put you in remembrance, though ye once knew this, how that the Lord, having saved the people out of the land of Egypt, afterward destroyed them that believed not" (**Jude 5**).

Scripture Reading: Jude 1–5

Introduction

When I was a little boy, my parents asked questions which at times seemed completely unnecessary to me. To avoid answering their questions, such as, "Did you do that?" or "Where were you?" or "What did you do with thus-and-so?" I remember answering, "I can't remember." As I reflect on these times, I must confess that my memory was not nearly as poor as my credibility. One sharp parental injunction remains with me. When I gave one of these flimsy, "I can't remember" answers, one of my parents would admonish, "Well, you'd better get your remembering cap on."

Jude seems to be voicing the heavenly Father's word to his children, "You'd better get your remembering cap on."

I. The point of their arrival.

"Therefore" indicates something has gone before.

A. The church was in danger of spiritual suicide.

B. The church had been infiltrated when "certain men crept in unawares."

C. These in the church but not of the church were the Trojan horse or the undetected cancer that constituted the real danger to the church.

D. There is a frightening parallel in some of our own church members today. Today church members subscribe to covenants they do not keep. We make pledges we will not pay and accept responsibilities we know we will not discharge. We employ church staffs we will not support and make promises we will not keep.

II. The principle of their survival.

"I will therefore put in remembrance, though ye once knew this...."

A. William Barclay said that seldom does a preacher of God say anything new, nor is he called upon to do so. He is called upon to remind the people of what they already know for the larger part of his message.

B. This principle of revival through remembrance runs through the Bible.

1. "Remember Abraham, Isaac, and Jacob" (Ex. 32:13).
2. "Thou shalt remember the Lord thy God" (Deut. 8:18).
3. "Remember now thy Creator in the days of thy youth" (Eccl. 12:1).
4. "And his disciples remembered" (John 2:17).
5. "Peter remembered the word of the Lord" (Luke 22:61).
6. "He shall ... bring all things to your remembrance" (John 14:26).
7. "I stir up your pure minds by way of remembrance" (2 Peter 3:1).
8. "Remember therefore from whence thou art fallen" (Rev. 2:5).

III. The parallel for their revival.

"The Lord, having saved the people out of the land of Egypt, afterward destroyed them that believed not."

A. It is reported at the first Passover that they believed God (Num. 13:14).

B. Some murmured (Num. 14:1–3).

C. The people had faith to go from Egypt but not to go into the Promised Land. They were for the Passover but not for the pass-in. They were all for escape from Egypt, but they were not all for engagement in Canaan.

Conclusion

God will not continue to put up with unconfessed, unforgiven sins of his people. God expects his liberated people to be a consecrated people, claiming in active combat their promised territory. We can have "revival through remembrance," which means that we have to get back to God's basics for living the Christian life before we go forward.

SUNDAY MORNING, JULY 31

Title: Quality of Discipleship—Humility (The Parable of the Pharisee and the Publican)

Text: "I tell you, this man went down to his house justified rather than the other: for every one that exalteth himself shall be abased; and he that humbleth himself shall be exalted" **(Luke 18:14)**.

Scripture Reading: Luke 18:9–14

Hymns: "Love Divine All Loves Excelling," Wesley

"Christ Receiveth Sinful Men," Neumeister

"Amazing Grace," Newton

Offertory Prayer: Our Father who art in heaven, we approach you boldly because you are our Father. We come humbly because you are in heaven. Our sense of need because of our sins is the most eloquent petition we can offer. Encouraged by your promises and by the example of the publican whom you pronounced justified, we humbly pray as he did, "Lord, have mercy on me, a sinner." For your justification, we give you the thanks of dedicated lives in Jesus' name. Amen.

Introduction

This is the first of a series of messages concerning qualities of discipleship as illustrated in some of our Lord's parables.

The parable of the Pharisee and the publican allows us to hear two men at their private prayers. Both men seem to be sincere. It is this quality that tells us so much about them. It is not often that one is privileged to listen in on another's private prayer. The heart test is the true test of character. "For as he [man] thinketh in his heart, so is he" (Prov. 23:7). This does not mean that what one thinks he is, so he is; it means rather that what a man thinks in his inmost being is the kind of person he is. Only God can know this. "For the Lord seeth not as man seeth; for man looketh on the outward appearance, but the Lord looketh on the heart" (1 Sam. 16:7). The judgment of God with reference to these two men was doubtless a curious reversal of the judgment of the people who judged by appearance rather than according to the heart.

Let us note the sure portrayal of the story: "Two men went up into the temple to pray; the one a Pharisee, and the other a publican" (Luke 18:10). They probably went at one of the times designated for prayer. There is no evidence that either went for show. The Pharisee was a member of the strictest religious sect. The publican, or tax collector, was counted as a sinner by the Jewish people because he worked for the hated Roman conquerors.

I. The prayer of the Pharisee.

A. "The Pharisee stood and prayed thus with himself" (Luke 18:11). He began, "God, I thank thee, that I am not as other men are" (Luke 18:11). He thought that he was in a class by himself. In his own eyes, all other men were inferior. Remember that Jesus "spake this parable unto certain which trusted in themselves that they were righteous, and despised others" (Luke 18:9). The Pharisee also was uncharitable in his estimate of others whom he considered as "extortioners, unjust, adulterers," and although he did not know the publican personally, he condemned him because he belonged to a class of people who were generally condemned.

B. Having thanked God for his virtues of omission, the Pharisee next commended himself for his virtues of commission. He fasted twice a week, which was more than the law required. He gave tithes of all he received. Perhaps he was as careful as those in Matthew 23:23 to "pay tithe of mint and anise and cumin," the household spices. He did not ask for forgiveness. He seemed not to be conscious that he needed such.

II. The prayer of the publican.

The publican presented quite a contrast to the Pharisee. "And the publican, standing afar off, would not lift up so much as his eyes unto heaven, but smote upon his breast, saying, God be merciful to me a sinner" (Luke 18:13). He recognized his uncleanliness and felt that he was in a class by himself. One is reminded of Paul, who, under conviction for sin, considered himself the chief of sinners (see 1 Tim. 1:15). The publican had come to pray out of a conviction of a deep need. He dared to believe that God would be merciful. He pleaded nothing of his own righteousness but threw himself upon God's mercy.

III. Why the condemnation of the Pharisee?

A. He was condemned not:
   1. Because he was a Pharisee. Other Pharisees were saved.
   2. Because he was honest.
   3. Because he was just.
   4. Because he was moral.
   5. Because he fasted and tithed.

B. He was condemned because his heart was not right. He was unsaved. His motives were wrong.
   1. His prayer reveals a wrong opinion of himself. He completely overlooked his faults.
   2. He had a wrong opinion about others. He wanted to believe the worst rather than the best about others. The black background of the publican's sins helped to show off the Pharisee's virtues.
   3. He had a wrong view of God. God must surely be proud of him, thought the Pharisee, and be eager to congratulate him for well-deserved honors.
   4. He had a wrong idea about salvation. If he thought of it at all, salvation was an attainment, the just reward for good works. God owed it to himself to be very proud of him.

IV. Why the commendation of the publican?

A. He was commended not because of his sins. They were horrible in God's sight as indeed they were in his.

B. He was commended because of his repentance. He did not blame others for his sins. He did not excuse himself by pleading extenuating circumstances. He was sorry for his sins. His condemnation would be just. He was willing to confess his sins and to turn from them. Scripture says, "He that covereth his sins shall not prosper: but whoso confesseth and forsaketh them shall have mercy" (Prov. 28:13). He dared to act on God's promise.

Conclusion

"This man [the publican] went down to his house justified rather than the other" (Luke 18:14). He was saved. His sins were forgiven. He was given right standing with God. He was regenerated. He became a child of God.

We can only imagine the rest of the story. If we could have seen the publican later, he would doubtless have been able to say, "I am not an extortioner; I am not unjust; I am not an adulterer. I fast, give tithes, and go to the church." How then was he different from the Pharisee? In heart attitude, in love for God, in concern for others, and in humility before God. "For every one that exalteth himself shall be abased: and he that humbleth himself shall be exalted" (Luke 18:14).

No sins are so black that God cannot forgive. No person is so good that he or she does not need God's forgiveness. No deeds can save one whose heart is not right. If one's heart is right, good deeds will follow, for good deeds are the fruit rather than the root of salvation.

SUNDAY EVENING, JULY 31

Title: Character of God—Sovereignty (The Parable of the Laborers and the Hours)

Text: "Don't I have the right to do what I want with my own money? Or are you envious because I am generous?" **(Matt. 20:15 NIV)**.

Scripture Reading: Matthew 19:30–20:15

Introduction

Jesus begins his parables with "For the kingdom of God is like," and then he tells a story that will in some way illustrate the way God reigns.

The parable of the laborers and the hours is difficult to interpret. It is not an allegory. It sheds light on how God deals with humankind. Here in brief is the story: A householder who needed laborers to harvest his grapes went out early in the morning to hire laborers. He found some and agreed to pay each of them a denarius (the usual wage) for the day's work. At 9:00 a.m. he went back to the marketplace seeking laborers. He hired some and agreed to give them whatever was right. This he did again at noon, at midafternoon, and at one hour before the day's end. The laborers indicated that they were idle because no one had hired them. When the day's work was over, this employer, beginning with the last hired and going to the first hired, paid each one a denarius, a full day's wage. Although he had paid every man as much as agreed, those who had worked all day in the heat complained about his generosity. "But he answered one of them, 'I am not being unfair to you, friend. Didn't you agree to work for a denarius? Take your pay and go. I want to give the man who was hired last the same as I gave you. Don't I have the right to do what I want with my own money? Or are you envious because I am generous?'" (Matt. 20:13–15 NIV).

Both at the beginning of the parable and again at the end in Matthew 19:30 and 20:16, Jesus says, "But many that are first shall be last; and the last shall be first." We conclude that this is the truth illustrated: God's judgment will curiously differ from man's judgments. Every kingdom worker is precious in God's sight. Lack of opportunity will not be a hindrance to one's reward.

I. The sovereignty of God.

"Don't I have the right to do what I want with my own money?" (Matt. 20:15 NIV). God's ways seem as puzzling to us at times as the payment of equal wages to all of the laborers appeared to them. At first we are inclined to agree with the grumbling workers. It does not seem right to pay a man who has worked only one hour the same wages as one who has worked in the heat all day long. However, the workers who were not hired earlier had been ready. They were willing. They were idle not by choice but by necessity. They could honestly say, "No one has hired us." The man who went to work early at least knew that at the end of the day he would receive a day's wage with which to buy food for his family. The man waiting idly through the day must have worried about coming to his family without any money for their needs. Waiting was probably as difficult as working.

In ruling over his kingdom, God will take into account all of the facts, including motive and opportunity. When we know as he knows, we will see that his ways, which now seem strange to us, are just and right. "For my thoughts are not your thoughts, neither are your ways my ways, saith the Lord. For as the heavens are higher than the earth, so are my ways higher than your ways, and my thoughts than your thoughts" (Isa. 55:8–9).

II. God will do all he promises.

The laborers who first entered the vineyard bargained for so much money per day. The householder gave them what he promised. God promises to all who repent and obey salvation, eternal life, the indwelling of the Holy Spirit, heaven, and more. God will fulfill his promises.

In addition, on the basis of faithfulness and service, the Lord promises rewards according to his sovereign grace. In the parable of the talents in Matthew 25:14–35, the five-talent man and the two-talent man who were equally faithful received equal rewards. In the similar parable of the pounds, the one more faithful received more reward. The inequalities of the talents seem to recognize the inequality of human endowment. One pound to each servant seems to indicate that every person is potentially of equal value to God. God will take into account all of the facts.

III. God will do more than he promises.

A. The householder is more interested in the workers than in the work. God is concerned for his people.

B. The householder took into account the worker's opportunity. God in judgment will certainly consider one's opportunity. The assumption in the parable is that the workers accepted the first opportunity. They were not willfully lazy. They had not been hiding to avoid work.

Some people have heard God's call and have resisted. They are without excuse. Others have not heard the full gospel or have suffered under an unspiritual ministry. Others are excused by circumstances beyond their control. For example, let us imagine two sisters who answer the call of God for missionary service. Both make preparation by completing college and seminary. At the time for appointment, it is necessary for one of them to stay with their aged, sick parents. One of the sisters serves on the foreign field. The other remains with the parents. After the parents' death for whom she has cared tenderly, the second daughter is now past the age for foreign service. She serves faithfully in the homeland until her death. Who would call God unfair if he should give the same commendation to each of the sisters? Perhaps Andrew, the ordinary man, the personal soul-winner who brought his brother Peter to Jesus, will receive equal commendation to that of his gifted brother who preached to the multitudes.

IV. God will reverse many human judgments.

In Luke 16:19–31 the rich man certainly was considered a leading citizen of the community. His counsel would be sought by politicians. He was important among the businessmen. Lazarus was considered a common beggar. No citizen would have considered him among the first citizens. Lazarus, at death, however, was carried by angels to Abraham's side. "The rich man also died and was buried. In Hades, where he was in torment, he looked up and saw Abraham far away, with Lazarus by his side" (vv. 22–23 NIV). God's book of remembrance as to the great will be vastly different from the history books.

God takes into account the motive. The worker who was willing to work will be rewarded as the one who did work. David wanted to build the temple but could not. Solomon did build the temple. God said to David, "Whereas it was in thine heart to build an house unto my name, thou didst well that it was in thine heart" (1 Kings 8:18).

Conclusion

The murmuring workers did not share the spirit of the householder. They thought of work accomplished rather than of the welfare of the workers. They were like people who think that everyone ought to get exactly what he or she deserves or has earned. They leave no room for a merciful God who rejoices to give more than people deserve. The nearer we come to Jesus, the better we understand that the sovereign God has a right to do as he pleases and that because of his character he will do no wrong to anyone. The nearer we draw to him, the more we will rejoice in his grace and goodness to others.

Let us trust God enough to work in his vineyard. He will pay what he has promised—yes, vastly more. Work is better than idleness. How good it is to be able to work in God's vineyard!

SUGGESTED PREACHING PROGRAM FOR THE MONTH OF

AUGUST

■ Sunday Mornings

Continue with the theme "Qualities of Discipleship." This series will run through the end of September.

■ Sunday Evenings

Continue the series "Knowing the Character of God."

■ Wednesday Evenings

Continue the series of expository studies from the book of Jude.

WEDNESDAY EVENING, AUGUST 3

Title: Hell's Angels

Text: "And the angels which kept not their first estate, but left their own habitation, he hath reserved in everlasting chains under darkness unto the judgment of the great day" (**Jude 6**).

Scripture Reading: Jude 1–6

Introduction

By "Hell's Angels" I am not referring to the motorcycle gang, but to the real angels of hell talked about in the book of Jude.

I. The fact of angels.

A. The Old Testament mentions angels 108 times, and the New Testament mentions them 165 times.

B. Angels were created by God. "Praise ye him, all his angels praise ye him, all his hosts.... Let them praise the name of the Lord: for he commanded, and they were created" (Ps. 148:2, 5).

C. Angels were created superior to men. The Scriptures ask, "What is man, that thou art mindful of him?... Thou madest him a little lower than the angels" (Heb. 2:6–7).

D. Christ was made lower than angels in his incarnation but higher than the angels in his resurrection (Heb. 1:3–4, 9–10).

E. Angels do not reproduce, so there is a fixed number of angels. Jesus said of men and women, "For in the resurrection they neither marry, nor are given in marriage, but are as the angels of God in heaven" (Matt. 22:30).

F. Angels are innumerable—"an innumerable company of angels" (Heb. 12:22).

G. Some angels are holy—"when he cometh in the glory of his Father with the holy angels" (Mark 8:38).
H. Some angels are unholy. "Then shall he say also unto them on the left hand, Depart from me, ye cursed, into everlasting fire, prepared for the devil and his angels" (Matt. 25:41).

II. The function of angels.

A. They are called on to worship God (Ps. 148:2–5).
B. They are spiritual personalities; therefore they think and speak and have other personality traits.
C. They are beings who minister or serve (Matt. 4:11).
D. They are sent forth to minister to Christians. "But to which of the angels said he at any time, Sit on my right hand, until I make thine enemies thy footstool? Are they not all ministering spirits, sent forth to minister for them who shall be heirs of salvation?" (Heb. 1:13–14).

III. The fall of angels.

A. The explanation of unholy angels is that they are fallen angels. "For if God spared not the angels that sinned, but cast them down to hell, and delivered them into chains of darkness, to be reserved unto that judgment ..." (2 Peter 2:4). So angels are creatures of spiritual sensitivity and responsibility.
B. Pride is the prime sin of the prince of evil angels. "How art thou fallen from heaven, O Lucifer, son of the morning! how art thou cut down to the ground, which didst weaken the nations! For thou hast said in thine heart, I will ascend into heaven, I will exalt my throne above the stars of God: I will sit also upon the mount of the congregation, in the sides of the north: I will ascend above the heights of the clouds; I will be like the most High" (Isa. 14:12–14).
C. Rebellion to the point of hostility is the basis for expulsion of the angels from heaven (Rev. 12:7–9).

IV. The fate of fallen angels.

A. They fell from the life of heaven—"the angels which kept not their first estate, but left their own habitation" (Jude 6).
B. They fell from the liberty of heaven—"he hath reserved in everlasting chains" (Jude 6).
C. They fell from the light of heaven—"under darkness unto the judgment of the great day" (Jude 6).

Conclusion

God created angels to be good, but some of them—scholars believe about one-third—joined Lucifer's rebellion and are now fallen and evil. They have received eternal punishment. Jude teaches us that if even the angels of heaven cannot get away with pride and rebellion without an accounting punishment, neither can people inside or outside the church.

SUNDAY MORNING, AUGUST 7

Title: Quality of Discipleship—Astuteness (The Parable of the Unjust Steward)

Text: "I tell you, use worldly wealth to gain friends for yourselves, so that when it is gone, you will be welcomed into eternal dwellings" **(Luke 16:9 NIV)**.

Scripture Reading: Luke 16:1–9

Hymns: "Sing the Wondrous Love of Jesus," Hewitt

"There Is a Name I Love to Hear," Whitfield

"I Lay My Sins on Jesus," Bonar

Offertory Prayer: Our Father, grant that we may be as wise and as zealous in promoting your kingdom as we are in promoting our own interests. No, rather, help us to make your interests ours so that our only concern will be to administer the trust that you have given to us in accord with your righteous will. Grant to us as individuals and as a church wisdom to distribute the gifts we bring to you in the wisest possible way as responsible stewards of your bounty, for yours is the kingdom, and the power, and the glory, forever. Amen.

Introduction

Of all Jesus' parables, the parable of the unjust steward is probably the most difficult to interpret. Did Jesus commend the embezzler, a servant who defrauded his master? Yes, but his commendation was not for his character; it was for his astuteness.

This story is a parable, not an allegory. An allegory is typical, and the likeness can be traced all the way through as, for example, in the allegory of the good shepherd: the shepherd, the sheep, the sheepfold, and the door all have typical meanings. A parable is illustrative, and the parable may touch the truth at only one point. For example, in Luke 12:39–40 the coming of the Son of Man and of the thief are alike only in their unexpectedness. They are not at all alike in character, in the purpose for which they come, or in any other manner contemplated by the parable. If one says, "A watch is like a sundial, and both are like an hourglass," the similarity would be only that they are methods of telling time. Any comparison as to substance, weight, color, and so on is not intended. Any effort to interpret the parable of the unjust steward as an allegory will end in fanciful folly and error.

I. Note the story carefully (Luke 16:1–2).

A. A steward often had wide latitude in the oversight of his master's properties, enterprises, and goods. Potiphar's trust of Joseph is an interesting illustration. "And Joseph found grace in his sight, and he served him: and he made him overseer over his house, and all that he had he put into his hand" (Gen. 39:4). The fact that a master would trust a servant with all of his goods made embezzlement easier but also more blameworthy. A rich master would most likely learn of his steward's mismanagement by the testimony of a third party.

B. The steward faced the facts (16:3–7). When ordered to get his accounts in shape for an accounting, he knew that the verdict would be "guilty." He was not strong enough to do manual labor and was too ashamed to beg, so he resolved to follow a shrewd scheme of contacting his master's debtors and allowing them to lower the amounts of the notes owed to his master. He knew that his customers could be bought, and he knew how much it would take to buy each one. His hope was that when he was fired they would remember his kindness and share their ill-gotten gain with him.

C. The strange commendation (16:8). The men listening to Jesus narrate the story expected to hear him say that the rich master condemned the wicked steward. How surprised they must have been to hear Jesus say, "The master commended the dishonest manager because he had acted shrewdly. For the people of this world are more shrewd in dealing with their own kind than are the people of the light" (v. 8 NIV). Note that the master commended him, not for his motive, but for his astuteness; not for his fraud, but for his foresight. We may assume that the servant was summarily dismissed.

Have you ever had a swindler take you for some money in such a clever way that in spite of yourself you admired his astuteness? Surely a confident man as clever as he could make an honest living if he desired to do so.

II. The meaning of the parable (Luke 16:8).

A. If unsaved people, for selfish, unworthy ends, can display such astuteness, foresight, and dedication to their worldly goals, how much more should Christians use intelligence, foresight, and zeal for kingdom interests? Take, for example, great athletes or great musicians who are famous for their performances in the secular realm. They must devotedly dedicate their time and energy to their work to become skilled. Does the cause of Christ deserve less devotion? Can we justify an inferior dedication to preparing for the worship and service of God?

B. This parable is a challenge to foresight. The unjust steward looked ahead. He made provision for the future. Jesus said, "Use worldly wealth to gain friends for yourselves, so that when it is gone, you will be welcomed into eternal dwellings" (Luke 16:9 NIV). We are to use the treasure of this life in such a manner that when death comes, we will have a welcome in heaven. Entrance into heaven depends on one's salvation. Rewards in heaven depend on the faithful way one has served others in Jesus' name. One is to use the treasures of this life (specifically money) so as to lay up treasures in heaven. Note carefully other teachings of Jesus about heavenly treasure in Matthew 6:19–20; 10:42; 25:31–41; and Revelation 14:13.

Conclusion

Are the children of this world really wise? No, their wisdom is only "in this generation." In other words, they have mere worldly wisdom. They are fools who build the house of life on shifting sands. The truly wise are those who build on the solid rock and seek first the kingdom of God and his glory. Jesus is their Captain, God is their Father, the Holy Spirit is their Guide. Even now in earthly tabernacles they have eternal life and journey toward the heavenly city.

SUNDAY EVENING, AUGUST 7

Title: Character of God—Seeking (The Parables of the Lost Sheep, the Lost Coin, and the Lost Sons)

Text: "For the Son of man is come to seek and to save that which was lost" **(Luke 19:10)**.

Scripture Reading: Luke 15

Introduction

Three companion parables in Luke 15 reveal God as the loving Father who seeks the lost. Jesus told these stories to answer the accusation of the scribes and Pharisees that "this man receiveth sinners, and eateth with them" (v. 2). In effect, Jesus replied, "As a lost sheep needs a shepherd, as a lost coin needs to be found, as a son needs a father, so sinners need God."

I. The parable of the lost sheep (Luke 15:3–7).

A. Lost. A shepherd having a flock of one hundred sheep brought them at the close of the day to a fold in the wilderness. This fold was a stockade built mostly of rocks. A porter (usually one of the shepherds) guarded the door during the night. As the shepherd counted his sheep, he found that one was missing. The shepherd was not satisfied that only 99 percent of his sheep were safe, so he left the ninety-nine safe with the porter in the wilderness and went out into the night to search for his lost sheep. His purpose was to seek until he found it.

B. Found. What joy the shepherd had when he found the sheep still alive though so weak that it had to be carried to the fold. He was so happy that when he brought his sheep back home he called his friends and neighbors to rejoice with him.

C. Application. God loves every person and wants all to be saved. He is not satisfied with a good percentage. He seeks for the lost, and his Holy Spirit convicts of sin and invites to salvation. He rejoices "over one sinner that repenteth, more than over ninety and nine just persons, which need no repentance" (v. 7). One repentant sinner pleases God more than a multitude of religious people with no sense of guilt.

II. The parable of the lost coin (Luke 15:8–10).

A. The lost coin was valuable to the woman. She searched diligently, turning the place upside down until she found the coin.

B. Found. Joy needs to be shared. On finding the coin, the woman called her friends and neighbors to rejoice with her. The value she placed on the coin is reflected in the joy of finding it.

C. Application. Every person is potentially valuable to God, but that value is potential only so long as one is lost. The coin must be found for value to become actual. So the lost must be found for potential value to become actual. "Joy in the presence of the angels of God over one sinner that repenteth" (v. 10) must mean joy in the heart of God himself.

III. The parable of the two sons (Luke 15:11–32).

A. The younger son (vv. 11–13).

1. The departure. The younger son asked his father to give to him the portion of the estate that he would inherit upon his father's death. The son thought that he could be happier away from home. His request was willful and selfish. It must have pained the father greatly, but if the son were forced to stay home, then home would be a prison; so, with sadness of heart, he divided his estate between his two sons. In accord with custom, the older son received twice as much as the younger. The younger son took his inheritance and set out for a far country.
2. Destination (v. 13). The younger son thought that living far away from home would bring him happiness, for he would no longer have any parental restraints. He acted on the lie that his father's restraints were grievous. He believed Satan's lie that sin brings pleasure. As Satan caused Adam and Eve to doubt God's good purpose by asking, "Hath God said?" so the younger son doubted his father. Anywhere outside the will of God is a far country.
3. Destitution (vv. 13–15). The far country promised freedom but actually enslaved the young man. While his money lasted, the young man had some fair-weather friends, but when the money gave out, he was reduced to destitution. He hired out to a Gentile to feed his hogs. He tried to eat hogs' food, but that was not food for a man. Man is made for fellowship with God. He can never find soul satisfaction in sin. As Augustine correctly perceived, "Thou hast made us for thyself, O God, and our hearts are restless until they rest in Thee."
4. Resolution to return (vv. 17–19). "When he came to himself" (v. 17) is a telling phrase. A demented person is sometimes said to be beside himself. Sin is moral insanity. The young man now came to his right mind about his father. He thought, *The hired servants at home fared well. Father is a good man. I'll go back to him, confess my sin, and ask to be a hired servant.* His conviction and contrition issued in action: he did it. How much better it was for him to go to his father than to drown his sorrow in drink or give up to the despair of suicide.

5. The reception (vv. 20–24). His father saw him when he was a great way off. The father had been hoping and looking for his son's return. The father ran to meet the son and embraced him and kissed him. The son started his confession, "Father, I have sinned against heaven, and in thy sight, and am no more worthy to be called thy son" (v. 21). The son did not get to request as he had planned, "Make me as one of thy hired servants." When the father heard the boy's confession, he pardoned him fully, gave him the insignia of sonship, and joyfully ordered a banquet saying, "For this my son was dead, and is alive again: he was lost, and is found." Jesus is saying that God is more merciful than we dare ask him to be and that his fatherly heart yearns to forgive.

B. The older son (vv. 25–32). How wonderful it would have been if the older son had said, "O how glad I am! The fact that my brother has come home shows that he has changed. I've missed him so much. I have prayed for his return. I've shared with Father concern for his safety. I must hurry to embrace him." But his reply was much different. The older son was not like his father in some very essential respects:

1. He lacked loving concern. Had he prayed for his brother's return? Did he rejoice at his return? Did he want to believe that he had sincerely repented? No! He showed lack of love for both his brother and his father. He was angry, and he refused to go to his brother's homecoming party. He doubted that his father had done what was right and believed the worst about his father rather than the best. The self-righteous older brother considered himself a slave rather than a son. He said, "'Look! All these years I've been slaving for you and never disobeyed your orders. Yet you never gave me even a young goat so I could celebrate with my friends. But when this son of yours who has squandered your property with prostitutes comes home, you kill the fattened calf for him!'" (vv. 29–30 NIV). His outburst revealed his ungratefulness. His father had provided all his needs and had also given him twice as much inheritance as he had given the younger son, yet he did not appreciate it.

   The older son showed a lack of love for his brother by accusing him of spending money on prostitutes without knowing whether it was true. He believed the worst about his brother and painted a dark backdrop of sin against which to display his own goodness. Instead of "my brother" he called him "thy son."

2. The older son had no place in his thinking for repentance and forgiveness. His idea was that one who sins should pay the penalty. His younger brother had made his bed, so let him lie in it. He, the older son, was sure of his own goodness. He merited much more than his father had ever given him. The older brother represents the scribes and Pharisees who thought that they were so good that they did not need God's forgiveness and that the publicans and harlots were so bad that they were beyond hope. They were wrong, of course, on both counts.

Conclusion

Some people are lost like a sheep who misses the way by careless drifting. Some, through life's circumstances, are misplaced like a lost coin. Others, like the young son, are lost through willful rebellion. Still others are lost as the older brother was—at home, yet far from the father; in church but full of hate, self-righteousness, prejudice, envy, and unforgiveness.

God is seeking lost persons as a shepherd out in the night, as a woman sweeping diligently, as a father earnestly watching.

When a sheep is found, the shepherd rejoices; when a coin is found, the woman rejoices; when a son is found, the father rejoices; when a sinner repents, God rejoices. Now is the day of salvation.

WEDNESDAY EVENING, AUGUST 10

Title: "Sodom and Gomorrah ... Likewise"

Text: "In a similar way, Sodom and Gomorrah and the surrounding towns gave themselves up to sexual immorality and perversion. They serve as an example of those who suffer the punishment of eternal fire. In the very same way, on the strength of their dreams these ungodly people pollute their own bodies, reject authority and heap abuse on celestial beings" **(Jude 7–8 NIV)**.

Scripture Reading: Jude 7–8

Introduction

In the court of human appeal, Jude presents the evidence. Exhibit I shows saved people. Exhibit II pictures destroyed people. Exhibit III deals with the angels. Now comes the plea for right thinking and right living in terms of God's recorded judgment on Sodom and Gomorrah.

I. A principle is seen.

A. God is interested in cities. He dealt with the cities of the plain: Admah, Zeboiim, Zoar, Sodom, and Gomorrah.

B. Review carefully God's keen interest in Rome, Ephesus, Tyre, Sidon, Jerusalem, etc.

C. God is still concerned with real "urban renewal." This embraces the character and integrity of a city's people. The souls of a city are more important than its streets. It is not traffic but truth, not industry but integrity, not money but people that make a city great.

II. A perversion is recorded.

A. Lot "pitched his tent toward Sodom," resulting in fateful consequences.

B. The name of Sodom is the parent word from which we get our word sodomy. So the infamy of that ancient city is written in every dictionary, in every courthouse, in every library and capitol of the land.

C. George Adam Smith said no event in history so impressed the Jewish people as did the story of Sodom. It is mentioned in the books of Deuteronomy, Isaiah, Jeremiah, Lamentations, Ezekiel, Amos, Zephaniah, Matthew, Luke, Romans, 2 Peter, and Revelation.

D. Sodom became known as an immoral city. The merchandising of Lot's own daughters, his own mocking attitude, and the fearful consequences recorded in Genesis 19 mark the city forever.

E. Jesus used Sodom as an example of wickedness and judgment (Matt. 10:15; 11:24–25).

III. A punishment is given.

"Then the Lord rained upon Sodom and upon Gomorrah brimstone and fire from the Lord out of heaven; and he overthrew those cities, and all the plain, and all the inhabitants of the cities, and that which grew upon the ground" (Gen. 19:24–25).

IV. Parallel is noted.

The text declares that Sodom is set forth as an example.

A. Dreamers. They are filthy dreamers. This is not, of course, a natural sleep. It is the fantasy of rotten imaginations, daydreaming about immoral garbage.

B. Defilers. These people were not only corrupt, but they also were sources of moral and spiritual pollution in a perversion that threatened the spiritual ecology of the day.

C. Despisers. These people flouted constituted authority. There are parallels around us everywhere today.

D. Declarers. It is no surprise that from their mouths should come the issues of their hearts. They spoke evil of celestial beings, which means that their wicked impulses were released both horizontally and vertically—against other people and celestial beings.

V. A prevention is suggested.

G. Campbell Morgan said, "A text without the context is a pretext." In the context of our text there is the pull of history, the example of municipal judgment, and the curse of the city. But there is also the appeal of repentance. There is a call to the called, a bulletin for believers. Jude's message is not a sealed obituary. It is an evangelistic sermon.

Conclusion

1. A look into the rearview mirror of history can help us in the traffic ahead.
2. The God of love and compassion is also one of firm judgment.
3. We can find hope in God's power and presence.
4. History need not repeat itself. There is hope!

SUNDAY MORNING, AUGUST 14

Title: Quality of Discipleship—Sympathy (The Parable of the Rich Man and Lazarus)

Text: "Son, remember that thou in thy lifetime receivedst thy good things, and likewise Lazarus evil things: but now he is comforted, and thou art tormented" **(Luke 16:25)**.

Scripture Reading: Luke 16:19–31

Hymns: "Come, Thou Fount of Every Blessing," Robinson

"Break Thou the Bread of Life," Lathbury

"Make Me a Channel of Blessing," Smith

Offertory Prayer: Loving Father, we believe that you are full of compassion. Forbid that we should harden our hearts against the needs of others. Open our eyes to see the needs of our neighbors. May the gifts that we bring this day be used to extend the gospel and to help heal humanity's hurts. In helping others, we believe that we are serving you, for Jesus taught us, "Inasmuch as ye have done it unto one of the least of these my brethren, ye have done it unto me." In Jesus' name we pray. Amen.

Introduction

By telling the story of an unsaved man who did not have sympathy, Jesus conveys to his disciples the importance of being sympathetic and merciful. The parable of this rich man warns us against living as he did and ending up in hell.

There is much about the spiritual realities of the future that we mortals cannot know. To his disciples, Jesus said, "I have yet many things to say unto you, but ye cannot bear them now" (John 16:12). He had already told his disciples, however, that there is nothing in the future of which believers need be afraid: "Let not your heart be troubled: ye believe in God, believe also in me" (John 14:1).

The story of the rich man and Lazarus is a drama in two acts: Scene 1 is in this world; scene 2 is in the next world.

I. Scene I (Luke 16:19–22).

The rich man is sometimes called Dives from the Latin for "rich man." His clothing was the best quality. Purple was the clothing of royalty. His inner garment of fine linen was made with the choicest Egyptian flax. His table was set with exotic foods.

Lazarus, a beggar who was covered with loathsome sores, was carried daily and laid at the gate of the rich man's house. He apparently was unable to walk and was carried by friends. He fought with the scavenger dogs for the scraps from the rich man's table. He must have had some success, else he would not have returned daily.

Lazarus died, and we are not told whether his body was buried or left for the dogs. He (the spiritual person who had lived in the body) was carried by angels to Abraham's bosom. In accord with the custom of that day, people reclined to eat, and the place of honor was near the host. Recall that at the Last Supper John reclined next to Jesus and leaned on his bosom (John 13:22–25). In another place, Jesus said, "Many shall come from the east and west, and shall sit down [recline] with Abraham, and Isaac, and Jacob, in the kingdom of heaven" (Matt. 8:11). Thus the bosom of Abraham represents the bliss of heaven.

The rich man also died. The record specifically says that he was buried. The funeral doubtless was a big, expensive one. He probably was eulogized as a great citizen, a pillar of the community, but he (the spiritual person who had lived in the body) went to hell.

It would be a serious error to jump to the conclusion that the rich are always bad and the poor are always pious. Abraham is just one example of a godly rich man. Jesus was a guest in the homes of the wealthy, and he never condemned the rich because they were rich or elevated the poor simply because they were poor. His own clothes were valuable enough for the soldiers to divide at his death. They even gambled for one of his garments. For the purpose of this story, Lazarus is a godly poor man. By his actions, the rich man proved that he was ungodly. He was not a thief or embezzler or murderer. He was unsympathetic. He let human need for which he should have cared go unrelieved. His wealth was not his sin; it was his opportunity. His sin was self-love without sympathy.

II. Scene 2 (Luke 16:23–31).

The story seems to affirm that at death one goes without delay either to Abraham's bosom (paradise) or to hell. This view is confirmed by Jesus' promise to the repentant robber in Luke 23:43, the experience of Stephen who was welcomed by Jesus in Acts 7:56, and the vision of John who saw the redeemed in paradise in Revelation 7:9–17.

Memory and conscience both survive death. Father Abraham, speaking as the voice of eternal truth, called on the rich man to remember. Memory will recall through eternity poor bleeding Lazarus, and conscience will goad him for his neglect. Memory and conscience may be the twin fires of torment.

The rich man still considered Lazarus as a subordinate, as revealed by his imperative, "Send Lazarus, that he may dip the tip of his finger in water, and cool my tongue; for I am tormented in this flame" (v. 24). Abraham replied that there is a chasm between heaven and hell over which there is no passing.

The rich man requested that Lazarus be sent to warn his five brothers. Is this unexpected compassion for his brothers, or is it a suggestion that he was not adequately warned in life? Father Abraham affirmed the sufficiency of divine revelation. He also affirmed that no one returns from paradise or from hell to this earth.

Dives's suggestion almost wins our approval. Let someone return to witness of the joys of the saved and the torments of the damned. But would people turn? What credentials could someone else bring that Jesus does not have? He had character; he had miraculous power; he arose from the dead. God said, "This is my beloved Son, in whom I am well pleased; hear ye him" (Matt. 17:5). If Moses and the prophets had light enough for judgment, "How shall we escape, if we neglect so great salvation?" (Heb. 2:3).

Conclusion

Some people hold to the hope that there will be opportunity for repentance beyond the grave. We devoutly wish that we could believe it, but it is not taught anywhere in God's Word. The gulf between heaven and hell is final. Eternal destiny is fixed forever on this side of the grave.

Why should you wait for a second chance? If you are ever to give your heart to Christ, do it now. "He that believeth on the Son hath everlasting life: and he that believeth not the Son shall not see life; but the wrath of God abideth on him" (John 3:36). "Behold, now is the accepted time; behold, now is the day of salvation" (2 Cor. 6:2).

Your attitude toward Lazarus at your door may be either a confirmation or a warning about your salvation or damnation.

SUNDAY EVENING, AUGUST 14

Title: Character of God—Prayer-Hearing (The Parables of the Friend at Midnight and of the Importunate Widow)

Text: "And he spake a parable unto them to this end, that men ought always to pray, and not to faint" **(Luke 18:1)**.

Scripture Reading: Luke 11:1–13; 18:1–8

Introduction

These parables of the friend at midnight and of the importunate widow probably are based on boyhood experiences of Jesus.

The first is a humorous story. A certain person had an unexpected guest arrive during the middle of the night. He had no food to place before him. His embarrassment was so great that he knocked on his neighbor's door and called out, "Friend, lend me three loaves; for a friend of mine in his journey is come to me, and I have nothing to set before him" (Luke 11:5–6). Now this man had bedded his family down for the night. As was frequently the custom, the children slept in the same room with the parents. For the man to get up would mean to wake the children. The baby would surely cry again. He was simply not willing to get up. But the embarrassed neighbor kept on knocking—persistently, shamelessly. Now thoroughly awake (doubtless the children were awake also), the gruff neighbor loaned him as many loaves as he needed.

The second parable is serious, almost tragic, but is relieved by a touch of humor and a happy ending. Did Mary, Jesus' widowed mother, have someone try to take advantage of her? There were men in Jesus' day, even men who professed religion, who would rob widows. Jesus condemned them soundly (see Matt. 23:14). The widow sought the aid of a judge—who had no sense of right before God or man—to get for her justice from her oppressor. She had no power to compel; she had no money to bribe; she could only beseech. This she did continuously, at home, at his office, on the street; morning, afternoon, and night she pled her case. She pestered him so much that he got justice for her just to get rid of her.

I. God does hear our prayers?

A. What is Jesus telling us about God in these stories? Is he saying that God is like a gruff neighbor who hesitates to get up? Is he an unjust judge who must be begged until in self-interest he attends to the suppliant's plea? Far otherwise. The point is in the a fortiori logic of which Jesus was so fond. If a gruff neighbor will answer the persistent pleas of an embarrassed friend at midnight, how much more will the heavenly Father hear the pleas of his children? If a venal judge will hear the pleas of a persistent widow, "Shall not God avenge his own elect, which cry day and night unto him, though he bear long with them? I tell you that he will avenge them speedily" (Luke 18:7–8).

B. Jesus enforces the argument beautifully and logically: "If a son shall ask bread of any of you that is a father, will he give him a stone? Or if he ask a fish, will he for a fish give him a serpent? Or if he shall ask an egg, will he offer him a scorpion? If ye then, being evil, know how to give good gifts unto your children: how much more shall your heavenly Father give the Holy Spirit to them that ask him?" (Luke 11:11–13).

If earthly parents, the best of whom are evil as compared to the holy God, would not give a child who asked for a biscuit a stone, nor for a fish a snake, nor for an egg a scorpion, then how much more can we depend on God, who is better than us, to do better than we do? Jesus is affirming that God hears our prayers and will give "good things" (see Matt. 7:11) to those who ask him. God will not be worse than the best of his creation.

II. The fatherly character of God is an encouragement to prayer.

A. According to Luke, Jesus spoke the parable of the importunate widow "to the effect that they ought always to pray and not lose heart" (Luke 18:1 RSV). Doubtless, the parable of the friend at midnight had substantially the same purpose.

B. God will not give us bad things. If a parent would not give a little boy a sharp razor no matter how earnestly he pleaded for it, how much more can we depend on God to deny our foolish petitions? We would be afraid to pray if God granted everything we asked. This would substitute our fallible, limited judgment for God's infallible judgment. There would be no challenge, no courage, no heroism, no sympathy, no faith. Let us thank God for unanswered prayer.

C. God desires to give us good things (cf. Matt. 7:11; Luke 11:13).

1. Prayer is a means of soul growth.

   a. By prayer we mean more than saying prayers. One's prayer is that which one really desires. We may or may not use words to relate that desire. James Montgomery's beautiful hymn expresses the meaning accurately:

Prayer is the soul's sincere desire,
Unuttered or expressed;
The motion of a hidden fire
That trembles in the breast.

b. One purpose of prayer is to get the petitioner's will in harmony with God's will. Jesus' primary prayer in Gethsemane was not, "O my Father, if it be possible, let this cup pass from me." It was rather, "Nevertheless, not as I will, but as thou wilt" (Matt. 26:39). Prayer "in Jesus' name" is a prayer so in accord with our Lord's will that he could sign his name to it. If God's will is best, then believers need to come to the place where their wills conform to God's will. Prayer helps to do this. God's delay in answering our prayers may be the means of clarifying our motives and desires.

2. God's "no" or "wait" or "something else" will prove to be better than our own desires.

Second Corinthians 12:7–9 narrates how Paul prayed earnestly that the thorn in his flesh might be removed. He thought this thorn in his flesh hindered his ministry. He believed its removal to be God's will. God did not take away the thorn in the flesh, but he did give Paul the grace to bear it. Paul lived to see that he was a better minister of Christ because the Lord did not give him what he asked for.

All mature Christians have had similar experiences. We look back and thank God for unanswered petitions but answered prayers.

Some Christian has expressed this thought as follows:

How God Answers

He prayed for strength that he might achieve;
He was made weak that he might obey.
He prayed for wealth that he might do greater things;
He was given infirmity that he might do better things.
He prayed for riches that he might be happy;
He was given poverty that he might be wise.
He prayed for power that he might have the praise of men;
He was given infirmity that he might feel the need of God.
He prayed for all things that he might enjoy life;
He was given life that he might enjoy all things.
He had received nothing that he asked for—all that he hoped for;
His prayer was answered—he was most blessed.

—*Author unknown*

III. Delayed answer may be necessary to develop earnestness.

God's blessings will not be bestowed in response to a superficial prayer. Prayer for God's will to be done on earth implies that the one praying will allow

God's will to be done in his or her life. Prayer for the salvation of the lost implies one's willingness to live an exemplary Christian life and a willingness to seek the leadership of the Holy Spirit in witnessing to the unsaved. A prayer for peace implies that one is both peaceable and a peacemaker. One's prayer for justice and mercy implies that one will be just and merciful.

Conclusion

Is your prayer in Jesus' name? Are you praying in God's will? Are you seeking first the kingdom of God and his righteousness? (See Matt. 7:33.)

Believe that God will work out the situation you are praying about for good. Jesus says that you are not to give up. Keep on asking, keep on seeking, keep on knocking. The heavenly Father may not give what you ask for, but he will give you better than you ask. He will not be deaf to your entreaty.

God promises some things when you ask in sincerity: for example, forgiveness of sins, salvation, eternal life, the presence of the Holy Spirit, and heaven as your eternal home. He has not promised health, freedom from pain, material prosperity, long life, or escape from death. He does promise that whatever the trial, "My grace is sufficient for thee: for my strength is made perfect in weakness" (2 Cor. 12:9).

The purpose of prayer is not to get God to do our will. Rather, it is to get God's will done through us.

WEDNESDAY EVENING, AUGUST 17

Title: Michael, Moses, and Men

Text: "But even the archangel Michael, when he was disputing with the devil about the body of Moses, did not dare to bring a slanderous accusation against him, but said, 'The Lord rebuke you!' Yet these men speak abusively against whatever they do not understand; and what things they do understand by instinct, like unreasoning animals—these are the very things that destroy them" **(Jude 9–10 NIV)**.

Scripture Reading: Jude 9–10

Introduction

Let us examine this passage from Jude as if looking at a drama with a plot and characters.

I. The characters.

A. Michael. Michael is the archangel whose name means "like unto God." No wonder so many parents name their sons Michael. In the language of our day, Michael would be called God's right-hand man. God sent Michael as a warrior to settle disputes with satanic forces.

Michael is mentioned also in the following Scriptures, and reviewing the passages indicated (Dan. 10:13, 21; 12:1; Rev. 12:7–9) will enrich this study.

B. Moses. There is so much biblical material on Moses that it is not possible to reduce 120 years of his wonderful life to a few moments of time. However, for the purpose of our focus here, care should be given especially to the account of his death as found in Deuteronomy 34:1–6.

C. The devil. Called by various names, the devil is presented as a reality throughout the Bible. We see evidence of his work in the world around us.

II. The contention.

A. Where did Jude get the story of Michael and the devil contending for the body of Moses?
   1. From the Bible? No.
   2. From The Assumption of Moses, an apocryphal book? Possibly.
   3. From God? Yes. Jude received the story through divine inspiration.

B. Why the contention?
   1. If the body is evil, as many have believed and continue to believe, it rightly belonged to the devil.
   2. Since Moses had sinned (he had murdered and had struck the rock rather than speaking to it, etc.), for Satan to get his body would prove that any who sin or disobey God are turned over to Satan.
   3. The devil would have delivered Moses' body to Israel, and the people may have carried his remains with them and worshiped him, thus effecting a sort of idolatry. Such a religious idolatry may well be the worst kind of all.
   4. Or they may have returned the body to the grave and made a shrine of the place.
   5. They may have used the body to frustrate (at least in the minds of the people) the doctrine of the resurrection.

III. The contrast.

A. Michael brought no railing accusation, but simply said, "The Lord rebuke you!"

B. These evil men "speak abusively against whatever they do not understand." This is unregenerate human nature, since it seeks to preserve the ego at any price.

C. Michael's understanding was due to his relationship to his Maker. The understanding of these dreamers was on the level of beasts.

D. Michael did not use what he knew in self-inflicted injury. The resources of these vile men were used in pitiful self-destruction.

Conclusion

1. The conflict continues unceasingly and will for the "duration."
2. "Railing" is a sure way of failing; it settles no battle.

3. Final judgment belongs to the final Judge.
4. God has left some unique things for us; let us leave some things with him (Ps. 37:1, 7–8).

SUNDAY MORNING, AUGUST 21

Title: Quality of Discipleship—Forgiveness (The Parable of the Unmerciful Servant)

Text: "For if ye forgive men their trespasses, your heavenly Father will also forgive you: But if ye forgive not men their trespasses, neither will your Father forgive your trespasses" **(Matt. 6:14–15)**.

Scripture Reading: Matthew 18:21–35

Hymns: "We Praise Thee, O God," Mackay

"O Safe to the Rock," Cushing

"Wonderful, Wonderful Jesus," Russell

Offertory Prayer: Loving Father, we rejoice that your forgiveness is without limit. "There is therefore now no condemnation to them which are in Christ Jesus, who walk not after the flesh, but after the Spirit." Grant that we may be kind one to another, even as you for Christ's sake have forgiven us. To that end we confess our sins, in Jesus' name. Amen.

Introduction

The parable of the unmerciful servant climaxes a whole chapter recording teaching of our Lord about the importance of right personal relationships.

The immediate occasion was Peter's question, "Lord, how oft shall my brother sin against me, and I forgive him? till seven times?" On the basis of the prophet Amos's repeated phrase "for three transgressions and for four," the rabbis taught three times as the limit. Peter thought he was being very magnanimous in suggesting seven times. Whether Jesus' reply is seventy-seven or seventy times seven (an analogy of Gen. 4:23–24), his answer clearly means that there is no numerical limit on the number of times a Christian must forgive one who seeks forgiveness. Instead of Lamech's unlimited revenge, Jesus proclaims unlimited forgiveness. From the cross he prayed, "Father, forgive them; for they know not what they do" (Luke 23:34).

The theme enforced by the parable is this: Unless one has a right heart attitude expressed by willingness to forgive others, he or she has no forgiveness from God. Unforgiveness bars God's forgiveness and incurs guilt. So states our text.

This parable is not an allegory. It deals with principles and relationships rather than with persons. Erroneously identifying the king as God will result in many contradictions. This story illustrates the way that God rules.

I. The magnitude of the debt (Matt. 18:23–25).

Jesus showed humor in making the debt of the servant to the king so great. One talent was six thousand denarii (pence). Ten thousand talents would be 60 million denarii. A denarius in the parables was usually a day's wage. The historian Josephus records that the annual imperial taxes of Judea, Idumea, and Samaria were only six hundred talents. Ten thousand talents was an impossible sum! A day laborer could as easily pay off the national debt as that servant could pay off the king. He was utterly, completely insolvent. Yet, in his pride and desperation he cried, "Have patience with me, and I will pay thee all" (v. 26).

In a similar way, all people owe a sin debt to God that they can never pay. Sinners are "dead in trespasses and sins" (Eph. 2:1), and dead people cannot save themselves. Human pride thinks, I can atone for my sins by good deeds. Good deeds cannot atone for past sins, and all our deeds will not be good. "For all have sinned, and come short of the glory of God" (Rom. 3:23).

II. The forgiveness of the debt (Matt. 18:26–27).

A. On the basis of the debtor's pitiful plea, the king compassionately forgave him the debt and freed him and his family from bondage.

B. This portion of the parable suggests the greatness of God's mercy in forgiving the sin debt of those who call on him in sincerity. God's forgiveness is offered to all people. He offers to forgive all sins for all time. This offer is free yet costly. The death of Christ on the cross shows that God's offer is not cheap grace. "For God so loved the world, that he gave his only begotten Son, that whosoever believeth in him should not perish, but have everlasting life" (John 3:16). "All we like sheep have gone astray; we have turned every one to his own way; and the Lord hath laid on him the iniquity of us all" (Isa. 53:6). "[Christ] gave himself for us, that he might redeem us from all iniquity" (Titus 2:14). "There is therefore now no condemnation to them which are in Christ Jesus" (Rom. 8:1).

III. The terms of forgiveness (Matt. 18:28–34).

A. The king in the parable was fooled about the nature of the servant on whom he had compassion. He expected that the servant would show a like compassion to others. Instead, the servant found a fellow servant who owed him a mere one hundred pence (only 1/60,000 of that which he had been forgiven). The plea of the fellow servant in the exact words that he himself had used to the king fell on deaf ears. Without compassion he cast him into prison. Fellow servants who were grieved at his action carried word to the king. The king was angry and called the servant before him, reversed his decision, and delivered him to the tormentors.

B. God never makes a mistake as did the king. God never forgives until a person genuinely repents. Repentance is more than being sorry for the effects of sin. Repentance is a change of mind that comes to see sin as God sees it, which is to hate it and to be willing to turn from it. Repentance is essential to God's forgiveness (see Luke 24:47; Acts 20:21). Repentance and faith are conjoined twins: there can be no turning from sin without turning to God in believing faith.

When God forgives, he justifies (sets sinners right with himself) and regenerates (gives them a new heart attitude that loves the Lord and hates sin). It is a moral impossibility to be forgiven of God and to desire the damnation of others. Redeemed people who are now children of God through faith in Christ Jesus will partake of the nature of their heavenly Father.

C. Even God cannot forgive people who are not willing to be forgiven. God always desires to forgive. Christ died to make forgiveness possible so that God can be just to himself and forgive us sinners (see Rom. 3:23–26). However, even God must sadly see unrepentant people go unforgiven.

D. As does our heavenly Father, so do we desire to live in right relations with all persons. If we have offended anyone, we are to seek reconciliation immediately (see Matt. 5:23–24). If our brother has sinned against us, we are to go to him in the hope that he will repent as instructed in Matthew 18:15–17 and Luke 17:3–4.

Conclusion

"If ye ... forgive not" (Matt. 18:35). Unforgiveness in the heart is evidence that a person has not been saved. When, as it were, one accepts forgiveness for his ten thousand talents of debt to the Lord, the one hundred pence his neighbor owes him is as nothing.

Sometimes one hears the statement, "Revenge is sweet." How absolutely untrue. Revenge shows a wicked spirit. Christians never pray, "Father, damn them," but always, "Father, forgive them." Christians may have to defend themselves from enemies, but even then they are praying that their enemy will be saved, become a friend, and cease fighting. If any punishing needs to be done, that is God's task. The Lord says, "It is mine to avenge; I will repay" (Heb. 10:30 NIV).

A forgiving spirit brings a peace that passes understanding. It is godlike to love and to forgive. Jesus said, "Love your enemies, bless them that curse you, do good to them that hate you, and pray for them which despitefully use you, and persecute you; that ye may be the children of your Father which is in heaven" (Matt. 5:44–45).

SUNDAY EVENING, AUGUST 21

Title: Character of God—Hopeful (The Parable of the Wicked Husbandmen)

Text: "And when the time of the fruit drew near, he sent his servants to the husbandmen, that they might receive the fruits of it" **(Matt. 21:34).**

Scripture Reading: Matthew 21:33–46

Introduction

The parable of the wicked husbandmen was addressed to the chief priests and others (see Matt. 21:23) in the court of the temple by our Lord on the Tuesday before his Friday crucifixion. Those to whom Jesus addressed this parable knew that he was preaching to them and reacted violently.

"Hear another parable," Jesus said (Matt. 21:33). Those around Jesus had just listened to the parable of the two sons with its pointed application (see vv. 28–32). Now he told this story: A man planted a vineyard with the full expectation that it would bear fruit and that he would enjoy the fruit. Doubtless, as in the earlier story in Isaiah 5:1–7 on which the parable is based, he "planted it with the choicest vine." The hedge about it would keep out the animals. The tower provided a place for the watchmen and a lodging place for the workers. His hope of fruit was such that he dug a winepress out of the rock. He leased the vineyard to agriculturalists who were to pay him a portion of the harvest as rent. Then the owner went on a journey. At the appointed time of the harvest, the owner sent his servants to collect the rent. Those who had leased the vineyard beat one, stoned one, and killed another. At last the owner decided to send his son. He hoped that they would respect the son. On the contrary, "They said among themselves, This is the heir; come, let us kill him, and let us seize on his inheritance" (v. 38). This cruelly they did. Jesus asked those who listened to his story what the owner of the vineyard would do to those tenants when he came. They answered, "He will miserably destroy those wicked men, and will let out his vineyard unto other husbandmen, which shall render him the fruits in their seasons" (v. 41).

We recognize, as did those who heard the story, that the householder or lord of the vineyard represents God. The vineyard is Israel, God's people, or more particularly, the vineyard represents God's plans and purposes "to redeem us from all wickedness and to purify for himself a people that are his very own, eager to do what is good" (Titus 2:14 NIV). The vineyard represents the methods God uses to accomplish his reign and in verse 43 is called "the kingdom of God" or "the reign of God." The wicked husbandmen entrusted with the vineyard are the religious leaders of the people. The servants are the prophets of God who had come from time to time to collect the fruit of righteousness but who had been shamefully mistreated. The son was the Lord Jesus whom the religious leaders were even then plotting to kill.

I. God called Israel as a special people.

A. God made known to Abraham that his seed would be a special people. He did this at the time he called Abraham to leave his father's house and go to the Promised Land: "Get thee out of thy country, and from thy kindred, and from thy father's house, unto a land that I will shew thee: and I will make of thee a great nation, and I will bless thee, and make thy name great; and thou shalt be a blessing: and I will bless them that bless thee, and curse him that curseth thee: and in thee shall all families of the earth be blessed" (Gen. 12:1–3). The promise was renewed to Abraham at the time he was willing to offer up Isaac as recorded in Genesis 22:15–18. It was renewed with Isaac and Jacob.

At Mount Sinai the covenant with Israel through Moses was conveyed in these words: "Ye have seen what I did unto the Egyptians, and how I bare you on eagles' wings, and brought you unto myself. Now therefore, if ye will obey my voice indeed, and keep my covenant, then ye shall be a peculiar treasure unto me above all people: for all the earth is mine: and ye shall be unto me a kingdom of priests, and an holy nation. These are the words which thou shalt speak unto the children of Israel" (Ex. 19:4–6). The Israelites were to be a special missionary people to all others. Like a vineyard specially planted, God expected that they would be his own special people to tell of his love to all nations.

B. God in love sent to them prophets culminating in the sending of his only begotten Son. As the author of Hebrews states the case so beautifully: "God, who at sundry times and in divers manners spake in time past unto the fathers by the prophets, hath in these last days spoken unto us by his Son, whom he hath appointed heir of all things, by whom also he made the worlds; who being the brightness of his glory, and the express image of his person, and upholding all things by the word of his power, when he had by himself purged our sins, sat down on the right hand of the Majesty on high" (Heb. 1:1–3).

C. The Jewish people rejected and mistreated the prophets. They put Jeremiah in stocks (see Jer. 20:1ff.; 37:15–16) and threw him in the pit (see Jer. 38:6). The prophets of God had to hide for their lives in the time of Elijah. Zechariah was stoned to death (see 2 Chron. 24:21). John the Baptist was beheaded. Jesus summed up the accusations: "Wherefore ye be witnesses unto yourselves, that ye are the children of them which killed the prophets" (Matt. 23:31). "Wherefore, behold, I send unto you prophets, and wise men, and scribes: and some of them ye shall kill and crucify; and some of them shall ye scourge in your synagogues and persecute them from city to city: that upon you may come all the righteous blood shed upon the earth, from the blood of righteous Abel unto the blood of Zacharias son of Barachias, whom ye slew between the temple and the altar" (Matt. 23:34–35). As a climax to these rebellious acts, they would slay Jesus, the Son of God.

D. The religious leaders rejected Jesus. Peter preached, "Therefore let all the house of Israel know assuredly that God hath made that same Jesus, whom ye have crucified, both Lord and Christ" (Acts 2:36). The religious experts rejected Jesus and in so doing fulfilled the Scripture, "Did ye never read in the scriptures, The stone which the builders rejected, the same is become the head of the corner: this is the Lord's doing, and it is marvelous in our eyes?" (Matt. 21:42).

On the basis of this disobedience and rejection, the privilege of being the special people of God to bring in the kingdom was taken from the posterity of Abraham and given to the spiritual seed of Abraham, those who have faith in God as did Abraham—that is, to Christians.

Note that God did not give up. He has hope in humankind. He called another people.

II. God calls Christian people to care for his vineyard.

A. Jesus affirmed that the kingdom of God was taken from the Jewish people and given to another people who hopefully would bring forth the fruit thereof (see v. 43). Peter, in almost the same words that God used to call Israel, wrote to the scattered Christians of the Roman provinces: "But ye are a chosen generation, a royal priesthood, an holy nation, a peculiar people; that ye should shew forth the praises of him who hath called you out of darkness into his marvellous light: which in time past were not a people, but are now the people of God: which had not obtained mercy" (1 Peter 2:9–10).

B. God gives Christians all they need for bearing fruit. In addition to the law and the prophets, Christians have the revelation through Jesus as recorded in the New Testament. They have the presence and power of the Holy Spirit for interpreting the words of Jesus and for witnessing.

C. Will Christians bring forth the fruit God expects? If yes, they will hear, "Well done, thou good and faithful servant: thou hast been faithful over a few things, I will make thee ruler over many things: enter thou into the joy of thy lord" (Matt. 25:21).

Christian people who are unfaithful will not cause God's purpose to fail. God will not be defeated, "for he must reign, till he hath put all enemies under his feet" (1 Cor. 15:25). Of the unfaithful servant, Jesus says, "Take therefore the talent from him, and give it unto him which hath ten talents" (Matt. 25:28). God purposes to place the kingdom of God in the hands of those who will render to the lord of the vineyard the fruits of the vineyard.

Conclusion

God trusts people. God, with courage and love, has created us in his own image, which includes the power of contrary choice. God has provided for the salvation of anyone who has used the power of choice to sin against his or her maker. "The Lord is … not willing that any should perish, but that all should come to repentance" (2 Peter 3:9). God hopes that every person will be saved and will bring forth the fruit of righteousness just as the owner expected to gather fruit from his vineyard.

God has loaned you a life. The owner did not sell the vineyard to the husbandmen. He loaned it to them. They were to possess it, to cultivate it, and to harvest it in accord with the will of the owner. They were then to render unto him the fruit of it. Similarly, God has not given up his rights as owner of your life. He has leased to you the opportunity to make choices. You have a life to direct but not to own.

You can be a good or a bad husbandman. The good husbandman follows the will of the Owner. He raises the crops the Owner wants raised in the manner prescribed. He welcomes the servants of God and rejoices to serve the Owner. He renders the fruit of the vineyard in season. He is the kind of servant the Owner of the vineyard wants him to be. He takes pride in his work and looks forward joyfully to his Master's "Well done." He has no fear that he will be removed from the vineyard. He especially welcomes the Son of the vineyard's Owner, for the Son is the image of his Father and brings the message of his Father's will.

The Owner of the vineyard, the husbandman, and the Son all rejoice when the husbandman serves faithfully in the vineyard, which is to say that there is joy in the heart of God and in the heart of the saved when one lives in the center of God's will.

WEDNESDAY EVENING, AUGUST 24

Title: Raising Cain and the Harvesttime

Text: "Woe to them! They have taken the way of Cain; they have rushed for profit into Balaam's error; they have been destroyed in Korah's rebellion" **(Jude 11 NIV)**.

Scripture Reading: Jude 11–13

Introduction

This is the seventh of nine studies in the little book of Jude, which gets bigger as we explore its historical references and ethical implications. The psalmist said that the Word was a lamp to his feet and a light to his path. It may be said that this portion of the Word, Jude, is a small light in measurement of size. But it is also one of "high density" as it shines on our way. Our previous discussions will serve as background for our present message.

I. The mistakes.

A. "They have taken the way of Cain" (read Gen. 4). Cain is remembered for his wickedness, especially for murdering his brother Abel. Even worse was his rejection of God's prescribed sin offering. The sin of attempting to save ourselves in our own way is that which puts us in Cain's category. The only way of salvation is by grace through faith in the Lord Jesus Christ.

B. "They have rushed for profit into Balaam's error" (read Num. 22). Balaam was sent to speak to the king of Moab. He refused to go, fearing the displeasure and the common fate of the Moabites. He refused three times. His donkey saw an angel standing in the road, became frightened, and scraped against a wall, and Balaam, in a fit of anger, beat the beast. It was then that the donkey spoke to him.

So Jude's description of the church member in terms of the experience of Balaam is of one who compromises so as to hurt no feelings nor risk any consequences.

C. "They have been destroyed in Korah's rebellion" (read Num. 25; 26:9–11). Korah was a Levite who led people in rebelling against Moses and Aaron. Korah was killed with some others when the earth opened and swallowed them, and 250 of his men were devoured by fire. Thus Jude describes the sin of not recognizing constituted authority.

II. The metaphors.

A. "These people are blemishes at your love feasts" (v. 12 NIV). In the fellowship feasts of the church, these deplorable members were like soiled spots.

B. "They are clouds without rain, blown along by the wind" (v. 12 NIV). They promise but do not deliver. They build people up only to let them down.

C. "Autumn trees, without fruit and uprooted—twice dead" (v. 12 NIV). Jude is saying that these church members have form but no fruit. They are like artificial Christmas trees, attractive but barren. They are sterile statues of pretense. They are fruitless because they are rootless, and indeed, Jude says, they are twice dead.

D. "They are wild waves of the sea, foaming up their shame" (v. 13 NIV). They are whipped by the winds of circumstance. They have no discipline and are activated by outside forces. Their raging foam and noise signal their own shame.

E. "Wandering stars, for whom blackest darkness has been reserved forever" (v. 13 NIV). They have no fixed path of purpose. They lack cooperation with a genuine spiritual galaxy. They are like shooting stars, losing their place and leaving the ordered mystery of the heavens. Sometimes these "wandering stars" wander from church to church, always critical, always searching.

Conclusion

Let us avoid the way of Cain, Balaam's error, and Korah's rebellion. Let us, with God's grace, determine to be fit partakers in feasts, clouds that deliver, trees that bear fruit, waves that deliver freight and sustain life, and stars that shine in harmony with God's galaxy.

SUNDAY MORNING, AUGUST 28

Title: Quality of Discipleship—Neighborliness (The Parable of the Good Samaritan)

Text: "Which now of these three, thinkest thou, was neighbour unto him that fell among the thieves? And he said, He that shewed mercy on him. Then said Jesus unto him, Go, and do thou likewise" **(Luke 10:36–37)**.

Scripture Reading: Luke 10:25–37

Hymns: "Praise Him! Praise Him!" Crosby

"Jesus Saves," Owens

"Something for Thee," Phelps

Offertory Prayer: Our heavenly Father, grant that our eyes may be open to see the needs of people who have been wounded and robbed on life's Jericho road. Give us hearts of compassion to go where they are and to give of ourselves and of our substance to help heal humanity's hurt. In the name of him who is full of compassion, we pray. Amen.

Introduction

This parable probably has built more hospitals, orphanages, and homes for the aging, and has raised more money for them and similar benevolences than any other words ever written. And if fully applied, this parable would remove all racial prejudice.

Jesus told this story in response to a lawyer's questions. The lawyer probably was a scribe who had copied the law of Moses so often that he was considered an expert in its interpretation. He asked, "Master, what shall I do to inherit eternal life?" His idea seemed to be: "How shall I live so that eternal life will be my lot at the judgment?" It was a perfectly proper question, but his purpose in asking it was wrong. He was not seeking an answer but rather was testing Jesus.

Jesus replied as if the lawyer were a sincere inquirer. "How," he asked, "do you understand it?" The lawyer's reply was brilliant and correct. He combined Deuteronomy 6:5, a part of the Shema, and Leviticus 18:5. On another occasion when another lawyer asked, "Master, which is the great commandment in the law? Jesus said unto him, Thou shalt love the Lord thy God with all thy heart, and with all thy soul, and with all thy mind. This is the first and great commandment. And the second is like unto it, Thou shalt love thy neighbour as thyself. On these two commandments hang all the law and the prophets" (Matt. 22:36–40).

The lawyer felt a little foolish that he had answered his own question so perfectly. So to justify himself, he asked a second question, "And who is my neighbor?" He wanted those who were listening to know that he had had some point to what he had asked. The Jewish people listening would have restricted neighbors to those of their own race and then probably would have excluded even some of their own race.

Jesus replied with the wonderful story of the good Samaritan.

I. Four classes of men.

A. "A certain man" seems to represent all persons. He was probably a Jew. He could have been otherwise. Perhaps Jesus intentionally does not say what race, because as the story unfolds, it becomes clear that Jesus is teaching that any person of any race whom we can help is our neighbor. This man was traveling down the road from Jerusalem on Mount Zion to Jericho in the Jordan Valley. It was a descent of more than three thousand feet in twenty-three miles. The winding road and limestone caves made it a favorite road for thieves to waylay travelers.

B. The thieves who robbed the traveler of his clothes, beat him, and left him half dead, represent ungodly, destructive persons. Their motto was, "What is yours is mine if I can get it." They used violence if necessary to prey on their fellow humans. People in this class today are not only those who rob people at gunpoint, but also those who cheat in their business, misrepresent their goods, or live off of the weaknesses of others by pushing drugs, producing pornography, running gambling establishments, and so on. Anyone who is willing to profit by another's misfortune stands with this robber crowd.

C. The priest and the Levite represent persons indifferent to the needs of others. One would expect the priest by race and by his sacred profession to have compassion. When by chance he saw the man, he went to the other side of the road and passed by. Perhaps he thought the man was already dead, in which case defilement by contact with a dead person would have kept him from his priestly duties in the temple. The Levite, one of a tribe from whom doorkeepers, singers, and helpers in the temple were chosen, did exactly as had the priest. He doubtless argued that if the minister did not consider this his responsibility, then surely it was not in the job description for the minister of music.

Why do we condemn the priest and the Levite? They did not rob the man. They did not profit by his robbery. They did not beat him. They did not aggravate his wounds. They did nothing. That is the condemnation: they did nothing.

D. The Samaritan was a most unlikely person to give help—at least in the consideration of the Jews who heard the story first. He was of a despised half-breed race. John, in relating the story of the woman of Samaria, explained, "for the Jews have no dealings with Samaritans" (John 4:9). This certain Samaritan proved himself a true neighbor.

1. He was kind at heart. "He had compassion on him" (v. 33). He was kind not because the law said to be kind, but because he was just that sort of person.
2. His service was not hindered by personal inconvenience. Was he not also on urgent business? Were not the same thieves lurking nearby? He did the best he could for the injured man. He cleansed the man's wounds with wine and soothed them with oil. Was it not inconvenient for the Samaritan to walk while his beast carried the man? Was not the money he offered in payment for the man's keep at the inn hard-earned?
3. He was a man of integrity. The innkeeper trusted him to keep his word that he would return and pay all.
4. He was not hindered by prejudice. The race and religion of the unfortunate man were other than his. He only seemed to know that this was a human being who needed help that he could give, without expectation of recompense. This was true neighborliness.

Conclusion

Jesus asked the lawyer, "Which now of these three, thinkest thou, was neighbour unto him that fell among the thieves?" (v. 36). The lawyer was so prejudiced that he could not say the word "Samaritan," but he did reply, "He that shewed mercy on him." "Go and do thou likewise" was Jesus' challenge to him and to us.

How can we obey the command of Jesus? First, we must be the right kind of people—that is, saved people who love God and love our fellow humans. This implies that we will never be found with the wicked thieves nor with the indifferent priests and Levites. Our concern for others ought not to be negated by their race, sex, or religion.

Second, we must join with all people of goodwill to provide government that will protect citizens against the thieves. Battles against such things as alcohol and drug abuse, crime, gambling, and prostitution must be pushed relentlessly.

Third, we must seek to help others provide for the basic needs of life.

1. Physical needs. Every person needs food, clothing, shelter, and medical care. When one is unable to provide for oneself because of age, disability, sickness, etc., the strong should help the weak. We join with fellow Christians in benevolences and seek for ways to help personally.
2. Social, political, and educational needs. Every person ought to have the opportunity to receive a good education. We heartily join with others in government and in church in providing education, recreation, and political opportunity for all.
3. Spiritual needs. Every person needs to know the true God and his Son, Jesus Christ, our Savior. Here the church is in a unique field. The church has many critics but no rivals in the work of reconciling people to God. If the church does not carry the gospel, it will not be carried. Only the church supports Sunday schools, worship, seminaries, and missionaries.

"Go and do thou likewise." Look about you. See how many ways there are to help. "Say not ye, There are yet four months, and then cometh harvest? behold, I say unto you, Lift up your eyes, and look on the fields; for they are white already to harvest" (John 4:35). "Inasmuch as ye have done it unto one of the least of the these my brethren, ye have done it unto me" (Matt. 25:40).

SUNDAY EVENING, AUGUST 28

Title: Character of God—Righteousness (The Parable of the Last Judgment)

Text: "Shall not the Judge of all the earth do right?" **(Gen. 18:25)**.

Scripture Reading: Matthew 25:31–46

Introduction

"Shall not the Judge of all the earth do right?" (Gen. 18:25). To Abraham's searching question, one's inmost being replies, "He ought to do right." The Word of God affirms that he is the "righteous Father" (John 17:25).

That all do not get justice in this life is obvious. A cartoon depicted a domineering woman speaking to a psychologist about her henpecked husband: "He has some foolish notion that a man's hell is on earth." It is true that judgment is not wholly reserved for the future. Good has reward in this life if only the reward of an approving conscience; evil has its judgment if only the condemnation of an aroused conscience; but so many sins go unpunished and so many good deeds go unrewarded that there must be a final day when God balances his scales. The parable of the last judgment or, perhaps better, the pageant of the last judgment, is the principal Scripture describing the judgment day.

We will do well not to be caught up in the details or its imagery but rather to seek the eternal principles of God's judgment. Hear the thoughtful words of John Broadus:

> How far this predictive imagery of a judgment scene will be literally fulfilled by actual assembly in a locality, etc., no one can tell. All descriptions and conceptions of things unseen and eternal are necessarily dependent on material analogies, even as our own mental action can be defined only in terms drawn from physical action. We may be very sure that the spiritual and eternal reality will be something far more solemn and instructive than any conception we are able to derive from the simplest or the most sublime images. (*An American Commentary on the New Testament*, vol. 1 [Philadelphia: American Baptist Publication Society 1886], 509)

I. The Judgment.

A. When? "When the Son of man shall come in his glory, and all the holy angels with him" (Matt. 25:31) is the time of the judgment. Matthew 24:27–31, 37–51, and the earlier portions of Matthew 25 make clear that Jesus is speaking of his second coming at the end of the gospel age.

B. Who? "And before him shall be gathered all nations" (Matt. 25:32), which means, of course, all people. Not one person who has once lived will be missing. "It is appointed unto men once to die, but after this the judgment" (Heb. 9:27). "So then every one of us shall give account of himself to God" (Rom. 14:12).

All the dead have at death either gone to Abraham's bosom, as did Lazarus (see Luke 17:19–31), or have gone to Hades, as did the rich man. The repentant robber went to paradise (Luke 23:43). Abraham's bosom and paradise seem to be synonymous for the place of the redeemed after death and before the final judgment. John has a vision of this happy state in Revelation 7:9–17. Peter affirms, "The Lord knoweth how to deliver the godly out of temptations, and to reserve the unjust unto the day of judgment to be punished" (2 Peter 2:9).

At the last judgment, the saints who have been in paradise will come with Jesus (see 1 Thess. 4:13–18) and will be reunited with their raised glorified bodies (see 1 Cor. 15:51ff.). They will be at the Lord's right hand. The saints who are living at Christ's return also will be glorified both soul and body and will be at his right hand. The unsaved will come from Hades and join the unsaved who are on earth on the Lord's left hand. They are apparently united with their resurrected bodies.

II. The Judge.

A. God in Christ is the Judge. This assures righteous judgment. "Because he hath appointed a day, in the which he will judge the world in righteousness by that man whom he hath ordained; whereof he hath given assurance unto all men, in that he hath raised him from the dead" (Acts 17:31).

B. Christ will be an understanding Judge. He knows humankind because he left heaven to take on a fleshly body. "For we have not an high priest which cannot be touched with the feeling of our infirmities; but was in all points tempted like as we are, yet without sin" (Heb. 4:15).

C. Christ knows all of the facts. There will be no reason to call witnesses, weigh testimony, ponder decisions. God knows the facts, including the thoughts and motives of every person. "But we are sure that the judgment of God is according to truth" (Rom. 2:2).

III. The nature of the Judgment.

A. As easily as a Syrian shepherd divided white sheep from black goats, Christ will divide all humankind. Every person's eternal destiny is fixed at death. The final judgment is not to decide that destiny but to make manifest the righteousness of God's judgment. Paul warned those who continued sinning "against the day of wrath and revelation of the righteous judgment of God" (Rom. 2:5).

B. Separating humankind into saved and lost is something only God can do. Judgment will be on the basis of a person's character, which is manifest in his or her attitude toward God as revealed in Jesus Christ as well as his or her attitude toward other persons. According to Paul, the righteous God "will render to every man according to his deeds: to them who by patient continuance in well doing seek for glory and honour and immortality, eternal life: but unto them that are contentious, and do not obey the truth, but obey unrighteousness, indignation and wrath, tribulation and anguish, upon every soul of man that doeth evil" (Rom. 2:6–9).

Character is manifest in deeds. A tree is known by its fruit. One's response to Jesus is a true indication of a person's character. John 3:16–21 reveals Christ as the divider of people. When one repents of sin and believes on Jesus, the merits of Christ's atonement are applied to cover his or her sins, and the Holy Spirit gives that person eternal life.

In this parable, verses 34–41, Jesus affirms that character is manifest by what persons do or do not do unto their fellow humans. Is not Jesus affirming that people who do not have the full light of the gospel will be judged by their response to the light they do have? All humankind has light enough to know that we ought to have goodwill toward our fellow humans. This is not to affirm that evil people can be saved by doing some good deeds. It is to affirm that good deeds may indicate that people's hearts are responsive to the truth they know; and if their response to the truth is right, they know that it is possible for God to apply the merits of Christ's atonement for their salvation, even though they are not personally aware of the grounds of their salvation. Jesus is the only Savior. It is possible, however, as this parable teaches, that people who have only a little light and do not know Christ personally can be saved by Christ on the basis of their heart response to what they do know.

Conclusion

This parable is another illustration of the righteousness and mercy of God. God wants to save. It would be unrighteous for him to save sinners without expressing his hatred of sin. God in Christ has provided the way whereby he can be just and justify those who believe in Jesus (see Rom. 3:23–28). This parable of Jesus also opens for us the hope that he can be just and justify those who respond in faith to the light they have.

The parable also has its darker side. If people have enough light to be saved, they also have enough light to be lost. Even the righteous God cannot save people as long as they will not repent of sin and follow the light God gives them.

How fortunate that Christ is the Judge. He will do right. He will be more merciful than we ask him to be. His purpose is to save, not to condemn.

Let each of us make his or her "own calling and election sure." Let us be good witnesses that others may know the Savior and on that great day hear the King say, "Come ye, blessed of my Father, inherit the kingdom prepared for you from the foundation of the world" (Matt. 25:34).

WEDNESDAY EVENING, AUGUST 31

Title: The Business and Benediction of the Church

Text: "To him who is able to keep you from stumbling and to present you before his glorious presence without fault and with great joy—to the only God our Savior be glory, majesty, power and authority, through Jesus Christ our Lord, before all ages, now and forevermore! Amen" **(Jude 24–25 NIV)**.

Scripture Reading: Jude 14–25

Introduction

The letter begins with a greeting to the church and ends with a benediction for and upon the church. And in the paragraphs in between, Jude warns of godless people who would try to destroy the church yet encourages his readers with the great hope of Jesus' return. He tells of God's just punishment on the wicked and of his reward for those who persevere and snatch others from the fire and save them. Our text is indeed a fitting close to this series of studies. It would be good to commit these last two verses to memory.

I. I believe in the church.

A. I believe in her Founder, foundation, function, fruits, and future.

B. The local congregation is the basic cooperative unit of the Christian enterprise. The church is the most needed institution in our national life. The maintenance of the home, the preservation of a sound economic and industrial order, the perpetuation of a vigorous and enduring state are all dependent on it. The church is the repository of humankind's spiritual heritage. It is the bearer of the evangel of Christ. It is the custodian of our deepest hopes. Through the influence of the church, the weak have been made strong, the discouraged have been strengthened, and the bewildered have found the light. In a chaotic and troubled world, it is the answer to our greatest need. Its gospel is the world's salvation, and in its fellowship we will find peace.

II. I believe in the dimensions of personal discipline in church membership.

A. Build up yourselves on a solid faith (Jude 20).

B. Bow down and pray in the Holy Spirit (Jude 20).

C. Stay in the effective circle of God's love (Jude 21).

D. Reach out to others in glad evangelism (Jude 22–24).

III. I believe in the God to whom the church belongs.

A. He is a powerful God: "now unto him that is able" (Jude 24).

B. He is a protective God: "that is able to keep you from falling" (Jude 24).

C. He is a personal God: "to keep you . . . and to present you" (Jude 24).

D. He is a presenting God: "to present you faultless" (Jude 24).

E. He is a praiseworthy God: "To the only God our Savior be glory, majesty, power and authority, through Jesus Christ our Lord, before all ages, now and forevermore! Amen" (Jude 25 NIV).

Conclusion

Who needs the church? We all do. We may not always be satisfied with what goes on in the church, but problems can be corrected more effectively from within than from without. If Jesus loved his church and gave himself for it, then we can afford to do no less. We must learn to love our fellow Christians and to serve with them to bring others into Christ's church.

SUGGESTED PREACHING PROGRAM FOR THE MONTH OF SEPTEMBER

■ Sunday Mornings

Continue the series from Jesus' parables, using "Qualities of Discipleship" as the theme.

■ Sunday Evenings

Use a series titled "We Preach Jesus Christ" on Sunday evenings in September.

■ Wednesday Evenings

Begin a new series this month on the prayers of Paul. Paul was a great man. He possessed a great mind, firm commitment, and strong prayer life. Four of the recorded prayers of Paul serve as the scriptural basis for the Wednesday evening messages.

SUNDAY MORNING, SEPTEMBER 4

Title: Quality of Discipleship—Faithfulness (The Parables of the Pounds and of the Talents)

Text: "His lord said unto him, Well done, thou good and faithful servant: thou hast been faithful over a few things, I will make thee ruler over many things: enter thou into the joy of thy lord" **(Matt. 25:21)**.

Scripture Reading: Matthew 25:14–30; Luke 19:11–27

Hymns: "I Love Thy Kingdom, Lord," Dwight
"What If It Were Today?" Morris
"Will Jesus Find Us Watching?" Crosby

Offertory Prayer: Heavenly Father, help us to consider our lives as precious to us as you have revealed that they are precious to you. Each one of us through faith in Jesus can expect to hear you say, "Come, ye blessed of my Father, inherit the kingdom prepared for you from the foundation of the world." Grant that through faithful stewardship we may also hear you say, "Well done, thou good and faithful servant: thou hast been faithful over a few things, I will make thee ruler over many things: enter thou into the joy of thy lord." In Jesus' name we pray. Amen.

Introduction

The parable of the pounds and the parable of the talents are similar. They both emphasize faithfulness as a quality of discipleship. Jesus spoke the former at Jericho just after the healing of blind Bartimaeus and the conversion of Zacchaeus. Jesus was on his way to Jerusalem, where he knew death and resurrection awaited him (see Luke 18:31–34). The disciples thought that he was going to Jerusalem to establish a political kingdom. Their attitude was reflected in the request of James and John for chief places (see Mark 10:35–45). Luke indicates that Jesus spoke this parable "because he was nigh to Jerusalem, and because they thought that the kingdom of God should immediately appear" (Luke 19:11). Jesus spoke the parable of the talents to the disciples on Tuesday after Jesus' triumphal entry on Sunday, as Jesus sat on the Mount of Olives (see Matt. 24:3; 25:14–30). Jesus used similar material with different audiences.

The parable of the pounds doubtless had a historical background that the people of Jericho knew. From Jericho, Archelaus, a son of Herod the Great, had journeyed to Rome to claim title to Judea. Herod the Great had first willed it to Antipas, then by a change of will to Archelaus. Caesar Augustus gave Archelaus the greater part of the kingdom with the title of ethnarch, although Antipas and fifty Jewish citizens went to Rome to protest. Upon his return to Palestine, Archelaus executed his opponents, rewarded his servants, and ruled with an iron hand.

If it seems improbable that Jesus would allow such a wicked person as Archelaus to represent himself, then remember some of the characters in the other parables: the unjust judge, the gruff neighbor, the unjust steward, and the thief. These are parables—not allegories. The stories do not touch reality at all points. In some specific way or ways, they illustrate God's dealings with people.

I. Interpretation.

In a similar way, Jesus is going away—as he did at the ascension. He will come again, at which time those who oppose him (the citizens) and those who have been his disciples (his servants) will receive judgment and reward according to merit.

A. The citizens who hated the nobleman (now the king)—the destroyed. Those who hate God, who despise God's Anointed, must face their doom. Those who use their lives to renounce and denounce their Maker will perish. "For the wages of sin is death" (Rom. 6:23). "So then they that are in the flesh cannot please God" (Rom. 8:8). There may have been some question as to whether Archelaus deserved loyalty, but there is no question about Jesus deserving loyalty.

B. The servants—Christian disciples. The parables of the pounds and of the talents are from this point on so similar that we can consider them together.

1. The entrustment. The nobleman, before going away, gave one pound to each of the slaves. The pound (Gk. mind) was a sum of money equal

to one hundred pence (Gk. denarius). A pence is used in the parables for a day's wage. Each servant's pound represents one life—one life to use for Jesus. The pounds still belong to the nobleman. The servants are to use them in accord with the will of the owner. They are to trade with them (use in business) until he comes back. Each person has one life for which he or she is responsible to God. Each pound is valuable to God. Perhaps the giving of one pound to each person suggests that every life is equally valuable to God.

A talent was a huge sum of money equal to six thousand pence, or sixty pounds. The master in the parable of the talents delivered his goods to his servants, "to every man according to his several ability" (Matt. 25:15). The master knew his servants. To one he gave five talents, to another two, to another one. This suggests the well-known fact of the inequality of human endowment. God is sovereign. It would be a monotonous world if we were all alike. In the accounting, each will be responsible for his or her own endowment and not for that entrusted to others.

God has given us valuable lives. Each life is valuable to him. One is to use his or her life in such a way as to bring glory to God. What does the Lord want you to do with your life? Certainly, to love him, love others, confess faith in Jesus, be baptized, be a church member, witness, give, do all things Jesus has commanded. In brief—each one is to do God's will. Paul says, "This, then, is how you ought to regard us: as servants of Christ and as those entrusted with the mysteries God has revealed" (1 Cor. 4:1 NIV). Peter wrote, "Each of you should use whatever gift you have received to serve others, as faithful stewards of God's grace in its various forms" (1 Peter 4:10 NIV).

2. The accounting. The nobleman (now the king) returned and called his servants for an accounting. One had gained ten pounds; another had gained five pounds. They received the same commendations as good and faithful servants. In accord with proved ability, the one who had gained ten pounds was made ruler over ten cities, and the one who had gained five pounds was made ruler over five cities. One servant did not use his pound as his master had commanded. Instead of investing it, he simply guarded it. He did not steal it. He simply did nothing. Doing nothing is doing wrong. His master called him not only lazy but also wicked.

The servant sought to justify his disobedience because of fear of his master's alleged austere character. He was afraid to trade for fear of facing his master if he should lose the principal amount.

Even in that case the master suggested he could have invested the pound with the bankers so that he would have received interest.

God is not a hard taskmaster. He does not ask his servants to make bricks without straw. He does, however, expect each believer to invest his or her life in his service. No one who obeys God fails, for reward will be on the basis of right heart motive and faithfulness. A disciple who rightly appraises our Lord will serve because of the constraint of love without fear, for "perfect love casteth out fear" (1 John 4:18).

Similarly, in the parable of the talents the man with five talents who had gained five more and the man with two talents who had gained two more received the same commendation: "Well done, thou good and faithful servant: thou hast been faithful over a few things, I will make thee ruler over many things: enter thou into the joy of thy lord." If the man with one talent had been equally faithful, he would have received the same commendation. As in the case with the servant who hid the pound, he hid his lord's money and tried to lay the blame on the character of his lord. The taking of the pound and the talent from those who hid them and giving them to those servants who used them seems to teach that one increases ability by use and loses ability by refusal to use his or her endowment.

Conclusion

What is the spiritual counterpart of the "ten cities" and of the "many things" over which faithful disciples will reign? In heaven "[God's] servants shall serve him" (Rev. 22:3). What joy to know that we will be with him and that we will serve him throughout all eternity.

If you have failed to use your life for God or have hidden or squandered the resources and talents God has given you, Jesus has a message for you: If you are willing to repent and yield your life to him, he will forgive you, redeem you, and help you to be a good and faithful servant.

SUNDAY EVENING, SEPTEMBER 4

Title: The Challenge of Jesus Christ

Text: "If any man will come after me, let him deny himself, and take up his cross, and follow me" **(Matt. 16:24)**.

Scripture Reading: Matthew 16:21–27

Introduction

There is no uncertain note in the trumpet sound of the New Testament concerning the uniqueness of Jesus Christ. Peter said, "Thou art the Christ, the Son of the living God" (Matt. 16:16). John the Baptist said, "Behold the Lamb of God, which taketh away the sin of the world" (John 1:29). Pilate said, "I find no fault in him" (John 19:6). The Roman centurion said, "Truly this man was the Son of God" (Mark 15:39). Judas Iscariot said, "I have sinned in that I have betrayed the innocent blood" (Matt. 27:4). The writer of Hebrews said, "Jesus Christ is the same yesterday and today and forever" (Heb. 13:8 NIV).

Not only does the New Testament declare Christ's uniqueness, but people of all ages have declared it. Augustine said of Christ that he is "God's mighty medicine." Thomas Carlyle called him "a light shining in the darkness." Will Durant said that Christ is "God's highest incarnation." Irvin S. Cobb said that Christ is the "greatest gentleman that ever lived." Charles H. Spurgeon called Christ "an incomparable being." And Philip Brooks declared, "In him all broken lines unite."

People never reach their full potential until they are challenged by Jesus Christ, to whom they can unselfishly give themselves. In the Scripture passage under consideration, Jesus Christ challenges us to discipleship. Let us consider some of the challenges of Jesus Christ.

I. The challenge of the person of Jesus Christ.

John, the beloved apostle, outlines Jesus' person in the prologue to his gospel.

A. Jesus Christ has eternity of being (1:1–2).
B. Jesus Christ is divine (1:1).
C. Jesus Christ is human (1:14).
D. Jesus Christ is the Creator of all things (1:3).
E. Jesus Christ is the Life and Light of human beings (1:4–5).
F. Jesus Christ is above others (1:15).
G. Jesus Christ declares God the Father (1:18).

II. The challenge of the example of Jesus Christ.

The world has known many great and moral teachers but none as great as Jesus Christ, for his teachings are superior to those of all other great religious leaders. He is unique because he exemplified perfectly his own teachings. People can find flaws and errors in the greatest of teachers, in the greatest of lives, but when they come to Jesus Christ, they are forced to the conclusion of Pontius Pilate: "I find no fault in this man" (Luke 23:4).

Jesus Christ said to his disciples, "As my Father hath sent me, even so send I you" (John 20:21). Jesus was sent into the world to reveal the love of God and to redeem people. In like manner, we are sent into the world to reveal Jesus Christ as Redeemer and to be a redeeming influence on people. He is our Lord and Savior, and he is our example in our mission in life.

III. The challenge of the claims of Jesus Christ.

What are the claims of Jesus Christ? "I and my Father are one" (John 10:30). "I am Alpha and Omega" (Rev. 1:8). "I am he that liveth" (Rev. 1:18). "I am the light of the world" (John 8:12). "I am the way, the truth, and the life" (John 14:6). "I am the bread of life" (John 6:35). "I am the true vine" (John 15:1). "I am the door" (John 10:9). "I am the good shepherd" (John 10:11). "I am the resurrection, and the life" (John 11:25). The claims of Jesus Christ are astounding, and they challenge us.

IV. The challenge of the calls and invitations of Jesus Christ.

Jesus Christ said to two of the disciples of John the Baptist: "Come and see" (John 1:39). Let us go to God's Word and see some of the calls of Jesus Christ:

A. He calls sinners to repentance (Luke 5:32; 13:3, 5).
B. He calls us to accept eternal life, abundant life as a gift from God (John 3:16; 10:10; 15:13).
C. He calls us to self-denial and cross bearing (Matt. 16:24).
D. He calls us to learn of him (Matt. 11:28–29).
E. He calls us to become fishers of men (Matt. 4:19).
F. He calls us to take the gospel to every creature, to all the world (Matt. 28:18–20; Mark 16:15).
G. He calls us to look for his return (Matt. 25:13; Rev. 2:25).

V. The challenge of the cross, the sufferings of Jesus Christ (Luke 9:22).

A. He suffered the loss of friends.
B. He suffered the insults of enemies.
C. He suffered physical abuses.
D. He suffered shame (Gal. 3:13).
E. He suffered for sin on the cross—my sins and your sins (Gal. 6:14).

Conclusion

While many are fleeing from Jesus Christ, let us rather turn to him and be challenged by him. While many are giving their lives over to destruction, let us rather turn to him who gives abundant life. While many are following an unending parade of novelties trying to find peace, let us turn to him who is the Prince of Peace.

I am challenged by Jesus Christ!

WEDNESDAY EVENING, SEPTEMBER 7

Title: A Prayer: The Knowledge of Truth

Text: "That the God of our Lord Jesus Christ, the Father of glory, may give unto you the spirit of wisdom and revelation in the knowledge of him" **(Eph. 1:17)**.

Scripture Reading: Ephesians 1:15–23

Introduction

The apostle Paul began his letter to the Ephesians with a doxology to God the Father, God the Son, and God the Holy Spirit. Having written of the blessings of being in Christ, the missionary in bonds broke forth in prayer.

I. The subject of the prayer.

Only one great subject or theme exists in this mighty prayer. The great theme is that God would give each of his children the Spirit of wisdom and revelation to know him better. This spiritual knowledge would result in the Christian's heart being flooded with light, "that he may know." The Lord intends not only to dispense grace, but also to reveal truth, as in the case of Paul (cf. Eph. 3:2–4). The Lord wants his children to walk in the light, not in the dark.

II. The object of prayer.

Spiritual knowledge consists of knowing the truth in Jesus. It includes learning of Jesus and hearing of Jesus (Eph. 4:20–21). Often Paul stated that he desired that the brethren not be ignorant of spiritual truths. The prisoner of the Lord described the outcome of knowing truth by using three statements that begin with the word "what."

A. What is the hope of his calling? Peter once asked the Lord, "We have followed, and now what do we get?" This whole epistle witnesses to the wealth, walk, and warfare of the child of God. In 1 Corinthians 2:12 this same author writes, "that we might know the things that are freely given to us of God." Truly, hope exists for the future of people in Christ, and hope exists for today as well.

B. What is the wealth of his inheritance? The Bible teaches that believers have an inheritance (1 Peter 1:4). The Lord invests greatly in each of his children. He guards both our inheritance in heaven and his inheritance in the saints.

C. What is the greatness of his power? Although God cannot fully explain his almighty power to finite creatures, Paul does share some tremendous insights into the scope of divine might as he closes this prayer.

1. God's power is resurrection power. In other words, the power at work in the believer also raised Jesus from the dead. Think of the potential for that same power in your life.
2. God's power is enthroned power. This power seated Christ as Lord at the Father's right hand. Note the phrase "far above all" (Eph. 1:21). Jesus reigns in the power of an endless life.
3. God's power is sovereign power. All things are under his feet. He rules over all the universe. Jesus Christ is head of the church by the same power that works in the believer's life.

Conclusion

This prayer petitions that Christians might know what life in Christ is all about. It is a prayer for today and should be prayed today—a "knowing" of the hope, the inheritance, and the power given us in our Lord.

SUNDAY MORNING, SEPTEMBER 11

Title: Quality of Discipleship—Love (The Parable of the Two Debtors)

Text: "Wherefore I say unto thee, Her sins, which are many, are forgiven; for she loved much: but to whom little is forgiven, the same loveth little" **(Luke 7:47)**.

Scripture Reading: Luke 7:36–50

Hymns: "Praise to God, Immortal Praise," Barbauld

"Jesus, Thy Boundless Love to Me," Gerhardt, trans. John Wesley

"My Jesus, I Love Thee," Featherston

Offertory Prayer: Loving heavenly Father, we thank you for salvation by grace through faith in Jesus Christ. No gift we could bring would merit your forgiveness. In loving gratitude we bring ourselves and a portion of that which you have entrusted to us to be used to bring good to others and glory to your name, for yours is the kingdom, and the power, and the glory forever. Amen.

Introduction

Jesus was frequently a dinner guest. There is no record in the Bible that he ever refused a dinner invitation. Often he was a guest in the home of friends, such as the home of Martha, Mary, and Lazarus. Occasionally he was invited by his enemies, as in Luke 14:1. In Luke 7:36–50 Jesus was a guest in the home of Simon, one of the Pharisees. His host did not seem antagonistic; nor was he very friendly. He was curious about Jesus, wondering whether Jesus was really a prophet.

One must recall the customs of that time to understand the situation. When eating meals, the guests reclined on couches with their feet extended. It was not considered improper for people to come in off the street and stand behind the guests. The host usually provided a servant to wash the feet of the guests who came barefoot or wore sandals. This was a normal courtesy in that day, much as offering to take a guest's coat and hat is in ours. And sometimes a host offered a guest oil to freshen up the hair or skin. Friends were embraced or kissed, as in many cultures to this day. Simon was hardly courteous, for he didn't provide water, a kiss, or oil for Jesus.

I. The man who loved little and the woman who loved much.

During the meal a woman came in and stood behind Jesus. Simon knew her. He knew her as a sinner—probably a prostitute. During one of Jesus' many conversations that are not recorded (see John 21:25), he had led this woman to salvation. She had accepted the forgiveness of God and was a sinner saved by grace. What would be more appropriate than to take the costly alabaster box of perfume—which she had used to make herself attractive to her customers—and anoint the feet of this man who had given her new life. As she looked at Jesus in adoring gratitude, her tears gushed forth. She had not meant to do this; so, perhaps with some embarrassment, she loosed her long tresses and wiped away the hot tears. Her gratitude caused her to grasp the feet of Jesus and kiss them again and again.

Simon was disgusted. He thought to himself, "This man, if he were a prophet, would have known who and what manner of woman this is that toucheth him: for she is a sinner" (Luke 7:39). Simon was wrong. Jesus knew the woman, and he did allow her to touch him. He knew Simon also, just as he knows you and me, so he told Simon a story to set him straight.

II. Jesus' explanation of the contrast.

Jesus told the story of the creditor who had two debtors. One debtor owed the creditor ten times as much as the other. When the debtors could not pay, the creditor forgave them both. Jesus asked Simon, "Which of them will love him most?" Simon correctly answered, "I suppose the one he forgave the most."

Simon had no love for Jesus. He had not asked for the forgiveness of his sins. He was not aware that he had any sins for which to ask forgiveness. His lack of affection for Jesus was demonstrated by his failure to provide water for his feet, oil for his hair, or an affectionate welcome. Lack of affection is demonstrated by what one omits as well as by what one does.

The woman was overcome by love for the one who had brought to her the assurance of God's forgiveness. She evidenced her love in a most spontaneous, prodigal way. She washed Jesus' feet with her tears and wiped them with her hair. She kept kissing his feet and poured all of the expensive perfume on his body. What she did evidenced a profound love, which was the result of a sense of great forgiveness.

Now, the point is not that the woman's sins were so much greater than Simon's sins. It is rather that she was greatly convicted of her sins. The magnitude and weight of her sins led to the greater joy of deliverance. Her sins were not forgiven because she was willing to offer her precious ointment to Jesus. Her actions were the fruits of a great forgiveness. The love she showed was the evidence of her forgiveness rather than the ground of it.

Simon never asked forgiveness for his filthy sins. Those nearest to God have the deepest sense of sin. Paul, one who was near to God, called himself the "chief of sinners." Those far from God may take God's name in vain. Those near to God would rather have their tongue jerked from their body than to profane God's name. Those far from God may use God's tithe for themselves. Those near to God would no more think of robbing God than of robbing their neighbor.

III. Love will manifest itself.

A. What do you think of Simon's love? You do not think much of it. In fact, you are not sure that he has any love at all. Love will manifest itself. Love cannot be hidden.

B. What do you think of the woman's love? It was certainly genuine. It was prodigal. It was selfless. Perhaps you might doubt the wisdom of what she did, but you cannot doubt her sincerity. It was wonderful.

C. What of your love for Jesus? What would you think of the love of a young man who could say to his sweetheart, "I love you with all my heart, but do not ask me to stand at the marriage altar and say so publicly. Let us just be secret lovers." You would not think much of a love that is secret. What do you think of the love for Jesus of a Christian who says, "I love you, Lord, with all my heart, but let me just be a secret disciple." Jesus wants public confession of faith in him. He said, "Whosoever therefore shall confess me before men, him will I confess also before my Father which is in heaven.

But whosoever shall deny me before men, him will I also deny before my Father which is in heaven" (Matt. 10:32–33).

Conclusion

No one can make you love Jesus. Love cannot be forced. It is a part of Christian experience, however, that when you are saved you will love the Savior. You cannot by an act of will make yourself love God. You can by an act of will repent of sin and give yourself to God. When you do, God saves you, and by experience you find that you love him. Obedience is the entrance to love. Love is the motive for a life of service.

SUNDAY EVENING, SEPTEMBER 11

Title: The Power of Jesus Christ

Text: "Then Jesus came to them and said, 'All authority in heaven and on earth has been given to me'" **(Matt. 28:18 NIV).**

Scripture Reading: Matthew 28:16–20

Introduction

The claim of Jesus Christ in Matthew 28:18 is astounding: "Then Jesus came to them and said, 'All authority in heaven and on earth has been given to me'" (NIV). Jesus Christ has the authority to command and expect others to submit to his commands. He has authority both in heaven and on earth by right of his incarnation, his matchless life, his vicarious and substitutionary death, his bodily resurrection, and his exaltation to the right hand of the Father. His power comes from his Father (John 17:2). Let us look at the various facts of his power.

I. The power of Jesus Christ is seen in his personality.

Jesus Christ is the greatest person in all the world. He has touched the world as no other person has. When Jesus Christ is preached as he is proclaimed in the Bible, the climate of thought and feeling change. Everywhere and in every land where the name of Jesus Christ has been proclaimed, ideals, individuals, and institutions have been transformed. Jesus Christ has literally turned the stream of history into new channels. In fact, history is His story.

The power of Jesus' personality draws, elevates, lifts, and renews. No pulpit of life has drawing power except Christ be uplifted therein.

II. The power of Jesus Christ is seen in his sinless character.

Jesus Christ is the only person who has ever lived perfectly. Paul wrote, "For he hath made him to be sin for us, who knew no sin; that we might be made the righteousness of God in him" (2 Cor. 5:21). There is no character in history, no character in literature, no character in the annals of time like Jesus. The worst thing said about him was that he received sinners and ate with them. His enemies accused him of letting a sinful woman touch his garment and of doing good on the Sabbath. No one could really accuse Jesus of sin, for he was sinless.

III. The power of Jesus Christ is seen in his great love.

Jesus Christ came to this earth from heaven to reveal the love of God. In doing this he reveals the greatest thing about God (John 3:16; 15:13; 1 John 3:1). The love of Jesus Christ is personal (Gal. 2:20), powerful (Rom. 8:35–39), permanent (John 13:1), and a pattern of love (Eph. 5:2).

IV. The power of Jesus Christ is seen in his death on the cross, in his ability to save.

It is written of Jesus Christ at his birth: "And she shall bring forth a son, and thou shalt call his name JESUS: for he shall save his people from their sins" (Matt. 1:21). Jesus Christ said of himself: "For the Son of man is come to seek and to save that which was lost" (Luke 19:10). "And I, if I be lifted up from the earth, will draw all men unto me" (John 12:32). Paul wrote to Timothy, "This is a faithful saying, and worthy of all acceptation, that Christ Jesus came into the world to save sinners: of whom I am chief" (1 Tim. 1:15).

Jesus Christ died a voluntary, violent, and vicarious death for sinners. By his death, he saves people from their sin. He changed rags into robes, screams into songs, hell into heaven. He saves from sin, from all sins.

V. The power of Jesus Christ is seen in his power to change lives, to lift up the fallen.

Jesus Christ cannot only save from sin, he can change lives. Jesus Christ changed Saul to Paul, a persecutor of Christians to a proclaimer of Jesus Christ. Jesus Christ changed a woman at the well. He turned her from wickedness and worldliness to a witness and witnessing.

Jesus Christ has power over evil, over demons, over alcohol, over drugs, and over Satan worship. He can lift the most depraved from the depths of degradation to the heights of holiness. He can help all—drunkards, drug addicts, liars, thieves, adulterers, and murderers. And he can lift you up.

VI. The power of Jesus Christ is seen in his power to comfort broken hearts.

Some of the most beautiful words of comfort in all the Bible are those Jesus spoke to his disciples on the night before his death (John 14:1–6). Hear him as he speaks to frightened disciples behind closed doors: "Peace be with you!" (John 20:19 NIV). Hear him as he speaks to a doubter: "Put your finger here; see my hands. Reach out your hand and put it into my side. Stop doubting and believe" (John 20:27 NIV).

Jesus Christ heals broken hearts. He does it by the cross (2 Cor. 1:5).

VII. The power of Jesus Christ is seen in his coming again (Luke 21:27).

A. His coming will be personal (Acts 1:11).

B. His coming will be sudden (Matt. 24:29; 1 Thess. 5:3).
C. His coming will be triumphant (1 Thess. 4:14–17; 2 Thess. 1:5–10).

Conclusion

You can trust the powerful Jesus Christ. Yield to him by faith today!

WEDNESDAY EVENING, SEPTEMBER 14

Title: A Prayer: The Knowledge of Him

Text: "The eyes of your understanding being enlightened; that ye may know what is the hope of his calling" **(Eph. 1:18)**.

Scripture Reading: Ephesians 3:14–21

Introduction

The first prayer in Ephesians is for spiritual revelation—"that ye may know." The second prayer in this letter is for spiritual realization—"that ye may be." Paul petitions that each believer yield to the indwelling power of the Lord by his Spirit. Interestingly, the prayer states its single request in two ways. Paul speaks of the indwelling Spirit in verse 16 and of the indwelling Christ in verse 17. He often uses these expressions of the work of God interchangeably (cf. Rom. 8:9–11).

I. The consideration of the prayer.

Paul anxiously prays that God's people understand God's work in their souls. A difference exists between "according to" and "out of" the riches of his glory. If wealthy people give ten dollars to a missionary offering, their giving is "out of" wealth. If people in a low income bracket give ten dollars to the same offering, their giving is "according to" their wealth. God always gives "according to" his wealth.

This prayer aims at the knowledge that the Lord Jesus lives in each believer's life. Think of the magnitude of this truth: Jesus, the Son of God, lives in his people by the Holy Spirit, "Christ in you, the hope of glory" (Col. 1:27).

II. The consequence of the prayer.

Paul notes the results of realizing that Christ lives within us. We recognize his loving presence, and love in turn flows from us. "The fruit of the Spirit is love" (Gal. 5:22).

A. The confirmation of that love. When Christians know not only their commitment to the Lord, but also the Lord's commitment to them, then they realize that the Lord loves them. To be "rooted and grounded" in love means learning to trust the Lord. Eugenia Price said, "Many people are suspicious of God because they are not sure that he loves them."
B. The comprehension of that love. Spurgeon wrote that he had found such an ocean of merit in the death of Jesus that his plummet sounded no

bottom and his eye discovered no shore. Walk as far as you will, and you will never walk beyond the boundaries of the depth, height, breadth, and length of the love of God.

C. The capacity of that love. The word "to know" also conveys the meaning "to personally experience." As you grow not only in grace, but also in the knowledge of the Lord, you have more capacity for his love. And he will respond by pouring more love into your heart (Rom. 5:5). What a beautiful expression: "all the fulness of God." What a grand dimension: "exceeding abundantly above all." Words fail the inspired writer to tell of Christ's love.

Conclusion

The apostle breaks into a doxology in verses 20 and 21. He attempts to record the unrecordable. He affirms that almighty God can do more than our fondest thoughts and highest prayers. God's works bring glory in the church now and forever.

SUNDAY MORNING, SEPTEMBER 18

Title: Quality of Discipleship—Preparedness (The Parable of the Virgins)

Text: "Watch therefore, for ye know neither the day nor the hour wherein the Son of man cometh" **(Matt. 25:13)**.

Scripture Reading: Matthew 25:1–3

Hymns: "Majestic Sweetness Sits Enthroned," Stennett

"It May Be at Morn," Turner

"Lo, He Comes with Clouds Descending," Wesley

Offertory Prayer: Eternal Father, you are Lord of life here and hereafter. Grant that we may be ready to live; then we shall be ready to die. May we live for you here and look forward to living with you hereafter. Your promise is, "Verily, verily, I say unto you, he that heareth my word, and believeth on him that sent me, hath everlasting life, and shall not come into condemnation; but is passed from death unto life." Surely this is a lamp that will never go out. May our concern not be whether we live here or there but that we live as redeemed, obedient persons ready to greet the Lord when he comes for us. Even so, come, Lord Jesus. Amen.

Introduction

The parable of the virgins probably reflects accurately the customs of a Palestinian wedding. Jesus' story may recount an actual incident. Wedding customs vary widely from country to country and from century to century. Imagine a modern reporter writing up a wedding without mentioning the bride!

According to the usual custom, the wedding took place at night at the home of the bride. The festivities celebrating the wedding took place at the home of the bridegroom. On the journey to the bridegroom's home, invited guests could join the wedding party. Each guest, however, must have a lamp. This probably was a small oil lamp with a wick mounted on a stick as a torch. The lamp itself would hold little oil so that if a person were to be out long at night, he or she would need to carry an extra supply. Our story is about ten bridesmaids who expected to join the bridegroom and the wedding party. Five wisely carried an extra supply of oil. Five foolishly took a chance. After all, it was inconvenient for maidens in beautiful dresses to bother with vessels of oil.

A part of the excitement of the occasion was that no one knew the exact time the bridal party would come. The bridegroom delayed beyond the expected time. The girls all began to nod and then fell asleep. No one blamed them for falling asleep. At midnight the servant came ahead of the bridegroom, calling loudly for all to trim their lamps and be ready to meet the bridegroom. Five made their lamps ready. The other five discovered that their lamps were flickering out. They asked the wise maidens to share their oil. They replied, "Not so; lest there be not enough for us and you: but go ye rather to them that sell, and buy for yourselves" (v. 9). No bazaars would be open at midnight. By the time they awakened some sleepy shopkeeper, secured oil, and returned, the bridegroom already would have come and gone. They that were ready went with him into the house for the marriage celebration, and the door was shut. The maidens came to the closed door and begged for admission, but in accord with custom they were not admitted.

The Lord himself pointed out the lesson he was enforcing by use of this parable: "Watch therefore, for ye know neither the day nor the hour wherein the Son of man cometh" (v. 13).

I. What is the Lord's coming?

Jesus Christ's return at the end of the gospel age is the theme of a group of parables of which this parable is one. The record of events of this Tuesday before our Lord's crucifixion on Friday is the fullest of that for any day in the gospel records. Early that morning as Jesus, accompanied by his disciples, went to the temple to teach, the disciples noted that the fig tree that Christ had cursed had withered. In the temple, Jesus defended his right to teach and told the parable of the two sons, the parable of the wicked householders, and the parables of the marriage feast and of the wedding garment. He gave honest answers to loaded questions about the tribute money, the resurrection, and the greatest commandment. He silenced his enemies with a pertinent question as to how the Messiah could be both David's son and David's Lord (see Matt. 21:18–22:46). Matthew 23 records Jesus' scathing denunciation of the hypocrisy of the scribes and Pharisees.

On the Mount of Olives that same day, our Lord spoke of the destruction of Jerusalem and of his second coming in a great eschatological discourse recorded in Matthew 24–25, of which the parable of the virgins is a part. He will come in great power and glory to end the age. The redeemed living on earth will join the redeemed he brings with him at the right hand of the throne of his glory. The unsaved all will be gathered on his left hand. He will pronounce the eternal states of all and will make manifest the righteousness of his judgments and of his rewards. He said that no one knows the day or hour of his coming. It will be at an unexpected time. As in the days of Noah when a flood came, people will be going about their usual activities when he comes. There will be no need to seek for the Lord when he comes again. His coming will be as plain as the lightning that is seen across the whole heaven. As easily and naturally as vultures find a carcass, all people will be gathered about Jesus at his second coming. Everyone will see him.

II. Be ready for his coming.

A. A series of parables that Jesus then told emphasizes this theme: "Watch therefore: for ye know not what hour your Lord doth come" (Matt. 24:42). They are the parable of the two women grinding at the mill (Matt. 24:41–42), the parable of the thief (24:43–44), the parable of the good and evil servants (24:45–51), the parable of the virgins (25:1–13), the parable of the talents (25:14–30), and the parable of the last judgment (25:31–46).

B. How does one watch for Jesus' return? How does one get ready to meet the Lord? In the parable, the requirement was that each bridesmaid should meet the bridegroom with a lighted torch.

It is required that one become a child of God by the new birth. God in love has provided salvation. One accepts that salvation by repentance and faith. When God saves, he justifies, regenerates, adopts, and gives eternal life. Those who are saved do not fear to meet the Lord, because their sins have been forgiven and they are seeking faithfully to do the Lord's will. They are as loyal servants who joyfully look for their master's return.

Each person must prepare for the Lord's return by believing for himself or herself. No one can believe for another. There is no proxy religion. "So then every one of us shall give account of himself to God" (Rom. 14:12). Just as the foolish bridesmaids could not borrow from the wise, no one can borrow another's salvation.

The foolish bridesmaids did not have time to make preparation after the bridegroom approached. The time to get ready to meet God is now. When he comes to end the age, it will be too late to get ready. "Behold, now is the accepted time; behold, now is the day of salvation" (2 Cor. 6:2).

III. Be ready to meet God at death.

The Lord may come to end the gospel age at any time. He may come before the end of your life, or he may not come for thousands of years. Every argument advanced for being ready to meet the Lord at his second coming is an argument for meeting the Lord in judgment at death. "It is appointed unto men once to die, but after this the judgment" (Heb. 9:27).

Conclusion

In solemn truth, we are not ready to live until we are ready to die; nor are we ready to die if we are not ready to live. One who is right with God can look forward with calm anticipation to meeting the Lord without anxiety.

Paul is a good example. To the Romans, he wrote, "If we live, we live for the Lord; and if we die, we die for the Lord. So, whether we live or die, we belong to the Lord. For this very reason, Christ died and returned to life so that he might be the Lord of both the dead and the living" (Rom. 14:8–9 NIV). From his Roman prison, Paul wrote to the Philippians, not knowing whether the issue would be life or death, "For to me, to live is Christ and to die is gain. If I am to go on living in the body, this will mean fruitful labor for me. Yet what shall I choose? I do not know! I am torn between the two: I desire to depart and be with Christ, which is better by far; but it is more necessary for you that I remain in the body" (Phil. 1:21–24 NIV). Paul escaped death during that imprisonment, but later, just before his martyrdom, he wrote to Timothy, "For I am now ready to be offered, and the time of my departure is at hand. I have fought a good fight, I have finished my course, I have kept the faith: Henceforth there is laid up for me a crown of righteousness, which the Lord, the righteous judge, shall give me at that day: and not to me only, but unto all them also that love his appearing" (2 Tim. 4:6–8).

Whenever the cry "Behold the bridegroom cometh" is given, whether by day or by night, in early life or later, let us be found among the wise who have prepared to meet God and who are ready to spend a happy eternity with him.

SUNDAY EVENING, SEPTEMBER 18

Title: The Ascension of Jesus Christ

Text: "And when he had spoken these things, while they beheld, he was taken up; and a cloud received him out of their sight" **(Acts 1:9)**.

Scripture Reading: Mark 16:19–20; Luke 24:50–53; Acts 1:1–11

Introduction

The risen Christ remained on the earth forty days after his resurrection. He remained this long that he might establish his resurrection, give encouragement to fearful disciples, impart closing instructions to his disciples, and present larger teachings about the kingdom of God.

The ascension of Jesus Christ is recorded in two of the gospels and in the book of Acts. Numerous other references are found in the New Testament. The ascension took place on the Mount of Olives near Bethany. The place of the ascension was a Sabbath's day's journey, or two thousand cubits, from the city of Jerusalem. There on the Mount of Olives, Jesus Christ lifted up his hands and blessed the disciples. While he was blessing the disciples, he was received up in a cloud out of their sight. He was on his way to heaven from the world whose sin sent him to the cross.

The ascension of Jesus Christ was no optical illusion, no subjective vision, but a literal objective fact. We will consider this stupendous event in this sermon.

I. The ascension of Jesus Christ speaks of the fulfillment of Scripture, of the lordship of Christ.

Jesus Christ ascended into heaven in fulfillment of his promises. He promised he would go to the Father (John 14:28; 16:10, 28; 20:17). He said that he would ascend to heaven and one day descend to earth again (Matt. 26:64; Mark 14:62; John 6:62).

Jesus' ascension also proclaims him as Lord. Paul said, "Wherefore God also hath highly exalted him, and given him a name which is above every name: that at the name of Jesus every knee should bow, of things in heaven, and things in earth, and things under the earth; And that every tongue should confess that Jesus Christ is Lord, to the glory of God the Father" (Phil. 2:9–11).

As Lord he is at the right hand of the Father to rule over both the hosts of heaven and the vast company of true Christians scattered throughout the earth.

II. The ascension of Jesus Christ speaks of his glorious intercession at the right hand of the Father.

The psalmist wrote with prophetic insight when he called for the warder to open the everlasting doors and let the King of glory in (Ps. 24:7, 9). At the ascension of Jesus Christ, the King of glory entered into his glorious destination at the right hand of the Majesty on high to make intercession for us (1 Tim. 2:5–6; Heb. 2:9; 12:2; 1 Peter 3:22; 1 John 2:1–2).

The Bible teaches that he ever lives to make intercession for us (Heb. 7:25).

III. The ascension of Jesus Christ speaks of the coming of the Holy Spirit and his work (Luke 24:49; John 16:7; Acts 1:4–5).

The Holy Spirit came after our Lord was ascended to heaven. He came to reveal the living Christ and not to take the place of an absent Christ. He came that our Lord might work everywhere on earth.

What is the work of the Holy Spirit? The Holy Spirit witnesses to lost people concerning Christ (John 16:13–15). The Holy Spirit develops Christlike character (Rom. 5:5; 14:7; Gal. 5:22–23). The Holy Spirit strengthens (Eph. 3:16), leads (Acts 13:2–4; Rom. 8:14), comforts (John 14:16–17), teaches us how to pray (Rom. 8:26), gives assurance (Rom. 8:16; Gal. 4:6–7; Eph. 1:13; 4:30), gives boldness in testimony for Jesus Christ (Acts 4:31), inspires hope (Rom. 15:13), and brings liberty (2 Cor. 3:17).

IV. The ascension of Jesus Christ speaks of witnessing (Acts 1:8; Mark 16:20).

After the ascension of Jesus Christ, the disciples became flaming witnesses. His resurrection from the dead and his ascension into heaven had equipped them for witnessing.

Just before Jesus Christ ascended into heaven, he said, "But ye shall receive power, after that the Holy Ghost is come upon you: and ye shall be witnesses unto me both in Jerusalem, and in all Judaea, and in Samaria, and unto the uttermost part of the earth" (Acts 1:8).

We are witnesses to the fact that Jesus Christ can save a soul, change a life, and give purpose and meaning to life.

V. The ascension of Jesus Christ speaks of blessings, praise, worship, and joy (Luke 24:50–53).

The ascension of Jesus Christ was not sunset for the disciples; it was sunrise. It meant blessings for the disciples. What were those blessings? We are not told, but Jesus may have lifted up his hands and blessed them with the old priestly benediction of Israel: "The Lord bless thee, and keep thee: the Lord make his face shine upon thee, and be gracious unto thee: the Lord lift up his countenance upon thee, and give thee peace" (Num. 6:24–26).

The fact that we have a risen Lord at the right hand of the Father should bless us and cause us to worship and serve him with joy!

VI. The ascension of Jesus Christ speaks of his coming again (Matt. 26:64; Mark 14:62; John 6:62; Acts 1:8; Phil. 3:20).

The disciples stood awestruck as Jesus ascended into heaven. The inevitable question came: "Is he ever to come back to this earth again?" Two men in white apparel, heavenly messengers, stood by to give the answer to the question: "This same Jesus, which is taken up from you into heaven, shall so come in like manner as ye have seen him go into heaven" (Acts 1:11).

Jesus is coming again!

VII. The ascension of Jesus Christ speaks of his preparation of a heavenly home for his people (John 14:1–6; Phil. 3:20–21).

Heaven is the sure destination of God's people. Heaven provides a perfect environment for perfect people, and Jesus is preparing a place for them there.

Conclusion

How will you respond to the ascended Savior? Let him come into your life today. He is a wonderful Savior and desires not only to save you but to bless you day by day!

WEDNESDAY EVENING, SEPTEMBER 21

Title: A Prayer: The Knowledge of His Desire

Text: "Being confident of this very thing, that he which hath begun a good work in you will perform it until the day of Jesus Christ" **(Phil. 1:6)**.

Scripture Reading: Philippians 1:3–11

Introduction

Paul wrote his letter to the Philippians from prison. Paul styled himself not a prisoner of Nero but of the Lord. This epistle allows us to look into the apostle's inner life. We hear his prayers, plans, and promises.

I. From the first day until now.

The missionary enjoyed having his converts look back to first things. He knew the motivation in recalling the purity of those first days.

A. They are in his prayers. His recall of the Philippians and their church causes thanksgiving. Prayer requests stream from his heart with every warm remembrance. We find Paul in the grand work of intercession.

B. They are in his fellowship. From the first day until now (the time when he wrote), a fellowship was maintained across the intervening miles. A partnership with the Lord results in steady communion and concern.

C. They are in his heart. Paul does not just remember names but also bears the believers upon his heart as did Aaron of old (Ex. 28:29). He calls on the witness of God himself that his longing for them is as the very beating of Jesus' heart. Love for fellow Christians is a needed teaching today.

D. They are in his defense. The word translated "defense" is literally "apology." The Philippian Christians joined the apostle in speaking out words of proclamation and confirmation. The letter writer was in bonds for the faith and would have his readers understand "that the things which happened unto me have fallen out rather unto the furtherance of the gospel" (1:12).

II. From now until the day of Jesus Christ.

The heart of this prayer is found in four "thats" that occur in verses 6, 9, and 10. The soldier of the cross had a purpose in his praying. He sets forth his desire for his brethren.

A. The continuance of a good work. Paul wrote elsewhere that salvation is by grace through faith unto good works. His desire is that God's initial good work of salvation carry on to its proper continuation and conclusion—that is, a holy life until the Master's return. This verse emphasizes the God who works "both to will and to do of his good pleasure" (Phil. 2:13).

B. The continuance of an overflowing love. The apostle often speaks of the "excess" or the "much more" of life in Jesus. Especially at the heart of this prayer is the matter of love against which there is no law. This abounding love will result in proper judgment and corresponding action.

C. The continuance of careful choices. The thought the author is trying to convey is that the child of God will sort among the possibilities and choices at hand and discern and perform the perfect will of God. Spiritual testings are necessary because the Christian life is filled with decisions.
D. The continuance of a holy walk. The believer should live to the praise of the Lord. Paul often mentions walking worthy of the Lord. The words spoken of Elisha are illustration of this thought: "I know that this man who often comes our way is a holy man of God" (2 Kings 4:9 NIV).

Conclusion

The imprisoned missionary has reflected on the life of the church from its early days. He has also formed some plans for the future days because a person cannot live long on last year's grace. So he writes to them of progress, of love, of discipline, and of holiness. But all that he says is said against the background of the return of the Lord Jesus Christ.

SUNDAY MORNING, SEPTEMBER 25

Title: Quality of Discipleship—Stewardship (The Parable of the Rich Fool)

Text: "And he said unto them, Take heed, and beware of covetousness: for a man's life consisteth not in the abundance of the things which he possesseth" **(Luke 12:15)**.

Scripture Reading: Luke 12:13–21

Hymns: "For the Beauty of the Earth," Pierpoint
"We Give Thee but Thine Own," How
"All Things Are Thine," Whittier

Offertory Prayer: Heavenly Father, we acknowledge that life and all that is necessary to sustain it are your gifts. You give us the power to acquire material things. Forbid that in the enjoyment of your gifts we should fail to remember you. Help us to be responsible stewards of material possessions. May we find by experience that true wisdom is found in doing your righteous will. In the name of him who prayed, "Not my will, but thine be done," we pray. Amen.

Introduction

On two recorded occasions, our Lord called a person a fool. In the closing illustration of the Sermon on the Mount, Jesus called a man foolish who did not build the house of life on the solid foundation of the Word of God (see Matt. 7:24–29). The covetous rich man of Luke 12:13–21 is a specific example of this kind of fool. He is an example of poor stewardship because he built life on material possessions rather than on being rich toward God.

Jesus sounded a warning against covetousness: "Keep a sharp eye and avoid every form of covetousness, for not even when one has abundance, does his life consist of his possessions" (Luke 12:15, trans. A. T Robertson).

I. The occasion of the warning (Luke 12:13–15).

Jesus was speaking to the multitudes about the Holy Spirit. One man rudely interrupted by saying, "Master, speak to my brother, that he divide the inheritance with me" (v. 13). This was not Jesus' business; it was a matter for the courts to decide. Jesus saw the man's covetous motive. The man's desire for material gain was, in his eyes, more important than the rights of others and than the spiritual ends of life.

II. Jesus told a story to illustrate the truth (Luke 12:16–21).

A. Picture the man whom Jesus called a fool. He apparently had many good qualities. His honesty was not questioned. He saved his money. He was a good businessman. He provided employment to many as he built bigger barns. He was no miser. Having received plenty of material things, he was willing to retire from the field. Having no evidence to the contrary, we assume that he was a good provider, temperate, and thrifty. In the eyes of his fellow humans, he was successful. Yet Jesus called him a fool.

B. Why did Jesus call him a fool?

1. He forgot God. In his soliloquy, he used "I" six times and "my" six times. He was an egotist. He spoke of "my fruits" and "my goods" and seemed to have no gratitude to God for fertility of soil, for the right amount of rain, for adequate sunshine, or for strength of mind and body to plan and execute the business operation.
2. He forgot his fellow men.
   a. He could not plow, sow, or harvest without the help of others. How could he build new barns without the help of others?
   b. He did not consider the needs of others. "What shall I do, because I have no room where to bestow my fruits?" (v. 17). Were there no poor people to help? Were there no hungry to feed? Was there no Lazarus at his door asking for food? He had no concern for others. His concern was for the amount of goods laid up for himself.
3. He was a spiritual pauper. He thought that the blessings of life consisted in goods. Think of how much in this world he must have missed. He knew nothing of worship. He had no sense of God's fellowship. He was foreign to the joy of sins forgiven. He had never rejoiced in the salvation of his children. He did not know the joy of sharing, helping, and loving.
4. Death came. He went into eternity unprepared. "Whose shall those things be, which thou hast provided?" (v. 20). Often when a person dies, someone asks, "How much did he leave?" The correct answer always is this: "He left it all."

   This man probably was unsaved. In a similar parable in Luke 16, the rich man went to torment. If he was a saved man, he was a pauper in heaven. He had sent on no heavenly treasure. The late Pat Neff, president of Baylor University and governor of Texas, said, "The way to send wealth to heaven is to invest in someone going there." There were no souls in heaven that the rich man had helped to win; no missionaries to thank him for their support. Jesus concluded, "So is he that layeth up treasure for himself, and is not rich toward God" (v. 21).

Conclusion

How can one avoid this man's folly? Only by the acceptance of life and all that pertains to it as a trust from God. God continues as the Owner. One is to use life for the purposes the Owner desires. Material possessions as servant can glorify God and help humankind. Material possessions as master are "covetousness, which is idolatry" (Col. 3:5).

God is concerned with the way his servants acquire wealth as well as with the way they use it. Good stewardship calls for Christian practices in the getting as well as in the giving.

When people travel from one country to another, they must have their currency converted to that of the country they are visiting. Material possessions are converted into heavenly treasures by using them for good purposes. Jesus made it clear that by helping others we are serving him.

> Then the King will say to those on his right, "Come, you who are blessed by my Father; take your inheritance, the kingdom prepared for you since the creation of the world. For I was hungry and you gave me something to eat, I was thirsty and you gave me something to drink, I was a stranger and you invited me in, I needed clothes and you clothed me, I was sick and you looked after me, I was in prison and you came to visit me."
>
> Then the righteous will answer him, "Lord, when did we see you hungry and feed you, or thirsty and give you something to drink? When did we see you a stranger and invite you in, or needing clothes and clothe you? When did we see you sick or in prison and go to visit you?"
>
> The King will reply, "Truly I tell you, whatever you did for one of the least of these brothers and sisters of mine, you did for me." (Matt. 25:34–40 NIV)

God wants us to be rich in heaven. "I am come that they might have life, and that they might have it more abundantly" (John 10:10). "Freely ye have received, freely give" (Matt. 10:8). "He which soweth sparingly shall reap sparingly; and he which soweth bountifully shall reap also bountifully" (2 Cor. 9:6). "Thou shalt be recompensed at the resurrection of the just" (Luke 14:14). "Whosoever shall lose his life for my sake and the gospel's, the same shall save it" (Mark 8:35).

Fools are not rich toward God. Wise people are rich toward God. In this life the latter have many added joys. In death they go to heaven where they enter the kingdom prepared for them and hear the Lord say, "Well done, thou good and faithful servant: thou hast been faithful over a few things, I will make thee ruler over many things: enter thou into the joy of thy Lord" (Matt. 25:21).

SUNDAY EVENING, SEPTEMBER 25

Title: The Second Coming of Jesus Christ

Text: "And then shall they see the Son of man coming in the clouds with great power and glory" **(Mark 13:26)**.

Scripture Reading: Mark 14:13–47

Introduction

The second coming of Jesus Christ is the great event of the future. No other future event in the Bible is so anticipated and so universally loved as this great climactic event. It is our blessed hope. How bright this event is for the child of God who cherishes the glorious coming of the great God and our Savior Jesus Christ (Titus 2:13).

Alexander Maclaren said, "The apostolic church thought more about the second coming of Jesus Christ than about death or heaven. The early Christians were looking not for a cleft in the ground called a grave, but for a cleavage in the sky called Glory. They were watching not for the undertaker but for the Uptaker" (quoted in Walter B. Knight, *Knight's Up-to-the-Minute Illustrations* [Chicago: Moody, 1974], 178).

The Bible says, "The Lord himself shall descend from heaven" (1 Thess. 4:16). Sooner than we think, Jesus is coming again. Let us consider some of the great truths taught in the Bible concerning the second coming of Jesus Christ.

I. The second coming of Jesus Christ is a biblical truth recorded in the Bible.

The Bible teaches beyond question that Jesus Christ will return to earth (Matt. 16:27; Acts 1:11; 1 Cor. 15:23; 1 Thess. 4:16; 1 John 2:28; Rev. 1:7).

All writers in the New Testament, gospel and epistle, early and late, looked forward to the second coming of Jesus Christ. They believed that he is coming again because he said so (Matt. 16:27; 24:30). Also, angels said that he is coming again (Acts 1:11). John the beloved disciple (Rev. 1:7) and Paul the great missionary apostle said that he is coming again (1 Thess. 4:16).

II. The Bible teaches that the time of the second coming of Jesus Christ is unknown.

A. The New Testament writers teach that the time of the second coming of Jesus Christ is unknown (Matt. 24:36; 25:13; Mark 13:32).

B. The New Testament writers had an attitude of constant expectancy toward the second coming of Jesus Christ. They felt his coming again was imminent (1 Cor. 15:51–52; 1 Thess. 4:17; 2 Tim. 4:8; James 5:7). Eagerness, longing, expectancy, and earnestness characterize the true Christian's attitude toward the second coming of Jesus Christ.

III. The manner of the second coming of Jesus Christ is revealed in the Bible.

A. Visible.
   1. Every eye shall see him (Matt. 24:26–27; Rev. 1:7).
   2. Every ear shall hear him (John 5:28–29).

B. Personal (Acts 1:11).

C. Sudden and unexpected (Matt. 24:27, 42, 44; Mark 13:35–36; Luke 17:24).

D. Glorious.
   1. With a shout (1 Thess. 4:16).
   2. With power and great glory (Matt. 24:30).
   3. With a glorious appearance (Titus 2:13).

E. Transforming (Phil. 3:20–21; Col. 3:4; 1 Thess. 4:13–17).

F. With his saints (1 Thess. 3:13; 2 Thess. 1:7–10; Jude 14).

   Jesus came the first time in lowliness. He will come the second time in power and dignity. He came the first time in poverty; he will come the second time in wealth. He came the first time in weakness; he will come the second time in strength. He came the first time in humiliation; he will come the second time in exaltation.

IV. The meaning of the second coming of Jesus Christ is set forth clearly in the Bible.

A. The second coming of Jesus Christ will be a time of revelation (1 Tim. 6:13–15; 1 Peter 4:13).

B. The second coming of Jesus Christ will be a time of reigning (Matt. 25:31; 2 Tim. 2:12; Rev. 5:10; 20:4).

C. The second coming of Jesus Christ will be a time of resurrection (John 5:28–29; 1 Cor. 15:51–54; 1 Thess. 4:13–17).

D. The second coming of Jesus Christ will be a time to receive his people (Matt. 24:31; John 14:1–3; 1 Thess. 4:14–17).

E. The second coming of Jesus Christ will be a time of rejection (Matt. 25:41, 44).

F. The second coming of Jesus Christ will be a time of reward (2 Tim. 4:8).

V. The Bible declares what our attitude should be toward the second coming of Jesus Christ.

A. Watchfulness (Mark 13:33–37).

B. Prayerfulness (Mark 13:33).

C. Purity, holiness (2 Peter 3:10–11; 1 John 3:3).

D. Diligence (2 Peter 3:14).

E. Sincerity (Phil. 1:10).

F. Readiness (Matt. 24:44).

G. Usefulness (1 Thess. 1:9–10).

Conclusion

About 380 verses in the New Testament refer to the second coming of Jesus Christ. As we look at our world through the prophetic Word, we are constrained to say, "The Lord's coming is near" (James 5:8 NIV).

Are you prepared? Are you watching for Jesus' return? What you do with Jesus Christ now determines where you will go hereafter. Accept him as your Savior and Lord!

WEDNESDAY EVENING, SEPTEMBER 28

Title: A Prayer: The Knowledge of His Will

Text: "We continually ask God to fill you with the knowledge of his will through all the wisdom and understanding that the Spirit gives" **(Col. 1:9 NIV).**

Scripture Reading: Colossians 1:9–14

Introduction

The apostle Paul passes from thanksgiving to petition in this brief epistle. The Greek word he uses for "desire" (Col. 1:9) carries with it the idea of requesting something for which one is entitled. Since Paul is coming to a King who had said that he would withhold no good thing from people who walk uprightly, the minister in bonds makes a large request.

I. The subject of the prayer.

Paul was persuaded that God desires each child to know his will. The Bible knows nothing of a reluctant heavenly Father hiding his will and demanding that his child find it. Rather, the Lord is more eager to reveal his will than most people are eager to know it. Nothing pleases God more than to see a Christian filled with the knowledge of his will. When we walk in wisdom and spiritual understanding, we fulfill God's will.

II. The object of the prayer.

The knowledge of the Lord's will is not for personal satisfaction or pride. The object or purpose in mind according to Scripture is a walk worthy of the Lord. Perhaps we need reminding that "to walk" in Bible language means not only the outer walk that our friends see, but the inner walk that our Best Friend sees. "Unto all pleasing" might be paraphrased: "satisfying him in every area of your life," or "meeting all of the wishes of the Lord."

III. The results of the prayer.

When we know and fulfill the will of God, the result is a worthy walk that can be identified and described.

A. A fruit-bearing life. There is much discussion of what bearing fruit for our Lord is all about. Some believe that fruit-bearing is simply the outworking of the indwelling life of Jesus Christ. So, in effect, it is the abiding principle of John 15:16.

B. A growing life. The apostle Peter spoke of growing in the grace and knowledge of our Lord Jesus Christ. The Christian life must be an informed life. We must know the Word of God so that we can understand God's principles and character. Too many of God's people know about church matters, policy, and organization but have little full or accurate knowledge of the Lord. To know about him and to know him are not the same thing.

C. A strong life. In verse 11 Paul uses three references to power in the disciple's life. This strength is not merely for show but rather to express itself in patience and endurance coupled with joyfulness. Only Jesus by the Holy Spirit could produce what is joined together in this marvelous verse.

D. A thankful life. Paul left us a goodly portion of this life of thanksgiving. He knew how to praise the Lord. He was not ashamed to publicly thank God the Father. Listen to his reasons for rejoicing.

1. God has qualified us to be partakers of the inheritance of the saints. In Jesus we are fitted for things beyond the natural body. Our citizenship is in heaven, and we are participating in the age to come.
2. God has delivered us from the power of darkness. Children of God have been rescued from the "authority" of darkness where we once walked "according to the prince of the power of the air" (Eph. 2:2). To be rescued is to be thankful.
3. God has transferred us into the kingdom of his dear Son. We were going to hell, "condemned already" (John 3:18), but we received a transfer. Christians have a new life, new power, new direction, and new destination. Thanks be to God!
4. God has given us redemption. Ours was no cheap salvation. We were purchased by the precious blood of Jesus Christ. Redemption means the forgiveness of sins. There is no Christian life apart from the forgiveness of sins.

Conclusion

Every child of God should be filled with the knowledge of God's will. The evidence of such a filling is a worthy walk before God and other people. Some of the proofs are mentioned in this prayer: fruit-bearing, growth, strength, and gratitude.

SUGGESTED PREACHING PROGRAM FOR THE MONTH OF
OCTOBER

■ Sunday Mornings

The theme for Sunday mornings is "The Positive Message of Christianity." A positive mental attitude toward God and life are essential for happiness and fruitfulness in Christian living.

■ Sunday Evenings

"The Need for Tall Heroes" is the suggested theme for a series of biographical sermons based on the response of some Old Testament people of faith.

■ Wednesday Evenings

Begin a series of messages based on selected psalms titled "Out of Human Experiences." The psalms contain God's message to us for the many different experiences of life. This series will run through the end of the year.

SUNDAY MORNING, OCTOBER 2

Title: I Believe in Tomorrow

Text: "For God hath not given us the spirit of fear; but of power, and of love, and of a sound mind" (**2 Tim. 1:7**).

Scripture Reading: 2 Timothy 1:7–11

Hymns: "O God, Our Help in Ages Past," Watts

"Standing on the Promises," Carter

"Onward Christian Soldiers," Baring-Gould

Offertory Prayer: Our Father, we thank you for this day that you have given us to prepare for the days to come. Take these gifts and bless their use in the spreading of your Word. Be with those people who give their offerings, and meet all the needs of each day. We thank you for fulfilling all your promises. We offer our gifts for the fulfillment of your work here on earth. We give ourselves for the fulfillment of your plan, through Jesus Christ our Lord. Amen.

Introduction

The heroes of history and poetry may be cruel, violent, self-seeking, ruthless, intemperate, and unjust, but they are never cowards frightened by what tomorrow may bring. They do not falter or give way. They do not despair in the face of almost hopeless odds. They have the strength and stamina to achieve whatever they set their minds to do. They would not be heroes if they were not people of courage and of confidence in tomorrow.

We must stand by the heroes of the Christian faith and assert our belief in God's sovereignty over tomorrow. The Christian has every reason and right to say, "I believe in tomorrow!"

I. I believe in tomorrow because of the failure of the past.

"This one thing I do, forgetting those things which are behind, and reaching forth unto those things which are before" (Phil. 3:13).

"The good old days" never existed. Whenever we become discouraged about the present and the future, the best tonic can be found in history. Truly, God must be in history for man to have survived himself!

A. We can never retreat to the past. The longer Israel was away from Egypt's suppression, the sweeter became the odor of garlic and onions (Num. 11:5–6)!

Because they misunderstand the past, some people desire to retreat to it. Israel misunderstood the past. God did not will for Israel to remain in bondage. Bondage was only one stage to pass through in the pilgrimage to the Promised Land.

Other people desire to retreat to the past as an escape from the responsibility of the present. Israel did not cherish the responsibility of fighting battles and running the risk of defeat. Life would have been far easier if Israel had done nothing in the past and thus had avoided the responsibility of the day (Josh. 7:7).

B. The past can help prepare us for the future (Prov. 24:30–34). The past teaches us that problems always have been and always will be with humanity. Contrary to history, we often think that the problems of today have never before been matched in history.

What about agricultural problems and food shortages? During one of the nation's worst droughts on June 18, 1887, the newspaper in Mason, Texas, reported the words found on a sign attached to an abandoned farmhouse near Blanco, Texas: "250 miles to the nearest post office, 100 miles to wood, 20 miles to water, 6 inches to Hell. God bless our home. Gone to live with wife's folks."

We have political problems today—and so did people in the past. We like to predict national disaster because of our political enemies. An early president of Yale, Timothy Dwight, said against a certain presidential candidate, "We may see our wives and daughters the victims of legal prostitution soberly dishonored and polluted; the outcasts of delicacy and virtue, the loathing of God and man." Who was the object of his denunciation? Thomas Jefferson—the author of the Declaration of Independence!

Labor problems occur today as they did in the past. More than a century ago, a large department store required its employees to work fourteen hours a day, six days a week. The store gave them one evening off a week in which they had to go to prayer meeting. Employees with "the habit of smoking Spanish cigars and being shaved at the barber's" would give their employer reason to doubt their integrity and honesty.

II. I believe in tomorrow because of pessimism's folly.

Even good people get discouraged. Ezekiel said, "The Lord hath forsaken the earth, and the Lord seeth not" (Ezek. 9:9).

Too many people feel that, having come so far, humankind can go no further—all great discoveries have been made, and all noble accomplishments have been achieved. We restrict our vision to current movements of the stock exchange and votes of Congress. We need to say with Paul, "We are perplexed. But not in despair."

A. Pessimism would limit God's activity to our generation. God works on a large canvas and takes a long time to complete his masterpieces. Here we need to recall God's words to Moses. "I have caused thee to see it with thine eyes, but thou shalt not go over thither" (Deut. 34:4). Similar to what God said to Moses, at times he must say to us, "You have accomplished much but my activity is not limited to your generation. After you are gone, Israel shall continue, and the greatest victory yet shall be won." God refuses to suspend his laws to satisfy our childish impatience.

B. Pessimism creates anxiety but offers no answers (Eccl. 2:23). History abounds with illustrations of this fact. In 1851 the Duke of Wellington said, "I thank God I shall be spared from seeing the consummation of ruin that is gathering around us."

Benjamin Disraeli said in 1849, "In industry, commerce, and agriculture there is no hope!"

In 1800 Bishop Wilberforce declared, "I dare not marry—the future is so dark and unsettled."

"Our world is full of corruption. Children no longer obey parents." These words were found chiseled on a stone tablet in Constantinople written by a prince to a friend 4,800 years ago!

We should not discount the serious problems faced today. Recognizing the long, painful journey of the human race helps us maintain faith, courage, and hope with which we can better face our problems.

III. I believe in tomorrow because of the faithfulness of God's promises (Ps. 121:8).

"Tomorrow is as bright as the promises of God" may be an old saying, but it is still true.

A. God has promised to save us (1 John 2:25).
B. God has promised to bless our efforts (Ps. 126:6).
C. God has promised to forgive our sins (1 John 1:9).
D. God has promised to answer our prayers (Matt. 7:7).
E. God has promised to meet our needs (Luke 12:31).
F. God has promised to claim us in heaven (John 14:3; Matt. 10:32).

Conclusion

As a Christian, you need not fear for tomorrow. In God's eyes and in the light of his promises, fearing tomorrow is an act of folly.

If you have not yet accepted Christ as your Savior, you have every reason to fear tomorrow. By turning your back on your sins and placing your future completely in the hands of Jesus Christ, you, too, can say, "I believe in tomorrow!"

SUNDAY EVENING, OCTOBER 2

Title: Because of Faith

Text: "And without faith it is impossible to please him. For whoever would draw near to God must believe that he exists and that he rewards those who seek him" **(Heb. 11:6 RSV).**

Scripture Reading: Hebrews 11:30–40

Introduction

Hebrews 11 has been described as "Faith's Hall of Fame." In this tremendous chapter, the inspired writer marshals a group of spiritual giants to the witness stand. Each of them gives testimony concerning how God blessed them in response to their faith.

The writer says that by faith they accomplished these great things. They accomplished these things not because of financial resources, academic achievement, scientific technology, military might, or hard work; they achieved significantly and rendered outstanding service primarily because of their faith in God and his promises.

I. Because of faith, God did great things to these people.

God does great things within us and to us. Until we let God change us, he will probably not do great things for us, with us, or through us.

II. Because of faith, God did great things for these people.

They came to know God through faith. They experienced him in a personal manner. They experienced forgiveness and gained a position of acceptance with God because of their faith.

The New Testament teaches us that we receive the gifts of life and sonship through faith in Jesus Christ. We receive an inward security that gives us poise and peace in the midst of turmoil.

III. Because of faith, God did great things through these people and with them.

Hebrews 11 lists great men and women who, because they outbelieved their contemporaries, were lifted to positions of privilege, prominence, and power. They rendered service to the kingdom of God and to their contemporaries and to their posterity. They were not exempt from struggle, suffering, and sacrifice. Their fount of motivation was their faith that made God real to them.

IV. How can we have a great and growing faith in God?

A. We can recognize that faith is a gift of God (Eph. 2:8). God reveals himself to us, and we can respond with faith. A distressed father prayed that the Lord would increase his faith (Luke 17:5).

B. Faith needs to be focused properly. God has given us the capacity to have faith. Some of us put faith in the wrong things. Some people even put faith in failure. We need to focus our faith on God and his promises.

C. Faith must be used if it is to be developed. All of God's gifts must be used or we will lose them. We develop a greater faith as we exercise the faith we have.

D. Faith comes by hearing and responding to the Word of God (Rom. 10:17). We should read God's Word to discover his great promises. We should listen as the Lord speaks, and we should harmonize his promises with the situations we face.

E. To have a great faith, we need to obey the known will of God in the present. Some people would like to have a great faith, yet they are not obeying that portion of the will of God that they know. If you want to develop a faith in God's person and promises beyond the range of your present experience, you must obey what you presently understand of God's will.

F. To have a great faith, you should get acquainted with people whose experiences with God can strengthen your faith.

G. To have a great faith, you should thank God for the blessings that he already has bestowed on you.

Conclusion

Jesus grieved because his disciples had such little faith (Matt. 8:26). He challenged his disciples to "have faith in God" (Mark 11:22).

WEDNESDAY EVENING, OCTOBER 5

Title: The Life That Rings True

Text: "For the LORD knoweth the way of the righteous: but the way of the ungodly shall perish" **(Ps. 1:6)**.

Scripture Reading: Psalm 1

Introduction

The author of Psalm 1 holds before us two verbal portraits. In verses 1–3 he presents the picture of the righteous person. In verses 4–6 he portrays the ungodly person. Let us look more closely at this contrast.

I. The blessedness of the godly (Ps. 1:1–3 RSV).

The psalmist began with a beatitude. "Blessed" embraces all that constitutes true happiness. It involves the conditions that follow: avoiding wickedness, delighting in God's law, and enjoying a glorious destiny.

A. The refusals (v. 1). The writer emphasized three refusals the righteous person must make. He must not walk in the counsel of the ungodly. He must not stand in the way of sinners. He must not sit in the seat of the scornful. Three sets of words depict the progression of evil: walk, stand, sit; counsel, way, seat; and wicked, sinners, scoffers. Each condition becomes progressively worse. The last words in the set depict a person in the farthest extremity from the Lord.

B. The pursuits (v. 2). The godly person finds great delight in the Word of God. He discovers that God's Word does not bind him but gives him freedom. He brings all of his life under the light of God's Word. He loves to study and to live God's truth, for he recognizes that it is the best for his life.

C. The rewards (v. 3). The psalmist depicted the enduring quality of the godly life. A healthy tree pictured beauty, stability, and prosperity. The godly person is like a tree, for he does not begin spontaneously. He is "planted." A tree near "streams of water" receives abundant provision of water. The point is that the godly person receives the continual provisions of the Lord. Because God lives within the redeemed, abundant fruits result. The godly also enjoys permanency. "Its leaf does not wither."

II. The blight of the ungodly (Ps. 1:4–6).

After holding the beautiful picture of the godly life before us, we look now at another picture. It is the description of the ungodly.

A. The worthlessness of the ungodly (v. 4). The ungodly go through life unattached. They are not like a tree, but they are like chaff. Chaff is the worthless part of the grain. A person without God is worthless for all the purposes God intended. Chaff is also helpless. Unless people are grounded by trust in God, every idea will move them. Chaff has no stability. The psalmist depicted a picture of the futile life of the ungodly.

B. The insecurity of the ungodly (vv. 5–6). The phrase "shall not stand in the judgment" means being unable to stand one's ground when judgment comes. God will cast off those who are not his covenant people. A different destination awaits the ungodly than the godly. The plans, purposes, and hopes of the ungodly will come to naught.

Conclusion

You do not need to be a specialist to judge these two portraits. Two vivid pictures are before you. The first portrait—the godly person—is beautiful. The second portrait is ugly; it is a picture of despair and doom. Which portrait describes you?

SUNDAY MORNING, OCTOBER 9

Title: The Therapy of Thanksgiving

Text: "In every thing give thanks: for this is the will of God in Christ Jesus concerning you" **(1 Thess. 5:18)**.

Scripture Reading: Psalm 92:1–5; 1 Thessalonians 5:18

Hymns: "Count Your Blessings," Oatman
"For the Beauty of the Earth," Pierpoint
"Love Lifted Me," Rowe

Offertory Prayer: Dear God, we thank you first for the joy of thanksgiving. Begin to reveal the blessings of giving as we bring these offerings today. We praise you for the renewal that is ours simply by giving back to you a part of all that you have given us. Fill us with your love that will cause us to give freely of all that we have. Make us aware of the great blessings we possess because of your love for us, and help us to know the joy of a life filled with thanks. Take these gifts as an offering of our thanks. In Jesus' name we pray. Amen.

Introduction

Practicing thanksgiving is therapeutic. When we learn to say, from the bottom of our hearts, "Thanks for everything," we are on the way to being healthy, happy people.

A man who had always been rather negative was constantly bothered by things. His health was poor; the world was in a terrible state; his business was failing. He always complained about himself and his circumstances. But one day people noticed that he had changed considerably. He was vital, vibrant, enthusiastic, and seemingly the picture of health. When asked to explain the marked change, he said, "It's the therapy of giving thanks."

Every night in bed this man thought of all the good things that had happened to him that day. Then he would pull the bedcovers up around his neck, say to the Lord, "Thanks for everything," turn out the light, and peacefully go to sleep.

The therapy of thanksgiving is amazingly therapeutic and health producing.

I. Thanksgiving encourages a grateful spirit (I Thess. 5:18).

Paul quickly asserted that the will of God is for you to have a grateful spirit—that "in every thing [you] give thanks." A grateful spirit makes a person happier and makes life better.

Just think of a few things for which you can be grateful.

A. Daily bread (Acts 27:35).

B. Christian friends (Rom. 1:8).

C. God's using you to spread the knowledge of him (2 Cor. 2:14).

D. Victory over temptation (Rom. 7:24–25).

E. The unspeakable gift of Christ (2 Cor. 9:15).

A pastor tells of a man who was on the verge of a nervous breakdown. He was an empty shell. Someone suggested that he could avoid further breakdown by practicing the therapy of thanksgiving. He was told to make a list of everyone who had helped him throughout the years. Then he was told to fill his mind with thanksgiving for all the things these people had done for him.

The third step included sitting down and writing a letter of thanks to a person who had especially blessed his life. He thought of a schoolteacher—a very old lady. He wrote her and expressed how much he loved and appreciated her.

Several days passed, and he received a reply. Calling him by his boyhood name, it read: "Dear Willy, As I recall all the children I have taught over the years, you are the only one who ever took time to write and thank me for what I did as a teacher. You have made me so very happy! I have read your letter through tears. I keep it by my bedside and read it every night. I shall cherish it until the day I die."

Thrilled by this reply, the man wrote letter after letter until he had written at least five hundred letters of thanks. He discovered that during these months he had become a changed man. The therapy of thanksgiving had lifted him above himself and opened to him the secret of real living.

II. Thanksgiving develops a positive attitude.

In 1 Thessalonians 5:18 Paul said in effect, "In spite of all that may happen, you are to continue being grateful—you are to maintain a positive attitude." Paul did not thank God for the possession of material abundance. He did not have an affluent standard of living. He had learned to be content in whatever state he found himself. He did not thank God for an easy time, for he had a "thorn" (2 Cor. 12:7). He knew the bitterness of persecution—he was stoned at Lystra, driven from Thessalonica, rejected at Athens, jailed at Philippi, apprehended at Caesarea, taken to Rome as a prisoner, and shipwrecked en route. He suffered imprisonment, was released then jailed again, put in a dungeon at Rome, and finally martyred.

Paul did not thank God for any superior standing among others. He was not like the Pharisee who prayed, "God, I thank you that I am not as other men."

The therapy of thanksgiving had developed a positive attitude that enabled Paul to forget the bad and to be grateful for the good.

When a Sunday school teacher asked her class what they were thankful for, one little fellow replied, "My glasses." "But why?" she asked. "Because they keep the boys from jumping on me and the girls from kissing me!" A positive attitude can always find something for which to be grateful!

Thanksgiving enables us to see the positive side of things. With so much bad news circulating today, we need to practice the therapy of thanksgiving so that we may see the positive side of things. For example, consider the millions of people last year who were not involved in crime, did not file for divorce, did not riot, but performed their jobs well and attended church.

III. Thanksgiving produces an attractive witness.

People want to be attractive. Americans spend millions of dollars each year on cosmetics. Christ wants his witnesses to be attractive too. Thanksgiving can make you the kind of witness that will attract others to Christ.

Paul may not have been eloquent, his physical appearance may not have been striking, but his witness always attracted people. He drew men and women wherever he went, from Jerusalem to Rome. The therapy of thanksgiving (practiced even in prison) had made Paul an attractive witness, and it can do the same for you!

C. H. Spurgeon said that "more flies are attracted by honey than by vinegar!" And another has said, "Unfailing gratitude makes a human magnet out of a common personality."

Conclusion

Are you in the "dumps"? Has life lost its glow? Do you no longer feel that you have a purpose for living? Has your whole world gone sour? Practice the therapy of thanksgiving every day for one full month, and you will make a wonderful discovery. You will develop a grateful spirit. Your attitude will become radiantly positive. And you will become an attractive witness for Christ!

SUNDAY EVENING, OCTOBER 9

Title: Faith and the Warnings of God

Text: "By faith Noah, being warned by God concerning events as yet unseen, took heed and constructed an ark for the saving of his household; by this he condemned the world and became an heir of the righteousness which comes by faith" **(Heb. 11:7 RSV)**.

Scripture Reading: Genesis 6:5–18

Introduction

Genuine faith in God includes believing that God is a personal being of great power, wisdom, and love.

Through faith we receive the blessings of God. "He rewards those who seek him" (Heb. 11:6 RSV). Some of God's rewards come here and now. Some of God's rewards do not come until we enter the next life. We may find ourselves in some difficulty if we limit God's activity on our behalf to the present. The heroes of faith did not always receive the fulfillment of their dreams immediately (Heb. 11:13). Genuine faith includes the positive response of the believer to the promises of God. This faith enables us to face all situations with a positive mental attitude, believing that God is working to bring good to people who trust him.

A believer responds to God's warnings with genuine faith. We live in a world that can be either dangerous or delightful. Noah comes to our attention primarily because he believed in God such that he heeded God's warnings. Noah was a righteous man who was blameless in his generation. He walked and talked with God and preached of righteousness. The exception in his day, he refused to compromise with that which was ungodly. He refused to become one of the crowd.

Genuine faith will heed the warnings that come from God.

I. God warns us against pathways that lead to self-destruction.

A. Adam was warned against the tree in the midst of the garden. Adam did not respond properly to the warning that God gave to him concerning the consequences of unbelief, disobedience, and selfishness.

The case of Adam should warn each of us against the peril of not trusting God. We should let his example warn us against greedily demanding our own way and rebelling against God. The calamity that befell the head of the race should warn us against the subtle destructiveness of pride.

B. Noah spoke loud words of warning.

1. God loves us, but his tolerance had limits.
2. God comes in wrath against entrenched evil. God wiped out Noah's generation and began again. God is interested not only in our creed but also in our conduct. Our faith should produce a proper effect in our morals.

C. The destruction of Sodom and Gomorrah reveals the divine wrath against sex perversion and moral destitution.

D. The book of Jonah reveals that individuals and nations should and can respond to God's warnings. Nineveh heard the warnings and responded, and God dealt with them graciously.

II. How does God warn people today?

A. God uses parents to warn children concerning ways that lead to ruin.

B. God warns us through the teaching of his Word if we will recognize its authority.

C. God may speak to us while we listen in our prayer closet.

D. God may disturb our conscience concerning some habit or contemplated path.

E. God may use the counsel of some godly man or woman to warn us.

F. God may warn us by our observation of wrecks along the road of life.

G. God may warn us through a Sunday school teacher or a pastor's sermon.

H. God may warn us through suffering and tragedy.

I. God uses the Holy Spirit who dwells within us to warn us against the ways that lead to ruin.

III. Some warnings from God.

A. Christ warns us against being mere hearers rather than doers of his Word (Matt. 7:24–27).

B. God warns us against reaping the wages of sin (Rom. 6:23).

C. God warns us against neglecting the great salvation that God offers (Heb. 2:4).

Conclusion

How do you respond to God's warnings? Do you believe that God is good and that he rewards those who seek him? Do your believe that when God speaks a word of warning, he has a benevolent purpose in mind for us—that is, that he is trying to keep us from damaging ourselves or others?

Do you ignore the warnings of God? Do you rebel against the warnings of God?

Do you rationalize the warnings of God, thinking that you are the exception and that you can somehow escape the consequences? Or do you receive the warnings of God with thanksgiving and with an obedient attitude?

Part of God's love for us comes in the form of warnings. Genuine faith recognizes and responds positively to these warnings.

WEDNESDAY EVENING, OCTOBER 12

Title: The Ideal Ruler

Text: "Be wise now therefore, O ye kings: be instructed, ye judges of the earth" (**Ps. 2:10**).

Scripture Reading: Psalm 2

Introduction

Psalm 2 was written at the coronation of a new king of Israel, probably David. Already Israel was looking for the ideal king for the future, the Messiah of God's kingdom.

I. Humankind's rebellion (Ps. 2:1–3).

The psalm portrayed people plotting a revolt against the king of Israel. "The heathen rage" in wild commotion. "The people imagine a vain thing" in conspiracy against God's ruler (vv. 1–2). The rebellion of the people against the new king was regarded as a revolt against the Lord because the king was ideally set apart as God's anointed ruler (v. 2). The rebels sought to break the bands of divine restraint (v. 30).

II. God's indignation (Ps. 2:4–6).

God responds to people who revolt against his rulers. The psalmist pictured God laughing at the revolutionaries (v. 4) and speaking with displeasure against them. One of the worst realities of life is to have God against you (vv. 5–6).

III. God's decree (Ps. 2:7–9).

In the day of coronation the king was acknowledged as God's son (v. 7). God acknowledged Jesus Christ as the ideal ruler: "Thou art my beloved son" (cf. Mark 1:11).

The vision of world dominion of the ruler in verse 8 goes beyond David's reign. Evidently the psalmist looked toward the Messiah as the ideal ruler.

The Messiah will rule by conquest. Ultimately, all of the world will be under the domination of God's Messiah. This does not mean that all ultimately will be saved. Instead, it means that God's Messiah will rule universally (v. 9).

IV. Humankind's admonishment (Ps. 2:10–12).

Both rulers and subjects were enjoined to submit to the Lord. Notice the admonishments: "Be wise ... be instructed ... serve the Lord ... rejoice with trembling ... kiss the Son" (vv. 10–12). People who submit to the Lord find a security and happiness in life (v. 12).

Conclusion

Just as the message of Psalm 2 was vital to Israel in the time of the kings, so it is vital to America today. If we want our country to prosper under God, we need to submit to the lordship of Jesus Christ.

SUNDAY MORNING, OCTOBER 16

Title: Try It—You'll Like It!

Text: "O taste and see that the Lord is good" **(Ps. 34:8)**.

Scripture Reading: Psalm 34:5–8

Hymns: "He Keeps Me Singing," Bridgers

"Make Me a Blessing," Wilson

"Sunshine in My Soul," Hewitt

Offertory Prayer: Heavenly Father, bless us now as we gather to worship you. Fill us with the joy that belongs to your children. Make us cheerful givers, both of our offerings today and of ourselves in the days to come. Use these gifts to build your kingdom so that more people may know the peace and happiness that your love brings. Strengthen us so that we may constantly offer your love to all people around us. Use our money and our lives to your glory. We ask in Jesus' name. Amen.

Introduction

"Try it—you'll like it!" That slogan once sold thousands of packages of Alka Seltzer that calmed many troubled stomachs. In Psalm 34:8 David used that same slogan in relation to God and the life that he made possible. "O taste and see that the Lord is good" is nothing more than sixteenth-century King James English for "Try it—you'll like it!"

Ever since our Savior invited Thomas to inspect his nail-pierced hands, the Christian faith has challenged people to test it. Because I personally believe in the abundant life made possible by Christ Jesus, without hesitation I challenge anyone to "try it" with the assurance that "you'll like it"!

I. Try looking on the bright side of things.

"And Caleb stilled the people before Moses, and said, Let us go up at once, and possess it; for we are well able to overcome it" (Num. 13:30).

A. Positive thinking will change your life. "For as he thinketh in his heart, so is he" (Prov. 23:7).

1. By eliminating destructive thinking. What do you do when you habitually think destructive thoughts? You constantly pump destructive thoughts out into the world around you. As a result, you destructively activate the world around you.

   Looking on the bright side of things—thinking constructive thoughts—will change your life by drawing constructive results your way. Many great thinkers have stated that you can change your life by your thoughts.

   Marcus Aurelius, a great Roman emperor and philosopher, said, "Our life is what our thoughts make it." Centuries later, Ralph Waldo Emerson wrote, "A man is what he thinks about all day long." William James, the father of American psychology, said, "The greatest discovery of my generation is that human beings can alter their lives by altering their attitudes of mind." That is, people can create constructive lives if they think right.

   Looking on the bright side of things will change your life by eliminating destructive thinking.

2. By making you more like Christ. "[Look] unto Jesus the author and finisher of our faith; who for the joy that was set before him endured the cross, despising the shame, and is set down at the right hand of the throne of God" (Heb. 12:2).

   The cross and the shame that went with it were not coveted by Christ, but he looked beyond them to his enthronement with God and the salvation of millions of men.

   You, too, can have the mind of Christ Jesus our Lord. Just think of it! You can have a mind free from all the negative things that destroy you. You can have a mind filled with all the glorious things that will create you.

B. Because it will change your world. Christ used the analyses of salt, light, and yeast to illustrate this truth.

II. Try being a part of the answer to problems.

"I plead with Euodia and I plead with Syntyche to agree with each other in the Lord. Yes, and I ask you, loyal yokefellow, help these women who have contended at my side in the cause of the gospel, along with Clement and the rest of my fellow workers, whose names are in the book of life" (Phil. 4:2–3 NIV).

The church at Philippi had a real problem. Paul asked for his coworkers there to be a part of the solution rather than the problem. When you see a problem, don't add to it by becoming part of it. Dedicate yourself to answering the problem.

III. Try listening more and talking less.

"Wherefore, my beloved brethren, let every man be swift to hear, slow to speak" (James 1:19).

A. Because you will learn more. "We have two ears, but only one mouth, that we may hear more and speak less" (Zeno). Learning with closed ears and open mouths is difficult—you just don't take in knowledge through an open mouth!

B. Because people will like you better. No one likes a "motor mouth." "He that blesseth his friend with a loud voice, rising early in the morning, it shall be counted a curse to him!" (Prov. 27:14).

1. You will be better liked at home. "A constant dripping on a rainy day and a cranky woman are much alike! You can no more stop her complaints than you can stop the wind or hold onto anything with oil-slick hands" (Prov. 27:15–16 TLB).
2. You will be better liked at work and in other groups. "Where no wood is, there the fire goeth out: so where there is no talebearer, the strife ceaseth" (Prov. 26:20).

IV. Try putting Christ first in your life.

In Luke 9:59–62 Christ is saying, "You must put me first in your life!" People who put him first liked it and were happy! People who did not put him first did not like it and were not happy, such as the rich young ruler who went away "sorrowfully."

A. Because it eliminates worry and anxiety. Jesus seems to say in Matthew 6:31–34, "Don't be anxious about tomorrow. God will take care of your tomorrow too. Live one day at a time."

B. Because life goes better. "I am come that they might have life, and that they might have it more abundantly" (John 10:10).

Conclusion

You have tried other things, and they have not worked. Try looking on the bright side of things, being part of the answer to problems, listening more and talking less, and putting Christ first in your life—you'll like it!

SUNDAY EVENING, OCTOBER 16

Title: The Patience of Faith

Text: "No distrust made him waver concerning the promise of God, but he grew strong in his faith as he gave glory to God, fully convinced that God was able to do what he had promised" **(Rom. 4:20–21 RSV)**.

Scripture Reading: Hebrews 11:8–16

Introduction

Faith unites us with God and makes possible the new birth within our souls (Gal. 3:26). Faith makes walking and talking with God possible. Faith makes it possible for us to see the invisible, to feel the intangible, and to hear the inaudible.

Abraham, the father of the faithful, trusted in God's goodness. He heard and heeded the promises of God and depended on God to be trustworthy.

I. Abraham's faith gave him a vision of God.

A. He left his homeland in obedience to God's call (Heb. 11:8).

B. He sojourned in the Promised Land without possessing it (Heb. 11:9).

C. Abraham looked for a city whose builder and maker was God (Heb. 11:10).

God took the initiative in calling Abraham. Abraham responded with faith, worship, and obedience (Gen. 12:7). He dialogued with the God who laid his claim to him (Gen. 12:8). We can assume that this prayer experience included praise, heart searching, dedication, rededication, and a spirit of sacrifice (Gen. 13:4).

II. Abraham's faith included a concept of eternity.

A. "He was looking for a city."

B. As a stranger in a land of promise, he sojourned with his eye upon God. "And Abram journeyed on" (Gen. 12:9 RSV). The lyricist Jim Reeves expressed a similar thought with the following words:

This world is not my home,
I'm just a passing through.
My treasures are laid up
Somewhere beyond the blue.
The angels beckon me,
From heaven's open door.
And I can't feel at home
In this world any more.

Paul declared that our citizenship is in heaven (Phil. 3:20). We can live in the present because of faith in the future.

C. A vision of eternity will encourage a willing detachment from the perishable present. Lot, Abraham's nephew, lived only for the present with no appreciation for the eternal future.

To some degree we all live under the painful pressure of the present, which can cause us to lose sight of eternal values.

D. A vision of eternity will encourage an enthusiastic investment in the permanent future. Faith has been described as the telescope that brings the future into the present. The decisions we make influence our future.

III. Abraham's faith in God's promises lifted him to spiritual greatness.

People in our era emphasize instant services. Always in a hurry, we want instant coffee, instant power, instant success.

During a tour of St. Peter's Cathedral in Rome, the tour guide emphasized the importance of working in the present with the future in mind. The tour guide indicated that such a structure could not have been built if people had not been willing to begin something that their grandsons would complete. With the eye of faith, we work in the present for the highest possible good in the future.

A. Abraham believed that God exists.

B. Abraham believed that God is vitally concerned about what happens to people in the present.

C. Abraham believed that God was trustworthy even when the evidence seemed to indicate that God was not going to keep his promises. Abraham continued God.

Conclusion

Abraham trusted God in the beginning. Abraham trusted God in the process of life. Abraham died trusting in God. This continual trust explains why his faith was counted to him as righteousness.

Faith should not be thought of as a gimmick to be used only in emergencies. In response to God, we should be faithful, trustworthy, dependable, and trusting, all the way to the point of death.

WEDNESDAY EVENING, OCTOBER 19

Title: The Multimedia of God's Communication

Text: "His going forth is from the end of the heaven, and his circuit unto the ends of it: and there is nothing hid from the heart thereof" **(Ps. 19:6)**.

Scripture Reading: Psalm 19

Introduction

Often we think communication is restricted to a spoken word. Modern studies in communication disprove this idea. People communicate both by verbal expressions and by nonverbal means.

God communicates to people. Few have heard God speak with an audible voice. Nonetheless, God speaks in many diverse manners. The psalmist examined some of the means of God's communication to humankind.

I. God speaks through nature (Ps. 19:1–6).

The psalmist leads us outside to the hillsides and shows us the glory of God in nature. God actually does speak through nature. Modern people need to listen to God's communication through nature. If we listened to God speaking through nature, what would we learn?

A. God's glory. "The heavens declare the glory of God" (v. 1). The psalmist depicted the heavens as a voice of God's glory. When we study the heavens, we are deeply impressed with the Designer. Just as a building is a tribute to its architect, so the universe is an honor to its Maker.
B. God's handiwork (v. 1). The psalmist selected the firmament as a voice of God's handiwork. Looking at the firmament causes one to be impressed with its beauty and order. Just as we are impressed with an artist when we observe his or her work, so are we impressed with God when we look at the world about us.
C. God's majesty (vv. 2–4). Each complete day is an incessant witness to God's majesty. Verse 1 seems to describe the past events of creation. Verses 2 and 3 depict the daily communication of God in nature. The day impresses us with certain wonders and the night with others.

   God's majesty can be seen by the entire creation (v. 4). Because people are in the world, they hear God communicating with them.
D. God's supremacy (vv. 4–5). Most people of the ancient world gave a supreme place to the sun. It was the center of their universe. Ancients viewed the sun as the source of the world, the ultimate destiny, and the sustaining factor of life. One is not surprised that many worshiped the sun.

   The psalmist called special attention to the sun (vv. 4–6). He pictured it as having a tent in the heavens. He compared it to a bridegroom in radiance and to an athlete in strength and endurance. The psalmist depicted the sun as a creation of God. God is supreme, not the sun.

II. God speaks through his Word (Ps. 19:7–11).

The psalmist brings us from the hills into the temple. He unrolls a scroll and tells us that God speaks through the Word.

A. The aspects of the law. The psalmist began by describing the law with different terms: law, testimony, statutes, commandment, fear of the Lord, judgments. These words describe various shades of God's great law.
B. The appreciation of the law. After examining the diverse aspects of the law, the psalmist described the law with a series of adjectives: perfect, sure, right, pure, clean, true. These descriptions should cause a profound appreciation for God's Word.
C. The appropriation of the law. When a person appropriates God's law, glorious results happen: souls are converted (renewed), wisdom is acquired, hearts are rejoiced, eyes are enlightened. God's Word endures forever and makes people righteous.
D. The accomplishment of the law. The psalmist closes his thoughts on God's Word by describing several effects of God's law. God's law is life's greatest possession—"more to be desired are they than gold, yea, than much fine gold" (v. 10). God's law brings satisfaction to life—"sweeter also than honey and the honeycomb" (v. 10). God's law warns against

rebellion—"moreover by them is thy servant warned" (v. 11). The law displays the good life—"in keeping of them there is great reward" (v. 11).

III. God speaks in life's experiences (Ps. 19:12–14).

The psalmist reveals the inward experiences of his life by telling how God spoke in these experiences. The heavens tell much. The Scripture tells more. But the soul tells most of all. What do life's experiences tell the psalmist and us?

A. Prevalence of sin. After scrutinizing God's law, the psalmist looked at his life. One fact was certain—he was a sinner. He mentioned "errors," sins committed by human weakness. He mentioned "secret faults," sins committed unknowingly (cf. Lev. 5:2). He also mentioned "presumptuous sins," sins committed in defiance of the Lord.

B. Power of God. God spoke to the soul of the psalmist, telling him that sin could not be conquered by human willpower (cf. Rom. 7:24–25). First, God said that he could not even know sin without the law. Second, only God could take care of the sin problem. God could cleanse from secret sins and restrain the psalmist from defiant rebellion. Uprightness and innocence are gifts available only from God. Third, God is always available in our thoughts and words as our Strength and Redeemer. As our Rock, God gives strength. As our Redeemer, God frees us from the tyranny of sin.

Conclusion

If you cannot hear God's communication, you are deaf. God speaks in many diverse manners. Listen to him!

SUNDAY MORNING, OCTOBER 23

Title: The Christian Answer to Anxiety

Text: "Do not be anxious about anything, but in everything, by prayer and petition, with thanksgiving, present your requests to God" **(Phil. 4:6 NIV)**.

Scripture Reading: Philippians 4:6–13

Hymns: "It Is Well with My Soul," Spafford

"How Firm a Foundation," attr. to John Keith among others

"Blessed Assurance, Jesus Is Mine," Crosby

Offertory Prayer: Father, we thank you for this time to come for a renewal of our spirits, and we ask that you would bless us now as we worship. Lift the burdens of the week so that we might draw closer to you. Take these gifts and use them to your greatest glory. Help us to go beyond these gifts and to give of ourselves. Remove the fears that prevent our being our best for you, and fill us anew with confidence that will render us the best tools in the work of your kingdom, through Jesus Christ. Amen.

Introduction

Anxiety is a painful uneasiness of mind over an anticipated ill. It produces worry and disquietness and robs peace of soul and any sense of tranquility. It takes a life, otherwise joyous and secure, and turns it into a prison of turmoil and distress.

Perhaps there is no other sin that more frequently appears in the lives of Christians than the sin of anxiety. The Bible has the answer to anxiety—it is an answer that confronts us with the exact image of what we are and with the means by which we may become what we ought to be. The answer is not simple, but it is one that will work if we will only accept it.

I. Communion with God.

The Bible tells us "Do not be anxious about anything" (Phil. 4:6 NIV).

A. Communion with God makes you mindful of God's blessings.
   1. God's blessings have met your needs every time before.
   2. God's blessings should remove self-pity and worry.

B. Communion with God affords you the privilege of request.
   1. Through request, you may unburden your soul. Psalm 55:22 says, "Cast thy burden upon the Lord, and he shall sustain thee: he shall never suffer the righteous to be moved."
   2. Through request, you may obtain God's help. This is illustrated in Moses, Jonah, and Paul in prison.

C. Communion with God brings peace.
   1. This peace is divine peace, and thus abiding (Phil. 4:7). Christ says, "My peace I give unto you; not as the world giveth, give I unto you" (John 14:27).
   2. God's peace is a guarding peace that "will guard your hearts and your minds" (Phil. 4:7 NIV). By using a military metaphor, Paul represents this peace as guarding their hearts as a garrison holds a fortress. At every inlet into their soul, this peace stands like an armed sentinel, keeping out all disturbing influences.
   3. God's peace is an indescribable peace "which transcends all understanding" (Phil. 4:7 NIV).

II. Control of thoughts (Phil. 4:8).

You can go to bed at night with nothing physically wrong and lie awake hour after hour worrying about tomorrow, about what someone said, or about personal prestige.

A. Control that limits thoughts to reality reduces anxiety. When the Bible says "whatever is true," it excludes all things speculative—things that "might have been" or "might occur."

B. Control limits thoughts to honorable things. Thinking of honorable things excludes unworthy words or deeds of others.

C. Control limits thoughts to righteousness. "Whatever is true" refers to thoughts that are in accordance with eternal and unchangeable righteousness.

D. Control limits thoughts to purity. This excludes a whole area of degrading and disturbing thoughts.

E. Control limits thoughts to that which produces love. There is no room for thoughts of hate, spite, or retribution when your thoughts are limited by love.

F. Control limits thoughts to that which is admirable. Things that are winning and attractive are always of a "good report."

III. Consistency in living (Phil. 4:9).

You may pray and you may control your thoughts and still be eaten within by anxiety because you know your life is inconsistent with your profession.

A. Consistency in living imparts a clear conscience. "And Paul, earnestly beholding the council, said, "Men and brethren, I have lived in all good conscience before God until this day'" (Acts 23:1).
   1. A clear conscience can come only when you are faithful.
   2. A clear conscience removes all guilt feelings.

B. Consistency in living is true to Christ's teachings (v. 9).
   1. Christ's teachings alone can develop self-respect.
   2. Christ's teachings alone can guide aright. "Your word is a lamp to my feet, a light on my path" (Ps. 119:105 NIV).

C. Consistency in living points others to Jesus.
   1. Others who would be on your hands.
   2. Others whose salvation gives you an occasion for rejoicing.

IV. Contentment in God's will (Phil. 4:11–12).

Much of our anxiety grows out of our inability to be content in God's will. We are not content with where it leads or with what it calls for us to do.

A. God's will may not meet all of your desires. "I know what it is to be in need, and I know what it is to have plenty" (v. 12 NIV).
   1. All of your desires are not necessities.
   2. Your desires, if met, may result in chaos.

B. God's will may call for personal sacrifice (v. 12). For Paul to be content in God's will meant for him to be content in personal sacrifice. Not only food, but other aspirations of life had to be surrendered. For instance, he had to give up his life as a Pharisee.
   1. Call for sacrifice of noble ideals that are not God's will.
   2. Call for sacrifice of time and talent in Christian service.

C. God's will is always best. "But seek ye first the kingdom of God, and his righteousness; and all these things shall be added unto you" (Matt. 6:33).
   1. God's will leads to fewer problems. The person who drops out of God's will is the one who has real problems.
   2. God's will is the will of a loving Father.

V. Confidence in Christ (Phil. 4:13).

A great deal of our anxiety stems from our failure to realize that we are not as important as we think we are. After all, God is in charge, and we are only instruments.

A. Confidence in Christ renews self-determination (v. 13).
   1. Confidence is necessary for success.
   2. Confidence is necessary for self-respect.

B. Confidence in Christ removes the fear of failure (v. 13).
   1. Fear results from a lack of trust in God.
   2. Fear results from a high estimation of self.

C. Confidence in Christ renders yourself God's instrument (v. 13).
   1. God's instrument to whom his strength is imparted.
   2. God's instrument through whom his power may be made known.

Conclusion

When nothing whereon to lean remains,
When strongholds crumble to dust,
When nothing is sure but that God still reigns,
That is just the time to trust.

—*Author unknown*

SUNDAY EVENING, OCTOBER 23

Title: When Faith Is Tested

Text: "By faith Abraham, when he was tested, offered up Isaac, and he who had received the promises was ready to offer up his only son, of whom it was said, 'Through Isaac shall your descendants be named' " **(Heb. 11:17–18 RSV)**.

Scripture Reading: Genesis 22:1–19

Introduction

Tests, trials, worries, disappointments, and frustrations are a part of every human life. We read in the Scriptures that Abraham was tested by God to bring out the good that was in him and to give him a tremendous testimony before his contemporaries. The manner in which Abraham was tested reveals something unique about the God of the Hebrews.

Let us look at some of the ways we are tested.

I. People are tested by Satan.

When Satan puts a person to the test, he does so to bring out evil. His motive is to hurt and destroy. It is interesting to note that our Lord was tempted and was victorious over these temptations that were designed to destroy him and to wreck God's great redemptive plan. Satan uses the same methods to tempt us today.

A. He promised Christ plenty if Christ would follow his suggestions (Matt. 4:3). People still desire pleasure, material goods, power, and other worldly things, and the devil has suggestions by which he promises us plenty.
B. He promises popularity and acceptance by our contemporaries if we follow his suggestions (Matt. 4:4–6). Satan suggested that Christ could accomplish his purpose by putting on an extravaganza. Satan comes to us with subtle suggestions that will lead us astray if we follow his guidance.
C. He comes to us with the promise of painless success if we will but follow his suggestions (Matt. 4:8–9). Satan was trying to tell Christ that it was unnecessary for him to suffer the ordeal of the cross in order to cause the kingdoms of this world to become the kingdom of God.

   Satan comes to us with all kinds of suggestions for shortcuts and substitutes for the right way. When Satan puts us through a trial or test, it is always to hurt and destroy.

II. People are tested by people.

One of the highest faculties with which we are endowed is the capacity to make judgments.

A. A variety of tests is utilized to eliminate the incompetent and the counterfeit. Some method of testing must be used, or we can be destroyed by people who would deceive us.
B. A variety of tests is given to discover the capable and to reveal the genuine.
C. A variety of tests is used to evaluate progress toward a desired goal in training or in the struggle of life.
D. A variety of tests is applied to develop character and leadership potential. These tests are used in the business world, and they are also used in the spiritual realm.

III. People are tested by God.

God needs people on whom he can depend. God needs people with whom he can trust the rich gifts of the Spirit for the good of others. God may not immediately reveal his purpose for testing people, but we can be assured that he has their best interests at heart.

A. The tests that come from God are designed by his love for us (James 1:2). A test that comes from God is a vote of divine confidence in us and is motivated by his love for us as he seeks to build character in us.
B. The tests that come from God are never beyond our power to conquer with divine help (1 Cor. 10:13). When God leads us into a difficult spot, he always promises his presence with us and his power to assist us if we will but trust him and be faithful to him.
C. The tests that come from God enable us to live more abundantly and to serve more effectively. Abraham became a greater man because he was faithful to God when God put him to the test.
D. The tests that come from God speak powerfully to people who will listen.

1. God is faithful and dependable, and we can trust him to be with us in every test and trial.
2. God is gracious and merciful, and every test is designed to bring out the good in us.
3. The tests reveal that God requires our very best.
4. The tests reveal that God is wise because he gives an appropriate test for each of us.
5. The tests reveal that God has a redemptive purpose for each of us and that he wants to use us to be a blessing to others.

Conclusion

The test to which God put Abraham reveals that God wants our best, deserves our best, and always is near to us with purposes of love as we face these tests. This experience of Abraham reveals that God is the great giver and that we cannot outgive God.

When God comes to test us, let us trust him and obey him no matter what (Heb. 2:18).

WEDNESDAY EVENING, OCTOBER 26

Title: The Abundant Provisions of God

Text: "The LORD is my shepherd, I lack nothing" **(Ps. 23:1 NIV)**.

Scripture Reading: Psalm 23

Introduction

Psalm 23 is perhaps the most familiar and best-loved portion of God's Word. Small children memorize the words before they can read. Many people facing crises or even death have repeated the words.

The words in their original setting comprised a confession of God's abundant provisions. It was David's testimony to the reality of God in every experience of his life. David was a shepherd, and he believed that if the shepherd provided abundantly for his sheep, how much more God provides for his people. Let us notice God's wonderful provisions for life.

I. God provides a relationship in life (Ps. 23:1).

A. An amazing relationship. The great name for God, Yahweh, is used. It depicts the fact that a holy God will associate with sinful humanity.

B. An analogous relationship. The word shepherd depicts a comprehensive and intimate metaphor of God relating to people. The ancient shepherd lived with the sheep and experienced an intimate relationship with them.

II. God provides the necessities of life (Ps. 23:1–3).

A. God provides the material necessities of life (vv. 1–2). The shepherd led the sheep to tender green grass, a rare sight in Judea. He provided waters that were at rest. He gave daily sustenance to the sheep by his intimate care. God provides the necessities of life for those who trust him. We need only ask him for "our daily bread."

B. God provides the moral necessities of life (v. 3). Sheep are dumb animals that need close supervision. Often they stray from the shepherd and trespass on the property of others. The shepherd of necessity has to guide the sheep. God provides moral guidance for his people. God leads us in the paths of righteousness. In these days of moral confusion, we need to follow the true Shepherd.

III. God provides strength through life (Ps. 23:4).

A. The inevitability of danger. In the experience of living, there are deep and dark ravines where wild beasts and robbers hide, ready to pounce on the sheep. Danger is an inevitable experience of living. The expression "valley of the shadow of death" (v. 4) describes the dangers of life. The Hebrew term refers to all dark and bitter experiences, one of which may be death.

B. The availability of the Lord. God's provision of strength does not come through removal of dangers. The presence of the shepherd banishes fear. The sheep know that the shepherd has the equipment to care for the sheep. "Thou art with me" is a statement that offers comfort in every experience of life. Life's most strengthening experience is the awareness of God's presence.

IV. God provides fellowship with him forever (Ps. 23:5–6).

A. A friend in life (v. 5). Old Testament scholars contend that the image of the shepherd changes in verse 5 to a host. Whatever the psalmist intended, we do know the truth remains the same. God pictured either as Shepherd or gracious Host provides a loving friendship. Verse 5 vividly portrays God's lavish hospitality to his people.

B. A friend through eternity (v. 6). God's people are portrayed by the psalmist as living with their Friend forever. The terms "goodness" and "mercy" suggest the steady kindness and support that one can count on between firm friends. These qualities endure forever.

Conclusion

Are you burdened with life's experiences? If the Lord is your Shepherd, God has abundant provisions for you. You dare not live another moment without a commitment to the Good Shepherd. He will lead you through life's journey and will take you to a glorious destination.

SUNDAY MORNING, OCTOBER 30

Title: How Do Disciples Become Christians?

Text: "In Antioch the disciples were for the first time called Christians" **(Acts 11:26 RSV)**.

Scripture Reading: Acts 11:19–26; Galatians 5:22–23

Hymns: "Holy, Holy, Holy," Heber

"Breathe on Me," Hatch

"Let Others See Jesus in You," McKinney

Offertory Prayer: For the beauty and the goodness of this day, we thank you, Father. For every good gift that you have bestowed on us, we offer our praise and gratitude. We come to give tangible expressions to our love, to our faith, and to the various ministries of your kingdom's work. We thank you for the ability to earn and to save and to give. As we bring our tithes and offerings, accept them and bless them and use them for the advancement of your kingdom and for the good of people, we pray in Christ's name. Amen.

Introduction

The Scriptures declare that the disciples of Jesus Christ were called Christians first in the city of Antioch, where the church was composed primarily of Gentile believers.

The inspired writer may be paying tribute to the work of the divine Spirit in the hearts of these disciples. Barnabas influenced the life and the spiritual growth of this congregation, and he is described as "a good man, full of the Holy Spirit and of faith." A large number of people were converted and added to the church through his ministry. With the assistance of Paul, these disciples ministered to the church and taught the people, and these people experienced spiritual growth. They let the Spirit produce his fruit within them, and they began to manifest the character traits and the graces of Jesus Christ. Others beheld the beauty of Jesus Christ in them. Thus they were called Christians.

Indira Gandhi, former prime minister of India, has been quoted as saying that if Christians would act like Jesus Christ, India would be at his feet. The greatest hindrance to the evangelistic effort of a local church or to the missionary effort of all of the churches is a poor example of Christianity. The low quality of life that some Christians display to the world is due to the fact that they have ignored and neglected the Holy Spirit and have even refused to let the Holy Spirit reproduce within them the character of Jesus Christ.

I. The term Christian has been cheapened, abused, and misused.

A. The term Christian has been claimed by many merely because they believe in the existence of God.

B. The term Christian has been applied to some merely because they live by a high moral code that produces respectability.

C. The term Christian has been applied by some to all who have received the rite of baptism. These labor under the impression that the rite of baptism makes a Christian out of the person receiving the baptism.

D. The term Christian has been used as a synonym for church membership. We often hear people say, "I'm a member of such-and-such church. Doesn't that make me a Christian?"

E. Some have considered being converted and becoming a Christian as one and the same thing. You have heard it said, "Well, Johnny became a Christian last night." The speaker actually is referring to a public profession of faith, but he equates this experience with being Christian. The misuse and the abuse of the term Christian has produced some tragic results. First, some people have the impression that the conversion experience is the sum of God's plan for their lives. Second, misuse of the term Christian has produced a low quality of life that does not reveal the radical and wonderful difference that Christ wants to produce in the lives of those who trust him as Savior and Lord. Third, some people have a nominal Christianity that is nothing but a thin veneer of the real thing yet wonder why they are not more successful in winning the unbelieving world to faith in Jesus Christ.

Many think of Christianity in terms of cushioned pews, agreeable music, and a comfortable worship service concluded with a monotonous sermon on Sunday, and then business as usual during the week. We need to rediscover what caused the people to start calling the disciples in Antioch Christians.

II. Some observations concerning how disciples do not become Christian.

The term Christian can be an adjective as well as a noun. It can describe a quality of life rather than just designating a person as a follower of Jesus Christ.

Let's note some good things, which in themselves do not produce Christians out of disciples.

A. Regularly attending worship services alone will not guarantee that you will be genuinely Christian in your life.

B. Regular Bible study is very profitable, but regular Bible study alone does not guarantee that one will become like Jesus Christ.

C. The habit of prayer should be formed and not broken. However, one can pray morning, noon, and night for a lifetime and not become genuinely Christian.

D. The practice of tithing can transform one's thoughts about the value of things, but this alone does not enable one to be genuinely Christian.

E. One can exercise superior willpower and practice good habits with persistence and still not be worthy to wear the title Christian.

To be Christians, people must let the life, the mind, and the Spirit of Jesus Christ so permeate their personalities that others will begin to recognize the transformation that has taken place.

III. Disciples become Christians as they make proper responses to the indwelling Holy Spirit.

The fact that God gives the gift of the Holy Spirit to the new convert has not been emphasized nearly as much as it should be. Many people who have trusted Christ as Savior are unaware that in the conversion experience the Holy Spirit took up residency within their innermost being and came to reproduce in their lives the character and personality of Jesus Christ (cf. Gal. 4:6–7). "But the fruit of the Spirit is love, joy, peace, patience, kindness, goodness, faithfulness, gentleness, self-control; against such there is no law" (Gal. 5:22–23 RSV).

A. These graces provide us with a verbal photograph of the person and Spirit of Jesus Christ. The apostle declares that these graces are the fruit of the indwelling Spirit of God.

B. These graces are the fruit of the indwelling Spirit for every believer. The gifts of the Spirit enable individuals to render specific ministries for the building up of the church and for the advancement of God's kingdom. These graces of the Spirit, which Jesus Christ personified perfectly, have to do with the character of the believer. People who have these graces in their lives will reflect and manifest the presence of Jesus Christ in their lives.

IV. Disciples become Christians when they make a proper response to the Holy Spirit.

There is no way for disciples of Jesus Christ to become fully Christian in their innermost beings or in their influence over others apart from the ministry and the work of the Holy Spirit in their lives. To become genuinely Christian, a person must make a positive response to the presence and the purpose of the indwelling Spirit.

A. We must believe the testimony of the Holy Spirit concerning our new relationship to God through faith in Jesus Christ (Rom. 8:16; Gal. 4:6–7).

B. We must recognize and respond to the indwelling Holy Spirit (1 Cor. 3:16; 6:19–20). The Holy Spirit cannot do his finest work unless his presence is recognized and unless there is a personal response of cooperation with him.

C. We must listen to the voice of the Holy Spirit and obey him (Rev. 2:7, 11, 17, 29; 3:6, 13, 22).

D. We must cooperate with the Holy Spirit as he works within us (Phil. 2:13).

Conclusion

The Holy Spirit invites the nonbeliever to put faith in Jesus Christ as Lord and Savior. The Holy Spirit is seeking continually to magnify and exalt Jesus Christ as the Savior who alone can bring the gift of forgiveness and new life into one's heart (John 16:13–14).

Trust Christ for forgiveness and cleansing, for new life, for hope for the future, for the power to live an abundant life, and for the gift of divine sonship and assurance of an eternity in the heaven of God.

SUNDAY EVENING, OCTOBER 30

Title: Christian Love: The Controlling Guideline

Text: "Therefore, if food is a cause of my brother's falling, I will never eat meat, lest I cause my brother to fall" **(1 Cor. 8:13 RSV)**.

Scripture Reading: 1 Corinthians 8:1–13

Introduction

In the chapter that serves as our Scripture reading, the apostle Paul is dealing with a practice that was common in the first century but is not familiar to us today. In America today, people generally either worship one god or no god. In ancient Corinth, there were many gods and many different religions. Sacrifices were made to these various idols, and then the meat offered in sacrifice was eaten by the worshipers and their guests. To eat meat offered to an idol was to engage in a form of worship and to receive nourishment and the hope of help from the idol god whose sacrifice was being consumed.

Those who were converted to faith in Jesus Christ forsook the worship of idols and recognized idols to be nothing. Some of these new converts insisted that since the idol had no reality, there was no harm in feasting at an idol temple or in purchasing the meat offered in sacrifice to idols.

Paul says that to participate in such feasts or to use the meat offered to idols could be harmful to those who had not yet come to a knowledge of the true God. He declares that not everyone has the knowledge of the truth as they had come to know it in Christ Jesus. He is eager that these new converts relate properly to those who are still pagans. In our text, he enunciates a principle that reveals that Christian love must be the controlling guideline for all of our conduct as it affects nonbelievers. As Phillips translates it, "This makes me determined that, if there is any possibility of meat injuring my brother, I will have none of it as long as I live, for fear I might do him harm."

I. We are responsible for our influence (Matt. 5:16).

Christian love will cause us to recognize our responsibility for our influence and cause us to beware lest we cause others to stumble.

A. We must not cause even those who are hostile toward Christ to stumble—"Give no offense to Jews" (1 Cor. 10:32 RSV).

B. We must not cause even those who are indifferent to Christianity to stumble—"Give no offense to ... Greeks" (1 Cor. 10:32 RSV).

C. We must not cause our fellow Christians to stumble—"Give no offense to ... the church of God" (1 Cor. 10:32 RSV).

II. We must be genuinely concerned about the welfare of weaker Christians.

We are warned against the consequences of sinning against weaker Christians and wounding their consciences. The conscience has been defined as "the faculty of responsible moral judgment."

A. Jesus warned against causing the weaker brother to fall into sin (Matt. 18:6).
B. To sin against the weaker brother is to sin against Christ (1 Cor. 8:12). It is interesting to note that the glorified Christ considered mistreatment of the church to be mistreatment directed toward him (cf. Acts 9:4).

   There are many ways by which the consciences of weaker Christians are injured by those who are more mature, or at least they think they are more mature. Social drinking, which may be controlled by some, is a deadly evil, because every person is a potential alcoholic. Even that which is considered to be harmless gambling can be very dangerous to some, because people can become addicted to gambling just as they can become addicted to alcohol. Some people habitually break the speed limit and think nothing of it. This can have a harmful effect on children who see parents recklessly disregarding traffic laws. The neglect of Bible study, prayer, and regular worship habits can have a harmful effect on weaker Christians who look to others for guidance and encouragement.

III. We must be builders rather than wreckers.

The apostle urged his readers to let love be the controlling guideline in all of their relationships with others. He rejoiced that these converts now had knowledge of the true God, which included an evaluation of idols as being nothing. However, he warned them against the peril of letting this knowledge create within them an attitude of arrogance. He encouraged them instead to relate to weaker Christians in loving concern.

A. Love always builds up rather than tears down.
B. Christian love is never self-centered. Christian love is always concerned about the welfare of others.

IV. The Christian's compelling objective: "That they may be saved" (1 Cor. 10:33).

With verse 33 the apostle brings a section of his epistle to a conclusion, and he reveals the basis for the counsel he has been giving. He was exceedingly eager that all groups might come to know Jesus Christ as Lord and Savior. It was essential that these new converts conduct themselves in such a manner as not to cast negative reflection on Christ or to violate the sense of propriety of those whom they were seeking to win.

A. Christians must relate to others in such a manner as to reveal to them that God loves them.
B. Christians need to relate to others in such a manner as to reveal that God has a wonderful plan for their lives.

Conclusion

What we do, what we say, and what we are wields an influence over the lives of others. One can no more escape from one's own influence that from one's shadow in bright sunlight. We must let love for the Lord and the Lord's love for the unsaved be the controlling guidelines in all of our conduct at all times.

SUGGESTED PREACHING PROGRAM FOR THE MONTH OF

NOVEMBER

■ Sunday Mornings

Our Lord taught that it is more blessed to give than to receive. He challenged his disciples to be givers with the observation that the rewards for a life of giving were great (Luke 6:38). The suggested theme for the morning messages is "The Need of the Giver to Give." We need to be tithers more than God needs our tithes.

■ Sunday Evenings

"Living the Grateful Life" is the suggested theme for the first three Sunday evenings. Our primary motivation is to stem from God's love for us.

On the last Sunday evening of the month, begin the series "God with Us at Bethlehem and God in Us at Pentecost." These messages prove that the Christ of Christmas is alive and working in our world today.

■ Wednesday Evenings

Continue the series of messages titled "Out of Human Experiences" based on selected psalms.

WEDNESDAY EVENING, NOVEMBER 2

Title: The Mastery of Fear

Text: "The LORD is my light and my salvation; whom shall I fear? The LORD is the strength of my life; of whom shall I be afraid?" **(Ps. 27:1)**.

Scripture Reading: Psalm 27

Introduction

Fear is one of the painful realities of our day. Modern psychology has coined more than seventy-five words based on variations of the Greek word phobia to describe our fears.

The psalmist had experienced some fearful situations. He had been tried and tempered by prevailing fears. Psalm 27 is a marvelous testimony of the mastery of fear. From these fourteen verses, we can learn how to control the numerous inward and outward fears of life.

I. Trust the Lord (Ps. 27:1–3).

The psalmist mastered his fears by trusting the Lord. His faith kept him from despair. Irrespective of raging fears, the psalmist trusted the Lord.

A. Trust in the present situation (v. 1). "The Lord is." The psalmist used the present tense to show that in the time of trouble he considered God as his "light," "salvation," and "strength." In all his bitter experiences, he discovered that trust in God kept him from being afraid. With God as the resource of his life, he had nothing of which to be afraid.

B. Trust in past experiences (v. 2). Looking back over his life, the psalmist wondered how he had mastered the enemies and foes of his life. He considered that God was greater than any of his enemies, and therefore he trusted the Lord.

C. Trust in future experiences (v. 3). The psalmist knew that trust in God was not protection against trial. Anything could happen—enemies, political oppression, or the horrors of war. Yet the psalmist affirmed that he would continue to trust.

You can master your fears by giving life to the care of God. He is capable of caring for all the assaults of life.

II. Meditate on God (Ps. 27:4–6).

The psalmist mastered his fears by meditating on the Lord. The more he learned of God, the less he feared.

A. See God's beauty (v. 4). The psalmist wanted to "behold the beauty of the Lord." The word translated "beauty" refers to the loveliness of God's character. The psalmist filled his mind with the glorious truths of God, which would sustain him in the troubles and perplexities of life.

B. Search further after God (v. 4). The psalmist wanted to "enquire in [God's] temple." He wanted to be taught God's ways. In the place of worship, we can have our minds enlightened. The more we know about God, the fewer perplexities we have.

The search will reveal some great truths about God. In time of danger, he will protect us. In the secrecy of our souls, he will be a dear Friend to us. He will give us a secure place. We will be able to rise above the fears (cf. 27:5–6).

C. Sing praises to the Lord (v. 6). The psalmist has found God to be greater than his fears; thus he shouts praises to God.

You can master your fears by meditating on the Lord. Preoccupation with yourself and your problems leads to devastating fears. Meditation on the Lord leads to serenity.

III. Pray to the Lord (Ps. 27:7–14).

The psalmist mastered his raging fears by honest prayer to God. He found that the fears were more than he could handle and submitted himself and his situations to God's control. He made specific petitions in his prayers.

A. He asked God to listen (vv. 7–9). The psalmist wanted God's attention. Though he trusted God and meditated on the Lord, he still felt that he must call on the Lord. The psalmist felt that even if his parents would not listen to his problem, the Lord would gladly listen.

B. He asked God for instruction and leadership (v. 11). He prayed that the Lord would teach him to act wisely.

C. He asked God for special strength (vv. 12–14). The psalmist's life would be robbed of strength. The efforts of his enemies would be too strong. Therefore he prayed that God would give him strength to endure severe hardships.

You can master your fears by prayer. God will listen to your prayers and grant what you need.

Conclusion

The psalmist concluded his message in verse 14. He invited others to trust the Lord, to meditate on him, and to pray to him. In times of danger and difficulty, the Lord will uphold us. Instead of being weighed down in despondency and despair, we will rejoice in the Lord.

SUNDAY MORNING, NOVEMBER 6

Title: Tithe to Tell the Story

Text: "I heard the voice of the Lord, saying, Whom shall I send, and who will go for us? Then said I, Here am I; send me" **(Isa. 6:8)**.

Scripture Reading: Isaiah 6

Hymns: "I Love to Tell the Story," Hankey

"Make Me a Blessing," Wilson

"Hark, the Voice of Jesus Calling," March

Offertory Prayer: Thank you, Lord, for your personal concern for each of us and for the revelation of yourself to us through Jesus Christ. As we give of our means today, help us to give because we love you and want to make it possible for the story of your love to be told to all people everywhere. In Jesus' name. Amen.

Introduction

To many people, "religion" is the study of a book—the greatest of all books—the Bible. To others, it is routine church attendance. To still others it is religious busyness. But real New Testament Christianity is more than any of these—it is the establishment and maintenance of a personal relationship with God through Jesus Christ, which issues in fulfilling God's will for one's life.

All the great men of the Bible were conscious of such a relationship with God. Enoch walked with God. Abraham was called the friend of God. Moses met with God on numerous occasions. Elijah was caught up by God in a chariot of fire. Jeremiah was personally called by God. And Isaiah was strangely moved by a tremendous worship experience with God.

I. Isaiah had a deepening personal experience with God.

While worshiping in the temple, Isaiah had a vivid consciousness of the presence, power, and holiness of God (Isa. 6:1–3). It happened in the year King Uzziah died. Many Christians are of the ordinary garden variety until they come face-to-face with God in a deep worship experience that changes the course of their lives. Such was the case with Moses (at the burning bush; Ex. 3:1–10) and with Jacob (Gen. 28:10–17).

Only when Christians live under the lordship of Jesus Christ can a continuing motivation of Christian service be sustained. If Christian people see a lost world with all its needs, they will do nothing about it if their hearts are cold. They will be like the priest and Levite in Jesus' parable of the good Samaritan and pass by them (Luke 10:30–34).

Our task is to begin by leading people to have a face-to-face confrontation with Jesus Christ. A story is told of a little delivery boy carrying a basket of eggs. He tripped on the curbstone, dropped the basket, and smashed the eggs. People gathered around as people do. One said, "What a pity." Another said, "He is crying; let's comfort him." Then one man stepped out of the crowd, put his hand in his pocket, and said, "I care half a crown." Turning to the man next to him, he said, "How much do you care?" The man replied, "I care a shilling." In a little time, they translated feeling into action. Only a personal encounter with the risen Lord will permanently motivate people into action.

II. Isaiah had a sense of belonging to God as his instrument of grace (6:5–7).

As Isaiah experienced God, he was convicted of sin—his own as well as the sin of Israel. Isaiah 1:1–6 describes what Isaiah felt in his heart about the sin of Israel. One of the main functions of worship is to get us to see ourselves as we really are so that we might cry with the psalmist, "Search me, O God, and know my heart: try me, and know my thoughts: and see if there be any wicked way in me, and lead me in the way everlasting" (Ps. 139:23–24).

When Isaiah confessed his sin, a seraph took golden tongs and picked up a glowing coal and touched it to Isaiah's mouth. Now with a cleansed heart, he wanted to do something to get his sinful people right with God. He wanted to be used.

First Peter 2:21–24 points out that the stewardship of Jesus was to fulfill the purpose of God in his life no matter what it cost him—and it cost him the cross. The Bible also reminds us that as Jesus' followers, we are to follow in his steps. Matthew 16:24 gives us the direction we should go. This concept of stewardship involves all that we are as well as all we possess. This is what God expects of us (2 Cor. 5:18–20; 1 Peter 4:10).

Isaiah saw himself as God's instrument. Do you?

III. Isaiah had a vision of God's strategy for redemption and committed himself to it (6:8–9).

God revealed to Isaiah that he wanted Isaiah to serve him in bringing the people back to him. And Isaiah volunteered to serve even though he knew the task would be difficult and that he would have limited success. However, God revealed to Isaiah that he would fulfill God's purpose.

God has a strategy for worldwide proclamation of the gospel, including a plan for financing the work—the tithe plus the offerings of God's people.

Conclusion

This is God's plan, and it includes your life and your resources. We are told that it took thirty thousand people and $400 million dollars to put the first man in orbit. There are millions of Christians, and God has given us the resources to win people to him. Let us lay our resources at the feet of our Master and give the whole gospel to the whole world—now!

Remember the word God spoke to Isaiah, "Go and tell this people." Let us "Tithe to Tell the Story."

SUNDAY EVENING, NOVEMBER 6

Title: Living Worthy of the Glad Tidings

Text: "Let your manner of life be worthy of the gospel of Christ" **(Phil. 1:27 RSV)**.

Scripture Reading: Philippians 1:27–30

Introduction

Paul wrote to his beloved Philippian friends from a prison cell. While he had many reasons for despair, his epistle radiates the joy of one who knew Jesus Christ to be very precious and very real. In fact, the apostle loved the Lord and had experienced his presence and power in such a manner as to cause him to want to go on and be with the Lord immediately. However, he came to the conclusion that it was best that he remain in order that he might encourage and assist others in their spiritual growth and service for Christ (Phil. 1:21–26). Paul encouraged his beloved friends to live in such a manner as to make the glad tidings they announced attractive to their listeners.

It is interesting to note how our text has been translated. The New International Version translates it, "Whatever happens, conduct yourselves in a manner worthy of the gospel of Christ." Phillips translates it, "Whatever happens, make sure that your everyday life is worthy of the gospel of Christ."

I. Traits that were and are desirable.

A. We must stand steady and faithful together as the disciples of our Lord (v. 27).

B. We must create and maintain a spirit of unity within the fellowship of the church (v. 27).

C. We must not be intimidated or terrified by those who oppose the gospel (v. 28). John Knox said, "Show a bold front at all times to your adversaries."

D. We must be willing to suffer for the sake of our faith and for the sake of the Christ who loved us enough to suffer for us (v. 29).

II. Right attitudes of mind and heart are essential if we are to live worthy of the glad tidings.

Christ is to be our model at all times as far as our conduct is concerned.

A. With humility and gratitude for salvation from the penalty of sin, we should give ourselves in service to others.

B. With confidence and trust in the power of our Lord, we should face the struggles of the present in the faith that God will give us victory.

C. Because the Lord has been so good in the past and is so good in the present, we can face the future with an attitude of confidence and joy.

III. Responding to our high privileges.

Paul wrote to those who had been blessed indescribably by the glad tidings of salvation through faith in Jesus Christ. He focused on some of their privileges and urged them to respond in a worthy manner.

A. We enjoy the privilege of believing in Jesus Christ as Savior.

B. We can rejoice in the privilege of being listed among his servants and helpers.

C. Paul pointed out that some enjoy the privilege of suffering for Christ's sake. Probably we have never really come to appreciate our Lord if we have not been willing to suffer for him.

D. We should live worthy of the glad tidings in order that we might have the joy of sharing Christ with a world that is still in spiritual darkness.

Conclusion

Each of us should make it our business to make certain that the manner in which we conduct our daily affairs is such as to demonstrate the difference that Jesus Christ makes. We need to participate in the work of our church so as to strengthen the witness of our church in the community and the world. Each of us, in our own individual world, must live worthy of the name that we wear if we are to identify with those who are called Christians.

WEDNESDAY EVENING, NOVEMBER 9

Title: A Glorious Pardon

Text: "Blessed is the one whose transgressions are forgiven, whose sins are covered" **(Ps. 32:1 NIV).**

Scripture Reading: Psalm 32

Introduction

A teenage member of our church exceeded the speed limit while driving through a small town. Also, the mufflers on his car were unlawful in that town. An alert marshall stopped the young man and charged him with speeding and having improper mufflers. It was such a blow to the young man that he came to see me, his pastor. He asked, "What can I do?" I replied. "Tell the judge that you are guilty and that you want to pay the fine."

The next day he went to court. Afterward he ran into my office, and with excitement in his voice, he said, "Pastor, guess what happened! I told the judge just what you said. He looked at me, and then he said, 'Young man, you are guilty, but this time I am going to pardon your offenses.'" The young man never forgot the generosity of that judge.

Offenders against God also can have a pardon. David, a man guilty of murder and adultery, admitted his guilt and repented. God pardoned David. No greater happiness awaits a person than forgiveness.

I. The contentment (Ps. 32:1–2).

The word "blessed" strikes the predominant note of the psalm. It is equivalent to the term happy. David was filled with overflowing joy and contentment because of what God had done with the evil in his life.

A. God forgives transgressions.
   1. Transgression is rebellion against God's rightful authority.
   2. To forgive means to lift up and to carry away. Perhaps it has reference to the scapegoat that was sent away into the wilderness.

B. God covers sin.
   1. Sin is failure to live according to God's standard.
   2. "Covers" means to conceal so that it will not appear.

C. God imputeth not iniquity.
   1. Iniquity means to be crooked.
   2. "Imputeth not" means not to charge to a person.

II. The confession (Ps. 32:3–5).

Perhaps David tried several methods to rid himself of the memory and guilt of sin. The only help he found was an honest confession to the Lord.

A. The burden of unconfessed sin.
   1. Rotting bones—the grief of his sin robbed David of strength.
   2. God's heavy hand—God brought the facts of sin to David's recollection.
   3. Sapped vitality—David possessed a distressed mind because of the conviction of sin.

B. The open confession.
   1. An acknowledgment—David confessed the fact of his sin to God.
   2. An uncovering—David resolved not to conceal his sin any longer.
   3. A confession—David placed the responsibility on himself and opened his life to the Lord.

C. The result of confession.
   1. God is willing to hear a sinner's confession.
   2. God forgives penitent sinners.

III. The commitment (Ps. 32:5–11).

After David's forgiveness, he made several commitments to the Lord. Forgiveness is not something merely transactional. It transforms one's lifestyle.

A. A sharing from experience.
   1. David urges everyone to call on the Lord.
   2. God will not allow a penitent person to be destroyed. He is our security.
   3. David once felt insecure, shut off from God. He testifies that forgiveness brings a sense of belonging to God.

B. The task of instruction.
   1. A forgiven man will be an instructor to others of the terrors of sin and the joy of forgiveness.
   2. A forgiven man will not be like a stubborn animal that has to be trained to do the master's will.

C. A contrast.
   1. The miseries of the wicked.
   2. The joys of the penitent.

Conclusion

Are you tired of the guilt of sin? Perhaps you have noticed a similarity in your experience as compared with David's. A glorious pardon awaits penitent sinners. When you acknowledge your sins and ask God to forgive, he will abundantly pardon.

SUNDAY MORNING, NOVEMBER 13

Title: Jesus Sat over against the Treasury

Text: "And Jesus sat over against the treasury, and beheld how the people cast money into the treasury: and many that were rich cast in much" **(Mark 12:41)**.

Scripture Reading: Mark 12:41–44

Hymns: "Take My Life, and Let It Be," Havergal

"Trust, Try, and Prove Me," Leech

"I Gave My Life for Thee," Havergal

Offertory Prayer: Our Father, we thank you for those who have succeeded greatly in life and who give generously from their abundance. We are grateful also for those who have little of this world's goods and give generously from their poverty. We are grateful that you look beyond the hand to the heart. In Jesus' name. Amen.

Introduction

It is my duty as a preacher to declare to you the whole Word of God. The Bible teaches the fact of the sovereignty of God; therefore, I preach about it. The Bible teaches the truth of the inspiration of the Scripture; therefore, I proclaim that truth. The central fact of the gospel is the atoning death of Jesus Christ. It is my privilege to proclaim this good news. Because the Bible teaches salvation by grace through faith without works of any kind, I preach it. The Bible tells us that there is a place called hell; therefore I warn people about hell. Christian stewardship also is taught in the Bible. I would not be true to my calling unless I preached Christian stewardship. I would not have you to be ignorant concerning what God has to say to us about this important matter. I do not preach on Christian stewardship simply as a means of making it possible for the church to receive more money. It is my conviction that those who are good stewards are happy, well-balanced, and fruitful Christians. I do not believe that people can know the full joy of Christian living until they have realized the blessing of God on their lives as a result of their faithfulness to his cause and kingdom.

Mark 12 records some of the teachings and activities of the closing days of Jesus' earthly ministry. Jesus was locked in a life-and-death struggle with the Pharisees, Sadducees, and scribes. He told them the parable of the wicked husbandmen, which demonstrated the wickedness of the hearts of the Hebrew religious leaders in rejecting him as the Son of God. Time and again they had tried to trap him, but time and again, with divine wisdom, he made their wisdom seem crudest ignorance. After lashing the religious leaders with caustic words (Mark 12:38–40), "Jesus sat over against the treasury" (v. 41).

I. Jesus is the Lord of his treasury.

This Scripture gives us a picture of Jesus' concern for the treasury of the house of the Lord. Jesus said more about stewardship than he did any other subject. Note Matthew 6:19–24, 33 as a classic example. Jesus is still Lord of the treasury of every church. As he was concerned then about people's giving habits, so he is today. Sometimes we feel that we are simply giving to a church budget—not so. This is not the preacher's church—it is the Lord's church. Everything in this church belongs to him. He is the head of this church and the head of the treasury. When we give, we give to further the gospel.

II. Jesus beholds our gifts (Mark 12:41).

"[He] beheld how the people cast money." Jesus was a spectator. The Greek word translated "beheld" means one looking at a thing with interest and for a purpose, usually indicating the careful observation of details. Jesus saw then, and he sees us today. He observes us as we give today. Our Scripture passage says that he saw the rich cast in much out of their abundance and witnessed the poor widow as she gave her little. Here is a drama if we care to see it: the people bringing their gifts to God and God in the shadows keeping watch over his own—his own people and his own treasury. What a sobering thought. We cannot escape this personal God. Psalm 139 tells us that there is no place we can go where God does not see us. He sees us as we earn money and as we determine in our hearts how much we are to give to the Lord's work through the church. He sees us as we write our checks. He knows whether we are really tithing or not. He looks not at the outward appearance but on the heart. A small gift is as great as a large gift if it is a right proportion and if it is given with the right motives.

III. Jesus judges our gifts.

Jesus not only noticed those who gave, but he also noted the amount of each gift. He did not condemn the rich for their large gifts. Thank God for those who make a lot of money and also give a lot—as much or more than a tithe. People ought to make all the money they can, as long as they make it honestly. God intends for all people to do the best they can in their area of business. Possessing possessions is not wrong until possessions begin to possess us. Jesus did not commend the widow because her gift was small; he commended her for the proportion she gave. He looked beyond the hand to the heart. The average person would bow and scrape to the one who gave the largest gift, but Jesus pointed out the one who gave the largest proportion. James had the spirit of Christ when he wrote James 2:1–4. The gift should be weighed, not counted.

IV. Jesus desires our gifts.

Throughout the Bible, we find the Lord being pleased with the gifts of those who loved him. Genesis 8:20 tells us that Noah built an altar unto the Lord and took of every clean beast and every clean fowl and offered burnt offerings on the altar. Verse 21 says that the Lord was pleased with Noah's gift. When the Lord commanded the building of the tabernacle, he told Moses to "take ... from among you an offering unto the Lord ... gold, and silver, and brass" (Ex. 35:5). Notice also Exodus 36:3–6. God delights in the offerings of his people whether they be of self or of substance. Notice what Paul tells us in 2 Corinthians 9:6–8. Jesus never completely gets you until he gets yours. Your gifts are needed, but more important than that, you need to give. Try tithing—that is, if you can do it with the right spirit. It will open the windows of heaven and also bring inner joy.

V. Jesus blesses our gifts (Mark 12:44).

Jesus commended the widow. Suppose she had said, "My gift is so small it will never do any good. It will not be missed if I keep it for myself." She would have missed the Lord's commendation. If you are not a good steward, you are missing many blessings. It is indeed far more blessed to give than it is to receive. Your gift is important—whether small or large. Look at what Jesus did with the five loaves and two fish. Notice this beautiful story found in John 6. The disciple Andrew said in verse 9: "There is a lad here, which hath five barley loaves, and two small fishes: but what are they among so many?" Is it not true that many times we feel that our tithe is not so much—it will not be missed—no one could tell the difference? But the individual who misses out on God's blessing can tell the difference. Jesus took those five loaves and two fish and fed more than five thousand men. If Jesus could do that with a little boy's loaves and fish, what do you think he could do with your life fully surrendered to him?

I believe that when Christian people give as God wants us to give, the Lord of the loaves and fish will miraculously make those gifts sufficient to meet the needs of the lost world. It is so with us here. When we love him enough to give in the proper proportion, the Lord Jesus will make what we give more than sufficient for our needs.

Conclusion

"And Jesus sat over against the treasury." He is here today. He will be here next Sunday and the next down through the years. He will be looking over your shoulder when you give. Is the Lord pleased with the proportion of your gifts? The widow gave all her material possessions. Jesus gave his life on the cross to redeem you. What will you give?

SUNDAY EVENING, NOVEMBER 13

Title: Internalizing the Law of the Lord

Text: "Blessed is the man who walks not in the counsel of the wicked, nor stands in the way of sinners, nor sits in the seat of scoffers; but his delight is in the law of the Lord, and on his law he meditates day and night" **(Ps. 1:1–2 RSV)**.

Scripture Reading: Psalm 119:97–104

Introduction

In recent years our nation has experienced great agony as a result of people rejecting and ignoring the law of God. This has given rise to a wave of paganism and lawlessness.

The law of God was addressed to the people of God who had been redeemed by his grace and power. The law was intended to provide guidance toward fulfillment in living the abundant life. The law of God is considered by some to be a negative list of restrictions against which people rebel. But people cannot live effectively without law. To attempt to do so is to invite disaster. The laws of God should be considered as the principles and guidelines that lift us and enrich us so we can live on life's highest plane. To ignore or to rebel against the laws of God is to experience a way of life that brings self-destruction and unhappiness.

In order for the law of the Lord to be the beautiful and powerful thing that he meant for it to be, each individual must internalize and make personal the good law of our Lord. The psalmist speaks of the value of God's commands when he says, "Moreover by them is thy servant warned; in keeping them there is great reward" (Ps. 19:11 RSV).

The law was not given by God as a ladder by which people might climb to heaven. The law was given to people who because of their faith were on their way to heaven. The law was given that the people of God might avoid self-destructive ways and that they might give themselves to constructive ways. The people of God should love the law of God rather than resent it. God was seeking to bless the race rather than to bring a blight upon it by the giving of his law.

I. The results of loving the law of the Lord.

The psalmist said, "Oh, how I love thy law! It is my meditation all the day" (Ps. 119:97 RSV).

A. To internalize the law of God brings happiness and prosperity (Ps. 1:1–3). People who have prosperous lives are those who delight in the law of the Lord and meditate on it day and night. They are blessed with stability and prosperity, refreshment and vigor, and a bountiful harvest. They enjoy the greenery of a tree that is planted by a river of flowing water. The psalmist describes the person who loves the law of the Lord as one who prospers in all that he does.

B. Loving the law of God brings refreshing restoration to the soul (Ps. 19:7).

C. Loving the law of the Lord makes the simple wise (Ps. 19:7).

D. Loving the law of the Lord brings rejoicing to the heart (Ps. 19:8).

E. Loving the law of the Lord brings enlightenment to the eyes.

F. Loving the law of the Lord provides us with warnings in the day of danger (Ps. 19:11).

II. The nature of the law of God.

A. The law of the Lord is perfect (Ps. 19:7).

B. The testimony of the Lord is sure (Ps. 19:7).

C. The statutes of the Lord are right (Ps. 19:8).

D. The commandment of the Lord is pure (Ps. 19:8).

E. The judgments of the Lord are true and righteous (Ps. 19:19).

III. How do you respond to the law of the Lord?

Your response can be stated either negatively or positively.

A. Negative responses.

1. The psalmist prays, "Let me not wander from thy commandments" (Ps. 119:10).
2. The psalmist determines, "I will not forget thy words" (119:16).

B. Positive responses to the law of the Lord.

1. We would be wise to choose the way of faithfulness to the law of the Lord (Ps. 119:30).
2. We would be wise to walk in the law of the Lord (Ps. 119:1).
3. We would be wise to keep the law of the Lord always in our hearts (Ps. 119:2).
4. We would be wise to keep our eyes fixed on the commandments of our Lord (Ps. 119:6.)
5. We would be wise to love the law of our Lord (Ps. 119:97).
6. We would be wise to trust in the law of our Lord (Ps. 119:81).

Conclusion

We are not saved by keeping the law of God perfectly. We are saved by putting our faith and trust in Jesus Christ, who kept the law perfectly. Not only was his life sinless, but he also met the demands of the law by dying under the penalty of it as a substitute for us. Christ filled the law full of meaning and lifted the demands of the law of the Old Testament.

When Christ comes into our hearts, he gives us the gift of the Holy Spirit. The Holy Spirit motivates us by the law of love. We must internalize and personalize the law of God if it is to be the blessing that God meant for it to be. Let God's law have its place in your heart and life. By so doing, you can live the truly grateful life.

WEDNESDAY EVENING, NOVEMBER 16

Title: Faith in Troubled Times

Text: "God is our refuge and strength, an ever-present help in trouble" **(Ps. 46:1 NIV)**.

Scripture Reading: Psalm 46

Introduction

During a Christian's lifetime, he or she faces many trials and vicissitudes of life. Experience teaches us that God does not always prevent tragedies and troubles from coming to Christians. But God is a present help in trouble.

Scholars believe that Psalm 46 was composed during troubled times. Probably it was penned during Sennacherib's invasion (2 Kings 18:13–19:37). The psalmist expressed his faith during these troubled times. He believed that God was greater and mightier than the crises.

I. God's protection (Ps. 46:1–3).

Verses 1–3 give evidence of the psalmist's serenity during tremendous earth-shattering crises. He did not panic. Instead, he maintained confident serenity.

A. The conflagrations. The psalmist mentioned several catastrophic possibilities: "Though the earth give way and the mountains fall into the heart of the sea, though its waters roar and foam and the mountains quake with their surging" (v. 3 NIV). The picture is the psalmist's conception of the worst that could happen.

B. The confidence. The psalmist expressed his confidence in God. "God is our refuge and strength, an ever-present help in trouble" (v. 1 NIV). God provides safety in the storms of life and strength for stability in life, and he is present every moment to help.

II. God's provisions (Ps. 46:4–7).

Verses 4–7 give evidence of the psalmist's security. He knew something that his enemies did not know. He had an unseen security.

A. The river. "There is a river." During the days of Hezekiah a tunnel had been dug to bring the waters of the Gihon Spring to a reservoir inside the city of

Jerusalem. The psalmist probably refers to this fact. The enemies did not know that the inhabitants of Jerusalem had an unfailing supply of water.

God's people have provisions that the unredeemed world does not know about. God supplies his people with marvelous provisions.

B. The city. In verse 4 the psalmist also refers to the "city of God." He recognized that Jerusalem was an invincible city. It had been captured many times by the enemy. Evidently the psalmist looked to the security of the new Jerusalem.

III. God's preeminence (Ps. 46:8–11).

Whatever the crisis the psalmist faced, it seemed to be predominant. Yet his faith looked to the Lord. He found that the Lord was greater than the crisis.

A. An exhibition of God's power (vv. 8–9). Here the psalmist calls attention to God's power over the enemies. He shatters bows, breaks spears, and burns chariots with fire. The scene is one of God's supremacy over the nations.

B. An exhortation to contemplation (v. 10). The psalmist called on his readers to stop and think. To seriously contemplate life will result in the realization of God.

C. An expression of personal confidence (v. 11). The psalmist expressed his confidence in the Lord. God will be with us in troubled times. He will be our refuge.

Conclusion

The times in which we live are tumultuous. The tensions of life are increasing. Amid these troubled times, we need to place our trust in the Lord. Accept the Lord as your refuge for troubled days.

SUNDAY MORNING, NOVEMBER 20

Title: A Psalm of Thanksgiving

Text: "I love the Lord, because he hath heard my voice and my supplications. Because he hath inclined his ear unto me, therefore will I call upon him as long as I live" **(Ps. 116:1–2)**.

Scripture Reading: Psalm 116

Hymns: "O Worship the King," Grant

"Count Your Blessings," Oatman

"A Mighty Fortress Is Our God," Luther

Offertory Prayer: Our Father, we are grateful this Thanksgiving for the blessings of salvation in Christ Jesus and for the blessings of family, material resources, and Christian friends. Help us to show our gratitude by sharing with others. In Jesus' name. Amen.

Introduction

One of the greatest Christian virtues is "thanksgiving," our grateful expression of thanks to God as we acknowledge him as the source of all blessings—blessings bestowed in grace (James 1:17).

Today we will consider a psalm (Ps. 116) that praises God for the personal triumphs he has brought to pass. The author of this psalm had suffered a severe illness and had been in the very jaws of death. We are told that he prayed with faith, even against all odds. This psalm is a glorious shout of thanksgiving because of deliverance from the illness that was already ushering him into the realm of the dead. He declared that because of God's grace he would keep on praising God. His love for God and his gratitude to him prompted him to do something for the one he loved.

I. The psalmist testified to what the Lord had done for him (Ps. 116:1–8).

A. "He hath inclined his ear unto me" (v. 2). How comforting it is to know that the Lord is interested in us as individuals. He is an intensely personal God.

I love to read Psalm 23 and meditate on the personal pronouns. "The Lord is my shepherd; I shall not want." Read the entire psalm with the personal pronouns in mind. We are not alone. Who can read Matthew 6:25–34 without a feeling of grateful security?

Listen to the comforting testimony of Jesus in John 14:16–18: "And I will pray the Father, and he shall give you another Comforter, that he may abide with you for ever; even the Spirit of truth; whom the world cannot receive, because it seeth him not, neither knoweth him: but ye know him; for he dwelleth with you, and shall be in you. I will not leave you comfortless: I will come to you."

B. "He hath heard my voice and my supplications" (vv. 1, 3, 4). The Hebrew verb translated "heard" in verse 1 indicates more than simply "to hear." It indicates that God heard and answered. God is always ready to provide.

The words of Jesus in Luke 11:9–11 are reassuring: "Ask, and it shall be given you; seek, and ye shall find; knock, and it shall be opened unto you. For every one that asketh receiveth; and he that seeketh findeth; and to him that knocketh it shall be opened. If a son shall ask bread of any of you that is a father, will he give him a stone? or if he ask a fish, will he for a fish give him a serpent?"

C. He offered his grace (v. 5). He indicated that the Lord is gracious, righteous, and merciful.

How grateful we should be this Thanksgiving season for the grace of God. Read with me Ephesians 2:8–10.

One Sunday when I visited a little northern Oklahoma Sunday school, the lesson was on grace. The teacher asked, "What is grace?" One man answered, "Grace is the unmerited favor of God bestowed on us unworthy sinners." Someone else added another thought. Then the teacher looked at a heavy-set old man dressed in overalls. He asked, "Bill, what do you say grace is?" Bill thought a moment and scratched his thinning gray hair. Finally, he said, "Well, I ain't for sure, but I think it means that God provides all the stuff."

D. He delivered him (vv. 6–8). Listen as I read verses 6–8. What a tremendous tribute to the grace and mercy of God! "For thou hast delivered my soul from death, mine eyes from tears, and my feet from falling" (v. 8).

The psalmist had a terrible plight. He was helpless—and God delivered him. In this light, how meaningful are the words in Isaiah 40:28–31:

> Hast thou not known? hast thou not heard, that the everlasting God, the Lord, the Creator of the ends of the earth, fainteth not, neither is weary? there is no searching of his understanding. He giveth power to the faint; and to them that have no might he increaseth strength. Even the youths shall faint and be weary, and the young men shall utterly fall: But they that wait upon the Lord shall renew their strength; they shall mount up with wings as eagles; they shall run, and not be weary; and they shall walk, and not faint.

II. The psalmist's response to God's goodness (Ps. 116:12–19).

A. "I will take the cup of salvation" (v. 13). "Salvation" here includes more than being saved in an initial experience. It includes salvation in the fullest extent with all its attendant blessings. Today think of the blessings of your salvation and thank God for them.

B. "I will ... call upon the name of the Lord" (v. 13). Here is a resolution to pray—to commune with God. The psalmist recognized prayer as a valuable ally.

C. "I will walk before the Lord" (v. 9). The psalmist testifies that he always will be conscious that God is looking upon his life, knowing every thought, word, and deed.

Listen as I read Psalm 139:1–5: "O Lord, thou hast searched me, and known me. Thou knowest my downsitting and mine uprising, thou understandest my thought afar off. Thou compassest my path and my lying down, and art acquainted with all my ways. For there is not a word in my tongue, but, lo, O Lord, thou knowest it altogether. Thou hast beset me behind and before, and laid thine hand upon me." In light of these facts, the psalmist wanted his life to be pleasing to the Lord.

D. "I will pay my vows" (vv. 14, 18). In his illness, the psalmist had made a vow to God. He promised to publicly praise God and give him the glory for his life. We must remember that a promise to God is sacred.

E. I will praise the Lord (v. 19). The psalmist not only indicated his own praise to the Lord but encouraged others to praise him.

Conclusion

This Thanksgiving season let us remember to "praise the Lord for his goodness, and for his wonderful works to the children of men" (Ps. 107:15).

SUNDAY EVENING, NOVEMBER 20

Title: What Can You Do If Life Caves In?

Text: "Out of the depths I cry to thee, O Lord" **(Ps. 130:1 RSV).**

Scripture Reading: Psalm 130

Introduction

In Psalm 130 the psalmist speaks from his heart in the midst of a time of difficulty and agony. All of us will sooner or later face the painful problem of suffering. What will you do if life seems to cave in on you? Have you developed a technique for dealing with failure, disappointment, defeat, disgrace, and trouble?

Suffering may come as a result of a combination of many different factors.

1. Some suffering comes as a result of the rule of law. The law of cause and effect always works.
2. Suffering may come as a result of the privilege of freedom we enjoy. We are free to do right as well as wrong. Others also have this freedom, and their misuse of it may harm us.
3. Some suffering comes as a result of joy of relationships that are precious. These relationships carry within them the potential for suffering and heartache.
4. Much suffering is due to the evil designs of Satan who seeks to destroy.
5. Some suffering is permitted by our loving God because of what we can learn through experiencing pain.

Other factors may also contribute to suffering. It is interesting to note what the psalmist did with the problem of suffering.

I. The psalmist gave himself to earnest prayer (Ps. 130:1–2).

A. By prayer we establish communion with God.

B. By prayer we offer petitions to God.

C. By prayer we intercede on behalf of others.

D. By prayer we listen to the voice of God as he speaks to us.

When suffering comes, there is no better thing for us to do than to give ourselves to prayer and especially to the type of prayer in which we let God speak to us.

Bible study can be thought of as the listening side of the prayer experience. Each of us would be wise to open up God's Word and give him the opportunity to speak his message to our hearts when we are in agony and when suffering threatens to destroy us.

II. The psalmist confessed his sin and trusted God for forgiveness (Ps. 130:3–4).

"What have I done to deserve this?" is usually the first question that comes to mind when we find ourselves in the midst of great suffering. This is a good question to ask, because much of our suffering is due either to our own ignorance or to our own error, or perhaps even to a deliberate choice we have made.

While all sin will result in suffering of one sort or another, not all suffering is due to some sin that has been committed by the person who is suffering.

A. Some deal with sin merely by ignoring it. They act as if there is no sin or error in their lives.

B. Some deal with sin by trying to cover it up.

C. Some deal with sin by means of rationalization, and they seek to blame their faults and mistakes on others.

D. The proper approach to the problem of sin is to confess our sin and forsake the love of sin, trusting God for forgiveness and cleansing (1 John 1:9). To confess sin means to sit in judgment on it and to view it from God's perspective. It means to be in complete agreement with God concerning the evil destructiveness of sin. The psalmist rejoiced in the fact that his God was the God who forgave sin. When God forgives, God forgets. He refuses to remember our transgressions against us. We need to accept God's forgiveness. We need to accept his love, mercy, and grace.

III. The psalmist encouraged himself in God's Word (Ps. 130:5–6).

There is no substitute for the devotional study of God's Word in which we let God speak to the needs of our hearts and lives. We should read God's Word not as a record of what happened in the ancient past, but we should read it as a revelation of what God wants to do for his people in the present.

A. We are to bring our burdens to the Lord and trust him to sustain us (Ps. 55:22). This is not merely a pious platitude. It should be looked upon as a precious promise of our Lord to bless us in our times of great need.

B. We should trust Christ for the strength that will enable us to adjust to all circumstances (Phil. 4:13). Paul is not making any boast concerning some stupendous achievement. Instead, he is registering his faith that through Jesus Christ he can adjust himself triumphantly to any circumstance in which he might find himself.

C. We should trust God to be with us as a helper in every trial and trouble of life (1 Cor. 10:13). Nothing can touch the life of one of God's children without his permission. God will not permit anything to come upon us that we cannot endure with the help he makes available.

To live a triumphant and grateful life in the midst of trouble, we must encourage ourselves in God's Word and let him guide and strengthen us.

IV. The psalmist commended the way of faith to others (Ps. 130:7–8).

By faith the psalmist believed that God works in all things for the good of those who love him, because the love of the Lord is a steadfast enduring love. The psalmist voiced his faith and kept silent concerning his fears. Instead of doubting his faith, he doubted his doubts and trusted in the trustworthiness of God.

Conclusion

What are you going to do when trouble comes? Let us hope and pray that it never comes, but in the meantime, let us develop a deeper faith in God's goodness. Let us discover the great promises of his Word. Let us listen to the voice of those who have been through trouble that we might be strengthened by their testimony. Let us beware lest difficulty discourage us and cause us to live a life of despair. Our God is as close to us when we are in the depths as he is when we are on the heights.

WEDNESDAY EVENING, NOVEMBER 23

Title: A Plea for Pardon

Text: "Create in me a clean heart, O God; and renew a right spirit within me" **(Ps. 51:10)**.

Scripture Reading: Psalm 51:1–17

Introduction

Psalm 51 represents a painful experience of David. After David committed adultery with Bathsheba and arranged for her husband's death, the prophet Nathan visited David and told him a simple story about two men in one city. One was poor, and the other was rich. The poor man treasured one small ewe lamb. When a traveler came to the city, the rich man took the poor man's lamb to feed the traveler, refusing to take one from his own flock. David was stirred by the story and wanted revenge. Courageously, Nathan said to David, "Thou art the man" (2 Sam. 12:7).

David penned Psalm 51 with the deep consciousness of sin. He threw himself on God's mercy, pleading for his pardon. The psalm opens for us the possibilities of sin consciousness and the pathway to repentance.

I. The cry (Ps. 51:1–2).

A. The God to whom David cries. He knew the traits of God's character: "lovingkindness" and "tender mercies" (v. 1). Though in destitution, sinners need to be aware of what kind of God they face. The second word for mercy ("tender mercies") comes from the Hebrew word meaning "womb." It suggests that God's mercy is comparable to a mother's love.

B. The sin to which he refers. David described his sin with three different words. "Transgression" means a willful revolt. "Iniquity" describes a twisting of God's ideal. "Sin" means to fall short of God's ideal. The predicament of sinners is seen from these three angles.

C. The forgiveness he desires. Three expressions describe David's great desire for forgiveness—"blot out," "wash me," and "cleanse me." The psalmist cried out to God, for he knew that only God could deal with his sin problem.

II. The confession (Ps. 51:3–5).

A. The painful knowledge of sin (v. 3). David was painfully aware of his sin. No one had to prove that he was a sinner. The fact of his sin haunted him, and he wanted to confess to the Lord.

B. The personal responsibility for sin (v. 4). David continually reiterated that the sin was "his." He did not blame the culture of the times, the attractiveness of Bathsheba, or even God. David assumed personal responsibility for sin.

C. The perpetuation of sin (vv. 5–6). Sin begets sin. In David's own experience, he confessed that one sin led to another. Man acts from an evil nature. David confessed that sin led nowhere except to more sin.

III. The cleansing (Ps. 51:6–12).

A. Cleansing involves deliverance from sin. David found deliverance from his sin problem. He was purged and washed. He wanted God to hide his face from his sins. He wanted his iniquities blotted out.

B. The creation of a new heart. Cleansing involved a totally new creation. The word create (v. 10) is used in Scripture only to describe the work of God. Only God can give genuine cleansing for sin.

C. The restoration to joy. One of the greatest benefits was the return of joy: "Make me to hear joy and gladness" (v. 8). God's Spirit is the source of a right and willing spirit.

IV. The commitment (Ps. 51:13–17).

A. The sharing of good news (v. 13). Being forgiven, David would now share his experience. Having received cleansing from God, he would help others to receive it.

B. The prayer for protection (vv. 14–15). David prayed that he would have no recurrence of the old self that would restrain his zeal to testify.

C. The offering of self (vv. 16–17). David felt that all of the sacrifices were not adequate to express the psalmist's thanksgiving and praise. The only sacrifice acceptable to God was a broken and contrite heart.

Conclusion

David pleaded for pardon from a merciful God, and he experienced God's forgiveness. All around us people are searching for a pardon. We need to share with them the message of Psalm 51 that everyone can receive God's pardon.

SUNDAY MORNING, NOVEMBER 27

Title: Christ Our Example—In Stewardship

Text: "For ye know the grace of our Lord Jesus Christ, that, though he was rich, yet for your sakes he became poor, that ye through his poverty might be rich" **(2 Cor. 8:9).**

Scripture Reading: 2 Corinthians 8:1–15

Hymns: "Something for Thee," Phelps

"All Things Are Thine," Whittier

"We Give Thee but Thine Own," How

Offertory Prayer: Thank you, dear Lord, for the example Jesus gave us as he came "to seek and to save that which was lost." May we follow in his steps as we seek to do your will in advancing your kingdom. We bring these gifts today out of hearts of love and gratitude. In Jesus' name. Amen.

Introduction

Jesus Christ is our example. Peter wrote, "Christ also suffered for us, leaving us an example, that ye should follow his steps" (1 Peter 2:21). In the Sermon on the Mount (Matt. 5–7), Jesus set the pattern for believers to follow. Christ Jesus is also our example in stewardship.

In 2 Corinthians 8:1–15 the apostle Paul set forth the stewardship of Jesus and indicated that the Christians at Corinth should emulate it. Paul had begun to take up a collection from Gentile churches for their poor fellow Christians in Jerusalem. The Macedonian churches gave liberally. The Corinthians were enthusiastic in pledging to give liberally but did not follow through by actually giving, so Paul wrote to them about their failure to act on their pledge.

I. Paul reminded the Corinthians of the stewardship of Christ (2 Cor. 8:9–10).

A. He told them of the riches of Christ before he came to earth. The life of Jesus Christ did not begin in the manger. Paul said, "He was ... he became." Only once did Jesus ever use the word *born* with reference to himself, and that was to Pilate, who would not have understood nor cared. But to Pilate he went on to explain, "For this cause came I into the world" (John 18:37; cf. John 14:28). Jesus came from the Father. He went back to the Father. He was rich. John said that all things are Christ's and that he made all things (John 1:3, 10). He enjoyed all power in heaven, and every knee bowed before him in adoration and with perfect obedience to his every command.

B. Paul told them that Jesus Christ became poor by coming to earth. "He became poor." He left his home in glory. There he was rich; here he had no place to lay his head (Luke 9:58). There angelic hosts bowed down before him; here he was rejected by humans (John 1:11; cf. Isa. 53:3, 7–8). There he had no physical limitations; here he became man (Heb. 4:15).

Jesus was rich in that he possessed divine fullness and independence; he became poor in that he took on himself human infirmity, dependence, and emptiness. As a prisoner, he was stripped of the little he possessed. His dying bed was a cross. His last resting place was a borrowed tomb. Jesus placed his life at the disposal of his Father. The whole drama of his coming was a story of pure stewardship.

C. Paul told them why he made this sacrifice (v. 9). The terms grace and love explain why Jesus "became poor"—he did it for "your sakes."

Jesus loves me, therefore he gave himself for me. How clearly Paul explained it in 2 Corinthians 5:21: "God made him who had no sin to be sin for us, so that in him we might become the righteousness of God" (NIV). The reason he saved us was not because we deserved it. "Herein is love, not that we loved God, but that he loved us, and sent his Son to be the propitiation for our sins" (1 John 4:10). Paul stated the same truth in a little different way in Romans 5:6–10. Jesus loved enough to be a perfect steward of his life. He pleased the Father perfectly with his life. His stewardship not only included the giving of himself so that we might be saved; it also included the perfect submission of his life to the will of his Father. Jesus plainly told his disciples, "My meat is to do the will of him that sent me, and to finish his work" (John 4:34). Here then is the example of the stewardship of Jesus Christ.

II. Paul gave the Corinthians an analysis of their stewardship.

Paul let them know that their stewardship was far below par. He told them that they were growing rich in everything else—in faith, expression, knowledge, and perfect enthusiasm. Then he admonished them to grow rich in gracious contribution. They had expressed much enthusiasm about giving generously to the poor saints at Jerusalem when Titus had talked to them about it some time before this. But they had never put their good feelings into action. They were sort of like the people James wrote about in James 2:15–16: "If a brother or sister be naked, and destitute of daily food, and one of you say unto them, Depart in peace, be ye warmed and filled; notwithstanding ye give them not those things which are needful to the body; what doth it profit?" The hungry in Jerusalem could not be fed with the enthusiasm and good intentions of the Corinthians. In like manner, the lost in the various parts of the world cannot hear the gospel as long as churches resolve to support mission programs but do not put money into missions. God holds us responsible as individuals for our stewardship; he also holds churches responsible for stewardship.

Paul urged them to compare their stewardship with the stewardship of Jesus Christ. The world is lost in sin and needs the Savior. The fields are already white unto harvest. We must not only put our money—our tithes and offerings—into the Lord's work; we also must give ourselves that the Lord might use us as preachers, teachers, missionaries, and educational workers on foreign fields. Take heed to the words of Jesus in Matthew 9:36–38.

Paul told them that what they did about this special offering would test the genuineness of their love.

III. Paul used the churches of Macedonia as an example of some churches who followed the pattern of Jesus Christ in stewardship.

A. These churches gave under very unfavorable circumstances. They were poor people (2 Cor. 8:2), yet they gave liberally. Many people say they cannot afford to tithe or even support the church with any finances. Some churches say they cannot afford to give much to missions. They say they are too poor. Anyone can tithe if he or she really wants to. Any church, no matter the size, can give generously from its budget to missions. The churches in Macedonia were poor, but they were giving far more than the church of Corinth.

B. They gave voluntarily. Christian liberality is accepted and rewarded according to willingness. Real Christian giving does not need to be commanded. We ought to tithe and give love offerings because we love the Lord and his work. The Macedonians actually begged for the privilege of helping. They wanted to have a share in this important work. They gave joyfully and were willing to share what they had with those who had need. They were like the Israelites in building the tabernacle (Ex. 35:4–10, 20–24; 36:3–7).

C. They first gave themselves to the Lord. It was easy for the Macedonians to surrender a part when they had already surrendered the whole. When our lives are brought into the will of God, he has all of us, and we will give whatever is necessary to carry on the kingdom work. This is true of individual Christians and of churches also. We are to follow the example of Jesus Christ in this matter of stewardship.

Conclusion

Jesus gave his best, his all. As his disciple, he expects you to do your best. He expects our church to do its best.

SUNDAY EVENING, NOVEMBER 27

Title: God in Us: As Counselor and Comforter

Text: "I will not leave you desolate; I will come to you" **(John 14:18 RSV)**.

Scripture Reading: John 14:16–19, 25, 26

Introduction

Running throughout the Old Testament is a thread of messianic prophecy that foretells the coming of the Savior. As we approach the Christmas season, we will be reading again and again the prophecies concerning the coming of the Christ child. With the shepherds, we should listen to the angels announce his birth. With the wise men, we should seek him and bow down before him, worshiping him as King of Kings and Lord of Lords. With the apostles, we should recognize him as the Son of God in human flesh.

In order for the miracle that was manifest at Bethlehem to have its full significance, we need to recognize and respond to the great truth that the gift of God that came at Bethlehem has been made permanent through the gift of God that came on the day of Pentecost.

The Old Testament not only promises the coming of the Messiah who was to be the Savior, but it also promises the gift of the Holy Spirit to the people of God (Ezek. 36:26–27; Joel 2:28, 32).

Shortly before our Lord ascended, he promised to his disciples the fulfillment of the Father's promise in the bestowal of the gift of the Spirit (Acts 1:4).

I. "He will give you another Counselor."

Each word in this phrase of promise from the lips of the Savior is significant. He is talking to his disciples concerning a gift of the Father God to his children. This gift is said to be "another Counselor." The word translated "Counselor" is *paraclete.* This word is in reality untranslatable in its full significance. It is a noun that is the result of combining a preposition and a verb. The preposition means "by the side of," and the verb means "to call." The *paraclete* is "one called to the side of." It is translated in some places "comforter" because the Holy Spirit does provide both comfort and strength for facing life. In other places, it is translated "counselor" because the Holy Spirit does serve as an adviser, a teacher, a confidant.

The word translated "another" is a significant word. In the language of the New Testament, two words are translated correctly with the English word "another." One of these words means "another of the same kind." It is significant that the word that appears in verse 16 means "another counselor of exactly the same kind." Jesus is promising to his disciples that the Holy Spirit will be to them exactly what he has been to them.

II. "To be with you forever."

Our Lord knew that his ministry was to be brief. The most accurate estimates would indicate that it was three and a half years at the most. We can easily understand why his disciples were distressed by news of his death and departure. Our Lord comforts them and seeks to motivate them to a great faith with this precious promise that the Comforter who will come from the Father will be with them forever.

III. "Whom the world cannot receive."

The word translated "receive" has a secondary meaning of "to seize, to arrest." Our Lord foresaw his arrest by the Jewish authorities and his death on the cross. He declared to his disciples that neither the ecclesiastical authorities nor the legal authorities would be able to arrest the Holy Spirit, because he is a spirit. He is invisible and intangible, yet he is real. The Counselor who is to come is not limited to a tangible, visible body.

IV. "He dwells with you."

The prophet had declared that the Christ child would bear the name Immanuel, which being interpreted is "God with us" (cf. Isa. 7:14; Matt. 1:22–23).

Our Lord was informing and challenging his disciples with the precious truth that in the Holy Spirit God was going to continue to be with his servants, even as Christ had been with his disciples during his public ministry.

V. "He will be in you."

We will miss the full significance of Christmas if we think of the birth of Christ as something that happened in the distant past without any present significance as far as the living presence of God is concerned. As Christ was born of the Virgin Mary and laid in a manger, so through faith in Christ we are born into the family of God. The divine Spirit of God comes to dwell within each of us, and we become a dwelling place for God the Spirit (1 Cor. 3:16; Gal. 4:6–7).

VI. "I will come to you" (John 14:18).

Jesus' promise here should not be interpreted as a prophecy concerning his victorious return to the earth at the end of the age. Instead, it is a promise that he was to fulfill on the day of Pentecost when in the Spirit he would return to dwell in the heart of each disciple and to take up his habitation in the church, which was to be his body in the world.

Conclusion

The Christ of Christmas has come to live in the heart of each born-again disciple. With the apostle Paul, we can declare, "Christ lives in me" (Gal. 2:20 NIV). The Christ of Bethlehem becomes Christ our contemporary because of what happened at Pentecost. Let us highly revere the Christ who came at Bethlehem. Let us respond to this same Christ who came in Spirit on the day of Pentecost and who came to dwell within us when we trusted him as our Savior.

WEDNESDAY EVENING, NOVEMBER 30

Title: The Benefits of Genuine Worship

Text: "My flesh and my heart faileth: but God is the strength of my heart, and my portion for ever" **(Ps. 73:26)**.

Scripture Reading: Psalm 73

Introduction

One day I decided to walk to the church building rather than drive my car. After I had walked about half the distance, a violent electrical storm erupted. Being afraid of lightning, I ran quickly to the nearest door of the church building. It happened to lead into the sanctuary. I sat in the sanctuary and listened to the rain and thunder. A wonderful truth came to me: the sanctuary offered a refuge from the storm.

The psalmist was caught in a storm. He was filled with doubt and uncertainty as he looked at life. He observed that the wicked prospered and the righteous suffered austerities.

In Psalm 73:3–14 the psalmist made several observations concerning the wicked. They were exempt from physical malady (v. 4), were exempt from trouble (v. 5), were proud (vv. 6–9), were recognized and honored (v. 10), were full of contempt for God (v. 11), and were materially prosperous (v. 12).

In the midst of his perplexities, the psalmist went to God's sanctuary where he found relief. People will find a difference when they worship God. Let us notice from the psalmist's experience how worship can change our lives.

I. Worship changes our minds.

A. The dismal perspective of the psalmist.
   1. Dismay over prosperity of the wicked (vv. 3–14).
   2. Disturbed over God allowing the wicked to prosper and the righteous to suffer (v. 12).

B. Worship brought new insights.
   1. The insecurity of the wicked (v. 18).
   2. The destruction of the wicked (v. 18).
   3. The futility of the wicked—like a dreamer (vv. 19–20).

C. Worship brings a new perspective.
   1. To the God above us.
   2. To life about us.

II. Worship strengthens the inner person.

A. The emotional disturbances of the psalmist (v. 2).
   1. Doubt (v. 2).
   2. Anxiety (v. 14).
   3. Depression (v. 16).

B. Lack of worship disturbs people.
   1. People continue to be bitter (v. 21).
   2. People fail to be informed (v. 22).

C. Worship strengthens the inner person (vv. 23–27).
   1. Look to God for stability rather than materialism.
   2. Rely on God's help rather than on the world's resources.
   3. Realize the permanence of God and the brevity of the world.

III. Worship gives people a task.

A. The experience in the sanctuary brought the psalmist near the Lord.
   1. The psalmist rejoiced over the presence of God (v. 28).
   2. The psalmist committed his life to the Lord (v. 28).

B. The experiences in the sanctuary were to be shared (v. 28).
   1. The psalmist shared what God had done for him.
   2. The psalmist shared some insights that the world does not possess.
   3. The psalmist urged people to observe that God is working in the world.

C. Genuine worship leads to a task.
   1. People go to worship God and experience his presence.
   2. People go from worship to share the lessons learned in worship.

Conclusion

People are tormented in these turbulent days. They will continue in doubt, uncertainty, despair, and frustration until they go to the sanctuary of God. A new way of life awaits people when they go to worship God. It changes their thoughts, feelings, and service.

SUGGESTED PREACHING PROGRAM FOR THE MONTH OF

DECEMBER

■ Sunday Mornings

When eyes and hearts are focused on the holiday season ahead, it seems wise to direct attention to "The Good News of Christmas." Announce the good news of what the birth of Jesus Christ really means.

■ Sunday Evenings

Continue the series "God with Us at Bethlehem and God in Us at Pentecost."

On Christmas, look toward the new year with the theme "Prayers for the Coming Year."

■ Wednesday Evenings

Complete the series "Out of Human Experiences."

SUNDAY MORNING, DECEMBER 4

Title: Personalities of Bethlehem—Joseph

Text: "And they went with haste, and found Mary and Joseph, and the babe lying in the manger" **(Luke 2:16 RSV)**.

Scripture Reading: Matthew 1:18–21

Hymns: "Thou Didst Leave Thy Throne," Elliott

"As with Gladness, Men of Old," Dix

"Good Christian Men, Rejoice," Neale

Offertory Prayer: Our gracious Father, we enter with eager expectancy the season of the year when the blessedness of giving is most significant. This is because we celebrate your greatest gift, your Son, who was born in Bethlehem so long ago. In response to that gift of love, we bring our gifts asking your blessings on each gift and each giver. In Jesus' name. Amen.

Introduction

When we think of the Christmas story, it is easy to get sidetracked. Artists have featured the shepherds and their sheep, the wise men and their gifts, the angel choir, and even the animals in the stable. However, there are three principal figures in the Christmas scene, and we will study them as we approach Christmas day. They are Joseph and Mary and the babe of Bethlehem, Jesus.

The forgotten participant in the drama of Christmas is Joseph. He played the role of father in Jesus' life. God gave him an important assignment as husband, father, teacher, provider, and protector. He was present at Jesus' birth. We are assured that he was admired and loved by this ideal Son.

We have very little biographical information in the Bible about Joseph. He never wrote a book. He traveled only a few miles from his birthplace all of his life. He was out of his little country only once, and that was to take his child to Egypt to preserve his life. He was not well educated, and he made his living at carpentry. Not a word he spoke is recorded in the Scriptures. He drops out of the picture when Jesus is twelve years of age, and we never see him again. In all likelihood, he died while Jesus was young, and this eldest Son succeeded him in the carpenter shop.

Joseph was not the father of Jesus in a physical sense, since Jesus was conceived by the Holy Spirit and born of Mary while she was still a virgin. But God chose Joseph to play the role of father in the young life of his Son.

I. Joseph was a man of great openness.

Joseph's faith was incredibly tested by the events preceding Jesus' birth. He was engaged to a young woman named Mary, and he learned before their marriage that she was carrying a child. Joseph was a man of integrity, and the news of Mary's pregnancy was a staggering blow to him. His integrity is revealed in his obedience to God's will upon being told by an angel of Mary's virgin conception.

II. Joseph was willing to believe the best.

Joseph believed in Mary's love, and he returned that love. He believed in her integrity, and he put his reputation and honor on the line as he came to her side. He believed in her purity, and he took her as his wife. He believed in Jesus' destiny and became a father to him.

Too often we are ready to believe the worst about a person. Even if the worst is true, we may not know the contributing circumstances. God is the Judge who knows all. When we set ourselves up as judges, we usurp the place of God.

Because of Joseph's exemplary ministry of fatherhood to Jesus, Jesus had a proper concept of fatherhood. Jesus' most precious revelation of God is as our Father. His master story, the parable of the prodigal son, is really the parable of the loving father.

Conclusion

Dr. John Claypool told of a young man named Mike who was taking drama lessons. The climax of the year was a play in which all the pupils participated. Mike was visibly disappointed when he was assigned a "bit part." He had only three lines, and they were close to the end of the play. His father told how he and his wife sweated through two hours until the time came for Mike's part. Summing up the lad's performance, the father said, "He said his lines—not too soon, not too late, not too loud, not too soft, not too fast, not too slow—he said his lines just right."

The father left the play thinking, This is a parable of my life. I am just a bit player in the great drama of history. But when the curtain comes down and the stage is vacant at last, I hope it can be said of me, "He said his lines—not too soon, not too late, not too loud, not too soft, not too fast, not too slow—he said his lines just right."

This can be said of Joseph, "He said his lines just right." Can it be said of you and me?

SUNDAY EVENING, DECEMBER 4

Title: The Wonder of the Gift of the Spirit

Text: "This Jesus God raised up, and of that we all are witnesses. Being therefore exalted at the right hand of God, and having received from the Father the promise of the Holy Spirit, he has poured out this which you see and hear" **(Acts 2:32–33)**.

Scripture Reading: John 16:7, 12–14

Introduction

Our text declares that the Holy Spirit is the gift of the Father to his Son and that in turn the Holy Spirit is the gift of the risen Christ to his disciples.

In order for us to properly appreciate the gift of the Spirit to the church on the day of Pentecost and the gift of the Spirit to each disciple in the moment of conversion, we need to have a better understanding of the work of the Holy Spirit in the Old Testament and in the life and ministry of our precious Lord.

I. Some illustrations of the activity of the Holy Spirit in the Old Testament.

A. Joseph was equipped by the Holy Spirit to be the prime minister of Egypt (Gen. 41:16, 33, 37–41).

B. God gave the Spirit to the seventy elders who were to assist Moses as judges (Num. 11:16, 17, 25).

C. The Spirit equipped Joshua to be the successor of Moses (Num. 27:18–19).

D. The judges were empowered to deliver Israel from their enemies by the power of the Holy Spirit.

1. The Spirit came upon Othniel (Judg. 3:10).
2. The Spirit came upon Gideon (Judg. 6:34).
3. The Spirit came upon Jephthah (Judg. 11:29).

E. The Holy Spirit came upon the kings of Israel.

1. The Spirit came upon Saul (1 Sam. 11:6) and later departed (1 Sam. 16:14).
2. The Spirit came upon David (1 Sam. 16:13), and David later feared the loss of the Holy Spirit (Ps. 51:10–12).

F. The Holy Spirit moved among the prophets and inspired them to be God's spokesmen.

II. The Holy Spirit and Our Lord.

A. The Holy Spirit effected the miraculous conception of our Messiah (Matt. 1:18, 20).

B. The Holy Spirit made it possible for Simeon to recognize the Messiah as an infant (Luke 2:25–27).

C. The Holy Spirit descended as a dove at the baptism of Jesus, and Jesus was thus identified as the Promised One (Luke 3:22).

D. Christ was led by the Spirit into the wilderness to be tempted by Satan (Luke 4:1).

E. After his victory over Satan's temptations, Christ returned in the power of the Spirit to begin his ministry (Luke 4:14).

F. The Holy Spirit equipped Christ for his redemptive ministry (Luke 4:18).

G. Christ performed his miracles in the power of the Spirit (Matt. 12:28).

Conclusion

When we look at the role of the Holy Spirit in the life of Old Testament spiritual leaders, we cannot help but be impressed. To recognize the role the Holy Spirit played in the life of our Lord is to be overwhelmed with the significance of the promise of our Lord to send this gift of the Spirit on his disciples (Luke 24:49; Acts 1:8).

Let us beware in this Christmas season lest we worship a Christ child of long ago and miss the tremendous significance of the indwelling Christ who comes to us as the Holy Spirit in the moment of conversion to do God's work in our lives that we might be a blessing to others. We need to recognize and respond to his presence in us moment by moment.

WEDNESDAY EVENING, DECEMBER 7

Title: The Gratitude of the Redeemed

Text: "O give thanks unto the Lord, for he is good; for his mercy endureth forever" **(Ps. 107:1)**.

Scripture Reading: Psalm 107:4–32

Introduction

God continuously rescued Israel from their numerous bondages. He freed them from Egyptian slavery and led them to the land of Canaan. Later he liberated them from the captivity of the Babylonians.

The psalmist found God to be the Redeemer, the Rescuer, and the Savior. Ultimately, God came to rescue the entire human race in Jesus Christ. Perhaps the title most used for Jesus is "Savior." The ministry of Jesus was a rescue operation to people held in the tenacious bondage of sin.

Psalm 107 is a call to gratitude for the salvation of the Lord. The writer had experienced redemption, and he wanted to express gratitude. He used four vivid pictures to tell about humankind's bondage and God's redemption.

I. Lost pilgrims (Ps. 107:4–9).

A. The terror of being lost. "They wandered ... they found no city ... their soul fainted." The picture graphically portrays that the travelers were lost in the pitiless desert sun. They could not find their way.

Many people in our world are lost like desert travelers. They vainly search for the true life.

B. The help for the lost. Travelers realized that they could not find their way, and they appealed to the Lord. "They cried unto the Lord." When the petition for direction came, God helped. "He delivered them.... He led them forth.... He satisfieth ... and filleth the hungry."

II. Separated prisoners (Ps. 107:10–16).

A. The experiences of the prisoners. The prisoners experienced "darkness ... shadow of death ... being bound." The people were portrayed as victims of their own moral folly. They did evil until the evil had them bound.

B. The release for the captives. The prisoners called on the Lord for help. "They cried unto the Lord." God delivered the prisoners. "He brought them out of darkness and the shadow of death, and brake their bands in sunder" (v. 14).

III. Afflicted people (Ps. 107:17–22).

A. The painful experiences of the afflicted. The Jews believed that sickness came on people as a result of their sin. Here those who were afflicted because of their sin are referred to as fools. They could not eat food, and they were close to death (v. 18).

B. The healing of the afflicted. Healing for the people enslaved by illness comes from God. "They cry unto the Lord." God healed them. "He saveth them.... He healed them, and delivered them."

IV. Sailors in a storm (Ps. 107:23–32).

A. The distress of the storm. The psalmist vividly sketched the stormy seas. The sailors were at their wits' end.

B. The deliverance from the storm. The only alternative was to turn to the Lord. "Then they cry unto the Lord." God brought marvelous deliverance: "He bringeth them out of their distresses.... He maketh the storm a calm.... He bringeth them unto their desired haven."

Conclusion

Four vivid pictures depict humankind's bondage and God's deliverance. These pictures are true to life's experiences. People are lost and cannot find the Lord's way in life. They are imprisoned by evil. They are sick with tormented guilt feelings. They are caught in the storms of life. People, like the sailors, are at their wits' end.

In all four situations, the people turned to the Lord. They found deliverance from their bondage. You can discover that God will rescue you from a desperate predicament.

SUNDAY MORNING, DECEMBER 11

Title: Personalities of Bethlehem—Mary

Text: "And behold, you will conceive ... and bear a son, and you shall call his name Jesus" **(Luke 1:31 RSV)**.

Scripture Reading: Luke 1:26–31

Hymns: "Hail, Thou Long-Expected Jesus," Wesley

"Gentle Mary Laid Her Child," Cook

"There's a Song in the Air," Holland

Offertory Prayer: Our heavenly Father, we thank you not only for the supreme gift of your Son, but also for the gift of love and obedience that characterized those who were most intimately associated with our Lord in days of his flesh. We thank you that we may bring our gifts of love and obedience, and our lives behind our gifts, to you today. Use our gifts to proclaim the glorious story of Christmas to all the world. In the name of the Lord Jesus we pray. Amen.

Introduction

It seems of tragic significance that the human mother of the Prince of Peace should herself have been the object of conflict and contention through the centuries. To some, she is an object of worship. To many, she is the one to whom they pray. There are others who swing to the opposite extreme and virtually ignore her. Although we do not worship Mary, we revere her memory and honor her as the human mother of our Lord.

I. The Mary of the Bible.

The accounts of Matthew and Luke reveal to us that Mary was a modest and pure young peasant woman in Galilee. She was engaged to a solid, moral, mature man named Joseph. She was deeply in love and looked forward to marriage and the fulfillment of her love.

Then came Mary's mysterious encounter with the angel Gabriel. The announcement he brought her was staggering. First of all, he proclaimed, "The favor of God rests upon you." We would think that this would mean that her pathway would be smooth. But the favor of God does not promise us an easy way. A simple maid in a small village was to give birth to a child who had no human father. To the neighbors, the child would be a baby who "came too soon."

How was Mary to reveal this staggering revelation to Joseph? Worse than wagging tongues and bitter gossip and slander was the probability that she would lose the man she loved. But God also revealed to Joseph his divine plan, and Mary and Joseph were married.

Mary had other problems too. She gave birth to her firstborn child in Bethlehem, seventy miles from home. None of her family was with her. No skilled and experienced women were present to supervise the birth of the baby. Only Joseph and the animals were around her.

The baby was born in a cattle stall and not in a clean room in the inn. While her Son was still a baby, Mary had to flee with him to Egypt to escape a cruel tyrant, Herod. When Jesus was a man, he left the carpenter shop at Nazareth and embarked on a ministry that seemed senseless.

Mary witnessed the wise men worshiping her Son, but she lived to see the religious leaders of her nation plotting his death. Truly, the sword was to pierce her heart.

II. Mary as symbolic of pure and chaste womanhood.

This noble woman Mary became a symbol of everything we see in Christian womanhood and motherhood. She was obedient to God's revelation and submissive to his plan. "Let it be according to thy word," she said. She laid everything she had on the altar, including her honor, her reputation, her love, and her home. Women of today would do well to imitate her.

III. Mary in history.

By millions of Roman Catholics today, Mary is looked upon as the mother of God and the queen of heaven. This doctrine was eighteen hundred years in the making. It began when theologians debated over the deity and humanity of Jesus. The doctrine was based on the premise that if Jesus had a human parent, he could not be sinless. So the miracle of the immaculate conception of Mary was conceived. This doctrine declared that Mary was conceived without sin and lived a sinless life. Since celibacy was considered as preferable over marriage, the church proclaimed the perpetual virginity of Mary. The other children in her home were not really hers. In recent years, the Roman Catholic Church created an equally amazing dogma, the assumption of Mary. Devout Catholics must now believe that Mary was taken bodily into heaven after her death.

Through this process, this simple and modest mother has been distorted and twisted into a strange and paradoxical figure. She is prayed to and worshiped. Hymns and feast days honor her memory and assume her spiritual presence. She seems to be a fourth person of the Trinity.

The last we see of Mary in Scripture is in a prayer meeting. "All these with one accord devoted themselves to prayer, together with the women and Mary the mother of Jesus, and with his brothers" (Acts 1:14 RSV). Here we find her not being worshiped but worshiping. We see her not being prayed to but praying like others. She had been favored of God and had done her work for him faithfully. Now she dropped back into the midst of the fellowship of God's people.

Conclusion

There is but one Mediator between God and man—Jesus Christ. We do not have to go through Jesus' mother to get the attention or the response of her Son. The intercession of Mary is unnecessary, superfluous, and impossible. Let us, like Mary, join in prayer in Jesus' name to a heavenly Father who hears and responds and keeps his promises.

SUNDAY EVENING, DECEMBER 11

Title: God in Us—Mystery and Miracle

Text: "And because you are sons, God has sent the Spirit of his Son into our hearts, crying, 'Abba! Father!' " **(Gal. 4:6 RSV)**.

Scripture Reading: Romans 8:9–17

Introduction

Mystery and miracle surround the great truths concerning the Trinity. We will never be able to fully comprehend how the one God can be Father, Son, and Holy Spirit at the same time.

It is our Christian faith that the eternal God became flesh in Jesus Christ and dwelt here on earth among men as Immanuel—God with us. And as the Old Testament prophets foretold, the Holy Spirit would come to dwell in the people of God subsequent to the coming of the Christ.

Mystery and miracle surround the birth of Christ, the life of Christ, the death of Christ, the resurrection of Christ, the ascension of Christ, and the glorious return of Christ.

Mystery and miracle surround the gift of the Holy Spirit to the church on the day of Pentecost and to individual Christians in the moment of their conversion.

To properly appreciate this mystery and miracle, let us be better informed about the personality and purpose of the divine Spirit who came to dwell within us at our conversion.

I. The Holy Spirit possesses intelligence.

A. He is said to know the things of God (1 Cor. 2:10–11).

B. He is described as having a will. He distributes his gifts to every person as he wills (1 Cor. 12:11).

C. He is described as having emotions. He loves and grieves (Eph. 4:30; 2 Tim. 1:7).

D. He has an appreciation for that which is moral. He reproves sin (John 16:9), and he guides into truth (John 16:13).

E. The personal masculine pronoun is always used in the original language in describing the Holy Spirit (cf. John 14:16–17).

II. Functions that can be performed only by a person are attributed to the Holy Spirit.

A. He hears, speaks, and guides (John 16:13).

B. He teaches and stirs up the memory (John 14:26).

C. He comforts God's people (Acts 9:31).

D. He calls to missionary service and gives guidance to God's people (Acts 13:2; 16:6–7).

E. He witnesses to us and prays for us (Rom. 8:16, 26).

III. The works of Deity are ascribed to the Holy Spirit who has come to dwell within us.

A. The work of creation was his (Gen. 1:2).
B. The work of inspiring Scripture was his (2 Peter 1:21).
C. The work of convicting the sinner of sin is his (John 16:8–9).
D. The work of regeneration is his (John 3:5; Titus 3:5).
E. The work of effecting the resurrection of the saints is his (Rom. 8:11).
F. The work of bringing about miracles is his (Matt. 12:28).

Conclusion

Christmas is the time when we focus on God's great gift of his Son for us. Is it possible that in concentrating our thoughts on the gift of the Son that we have missed the gift of his Spirit as a permanent dweller in the heart of each of his children? We have the privilege of hearing and listening to the Spirit (Heb. 3:7), of walking in the Spirit (Gal. 5:16), of being led by the Spirit (Gal. 5:18), and of being filled with the Spirit (Eph. 5:18), and we can also have the privilege of experiencing the fruit of the Spirit from day to day (Gal. 5:22–23). May the Lord help us to appreciate this great gift he has given to us in the Holy Spirit.

WEDNESDAY EVENING, DECEMBER 14

Title: The Folly of Omitting God

Text: "Except the LORD build the house, they labour in vain that build it . . ." **(Ps. 127:1)**.

Scripture Reading: Psalm 127

Introduction

A person is a fool to plan and to live life without including God. Jesus told a parable of a prosperous farmer who kept building bigger barns. There was only one blight on this farmer—he omitted God. For this folly, God labeled him a fool.

Psalm 127 deals with the folly of human experience that does not rely on the wisdom and goodness of God. The author presents four aspects that will end in failure if God is not considered.

I. God must be included in social life (Ps. 127:1).

A. Houses are vital parts of the social unit. The psalmist referred to people who considered social plans with a secular concept. People can construct an ideal social structure on paper and in their minds.
B. Houses must be built with God in mind. Building without God is folly. In Genesis people sought to build a tower without God, and it led ultimately to confusion. Jesus told about a person who built his house on the sand with disastrous results.

C. Social life in today's world must be structured with God in mind. Social problems abound because people have built selfishly rather than with God's help.

II. God must be included in the life of the city (Ps. 127:1).

A. Cities are strategic centers of life. The psalmist referred to people who lived in the city without God.
B. God secures life in the city. The safety of cities is not in the gates, nor in the council, nor in law enforcement. God brings safety to a city.
C. City life must be permeated with people who know the Lord. Cities that have become jungles of violence can become havens of peace.

III. God must be included in business (Ps. 127:2).

A. Work comprises a large portion of life. The psalmist referred to people who labored without reliance on God. The greatest labor according to God's Word is that which depends on God.
B. God must not be omitted from business. Though people work tirelessly from dawn until late at night, their labors will be fruitless unless they depend on God. Fretful anxiety results when people do not trust the Lord.
C. Business will be blessed when God is considered. If businesses depend on God and his principles, business will be great.

IV. God must be preeminent in domestic life (Ps. 127:3–5).

A. Families are symbols of God's blessing. The Old Testament regarded parents as experiencing God's special favor. Home is a strategic center of life.
B. God must not be left out of the family. Tragically, God is being left out of families. Marriages are being dissolved, and children lack serious responsibility and respect.
C. Godly families build a great nation. America can become stronger with God preeminent in domestic life.

Conclusion

Is there something missing in your life? You could be leaving God out of your social, civic, business, or domestic life. If so, your life will be lived in vain. Put God in the center of life, and allow him to permeate every aspect of your life.

SUNDAY MORNING, DECEMBER 18

Title: Personalities of Bethlehem—The Baby Jesus

Text: "For unto us a child is born" **(Isa. 9:6)**.

Scripture Reading: Luke 2:1–7

Hymns: "O Little Town of Bethlehem," Brooks
"Hark! The Herald Angel Sing," Wesley
"Silent Night, Holy Night," Mohr

Offertory Prayer: Our blessed Father, just as the wise men knelt before Jesus and worshiped him, so we worship him today. And just as they brought gifts and laid them at his feet as an act of worship, so do we worship him with our gifts and offerings. Make our gifts acceptable and pleasing to him. In Jesus' name. Amen.

Introduction

A little boy saved one piece of candy that had been given to him at a church Christmas party. When asked by his mother why he was saving it, he replied, "I'm saving it for the baby Jesus when he grows up." To many people, Jesus is still the innocent baby in the manger scene.

But Jesus advanced in wisdom and in stature and in favor with God and man. He grew into adulthood and became our Lord and Savior. He was God in human flesh who became man and dwelt among humanity. He still dwells in human flesh, our hearts, as we open our lives in faith and let him in.

Because Jesus was a baby that first Christmas, this season has a special significance for children. The eager anticipation, the thrilling excitement, the gracious generosity, and the genial goodwill of children somehow rubs off on us at Christmas. Something of the charm of our childhood returns each Christmas, and we are reminded of how much we have lost through our growth into adulthood.

Jesus said to adults, "Except ye become as little children ye shall not enter the kingdom of heaven." We have reversed his words and have said to our children, "Except ye become as adults ye shall not enter the kingdom." God help us to recover some of the childlike traits we have lost.

I. The sense of humility.

We have traded our childlike humility for crusty pride. To be humble means to be teachable. Children are easily taught. As we grow older, we grow more set in our opinions and are less open to truth. We become satisfied with our present knowledge and ignore new learning that is so easily available. Our Lord has much to teach us if only we will consent.

II. The sense of innocence.

We have exchanged the virtue of innocence for the depressing presence of guilt. We have been shut out of the Eden of our childhood as we have allowed our lives to be corrupted.

III. A sense of trust.

We have swapped trust for suspicion of the motives of our neighbors. We have lost our sense of wonder and have embraced in its place a cold sophistication. It is natural for children to trust others. They haven't been hurt many times, and they have quickly recovered from such hurt. Children have no cynicism, and there are no atheists in nursery schools.

IV. A sense of the present.

Children do not live in the past, for they have little past. They are not anxious about the future. "Now" is God's day and now is the possession of children. They recognize that this is the best hour of their lives.

Dr. Charles L. Allen, former minister of the First Methodist Church in Houston, told the story of a group of men out in the woods of northwest Canada who had labored several months away from civilization. When their wives joined them, they organized a celebration and brought in a band. Among the women who came was one who brought her baby. When the band started playing, the baby was frightened and started crying. A rough old woodsman jumped up and shouted, "Stop the band so we can hear the baby cry."

Science has made us richer, but it has not made us happier. Our homes and factories are stocked with labor-saving devices, but we are more exhausted than our grandparents who did everything by hand. We have more leisure time but are wearier than ever through boredom and emptiness. We have more to live with and less to live for.

We have nearly conquered outer space, but we have not conquered poverty and hunger. We have more knowledge today than ever before, yet we have less faith. We have exploded our superstitions, but we have undermined our reverence. We have gratified our curiosity and dulled our sense of wonder. We have built splendid cities and allowed the heart of those cities to rot in miserable slums. We have perfected our means of communication and have almost nothing to say.

It seems as if God is mocking us. Have we grown too big, too smart, too self-righteous, and too self-sufficient? As we have grown older, we have grown more cunning, more covetous, more grasping, and more cautious.

Conclusion

As we gather with our loved ones at this blessed season, let us pray for a childlike spirit. Let us pray for the excitement and glow of the spirit of our childhood to return to us. Let us shed our cynicism, our prejudices, and our fears. Let us believe the best about each other. After all, for the Christian, Christmas celebrates the conviction that God himself became a child that first Christmas.

SUNDAY EVENING, DECEMBER 18

Title: God with Us—We Can Face the Future with Courage

Text: "It is not you who speak, but the Spirit of your Father speaking through you" **(Matt. 10:20 RSV)**.

Scripture Reading: Matthew 10:16–23

Introduction

The servants of our Lord have not always had it easy. Nowhere did Jesus promise his disciples immunity from hardship, difficulty, disappointments, or death. He sent his disciples out in a difficult and dangerous world made up of imperfect people. He warned his disciples that they would face indescribable hardships and difficulties and persecutions, even to the point of being put to death. He encouraged them with the assurance that God would bestow the gift of his Spirit on them, and that by means of the presence and the power of the Spirit they would be equipped to give a worthy testimony of God's saving power.

Let us remind ourselves of our spiritual resources in the Holy Spirit, who came to the church on the day of Pentecost and to each individual believer in the moment of conversion.

I. Christ promised the Holy Spirit as a permanent Helper to his disciples (John 14:16–18).

Our Lord promised that in contrast to his brief ministry of three and a half years, the Holy Spirit would come to dwell with his followers forever. We can face the coming year and all of our coming years in the assurance that we have a divine Helper who has come to live within us.

II. Christ promised the Holy Spirit as an authoritative Teacher (John 14:26).

Our Lord was referred to time and time again as Teacher. The so-called Sermon on the Mount is in reality a "lecture of the Teacher" on the mount. Jesus came to teach us about God, about life, and about eternity.

Our Lord used simple methods to communicate the great truths of God because he found his disciples to be slow learners. There were many things he wanted to teach them, but they were sometimes slow to comprehend the truth (John 16:12–13).

A. The Holy Spirit will teach us all of the things that we need to know about God. The Holy Spirit uses the Scriptures as the primary medium for communicating the great truths of God to us. The Holy Spirit also uses the experiences of life and the needs of people.

B. The Holy Spirit is said to be a great reminder (John 14:26). Researchers tell us that we do not fully forget anything, that everything is stored in the computer of the human mind waiting to be triggered into recall by some incident. The Holy Spirit can recall to our memory any truth that we have learned about God or any Scripture passage that we have memorized. By so doing, he teaches us and often uses us as teachers about God.

III. Christ promises the Holy Spirit as a witness (John 16:14).

The Holy Spirit was given in order that he might glorify Jesus Christ. To glorify means to introduce or to make known. The Holy Spirit is seeking to bear testimony to each believer concerning who Jesus Christ is and what he wants to accomplish through us.

The Holy Spirit was promised that he might come and cause each believer to become a witness concerning the saving power and grace of the Lord Jesus Christ (Acts 1:8). It is interesting to note that Joel prophesied that when the Holy

Spirit came, people from all strata of society would be equipped to prophesy concerning Jesus Christ (Acts 2:17–18). To interpret prophecy here as prediction is to miss the point. To prophesy means primarily "to speak for God." The Holy Spirit came on the day of Pentecost so that all kinds of people might be able to speak for God concerning the wonderful things God does.

As we face the future, the Holy Spirit has come to dwell within us to equip us and to empower us that we might give our personal testimony concerning what Jesus Christ means to us. This testimony can be used by the Holy Spirit to impart the gift of faith to those who do not yet know Jesus Christ as Lord and Savior.

Conclusion

In this season of the year when we have been reminded of God's great gift in his Son, let us become aware also of his great gift to us in the Holy Spirit who has come to dwell within us. We must recognize and respond to the Holy Spirit who dwells within (1 Cor. 3:16). We must have faith in and trust implicitly in the Holy Spirit (John 14:26; Acts 1:8). And we must be obedient to the Holy Spirit's leadership (Acts 5:32). With joy let us determine to cooperate with the Holy Spirit as he does the work of God in and through us as we face the future with courage and cheer (Phil. 2:12–13).

WEDNESDAY EVENING, DECEMBER 21

Title: The Greatness of God

Text: "I will praise thee; for I am fearfully and wonderfully made: marvellous are thy works . . ." **(Ps. 139:14).**

Scripture Reading: Psalm 139

Introduction

Few things impress our generation. Several years ago we were amazed over jet travel, but now we treat it as an everyday affair. Sending a spaceship around the globe once caused perpetual conversation. Now rockets carrying supplies for the international space station are launched regularly and receive relatively little media coverage. With so many new things being thrown to our generation, we shall soon be labeled as "the age of the unimpressed."

The psalmist was deeply impressed with the glory and grandeur of God. Our age needs to discover the qualities of God the psalmist learned. It will cause us to exclaim, "My God, how great thou art!"

I. The knowledge of God (Ps. 139:1–6).

A. God has a perfect knowledge about our lives. He knows our strengths and weaknesses. He knows as no one else knows (v. 1).

B. Specific instances are cited of God's knowledge (vv. 2–3). God knows our daily schedule of life (v. 2), our thoughts before we think them (v. 2), our good and bad points (v. 3), and our words (v. 4).

C. The psalmist experienced reverential awe of God's knowledge (vv. 4–5). God's infinite knowledge was beyond his human comprehension.

II. The presence of God (Ps. 139:7–12).

A. The psalmist desired to escape from the presence of the God who knew all about him (v. 7).
B. The psalmist thought of several means of escape: heaven, depths of the earth, across the world, and even darkness (vv. 7–12).
C. The psalmist was impressed with God's presence (vv. 7–12). First, God was everywhere he went—"thou art there." Second, God's presence offered leadership—"thy right hand shall hold me." Third, God's presence would enlighten him.

III. The power of God (Ps. 139:13–18).

A. The psalmist praised God for the formation of life (vv. 13, 15, 16). The psalmist was amazed that God shaped him in his mother's womb. The power of God was demonstrative from the time the psalmist was an embryonic speck until the time God knitted together his bodily frame.
B. The psalmist praised God for the design of the human body (v. 14). The psalmist looked at the human body and marveled over God's power. To study the human body with its masterful design is to marvel over God's power.
C. The psalmist could not comprehend God's great power (vv. 16–18). God's power is beyond human calculation.

IV. The sovereignty of God (Ps. 139:19–24).

A. The psalmist realized that God was more powerful than his enemies (vv. 19–22).
B. The psalmist asked God to test the sincerity of his life (vv. 23–24). God's sovereignty is demonstrated by the fact that he searches, knows, and tests our ways and thoughts.

Conclusion

Has God become common talk to you? If he has, you need to know of his greatness. He is above and beyond our comprehension. Yet God has made himself known. Let us be thrilled over the grandeur of God's greatness.

SUNDAY MORNING, DECEMBER 25

Title: The Miracle of Christmas

Text: "For he grew up before him like a young plant, and like a root out of dry ground" (**Isa. 53:2 RSV**).

Scripture Reading: Luke 2:8–16

Hymns: "I Heard the Bells on Christmas Day," Longfellow
"Let All Mortal Flesh Keep Silence," Moultrie
"What a Wonderful Saviour!" Hoffman

Offertory Prayer: We are aware, heavenly Father, that Christmas is a time when we bring gifts to our loved ones and friends. But we remember that it is the birthday of your Son that we celebrate. Help us, then, to bring our most precious gifts to him, remembering that his greatest gift to us was his life, offered for an atonement for our sins. In Jesus' name. Amen.

Introduction

As one travels in the northwest part of the United States, he or she may come to a road sign that reads "Continental Divide." At this point, the watershed of the North American continent is found. A drop of water falling on the eastern side begins to journey toward the Atlantic Ocean or the Gulf of Mexico. A drop of rain on the western side flows to the Pacific Ocean.

The birth of Jesus Christ is the watershed of human history. It divides the events of the past and the future. It was the great and pivotal event of history.

When Jesus began his public ministry, word drifted back to his hometown about his teachings and miracles. Had there been a newspaper in Nazareth, it might have run the headline "Local Boy Makes Good." He was growing in fame and renown.

But when Jesus preached in Nazareth, his townspeople rejected both him and his claims. They could not accept as Messiah one whom they had known as a carpenter. They could not follow one as King whom they had viewed as fellow citizen. Jesus said, "A prophet is not without honor, except in his own country" (Mark 6:4 RSV). Mark records the reaction of Jesus' hometown in the words, "Many who heard him were astonished, saying, 'Where did this man get all this? What is the wisdom given to him? What mighty works are wrought by his hands!'" (v. 2 RSV). Bewildered, they asked, "Is not this the carpenter, the son of Mary and brother of James and Joses and Judah and Simon, and are not his sisters here with us?" (v. 3 RSV). In other words, they sought to account for him in human relationships and human terms.

Our text for this Christmas Sunday says, "For he grew up before him ... like a root out of dry ground." Dry ground suggests hard, arid soil, a most unlikely place for a plant to grow and flourish. It suggests (1) Unexpectedness. Jesus came, not full grown as expected, but as a tiny baby. He was born not in a palace or a mansion, but in a manger. (2) Miraculousness. He was born of a virgin mother. He was conceived by the Holy Spirit. (3) Unaccountableness. A gardener prepares the soil for planting and then keeps the ground moist and soft. If a plant grows out of dry ground or in the crevice of a mountain, it is shriveled and stunted. Jesus grew as a root out of dry ground, but he was no frail weakling. He was the Fairest of Ten Thousand. He was the Cedar of Lebanon in strength. He was the Lily of the Valley in purity and fragrance. He was the Rose of Sharon in glory and beauty. He was the best, the noblest, the highest, and the holiest of humankind. Look at the soil from which Jesus grew. You could no more account for him from that soil than you could account for the vigorous growth of a flower in a parking lot.

I. Nothing in his family could account for Jesus.

Heredity is a real factor in our lives. We sometimes make too much of it, but it is a part of our makeup. We not only inherit physical and facial characteristics, but also mental gifts and personal charm. A study of Christ's ancestry does nothing to explain him. He was a descendant of King David, but so were multitudes of others. God saw that he grew up in a good family, but no other child in the family compared with him.

II. Nothing in his environment could account for Jesus.

Next to heredity, our environment contributes most to what we are. The atmosphere in which we live and the company we keep have an influence on us. Jesus grew up in an ordinary village. His trade was that of a peasant carpenter. There was nothing in his upbringing that would explain him. So far as his environment was concerned, he was a root out of dry ground.

III. Nothing in the time in which he lived could account for Jesus.

There have been many times in history when several geniuses in literature or music or government lived at the same time. But never was there a genius like Jesus. The time in which Jesus lived was a barren time. For four hundred years there had been no prophetic voice. Formal religion was filled with legalism and hypocrisy. As far as fresh religious thought and revelation were concerned, he was a root out of dry ground.

IV. Nothing in his race or nationality could account for Jesus.

He was a Jew. The Jews had a genius for religion. They excelled in law, wisdom, poetry, and prophecy. They produced men like Abraham, Moses, David, Solomon, Elijah, Isaiah, Jeremiah, and Paul. But there was not another like Jesus. As far as his nation was concerned, he was a root out of dry ground.

However, there was nothing exclusively Jewish about Jesus. It is true that he loved his country, Jerusalem, and the temple, but there was nothing sectional or parochial about him. He belonged to the human race. The human race has produced many great people, but in wisdom and truth and holiness Jesus excelled them all. Others guessed at truth. He was the Truth. He was the greatest Teacher who ever lived. For two thousand years, he has inspired millions to live and even die for him.

We look at the human race—stained, defiant, and corrupt. Then we look at Jesus—sinless, obedient, and pure. We ask if so fresh and sweet a stream could flow from such a bitter fountain. If the human race could produce one Jesus, why could it not produce more? Human nature cannot explain Jesus. He was a root out of dry ground.

The Christmas story is the most logical account for Jesus. "For you know the grace of our Lord Jesus Christ, that though he was rich, yet for your sake he became poor, so that by his poverty you might become rich" (2 Cor. 8:9 RSV). His was not a mere human birth. The Word became flesh in a miraculous incarnation. Jesus was not simply the son of Mary. He was the Son of God.

Conclusion

It was a glorious day when God created man. It was an even greater day when God became man. It was a wonderful day when God made man in his image. It was an even more wonderful day when God made himself in man's image. This is the miracle of Christmas! Let us tell it to the world!

SUNDAY EVENING, DECEMBER 25

Title: Prayers for the Coming Year

Text: "Pray without ceasing" **(1 Thess. 5:17)**.

Scripture Reading: Matthew 6:5–13

Introduction

In our text, the apostle Paul encourages the believers in Thessalonica to develop the habit of praying and then not to break that habit.

As we approach the beginning of a new year, we can most appropriately and profitably spend some time in earnest prayer. It is suggested that we let some saints who were poets lead us in this time of prayer. Many of the hymns and songs in our hymnal take the form of earnest, fervent prayers. Let us join together on this last Sunday evening in the year in singing some prayers to our Lord.

I. Let our lives sing a prayer of adoration and consecration.

Fanny J. Crosby would lead us in praying:

I am Thine, O Lord, I have heard Thy voice,
And it told Thy love to me;
But I long to rise in the arms of faith,
And be closer drawn to Thee.

Consecrate me now to Thy service, Lord,
By the pow'r of grace divine;
Let my soul look up with a steadfast hope,
And my will be lost in Thine.

Refrain:
Draw me nearer, nearer, blessed Lord,
To the cross where Thou hast died;
Draw me nearer, nearer, nearer, blessed Lord,
To Thy precious, bleeding side.

II. Let our lives sing a prayer regarding Bible study for the coming year.

All of us need to spend some time with God's Word each day to grow spiritually (Josh. 1:8). Mary A. Lathbury voices for us a prayer that is appropriate when we open up God's Word and read.

Break Thou the bread of life, Dear Lord, to me,
As Thou didst break the loaves beside the sea;
Beyond the sacred page I seek Thee, Lord;
My spirit pants for Thee, O Living Word.

Bless Thou the truth, dear Lord, to me to me,
As Thou didst bless the bread by Galilee;
Then shall all bondage cease, all fetters fall;
And I shall find my peace, my All in all.

O send Thy Spirit, Lord, now unto me,
That He may touch my eyes, and make me see;
Show me the truth concealed within Thy Word,
And in Thy book revealed I see the Lord.

III. Let our lives sing a prayer for spiritual illumination.

Only God can open our eyes and help us see spiritual reality. Clara H. Scott wrote a prayer to God for us at this point.

Open my eyes, that I may see,
Glimpses of truth Thou hast for me;
Place in my hands the wonderful key
That shall unclasp, and set me free.

Open my ears, that I may hear
Voices of truth Thou sendest clear;
And while the wave-notes fall on my ear,
Ev'ry-thing false will disappear.

Refrain:
Silently now I wait for Thee,
Ready, my God, Thy will to see;
Open my eyes, illumine me, Spirit divine!

IV. Let our lives sing a prayer to the Master Teacher regarding prayer.

Our Lord's disciples requested not that he teach them how to preach or to teach but how to pray. He is the perfect Model and Master Teacher at this point. Albert Reitz voices our prayer for help.

Teach me to pray, Lord, teach me to pray;
This is my heart cry day unto day;
I long to know Thy will and Thy way;
Teach me to pray, Lord, teach me to pray.

Power in prayer, Lord, power in prayer!
Here 'mid earth's sin and sorrow and care,
Men lost and dying, souls in despair;
O give me power, power in prayer!

My weakened will, Lord, Thou canst renew;
My sinful nature Thou canst subdue;
Fill me just now with power anew;
Power to pray and power to do!

Refrain:
Living in Thee, Lord, and Thou in me;
Constant abiding, this is my plea;
Grant me Thy power, boundless and free:
Power with men and power with Thee.

V. Let our lives sing a prayer of commitment to personal witnessing.

Leon Tucker prayed the first stanza of the prayer that we will pray, asking our Lord to lay on us a new and deeper concern for the souls of the lost about us. With all sincerity let us join in this prayer.

Lord, lay some soul upon my heart,
And love that soul through me;
And may I bravely do my part
To win that soul for Thee.

Lord, lead me to some soul in sin,
And grant that I may be
Endued with power and love to win
That soul, dear Lord, for Thee.

To win that soul for Thee alone
Will be my constant prayer;
That when I've reached the great white throne
I'll meet that dear one there.

Some soul for Thee, some soul for Thee,
This is my earnest plea;
Help me each day, on life's highway,
To win some soul for Thee.

VI. Let our lives sing a prayer of personal commitment to our Savior as we face the coming year.

Take my life, and let it be
Consecrated, Lord, to Thee.
Take my moments and my days—
Let them flow in ceaseless praise;
Let them flow in ceaseless praise.

Take my hands, and let them move
At the impulse of Thy love.
Take my feet and let them be
Swift and beautiful for Thee,
Swift and beautiful for Thee

Take my voice, and let me sing
Always, only, for my King.
Take my lips and let them be
Filled with messages from Thee,
Filled with messages from Thee.

Take my silver and my gold—
Not a mite would I withhold.
Take my intellect and use
Every pow'r as Thou shalt choose,
Ev'ry pow'r as Thou shalt choose.

Take my will and make it Thine—
It shall be no longer mine.
Take my heart—it is Thine own;
It shall be Thy royal throne;
It shall be Thy royal throne.

—*Frances R. Havergal*

VII. Let our lives sing a song of faith for the new year.

Ours is not a dead Christ. He is alive from the dead to be our Leader and our King as we face the coming year. Let us rejoice as we respond to his living presence. Ernest W. Shurtleff wrote a prayer of triumphant faith.

Lead on, O King Eternal,
The day of march has come;
Henceforth in fields of conquest
Thy tents shall be our home:
Through days of preparation
Thy grace has made us strong.
And now, O King Eternal,
We lift our battle song.

Lead on, O King Eternal,
Till sin's fierce war shall cease,
And holiness shall whisper
The sweet amen of peace.
For not with swords' loud clashing
Nor roll of stirring drums;
With deeds of love and mercy,
The heav'nly kingdom comes.

Lead on, O King Eternal,
We follow, not with fears;
For gladness breaks like morning
Where-e'er Thy face appears.
Thy cross is lifted o'er us;
We journey in its light.
The crown awaits the conquest;
Lead on, O God of might.

Conclusion

When we pray, we let God come into our lives to help us. We also dedicate ourselves to helping him with his work in the world. Let us rejoice because of the year that is ahead of us.

WEDNESDAY EVENING, DECEMBER 28

Title: Praise the Lord!

Text: "Let everything that hath breath praise the LORD. Praise ye the LORD" **(Ps. 150:6)**.

Scripture Reading: Psalm 150

Introduction

The book of Psalms ends with a universal call to praise. Psalm 150 calls our world to praise the Lord. The intensity of praise increases with each additional musical instrument. The final verse makes a thrilling crescendo of instruments and voices praising the Lord.

Varied cries issue from the human heart in today's world. Doubts, fears, and frustrations comprise a large part of our feelings. Perhaps this psalm could teach us a new attitude—to praise the Lord. "Praise ye the Lord!"

I. The place of praise (Ps. 150:1).

A. The prepared place of worship—"Praise God in his sanctuary." God has instructed people to carefully prepare places of worship throughout history—tabernacle, temple, synagogue, church. The Lord instructs us in corporate praise. Nothing can replace assembling together in the fellowship of the risen Lord.

B. The praise from all creatures—"Praise him in the firmament of his power." God should be praised everywhere, not just on earth. Everything that breathes should praise God. Hymn writers include the concept that every creature should praise the Lord.

All creatures of our God and King,
Lift up your voice and with us sing
Alleluia! Alleluia!

—*St. Francis of Assisi*

"Firmament" means sphere. The entire creation becomes a sanctuary for the praise of God.

II. The reasons to praise (Ps. 150:2).

A. Praise for God's power. "Praise him for his mighty acts." God's ordering and controlling of the gigantic forces of nature demonstrate his power. We praise God when we behold his mighty power.

B. Praise for God's character. "Praise him according to his excellent greatness." This statement directs us to God's character. Recognizing how much God loves humanity and how much he has done for us, we should offer praise to the Lord.

III. The techniques of praise (Ps. 150:3–5).

A. The praise in all of life. In verses 3–5 the psalmist mentions numerous musical instruments: trumpet, psaltery, harp, timbrel, stringed instruments, organ, and cymbals. Most of these instruments were used in Jewish worship, but some were not. This suggests that all musical instruments, secular or sacred, should praise the Lord.

B. The praise in human souls. Praise resides within a person's soul. The greatest musical expression is worthless unless it comes from a heart of love (cf. 1 Cor. 13:1–3).

IV. The subjects of praise (Ps. 150:6).

A. The universality of praise. "Let every thing that hath breath praise the Lord." Nothing is excluded. All living things should offer praise to God. The psalmist considered all of creation as subjects for praising God.

B. The invitation to praise. "Praise ye the Lord." This concluding command invites people to praise the Lord.

Conclusion

Let us join together daily in praising the Lord. Life's greatest privilege occurs when people who are unworthy of praising God accept the invitation to "Praise ye the Lord!"

MISCELLANEOUS HELPS

MESSAGES ON THE LORD'S SUPPER

Title: An Example of Humility

Text: "A new commandment I give unto you, That ye love one another; as I have loved you, that ye also love one another" **(John 13:34).**

Scripture Reading: John 13:1–17

Introduction

One of the most moving accounts of our Lord's ministry is recorded in John 13, where he gives us a lesson in humility. We can grasp in small measure the depth of divine condescension when we see how the Son of God stooped low to wash his disciples' feet. In this priceless example of meekness and lowliness of heart, our Lord set forever the standard by which Christians can fashion their ideas of love and devotion.

On this occasion, Jesus brought faith down into the realm of the practical. So much religion is merely lip service and spends itself in mumbling meaningless holy words. Faith loses its reality when our thoughts are not followed by action. The upper room experience had a tremendous effect on the lives of the disciples. Their souls had been enriched, and they had been drawn closer to God.

I. Teacher and Lord.

Throughout the world, Jesus is recognized as the Great Teacher because he went beyond words and provided a living example of love by freely giving up his life that all who believe in him may have eternal life. We cannot compare Christian faith with other religions, because they cannot be compared. Christianity goes beyond the bounds of philosophy, which may be an end in itself with certain intellectual declarations as the goal, to claim the allegiance of people to Jesus Christ. He is Lord of all, and even those who refuse to bow their knees to him in this life will bow to him in the day of judgment (Phil. 2:9–11).

The apostle Peter's impulsive refusal to let the Master wash his feet is deeply indicative of rebellious human nature's refusal to surrender to divine command. While Jesus comes as the Great Teacher, he also claims to be the Lord of life. If people refuse his humble manifestations of love, they will have no true intimacy of fellowship with him. As Teacher, Jesus points to the way everlasting. As Lord and Master, he does for us what we cannot do for ourselves.

II. The call of service.

Jesus often impressed his disciples with words of instruction. Greatness could be found in no other way but in serving God and others. We lay up treasures in heaven as we lay out our lives in humble service. As Jesus performed the lowly act of foot washing, he climaxed all his teaching by a simple gesture of service.

In the first century, washing the feet of others was a common practice. In our day, the wearing of shoes has changed that custom. Yet there are other ways by which we can perform loving service to others. By faithful ministry at the bedside of one who is ill, by relieving suffering in poverty-stricken homes, and by supporting agencies of charity and institutions of mercy, we are practicing the principle laid down by Jesus. An upper room experience will always cause us to see the needs of the world through the eyes of Christ.

III. The motive of love.

Human love is a great thing, but divine love is greater. The disciples had known obedience to law. Now Jesus gave them a new commandment that could become objective in its expression. The true motive for all constructive Christian activity is not in answer to the call of duty, but to the call of love. This call of love has sent people to the far reaches of the earth to minister in Christ's name. Greater than the power that blasts mountains into dust, the power of Christian love can uproot selfishness, covetousness, envy, licentiousness, and greed in individuals; self is crucified, and serving Christ becomes one's passion in life. When hope grows faint and faith droops her wings, love toils on. His banner over us is love, and by this shall all people know that we are true disciples of the Master.

Conclusion

What a joy to have listened to the message of our Lord in the Upper Room today. Our spirits have been still as new resolutions of faith and service have come to challenge us to higher levels of living. Our eyes have been opened to multiplied opportunities of ministering to the needs of others. Again, we have come to acknowledge the motivating power of all service as the spirit of love impresses itself quietly in its invitation to send us out in the name of our Lord to minister to others. May all of us determine to dedicate our hearts and lives anew in the service of our gracious Lord.

Title: The Worth of Christian Character

Text: "Finally, brethren, whatsoever things are true, whatsoever things are honest, whatsoever things are just, whatsoever things are pure, whatsoever things are lovely, whatsoever things are of good report; if there be any virtue, and if there be any praise, think on these things" **(Phil. 4:8)**.

Scripture Reading: Philippians 4

Introduction

We have no choice in the matter of building character. It is a process that is taking place in our daily lives whether we think about it or not. The process does not blow a whistle or sound a cymbal, but it proceeds in a uniquely quiet way to leave its impression on our lives.

We may refuse to behold a beautiful sunset, or we may close our ears to the beautiful symphonies of Beethoven, but we cannot escape the silent influence that builds character in human lives. The law that governs the building of character is more powerful than the law of gravity or the law of motion. The law that builds character holds the destiny of people within its grasp.

I. Example of one man.

The apostle Paul believed in making his religion a reality. He did not believe that the spirit and the conduct of people could be separated. Therefore he devoted his life to making Christ real to believers. It was his greatest joy to enter the many spheres of their lives in times of happiness and in times of sorrow. He presented to them a pattern of humility.

Many times Paul's life was filled with tears of compassion and sorrow over others. He had become a part of every person he ministered to, and they in turn had contributed to the growth of his life.

In every area of life, Jesus invites us to put into practice those principles that will strengthen our daily activity. Verbal preaching is good, but it is made more impressive when it issues in the conduct of daily life.

II. Importance of teaching.

Character radiates from every person's life, and it has its origin in truth. The fruit that our lives bear, whether good or bad, can be distinguished by those who know us. The teaching that we receive has a strong bearing on our character; people will know whom we have been following by the fruit they see. If we put our confidence in the teaching of Christ, all who see us will know we are his disciples.

So, we, like Christ, have the ability to influence the character of others. Our ability to influence others depends largely on whether they can see the love of Christ in us. Nothing draws out the best in people like loving them and showing trust in them. The future is bright with promise for those who place themselves in an environment where truth has as its supreme objective the building of noble character.

III. Christian character.

Christian character does not become the possession of an individual all at once; it must grow. The moment people determine to become followers of Christ, they become a battleground on which the Holy Spirit contends with the flesh for the supremacy of the soul. Thus, all true development in Christian character comes when people follow God's will for their lives. Sin can no longer dominate, because their hearts and affections are set on things above. Their spirit and soul seek to conform to the high purposes of God.

Conclusion

These gracious moments have given us a time of sincere reflection on what God expects of those who determine to follow Christ Jesus. Peace of heart and mind are assured when obedience to God's will becomes a major concern in Christian discipleship. Obedience has ever been the key to successful spiritual experience.

Let us make this one of life's supreme moments. The day that is now passing has in it eternal issues. Once more we are in the valley of decision. Once more the glorious possibilities of the Christian life lie before us. Once more the call to definite consecration is heard. What will your response be? "Choose for yourselves this day whom you will serve" (Josh. 24:15 NIV).

Title: Beliefs That Make a Difference

Text: "If ye know these things, happy are ye if ye do them" **(John 13:17)**.

Scripture Reading: John 20:30–31; 1 Timothy 4:13–16; 1 John 5:1–15

Introduction

Our beliefs make a tremendous difference in how we conduct ourselves on a daily basis. We do things because we believe certain things. For example, advertisers continually pour out information that encourages people to believe certain things about their products. If boys repeatedly hear an ad that tells them they need a certain brand of basketball shoes to run faster and jump higher, they may begin to believe it and urge their parents to buy them a pair. Action grows out of belief just as truly as belief grows out of action. Just so, it is the business of the Scriptures to urge people to believe on Jesus Christ as Savior and Lord.

I. The writer's record.

Many of the works of Jesus were not written in one small treatise. "But these are written that ye might believe" (John 20:31). Scripture is a record of facts, not a volume of cunningly devised fables. The gospel is a record of events of no ordinary life and is written by eyewitnesses. Every reference the apostle John makes to Jesus points with deep significance to the total purpose of our Lord's ministry of forgiving sin and giving eternal life.

We read some books for entertainment and some for knowledge, but the purpose of the book of John is strictly to encourage readers to believe in Jesus Christ.

II. The believer's life.

As precious as it is, faith is but a means to an end. Faith is a posture of the soul; life is a state of the soul. Life is a natural result of faith. Every person's life is affected by what he or she believes. In fact, what we believe becomes the guiding principle of our conduct. It is so in politics, it is so in literature, it is so in art. A personal faith in a living Christ becomes the means toward a happy, enduring spiritual life. This spiritual life is eternal.

The life of the believer is hidden with Christ in God. It is eternal because he who gives it is eternal. Let the reader of this gospel ask, "Have I been led to believe that Jesus Christ is the true Son of God and to acknowledge him as my personal Savior?"

III. The Christian's example.

Christians must be humble and must deliberately strip themselves of distinctions that would identify them with anything but a Christian witness. The desire to serve Christ must be an obsession. Jesus is not only our pattern; he is also our motive. Further, by his wonderful indwelling Spirit, he is also the power that molds our selfishness into the likeness of his own perfect self-surrender. In the deepest sense of the word, the "mind which was in Christ Jesus" must be in us if we are truly Christian. If we do not have his Spirit, we are not his servants. If his Spirit lives in us, we, like him, will be girded with humility and will serve others.

Conclusion

The time we have spent around the Lord's table has been sacred. Once again we have been reminded that the Bible is the sole authority for faith and practice. Our hearts have been strangely warmed within us as the Holy Spirit has spoken to us about our eternal security with Jesus Christ as Savior and Lord. Our spirits have been impressed to "press toward the mark ... of the high calling of God in Christ Jesus" (Phil. 3:14).

God has called us to rededicate ourselves to things that make a difference. We ask ourselves these questions: Upon what is my heart set? To what is my life devoted? Are the aims of my life of such infinite importance that they redeem it from smallness and insignificance? Every person needs to have aims outside the circle of his or her own personal interest. Through this means alone can life be saved from spiritual barrenness. We need to consecrate ourselves to Christ and to the work he would have us do so that we may know what a blessed thing life can be.

Title: Intimate Fellowship with Christ

Text: "Ye are my friends, if ye do whatsoever I command you" **(John 15:14)**.

Scripture Reading: John 15:1–17

Introduction

Some people visit Christ; others abide in him. It was for this reason that Jesus was intensely eager for his disciples to understand that spiritual experience is far more than a studied academic assumption, more than stilted humanism, more than philosophical rationalism, and more than a professional connection with him. It is an abiding, realistic consciousness that Christ is not only in human life but actually is in control of life itself. There can be no other meaning in the beautiful account of the vine and the branches. He is the Vine, and we are the branches. The living, thriving, fruit-bearing branch is always a dependent branch. To be severed from the Vine means death and destruction. Without Christ we can do nothing.

I. Clean Christians.

Abiding in Christ is the one sure guarantee for a clean life. "Now ye are clean [because of me]" (John 15:3). We cannot reconcile or identify Christ with anything unclean, either in thought or action. We cannot think of our Lord participating in those practices that weaken and ultimately destroy moral character. We cannot believe that Jesus was a victim of those baneful habits that poison the human body, the temple of the Spirit. Neither can we entertain the thought that a person who is vitally related to Christ will deliberately consent to engage in activity that would impair the witness and strength of regenerated Christian personality. Christians should be the healthiest people in the world because of their clean lives.

II. New growth and fruitage.

Here the doctrine of regeneration is suggested and enforced. The old nature, the carnal nature, cannot produce fruit pleasing to God. The Lord's indictment against the present-day church is that there are too many professed followers who are strangers to his saving grace. How little is said today about repentance, the new birth, and faith!

Yet the Bible has not changed. Nor has human nature. Fruit-bearing is always a test of character. People who have the nature of Christ will produce fruits of the Spirit. The motive that moves Christians to action comes from within. They serve because they love. They serve not because they have to but because they want to. If churches are to meet the needs of a wayward generation and fulfill their mission in the world, they will have to take Christ more seriously. They must bear more fruit for the glory of God and live more consecrated lives.

III. Destiny and reward.

Fruit bearing is a test of our destiny. The three great arraignments of sin in the Bible are sins of omission: not doing, not believing, and not loving. Our Lord consigned the wicked to everlasting torment for not doing. They were fruitless.

We shall be judged according to the deeds done in the body. Faith without works is dead and has no reward. How faithful should Christians be in seeking to enlarge their capacities to do God's will? In his illustration of the vine and the branches, Jesus put it this way: "Ye are my friends, if ye do whatsoever I command you" (John 15:14). The surrendered life will obey his voice and find a joy beyond the reach of human treachery.

Conclusion

As we gather around the Lord's table, our hearts are deeply grateful for the blessing of our heavenly Father on our lives. We are reminded here in God's presence that new people, better people, cannot be explained apart from the working of the Spirit of Christ in our hearts. We have come to understand that people are not as high as they might be and ought to be until they are in some measure yielded to God's will. Indeed, Christians are not self-made people; they are God-made people. All that makes us different comes from our heavenly Father, and to his holy purpose we reconsecrate our hearts today.

MESSAGES FOR CHILDREN AND YOUNG PEOPLE

Title: Three Important Questions Teenagers Ask

Text: "I am the way and the truth and the life. No one comes to the Father except through me" **(John 14:6)**.

Scripture Reading: John 14:1–6

Introduction

Young people have changed greatly in this century, especially in regard to asking questions. The old saying "Children should be seen and not heard" was a common belief for many years. As a result, teenagers did not ask questions, some of which nagged at their inner being. But in recent years teenagers have won freedom—freedom to express themselves in many ways. Out of fears, anxieties, and loneliness, teenagers often ask these three questions: (1) Who am I? (2) What am I doing? and (3) Where am I going? Many people spend their whole lives searching for answers to these questions, and sadly, some never find the answers.

There was a young man whom many people today still have as their example. He knew who he was. He said, "You believe in God; believe also in me" (John 14:1 NIV). He knew what he was doing. Even at the age of twelve, he was about his Father's business. He responded fully to his relationship to God, to his family, and to his community. This man knew where he was going. He said, "My Father's house has many rooms; if that were not so, would I have told you that I am going there to prepare a place for you?" (v. 2 NIV). This young man died at the age of thirty-three, having finished the work that God wanted him to do. He knew the answers to these questions of life, what about you?

I. Do you know who you are?

You may say my name is ______, I was born in ______, and I live in ______.

A. Yes, that is you on paper, but who are you really? Have you taken a look at yourself through the eyes of God's Word?

B. Do you know the "you" who thinks those thoughts when you are alone?

C. Did you know that the person you see in your mirror is: (1) a creation of God and (2) a potential child of God? Yet that person is your biggest problem.

II. Do you know what you are doing?

The majority of young people I have asked that question to have said, "Yes, I know what I'm doing. I'm looking for all the happiness I can find in life."

A. Happiness in itself is an admirable goal, but the ways in which many people try to find it are not always admirable.

B. Satan gives happiness—temporarily. The Bible says there is pleasure in sin for a season. In *God's Super Salesman*, Bob Harrington gives ten things to do so that Satan can bring happiness ([Nashville: Broadman, 1970], 81–83).

1. Forget the Ten Commandments. We will have to have the "happiness" to do what we want.
2. Forget law enforcement agents.
3. Forget traffic laws.
4. Forget your health; Satan promotes fast living.
5. Forget about friends and family.
6. Forget about Calvary. Forget the fact that someone loved you enough to send his Son to die in your place.
7. Furthermore, don't die, because you will go to hell. (The wages of sin is death.)
8. Don't break down your body, because the diseases sin causes are hard to cure.
9. Don't run out of money or you will run out of friends.
10. Don't ask Satan for help; he has no time for his foolish victims.

C. Face reality. The Bible says that the pleasures of sin are for a season. This means that your happiness will soon leave you.

D. Only Jesus can give real lasting happiness. In John 10:10 Jesus said that he came that we might have an abundant life.

E. How do you accept his life?

1. Luke 13:5: "Except ye repent, ye shall all likewise perish."
2. Acts 16:31: "Believe on the Lord Jesus Christ, and thou shalt be saved."

III. Do you know where you are going?

A. You perhaps feel that your future is certain, but where are going?

1. Right now?
2. Tomorrow?
3. Next week?

B. It is definite that you are going into eternity. The question is, which eternity?

1. The eternity of death?
2. The eternity of life?

Conclusion

A teenager once told me that he was not sure about the next life. I told him that that is where we differ. I am not sure about some of the things this life has to offer, but I am completely sure about life after death. I always tell young people that they are not ready to live until they are sure about eternity.

Do you know who you are? What you are doing? And where you are going? Listen to Jesus: He said, "I am the way," and without him there is no going; "I am the truth," and without him there is no knowing; "I am the life," and without him there is no living.

Title: Three Great Truths

Text: "And ye shall know the truth, and the truth shall make you free" **(John 8:32)**.

Scripture Reading: Genesis 2:7; 3:1–7; Romans 12:1–2; 2 Timothy 3:7

Introduction

Evangelist Billy Graham once said, "Truth is timeless. Truth does not differ from one age to another, from one people to another, from one geographical location to another. Men's ideas may differ, men's customs may change, men's moral codes may vary, but the great, all-prevailing truth stands for time and eternity" (quoted in Cort R. Flint, *The Quotable Billy Graham* [Anderson, SC: Droke House, 1966], 201).

Volumes have been written on the subject "What is truth?" To many people truth seems to be an elusive dream, while to others truth seems to be a way of life. Why is there this discrepancy in people's thinking about truth? Perhaps it is because some people feel they have to experience truth before it is truth. Yet there are those who know that truth is always consistent no matter what their own personal experience. Personal experience does not create truth; it only makes truth become a reality in our lives.

I would like for us to consider three truths. Perhaps these truths can become realities in your life today. These three truths are (1) God formed us, (2) sin deformed us, and (3) Jesus Christ transforms us. In this sermon, we will look at these three "all-prevailing truths."

I. God formed us (Gen. 2:7).

A. Many have a theory about where and how humans were formed.

1. Some people believe humans "just happened." Some people believe life began as a result of a big cosmic explosion and that humans evolved from one-celled life forms. This theory is about as sound as saying that as a result of an explosion in a machine shop, a jumbo jet was formed. Something of that precision takes time and planning.
2. Scripture reveals the truth about how humans were formed by God (Gen. 1–2). Those who believe that humans evolved from lower life forms have been unsuccessful in finding any missing links of proof. In fact, the fossil record supports creation.

B. God's Word, the source of truth, records that "God formed man." Nevertheless, some people choose to believe a lie (Rom. 1:18–25).

II. Sin deformed us (Gen. 3:1–7).

A. Humans were created in God's image, but because of sin, that image has been marred.

B. Sin deforms. Many people believe they can "get away" with sinning, not knowing that in some way they are being deformed.
   1. Physically—sin deforms physically because of drugs and alcohol, the misuse of sex, etc.
   2. Spiritually—sin deforms spiritually, robbing us of joy, peace, and most of all, eternal life.

C. Sin will find you out.
   1. In your face.
   2. In your body.
   3. In your character.
   4. In your conscience.
   5. In your children.
   6. In judgment and death.

D. Sin is:
   1. Vain labor. After we have worked for what we want, what do we have? Only an empty feeling that craves to be filled.
   2. Extremely unsatisfying. Sin is something that never gives lasting contentment.
   3. Costly. Sin is not free; it costs us character, influence, reputation, health—the list could go on, but most of all it costs us life.

III. Only Jesus Christ can transform (Rom. 12:1–2).

A. People are looking for ways to transform themselves from what they are into something or someone else. They look for many different ways to transform themselves.
   1. Through education. As good as education is, it does not transform us for eternity (2 Tim. 3:7).
   2. Through working at being good. Many work and meditate as much as possible to help bring a transformation, but the Bible says, "By grace are ye saved through faith; and that not of yourselves; it is the gift of God: not of works, lest any man should boast" (Eph. 2:8–9). Many try to clean themselves up on the outside, always knowing that trouble is on the inside.
   3. Through being religious. Many feel that by going to church and going through the motions, this will transform them. But this is as fruitless as good works.
   4. Through drugs, alcohol, etc. After repeated failures of transformation, many people turn to drugs or alcohol. These do not produce transformation; they only increase despair.

B. Though people may seek many ways of transforming themselves, the only true transformation can be done by God through Jesus Christ.

1. Jesus can transform your past. He can blot out your sins and separate them from you as far as the east is from the west. Jesus forgives and forgets.
2. Jesus can transform your present. He can take your life and lift it out of loneliness and despair to joy and peace that passes all understanding.

   Jesus can transform your destiny. No matter where you are headed right now, Jesus can change your direction. He can take a life destined to an eternity of hell and change its direction to a life destined for an eternity of heaven.

Conclusion

Make your decision today to let Jesus Christ become real to you by trusting him as Savior or by letting him become Lord if you have already received him as Savior.

Title: What Do You Weigh?

Text: "Thou art weighed in the balances, and art found wanting" (**Dan. 5:27**).

Scripture Reading: Daniel 5:1–5, 27

Introduction

Weight is an issue that most people today cannot ignore. Americans spend billions of dollars each year on weight-loss and weight-control products. And companies continue to produce hundreds of new lower-fat, fewer-calorie food products. With all this interest in people's weight, perhaps we should think of our spiritual weight. Have you weighed yourself spiritually lately?

I. What do you weigh on your own scales?

A. This set is individual and belongs to you.
   1. No one can see the face of this scale but you.
   2. There are many things about you that no one else knows! In fact, psychologists have told us that, at one time or another, all of us have a need to either reveal or conceal something about ourselves.
   3. You know yourself better than anyone else in the world knows you!
   4. What do you weigh on your own little private set of scales?

B. Paul said, "Let a man examine himself."
   1. What are the desires of your heart?
   2. What are the things you yearn for "deep down"? Are they beautiful things?
   3. To what do you aspire?
   4. What is the purpose of your life?
   5. What kind of pictures do you hang on the walls of your imagination?
   6. Do you have ugly, vulgar pictures, or is your mind filled with pure, lovely thoughts and wishes?

C. Remember, "As a man thinketh in his heart, so is he" (Prov. 23:7).
   1. What you weigh on your own scales is very important.
   2. The thoughts of your heart can bring you happiness and exhilaration. They can add zeal to life and help you face the dawn of a new day with joy and confidence.
   3. On the other hand, what you hide in your heart can make you feel unworthy, unclean, and unfit to live.

D. How you weigh yourself can make the difference in having the abundant life of Jesus or just a miserable existence. What do you weigh on your own scales?

II. What do you weigh on others' scales?

A. These are scales you cannot see!

B. Many people say, "Do your own thing. Don't worry what people think."
   1. Yet it is important what people think, because the only Bible some people will read is the open book of your life as a Christian. What are they reading in your life?
   2. Are people better because their lives come in contact with yours?
   3. Are people better because they know you?
   4. Do you bring happiness to those you meet?
   5. Influence could almost be sacred. What are you doing with yours?

III. What do you weigh on the scales of God?

The greatest question we can ever ask ourselves is what we weigh on God's scales.

A. If God were to put us in his balance today, and on the other side place what he expects us to be and what we should be, how would the scales balance out?

B. God's scales weigh such things as integrity, courage, zeal for the work of the kingdom, honesty, sincerity, earnestness, and especially faith!

Conclusion

One day all of us will be in God's scales. Will he look at us and have to say, "You have been weighed in the balances and are found wanting. Depart from me, for I never knew you"? Or will he be able to say, "Well done, good and faithful servant"?

FUNERAL MEDITATIONS

Title: Death Is a Door

Text: "Truly, truly, I say to you, he who hears my word and believes him who sent me, has eternal life; he does not come into judgment, but has passed from death to life" **(John 5:24 RSV).**

Scripture Reading: Romans 8:38–39

Introduction

We all can vividly remember our first encounter with death, whether it was when a pet, a grandparent, or even a friend died. If it was the death of a person, the pale unsmiling faces, the hushed tones, and the unusual events were a maze of bewilderment to us. No one could explain this powerful force that took away our friend or family member for good.

I. Death closes the door of life (Job 14:1).

Death, sorrow, and tears are as real as life. Death is the close of one's earthly life, and then it is time for a final service and a last tribute. Fragile life, likened in the Bible to a vapor, a flower, and a cut blade of grass, has ceased; and all the talking in our world cannot make death anything but death.

II. Death opens the door of eternal life (John 5:24).

People are born to live in two worlds, and when death closes the door to this one, it also opens the door to the next one. As the storm door on our house closes behind us, the inner door opens to admit us to the wonderful presence of all we call our home. The same is true when we leave all the storms of life behind us and are ushered into all that God has prepared in our heavenly home.

Conclusion

One door has closed, another has opened, and a swelling dimension of living that defies description is being enjoyed by the deceased. Let us thank God for sending his Son to make it all possible (John 3:16).

Title: The Sympathetic Savior

Text: "Jesus said to her, I am the resurrection and the life; he who believes in me, though he die, yet shall he live" **(John 11:25 RSV)**.

Scripture Reading: John 11: 23–26

Introduction

There is no time in a family's life when there will be more expressions of love and sympathy received than at the death of a loved one. With cards, letters, flowers, food, phone calls, and spoken words, friends let their love be known. The presence of this crowd is also a silent but eloquent way of expressing love and appreciation.

I. Jesus attended funerals.

The Bible tells us that no sparrow falls to the ground in death but that it is noticed by the Lord. We are of greater worth than that sparrow. Jesus walked into the home of Jairus when his daughter died and was of great comfort to the family (Mark 5:23). He stopped a funeral procession and encouraged the widowed mother not to weep for her son (Luke 7:13). At the tomb of Lazarus, Jesus wept and then spoke lifting words about his people never dying (John 11:35).

II. Jesus is present at this funeral.

Anywhere his people are gathered for any reason, Jesus is there. This death did not surprise Jesus, and he sees it as a precious time, for one of his has been released from the body and has come home. Yet he is fully aware of your heartache, tears, numbing grief, and loneliness, for he is a man of sorrows and well acquainted with the hurt of loneliness.

Conclusion

We need only to recognize Christ's presence here to be comforted. Jesus is here to freely give the same peace, love, encouragement, and hope of the hereafter that he spoke of at Lazarus's tomb. We need only to reach out to him in faith and prayer.

Title: A Loss and a Hope

Text: "Can I bring him back again? I shall go to him, but he will not return to me" **(2 Sam. 12:23 RSV)**.

Scripture Reading: 2 Samuel 12:15–23

Introduction

Officiating at a child's funeral is one of the more difficult tasks of a minister. The loss of a life that scarcely has begun, the diminutive casket, and the collective grief of the family and of all those who mourn with them make for a sad setting.

I. David's loss (2 Sam. 12:15–19).

This father simply would not give up when he was told of the impending death of his infant son. He refused to eat and spent much time before God in prayer. His servants tried to be of assistance, but David kept his vigil. On the seventh day, the child died, and the father had the same feelings of sorrow that you are experiencing and that all other parents who have lost a child have suffered.

II. David's hope (2 Sam. 12:20–23).

After the child died, David arose from his prostrate position before God, bathed, changed his clothing, and went to the house of God and worshiped. Then he went home and asked for food.

The servants were puzzled and said so. Their master replied that while the child was alive, he fasted and prayed in hope that God would be gracious and spare the child's life. After the child died, there was no use to do either. Then he asked and answered a question: "Can I bring him back again? I shall go to him, but he will not return to me" (v. 23).

Conclusion

Babies belong to God, and if parents wish to spend eternity with them, they must belong to God also. This can come about by a simple but sincere prayer of faith in Jesus Christ in which we ask for forgiveness of sin and salvation of our souls. A reunion is then assured, and the hope David had can be a reality that helps us to endure the sorrow (John 3:17).

Title: The Resurrection of Jesus Christ

Text: "He is not here: for he is risen, as he said. Come, see the place where the Lord lay" **(Matt. 28:6)**.

Scripture Reading: Matthew 28:1–8

Introduction

There can be no true gospel that leaves out the biblical account of the bodily resurrection of Jesus Christ. Even though no one witnessed the resurrection, many saw the risen Lord.

The most authenticated miracle in the New Testament is the resurrection of Jesus Christ. All competent scholars admit that the tomb was empty on the Resurrection Sunday morning.

The witnesses to the resurrection of Jesus Christ in the Gospels are: (1) Mary Magdalene and other women (Matt. 28:9–10; Mark 16:9–11; John 20:11–18); (2) the eleven disciples (Matt. 20:16–20; Mark 16:14–15; Luke 24:36–53); (3) Thomas and the disciples (John 20:26–29); (4) the seven fishing disciples (John 21:1–25); and (5) the two disciples as they walked the Emmaus road (Mark 16:12–13; Luke 24:13–25).

The witnesses to the resurrection of Jesus Christ in 1 Corinthians are: (1) Cephas, or Peter (15:5); (2) the Twelve (15:5); (3) five hundred brethren (15:6); (4) James (15:7); (5) all the apostles (15:7); and (6) Paul (15:8).

The resurrection of Jesus Christ is a cardinal doctrine, and it declares many great truths to us. What are some of them?

I. The resurrection of Jesus Christ is a mighty revelation.

A. The resurrection of Jesus Christ reveals his glorious victory (Heb. 2:14; 1 Cor. 15:55, 57).

B. The resurrection of Jesus Christ reveals his mighty power (Luke 24:5–8; John 10:17–18).

C. The resurrection of Jesus Christ reveals the Father's approval of him (Acts 2:32).

II. The resurrection of Jesus Christ is a ringing testimony.

A. The resurrection of Jesus Christ is a ringing testimony to his deity (Acts 2:22–24, 32–36).

B. The resurrection of Jesus Christ is a ringing testimony to the complete justification of people (Rom. 4:25).

C. The resurrection of Jesus Christ is a ringing testimony to the promise of the Christian's resurrection (1 Cor. 15:20–22).

III. The resurrection of Jesus Christ is a wonderful assurance.

A. The resurrection of Jesus Christ assures us of the truthfulness of Jesus (Matt. 16:21; 20:18–19; 27:63; Luke 24:6–8).

B. The resurrection of Jesus Christ assures us that God approves his sacrifice for our sins (Acts 17:31).

C. The resurrection of Jesus Christ assures us that our faith is not in vain (1 Cor. 15:12–19).

D. The resurrection of Jesus Christ assures us of his intercession for us (Rom. 8:34; 1 Tim. 2:5; Heb. 7:25; 9:24; 1 John 2:1–2).

E. The resurrection of Jesus Christ assures us of the power for victorious living (Matt. 28:16–20).

F. The resurrection of Jesus Christ assures us of the blessed hope and of our resurrection (1 Cor. 15:23, 45; Phil. 3:20–21; 1 Thess. 4:14).

G. The resurrection of Jesus Christ assures us of his presence (Matt. 28:20).

Conclusion

Our Lord is the risen Lord. Our Lord is the Savior who was crucified, buried, and raised from the grave. He lives!

Up from the grave he arose,
With a mighty triumph o'er His foes;
He arose a victor from the dark domain,
And He lives forever with His saints to reign.
He arose! He arose! Hallelujah! Christ arose!

—*Robert Lowry*

WEDDINGS

Title: Wedding Ceremony 1

The Bible declares, "Therefore shall a man leave his father and his mother, and shall cleave unto his wife: and they shall be one flesh" (Gen. 2:24).

First and noblest of all human contracts is marriage. Marriage is ordained by God and is taught in his Word. He spoke the first nuptial words to Adam and Eve in the Garden of Eden before the tempter had touched the world. Jesus the Savior performed his first miracle at a wedding in Cana of Galilee. Paul said that marriage is like the relationship that exists between Christ and his church. He told the husband to love his wife as Christ loved the church and gave himself for it, and the wife to be faithful as the church is faithful to Christ in all things.

You [groom] and you [bride], having signified to me your desire to be united in marriage, and being assured that no legal, moral, or religious barriers hinder this union, I request that you join right hands and repeat after me your marriage vows:

I, [groom], take thee, [bride], to be my wedded wife, to have and to hold from this day forward, for better, for worse, for richer, for poorer, in sickness and in health, to love and to cherish till death do us part, according to God's holy teaching; and thereto I pledge thee my faith.

I, [bride], take thee, [groom], to be my wedded husband, to have and to hold from this day forward, for better, for worse, for richer, for poorer, in sickness and in health, to love and to cherish till death do us part, according to God's holy teaching; and thereto I pledge thee my faith.

From time immemorial the ring has been used to seal important covenants. When the race was young and there were no parliaments, the great seal of the state was fixed upon the ring worn by the reigning monarch, and its stamp was the sole sign of imperial authority. Friends often exchange the ring as evidence of goodwill and friendship. From such impressive precedents, the circlet, the most prized of all jewels, comes to its loftiest meaning here at the marriage altar. Its untarnishable material and unique form become the precious tokens of an abiding and pure love.

[Groom], please take this ring and put it on the third finger of [bride's] left hand and repeat after me your vow: With this ring I thee wed; with loyal love I thee endow; and all my worldly goods with thee I share. Where thou goest, I will go; thy people shall be my people, and thy God my God.

[Bride], please take this ring and put it on the third finger of [groom's] left hand and repeat after me your vow: With this ring I thee wed; with loyal love I thee endow; and all my worldly goods with thee I share. Where thou goest, I will go; thy people shall be my people, and thy God my God.

Having pledged your faith in and love to each other and having sealed your marriage vows by giving and receiving the rings, acting in the authority vested in me by the laws in this state, and looking to God for divine sanction, I pronounce you husband and wife in the presence of God, your family and friends, and these assembled witnesses. Therefore let all people take care in the sight of God that the covenant you have made together shall forever remain sacred.

Title: Wedding Ceremony 2

Friends, we are gathered here on this occasion to unite in the bonds of holy matrimony [groom] and [bride] by the authority of this license bearing the date ______.

[Groom's first name] and [bride's first name], marriage was God's first institution for the welfare of the human race. God saw that man could not live alone, so he created a helpmate for him and established the rite of matrimony while heavenly hosts witnessed this wonderful scene.

As an institution of divine appointment, it was given in wisdom and kindness to increase our human happiness and to support our social order. So marriage is honorable in all things and must so remain until the end of time.

To the end that you would establish a home that would honor God, I commend to you that you build your home and your home life on the great eternal spiritual principles that are found in the Word of God. Building with God, you can build securely. Building with God, you can build permanently. Building with God, you cannot fail.

Prayer by the officiating person.

And now [groom's first name] and [bride's first name], in token of your decided choice for each other as partners for life, I will ask you to join your right hands. [Groom] do you solemnly promise before almighty God and in the presence of these witnesses to accept [bride] as your lawful wedded wife, pledging yourself to perform those duties that encourage the building of a successful home life, to love, honor, and cherish her until this union into which you are now entering is dissolved by death?

The groom responds: I do.

[Bride] do you solemnly promise before almighty God and in the presence of these witnesses to accept [groom] as your lawful wedded husband, and pledging yourself to perform those duties that encourage the building of a successful home life, to love, honor, and cherish him until this union into which you are now entering is dissolved by death?

The bride responds: I do.

And now, you present these rings by which you would seal the sacred bonds of this union. The ring has been used through the centuries to seal important contracts and covenants. It is deeply significant that it shall be used on this occasion. In making this exchange of rings, each of you will repeat after me these words.

As the groom places the ring on the ring finger of the bride's left hand, he will repeat these words: With this ring I thee wed, with loyal love, I thee endow, and all my worldly goods with thee I share.

As the bride places the ring on the ring finger of the groom's left hand, she will repeat these words: With this ring I thee wed, with loyal love I thee endow, and all my worldly goods with thee I share.

That we might further seal this new relationship in words of Holy Scripture, we turn to Ruth 1:16 in the Old Testament. The message reads, "Intreat me not to leave thee, or to return from following after thee: for whither thou goest, I will go; and where thou lodgest, I will lodge: thy people shall be my people, and thy God my God."

And now by virtue of the authority vested in me as a minister of the gospel, according to the laws of the state of ______, and according to the vows you have taken, I do now pronounce you husband and wife; henceforth in interest, in destiny, and in affection you are one, and what God hath joined together let no one put asunder.

Closing prayer and benediction.

Title: A Short-Form Marriage Ceremony

Dear friends, we are assembled here in the presence of almighty God and the fellowship of these friends to join in the bonds of holy matrimony [groom] and [bride].

This mystical union was God's first means of approving and honoring the holy estate of marriage as the foundation for the building of a home. It is not to be entered into without a most serious reflection upon the sacredness of the vows that hold the prospect of establishing a relationship that will honor God.

So by virtue of your decided choice of each other as partners for life, I will ask you to join your right hands. Please listen carefully to the vows you shall make on this most significant occasion.

[Groom], do you accept this woman to be your lawful wedded wife, and do you promise to live together after God's ordinance in this holy estate? Do you promise to love her and comfort her in sickness and in health until this bond of marriage is dissolved by death?

The groom will respond: I do.

[Bride], do you accept this man to be your lawful wedded husband, and do you promise to live together after God's ordinance in this holy estate? Do you promise to love him and comfort him in sickness and in health until this bond of marriage is dissolved by death?

The bride will respond: I do.

As the groom places the ring on the ring finger of the bride's left hand and repeats after the officiating minister in phrases of three words: With this ring ... I thee wed.... With loyal love ... I thee endow.... And all my worldly goods ... with thee I share.

When the bride presents a ring, the same procedure will be followed during the ring ceremony.

The minister will say: And now according to the vows that you have taken in the presence of these witnesses, and before almighty God, I do now pronounce you husband and wife. What God hath joined together, let not man put asunder.

The benediction: The Lord bless you and keep you. May his mercies, love, and favor be upon you and fill you with spiritual benediction and grace. May you so live together in this life that in the world to come you shall know the joy and peace of life everlasting. In the name of the Father and the Son and the Holy Spirit. Amen.

Sentence Sermonettes

Tragedy can make you bitter or better.

Courtesy often stumbles on the rock of forgetfulness.

Prayer is heaven's company credit card.

Stop trying and start trusting.

Death is life's crowning adventure.

Performance speaks louder than words.

Is your eternal destiny with God?

Giving up the world's wisdom is no loss when God's wisdom supplants it.

Satan fears prayer because God hears prayer.

Work is love made visible.

If you would not fall into sin, keep away from the brink of temptation.

Recipe for having friends: Be one.

Better not to have been born at all than never to have been born again.

The world crowns success; God crowns faithfulness.

Kindness is the oil that takes the friction out of life.

The world needs the peace that passes all misunderstanding.

No man has ever hurt his eyesight by looking on the bright side of life.

A smile is a curve that can set a lot of things straight.

A smooth sea never made a successful sailor.

God made each person to be somebody.

God meant for people to possess their possessions not to be possessed by them.

We should be glued to the good.

Resistance to constituted authority is resistance to God.

True love demands self-forgetfulness.

We must use things and love people.

The secret of life is not what happens to you but what you do with what happens to you.

Pray for power equal to your task.

Nothing great was ever achieved without enthusiasm.

Prayer can turn tragedy into triumph.

Selfishness and love are forever opposed to each other.

Prayer opens up a person's life to God's goodness.

A friend is a present you give yourself.

All negative thoughts are like a boomerang.

No person is immune to trouble.

It is always too soon to quit.

Disappointments in life often prove to be His appointments.

Real living is being and not just having.

Give your offerings as though you were placing them in the nail-pierced hands of Jesus.

Trust is man's answer to God's truth.

Few things are more contagious than meanness.

There is no right way to do the wrong thing.

Each of us is a slave to something or to someone.

Tomorrow, today will be yesterday.

The perfume of kindness travels even against the wind.

The good can be the enemy of the best.

Trust God for too much rather than for too little.

God does not have favorites, but he does have intimates who walk and talk with him.

Beware of the tranquilizers of the devil.

Index of Scripture Texts

Subject Index